OPEN HOUSING

Juliet Saltman

OPEN HOUSING

Dynamics of a
Social Movement

PRAEGER PUBLISHERS
Praeger Special Studies

New York • London • Sydney • Toronto

Library of Congress Cataloging in Publication Data

Saltman, Juliet Z
   Open housing.

   Bibliography: p.
   Includes index.
   1. Discrimination in housing--United States.
2. Discrimination in housing--Ohio--Akron.
3. Social movements--United States. 4. Social
change. I. Title.
HD7293.S253   301.24'2   78-19464

ISBN 0-03-022376-8

PRAEGER PUBLISHERS
PRAEGER SPECIAL STUDIES
383 Madison Avenue, New York, N.Y. 10017, U.S.A.

Published in the United States of America in 1978
by Praeger Publishers,
A Division of Holt, Rinehart and Winston, CBS, Inc.

89   038   987654321

To all those who continue the struggle for equal access to shelter—with admiration and appreciation for their courage, vision, and stubbornness.

PREFACE

THE TEN PAINS OF DEATH

To wait for one who never comes,
To lie in bed and not to sleep,
To serve well and not to please,
To have a horse that will not go,
To be sick and lack the cure,
To be a prisoner without hope,
To lose the way when you would journey,
To stand at a door that none will open,
To have a friend who would betray you,
These are the ten pains of death.

Second Fruits, Giovanni Florio, 1591

[Author's emphasis]

It would almost be correct to say that I did not deliberately choose to study the open-housing movement, but that it was thrust upon me. There were five stages of my involvement with the movement. I began as a sociologist, then became an active participant, turned into a participant observer, then back into an active participant, and again into a sociologist. This division is, of course, an artificial one, since the roles overlapped.

In 1964, as a university professor of sociology, I was asked by an Akron human relations group to present evidence to the city council concerning the need for open (fair) housing in the city. An emergency ordinance had been prepared by the one black councilman, which cited six reasons for such legislation. I was asked to document these reasons for the legislative body.

In July the open-housing ordinance was passed as emergency legislation, but it was defeated in November in a public referendum spearheaded by the local real estate board. Thus, Akron had the dubious distinction of having had a fair-housing law for a shorter time than any other city in the nation.

A few months later, local civil rights groups decided that with or without a law, we would explore the possibilities of setting up a volunteer listing service as a fair-housing group. The National Committee Against Discrimination in Housing (NCDH) was contacted, and furnished names and addresses of some twelve well-functioning fair-housing groups throughout the country, which sent us materials helpful in forming a new fair-housing organization. With these, we developed a plan for a local volunteer fair-housing group.

As the first secretary of the organization, I organized and coordinated the local effort. During the first years we maintained close contact with the NCDH and other community fair-housing groups. After our first successful year, the National Committee advised us to prepare a proposal for funding through the Office of Economic Opportunity (OEO). We did this, but were turned down. We submitted the proposal to several foundations and to other government agencies, but without success.

At the end of our third year, in late August 1968, we were funded through OEO with almost $60,000 to open an office and hire a staff by October 1. This marked the end of the second stage of my involvement and the beginning of the third stage as participant observer.

I had accepted a grant to work on my doctorate, and began my doctoral studies with the thought of doing my dissertation on the open-housing movement. At first I thought of studying only the local group in its volunteer phase. But after the first painful months of transition after funding, I began to recognize that what was happening in Akron was the institutionalization of a movement, and I knew I had to study this phase, too. Then I decided to examine the national level also, and to compare the Akron experience with four other communities.

I cannot describe here the difficulty of being a participant observer, as in the first funded two-year period of the Akron case study. To experience anguish and to be analytical about it is truly being what George Simmel called "inside and outside at the same time."* In terms of objectivity, my close and intense involvement has often been a liability, but in being able to perceive small and large changes in direction as well as morale, my involvement was a distinct asset.

When the difficulties of my role as an involved and covert participant observer became too painful, I was comforted by Kenneth Clark's observations in the introduction to his Dark Ghetto:

> Distortion of vision and confusion may harass the
> involved observer, but the inevitable pressures of
> his role bring, also, gnawing self-doubt. It is the

---

*Kurt H. Wolff (trans.), The Sociology of George Simmel (New York: Free Press, 1950).

ultimate test of strength, which this observer did
not always pass, as the pressures intensify. . .to
discipline himself and attempt to control his defen-
siveness, his doubts concerning adequacy of self,
and above all, his desire to escape before the completion of his task.*

After the painful two-year period of participant observation,
which ended with the renunciation of funding by the Akron group, I
was able to be just an active participant, since my writing labors
were ended. From 1970 to 1974 I continued to work on the volunteer
board of directors, and in 1972 became the fifth president. During
this period, the Akron group won the National Volunteer Award for
the country, a most unanticipated event. After my two-year term
as president was over, I left the board in 1974 after ten years of
service, for reasons explained toward the end of Chapter 4.
   In the case study, I am the only person openly identified—as
the founder, the volunteer board secretary, later the public relations
chairperson, and J. S. All other initials and occupations are changed
to preserve anonymity. These are people whose friendship I cherish,
and I would not want them to be embarrassed in any way.

Seven Years Later

The first study was published in 1971 as Open Housing as a
Social Movement: Challenge, Conflict and Change. So much happened after 1970 to Akron's group, to the others in the comparative
analysis, and to the development of social-movement theory, that
this book seems very much out of date. The Denver group folded,
Seattle's died, the one in Los Angeles revived, and New York's
kept going.
   So it seemed important to me to bring events up to date, answer
some questions, and share my thinking with those who found the earlier book helpful and with new readers. Probing for answers to why
Denver's group folded and Seattle's died (despite my assessment
of it as the most successful in the country) was necessary and satisfying, though disturbing.
   Refreshed by this nostalgic and fact-finding journey, I offer a
second expanded version of my work on open housing. Much of the

_____

   *Kenneth Clark, Dark Ghetto (New York: Harper and Row,
1965).

review of the literature in the first chapter is new. The third chapter contains some historical material not included in the first book. The fourth phase of development (since 1970), in the third, fourth and fifth chapters, is all new. The fifth chapter contains new material relating to the earlier phases of development in each movement organization. The profiles of movement organizations across the country, also in the fifth chapter, are new. The final chapter contains new thoughts about social movements generally, and the open-housing movement specifically. I do not plan to write a third book about open housing. Any errors of judgment this time will have to stand.

ACKNOWLEDGMENTS

The writer gratefully acknowledges the cooperation of Edward Rutledge and Margaret Fisher, formerly of the National Committee Against Discrimination in Housing (NCDH). Mr. Rutledge granted a personal interview in San Francisco on August 27, 1969, and arranged for access to materials in the New York office when needed. Miss Fisher granted an interview on April 22, 1970 in New York, and made two files available to the writer. One file contained documents of the earliest period of NCDH's development. The second file contained 14 years of newspapers (Trends in Housing), which the writer was permitted to borrow for a limited period. It would have been impossible to write the third chapter without these materials. My thanks to Ed Holmgren, executive director of NCDH, for many things over the years, but here specifically for the long searching interview he gave me on July 1, 1976.

For their patience, time, and helpful suggestions the first time around, the writer is deeply indebted to Professors Sidney M. Peck, Irwin Deutscher, and Lloyd Rogler of the Department of Sociology at Case Western Reserve University, Professor James Blackwell of the Department of Sociology at the University of Massachusetts, and Professor Elliott Rudwick of the Department of Sociology at Kent State University.

The first version of this book was written as a Ph.D. dissertation in sociology for Case Western Reserve University, under a National Defense Education Act fellowship. The first dedication was to the memory of my former professor at the University of Chicago, Louis Wirth, "who taught me long ago that housing is a sociological and social concern."

To my family—Will, my husband, and our children (now grown), Dave, Nina, and Dan—goes my constant appreciation and love, for without their cooperation and understanding, none of this would have been possible. Together, we've all grown up with the open-housing movement.

CONTENTS

Chapter   Page

LIST OF TABLES AND FIGURES

TABLE

LIST OF ACRONYMS

AEC	Atomic Energy Commission
BNI	Baltimore Neighborhoods, Inc.
BUS	Black United Students
CAC	Community Action Council
CD	Community Development
CDA	Housing and Community Development Act (1974)
CDBG	Community Development Block Grant
CETA	Comprehensive Employment Training Act
CORE	Congress on Racial Equality
EO	Equal Opportunity
FEPC	Fair Employment Practices Commission
FHA	Federal Housing Administration
FHC	Fair Housing Council, Fair Housing Center
FHCS	Fair Housing Contact Service
FHLS	Fair Housing Listing Service
GDHOC	Greater Dallas Housing Opportunity Center
HCD	Housing and Community Development
HCG	Heights Community Congress
HEW	Health, Education and Welfare
HMPS	Housing Market Practices Survey
HOC	Housing Opportunities Center
HOME	Housing Opportunities Made Equal
HUD	Department of Housing and Urban Development
LCMOC	Leadership Council for Metropolitan Open Communities
LWV	League of Women Voters
MARC	Metropolitan Applied Research Center
MCFH	Mid-Peninsula Citizens for Fair Housing
MDFHC	Metro Denver Fair Housing Center
MHA	Metropolitan Housing Authority

MLS	Multiple Listing Service
MO	Movement Organization
NAACP	National Association for the Advancement of Colored People
NAREB	National Association of Real Estate Boards
NCDH	National Committee Against Discrimination in Housing
NN	National Neighbors
NOACA	Northeast Ohio Area Coordinating Agency
OC	Open City
OE	Operation Equality
OEO	Office of Economic Opportunity
OHC	Open Housing Center
OOC	Operation Open City
OS	Operation Sentinel
PHA	Public Housing Administration
SFV	San Fernando Valley
SMSA	Standard Metropolitan Statistical Area
UL	Urban League
VA	Veterans Administration

1

THE STUDY OF
SOCIAL MOVEMENTS

INTRODUCTION

The literature on the general study of social movements seems to suggest a curious sequential paradox.

- Unsuccessful social movements usually fail before reaching the stage of institutionalization.
- The ultimate success of a movement, then, is symbolized by institutionalization.
- Yet, institutionalization leads to the decline and eventual failure of a movement.
- Thus, successful movements must eventually fail.

This study explores one aspect of the above paradox: Does institutionalization lead to the decline of a movement? Institutionalization has been described by Ralph Turner and Lewis Killian as

> . . .the stage when a movement reaches a high degree of internal stability and has achieved societal recognition, and when the movement is seen as having some continuing function to perform in the larger society, and is accepted as a desirable or unavoidable adjunct to existing institutional arrangements.[1]

They contend that a social movement cannot continue indefinitely, since its very nature is dynamic. When the dynamic quality is lost, a social movement either disappears or becomes a different social form. Thus, success leads to the transformation and end of a movement.

Other scholars hold similar views of the stage of institutionalization. Kurt and Gladys Lang regard institutionalization as the end product in the career development of a movement, and institutionalization is equated with bureaucratization.[2]

Neil Smelser also considers institutionalization as the last phase of the development of a movement,[3] and sees it as settling into either a decline or routine day-by-day activity. He states that movements are bound to fail, since fears and hopes are exaggerated by generalized beliefs and there is always a residue of disappointment. Though he does not define success, Smelser contends that a successful movement usually begins to focus on other related reforms, or else guards the changes it has achieved. Thus in their later stages, successful and unsuccessful movements resemble each other, and both assume new functions in place of their original purposes.

Hans Toch, in discussing the life cycle of a social movement, views institutionalization as a "process characterized by the tendency to relegate ideology more and more to a position of a means to ends."[4] He states that whenever a belief becomes an impediment to public acceptance, it is modified or abandoned. Thus, to survive in a changing world, social movements must undergo adaptive transformations that are designed to increase their appeal in competition with the outside. These kinds of changes, according to Toch, tend to convert a successful social movement into an institution. When adaptive changes continue beyond this point, the institution tends to lose its identity and merges into the larger society.

Though C. Wendell King does not explicitly equate institutionalization with decline, he does suggest that institutionalization is the fourth and final stage of development of a social movement. According to King, this stage is marked by internal stability and integration with the society at large.[5]

Joseph Gusfield does not agree with those scholars who have indicated a natural tendency for movements to become accomodative and then decline; that is, they simply grow old and die. But he does recognize the implications of the institutionalization of a movement, as revealed in the statement:

> The development of at least a semipermanent organizational structure is often essential to the realization of the goals of a movement. However, such organization often sets in motion influences which defeat the ideals that gave birth to it. This is the paradox: that which is a needed means to an end is often the means which frustrates attainment of the end.[6]

Flowing from the initial question of whether institutionalization does, in fact, lead to the decline of a movement, are others. How does one determine at what point a movement is institutionalized? What happens to a social movement when it becomes institutionalized? Does the movement, indeed, have to die after institutionalization? If so, what precise factors lead to its failure? Is it the institutionalization itself, or the change of leadership, or other factors? Do internal or external factors, or both, account for failure? If the movement does not die, what factors contribute to its continued growth and development? And how can the success or failure of a movement be measured? The last three questions have come to be the most critical ones for this study.

In an attempt to answer the above questions, this study examines a changing social movement—the open-housing movement—before and after institutionalization, on national and community levels. In order to assess the validity of studying open housing as a social movement, one must first try to understand what a social movement is.

THE CONCEPT OF THE SOCIAL MOVEMENT

It is intriguing to note that in spite of an ever-present recognition and awareness of change among social scholars throughout the years, there are relatively few works devoted to the general study of social movements. Yet the study of social movements in modern society is especially vital in yielding insight and understanding of the process of social change.

The works that do deal with the general study of social movements may be categorized in terms of three perspectives: the collective-behavior approach, the psychological approach, and the sociological approach. The sociological approach may be divided into two types: the conflict perspective—which may be further subdivided into Marxist and non-Marxist—and the organizational perspective.

There are two primary features that distinguish the collective-behavior approach from the sociological approach. The collective-behavior approach considers the social movement only as a special type of collective behavior—a type that requires more organization than other more elementary types. The collective-behavior approach also presents a diffused conception of the social movement, one that encompasses a much wider range of collective activity than is found in the sociological approach. Thus movements that are directed to personal transformation are included in the concept, as well as those oriented to societal change. Examples of the collective-behavior approach are the works of Herbert Blumer, Turner and Killian, Lang and Lang, and Smelser.

The sociological approach, on the other hand, is a societal one which focuses on collective action strictly oriented to some form of societal change, rather than individual change. Moreover, it views social movements as unique, separate, organized, enduring entities rather than merely as one type of general collective behavior.

Within this framework, the conflict perspective stresses power differentials in society as the generating force of discontent leading to social movements. The Marxist subtype of the conflict perspective focuses primarily on an economic model of differentiation, suggesting that social movements arise out of the contradictions present in a class-based society. The organizational perspective examines internal and/or external structural conditions relating to the mobilization and development of movements. Recent theoretical developments within the sociological approach have prompted this distinction, which is perhaps useful only for analytical purposes. Actually, a number of these approaches overlap and are not so easily categorized.

The general sociological approach is represented in the works of Rudolph Heberle, C. Wendell King, James VanderZanden, William Cameron, Joseph Gusfield, and Robert Lauer. The conflict perspective is found in the works of Roberta Ash, Gary Rush and R. Surge Denisoff, and Ron Roberts and Robert Kloss. The organizational perspective is seen in the works of Mayer Zald and Roberta Ash, Moyer Zald and John McCarthy, Anthony Oberschall, and John Wilson.

The psychological approach is primarily oriented to the study of individuals who become part of a movement, and focuses on their motivations and individual development. This approach does not examine the societal structure, nor is it concerned with developmental aspects of a movement. It does not consider the organization and structure of social movements and their crucial interrelationship with the society at large. The psychological approach does not analyze the strategy and tactics of a movement, and it ignores the impact of a movement on the larger society. This approach does help in understanding one facet of the social movement—the participants—but not in understanding all the other vital aspects of social movements. The psychological approach is illustrated in the works of Hadley Cantril, Eric Hoffer, and Hans Toch.

The concept of the social movement as it is treated in each of the three approaches will be examined in terms of the definition, structure, and process of a social movement. A comparative analysis of the literature in all three approaches reveals some similar core concepts relating to definition, structure, and process of social movements, but more that are dissimilar.

Despite a vast array of definitions, characteristics, properties, components, stages, and types offered in each of the three approaches, there has been scanty theoretical development in the field of social movements. Scholars in the sociological approach have only recently begun to interrelate the network of factors suggested in the many sets of taxonomies offered. It is somewhat comforting to recall here John

Wilson's suggestion: "Classification is a necessary prerequistie to analysis."[7] Through a synthesis of the three approaches, an ideal-type* concept of a social movement can be developed, and in addition, its distinguishing features can be identified.

Definition

The Collective-Behavior Approach

The classic treatment of social movements within the framework of collective behavior is that of Herbert Blumer. Blumer contrasts collective behavior with small-group behavior and more established behavior, suggesting key differentials such as physical and cultural criteria, psychological and interactional factors, plus mobilizational and rationality variances. Though the relationships among these criteria are unclear, Blumer illustrates the transition from elementary collective behavior to organized behavior in his discussion of social movements:

> During its development, the social movement acquires organization and form, a body of customs and traditions, established leadership, enduring division of labor, social rules and values—in short, a culture, an organization, and a new scheme of life. [8]

Blumer defines a social movement as a collective enterprise to establish a new order of life, and suggests three major types as general, specific, and expressive.

Turner and Killian, in their general work on collective behavior, consider and examine social movements in terms of character and process and as a special type of collective behavior. They view social movements as having a considerable degree of organization, regulations, stability, and continuity. Their definition of a social movement does not quite encompass all of these, however: "A social movement is a collectivity acting with some continuity to promote a change or resist a change in the society or group of which it is a part."[9]

Lang and Lang, in their work Collective Dynamics, define a social movement as ". . .a large-scale, widespread, and continuing elementary collective action in pursuit of an objective that affects

---

*An ideal-type is a model or mental construct, as developed by Max Weber.

and shapes the social order in some fundamental aspect."[10] They
claim that every social movement leaves changes that are apt to
endure and has activities that are coordinated by some core group.

Smelser's Theory of Collective Behavior does not treat social
movements separately as such, but rather includes "norm-oriented"
and "value-oriented" movements in this general analysis of collective
behavior. In considering the norm-oriented movement, Smelser first
defines this as an "attempt to restore, protect, modify, or create
norms in the name of a generalized belief." Value-oriented movements
include religious movements, utopian movements, political revolution,
charismatic movements, and many others. Many norm-oriented movements occur independently of value-oriented movements, which call
for more sweeping changes. Norm-oriented movements do not challenge the legitimacy of values, whereas value-oriented movements
do.[11]

The Psychological Approach

Hadley Cantril's work,[12] frequently cited in bibliographies on
social movements, is devoted first to the individual's mental context,
motivation, and pursuit of meaning as related to social movements.
The remainder of the work is a series of accounts of five individual
social movements: Father Divine's movement, the Oxford Group,
the Townsend Plan, the Nazi party, and the Lynching Mob. One can
only agree with Heberle's evaluation of the Cantril work as "a series
of case studies, with no systematic comparative theory of social
movements, not enough on the organization and structure of movements, and focusing entirely on the socio-psychological foundations
of social movements."[13] This criticism has already been extended
to the other representatives of the psychological approach to the
study of social movements.

Like Cantril, Eric Hoffer offers no definition of a social movement. Toch, however, states that "a social movement represents
an effort by a large number of people to solve collectively a problem
that they feel they have in common."[14]

The Sociological Approach

Heberle's work, which contains the above critique of Cantril,
seems to be one of the first sociological approaches to the study of
social movements. Heberle maintains that a social movement aims
to bring about fundamental changes in the social order, to change the
patterns of human relations and social institutions. Ferdinand Tonnies's
term "social collectives" is utilized in Heberle's treatment of social
movements as a special kind of social group, of a peculiar unorganized
structure. A sense of group identity and solidarity is required, and a
social movement must be large enough to continue its existence even
with a change in membership.[15]

Another sociological approach is found in King's Social Movements in the U.S. King offers a cogent analysis of social movements and raises five issues for consideration: the nature of movements and the societies in which they occur, the development and ongoing process of a movement, the reactions of members to change, the growth or decline of the movement as a reflection of its elements, and the influence of the external setting. The distinguishing features of social movements, according to King, are change as the purpose, their use of organization, their durability, and their geographical scope. He defines a social movement as "a collective ready for action by which some kind of change is to be achieved, some innovation to be made, or some previous condition to be restored, extending beyond a local community or single event."[16]

An interesting view within the sociological framework is found in a very brief article by VanderZanden.[17] Here he points out the fact that social movements have traditionally been defined so as to exclude movements resisting change, and thus are studies of reform and revolutionary movements. This closes the door on much of the dynamics of change and yields only sterile studies, he contends. But social movements often stimulate the rise of movements opposed to change, and the study of the countermovement that arises is essential to the analysis of the interaction. He maintains that the countermovement frequently influences the speed, degree, and nature of social change. The function of the countermovement is seen as a gradualization of the process of social change, thus preventing sharp and sudden social dislocations, and providing for a less traumatic transition to a new social order.

Thus VanderZanden concludes that a more satisfactory definition of the social movement would be, "a more or less persistent organized effort of a considerable number of members of a society either to change a situation defined as unsatisfactory or to prevent change in a situation they define as satisfactory."[18] Turner and Killian's work includes resistance to change in their definition, other authors also consider at length the "opposition" as a significant force in social movements, though they do not include this in their definitions.

William Cameron's recent work, Modern Social Movements, attempts an analysis of social movements as "an area of problems." Cameron considers four aspects of social movements: general characteristics, membership, structure and rationale, and methods of social action. Each aspect is illustrated with a specific social movement, such as the Black Muslims, the Communists, civil rights, and passive resistance. He defines a social movement as "occurring when a fairly large number of people band together to alter or supplant some portion of the existing culture or social order."[19]

"The Study of Social Movements," by Joseph Gusfield, in the Encyclopedia of the Social Sciences, offers a definition of a social movement as "socially shared demands for change in some aspects of the social order." He adds, . . ."a social movement. . .has the character of an explicit and conscious indictment of whole or part of the social order, together with a conscious demand for change."[20]

A social movement is defined by Zald and Ash as "a purposive and collective attempt of a number of people to change individuals or societal institutions and structure."[21] Though Zald and Ash include individual change within their definition, their approach generally is a sociological one, focusing on movement organizations through which they say social movements manifest themselves.

Rush and Denisoff define social movements as collective organizational phenomena which function in relation to some form of social change.[22] Movements have a problem orientation, and they are not perceived as legitimate in the eyes of the public.

Ash also uses a conflict perspective in her definition: "A social movement is a set of attitudes and self-conscious action on the part of a group of people directed toward change in the social structure and/or ideology of a society, and carried on outside of ideologically legitimated channels, or which uses these channels in innovative ways."[23]

Finally, John Wilson sees a social movement as "a conscious, collective, organized attempt to bring about or resist large-scale change in the social order by noninstitutionalized means."[24]

Through a synthesis of the foregoing definitions, it is possible to produce a comprehensive definition of a social movement as "a collectivity acting with some continuity to promote or resist change, extending beyond a local community or single event." The distinguishing features of social movements may also be cited as change-oriented goals, the use of organization, durability, and geographical scope. It should be noted, however, that this represents an ideal-type definition and that an actual social movement may not correspond exactly to this final synthesis.

Structure

There is more to the concept of the social movement than a mere definition, however. An examination of the many component characteristics and parts of a social movement, as revealed in each of the three approaches, suggests that these might be combined into three key structural features: organization, ideology, and strategy. The many classifications of types of movements seem to be related to the particular kind of ideology or strategy that characterizes a movement.

Organization: Leaders and Followers

Organization seems most frequently to be conceived, in all three approaches, in terms of leadership and membership or following, though the psychological approach focuses primarily on membership.

The treatment of leadership in the literature on social movements can be traced back to Max Weber's distinction among charismatic, traditional, and legal-rational authority types.[25] Similar typologies have been offered by a number of other scholars. Among the collective behaviorists, for example, Blumer suggests four types: the agitator, the prophet, the statesman, the administrator. He recognizes that more than one of the types may perform more than one of the roles, and no necessary progression is implied.[26] Turner and Killian use the terms charismatic, intellectual, and administrative,[27] and discuss the leader as symbol and decision maker. Several types of leaders are referred to, drawing on previous writings of other scholars. The authors suggest that although leader decisions are often passive responses to the cultural or historical situation, occasionally such decisions are crucial and can affect the course of history. The role of the leader may develop leadership qualities and even charisma. Members' motivations are viewed in terms of personal characteristics cited as prestige, isolation, inadequacy, and simplistic (narrow-minded) life views. This seems a surprisingly negative interpretation of membership in an otherwise straightforward presentation of the general subject matter.

Lang and Lang, also collective behaviorists, note that leadership needs in a movement change as the movement changes. Early leaders serve to unify the followers and also act as instigators or initiators who supply an example or model. The active direction of a recognized leader or core group in the early stages is seen as necessary for offering a plan or ideology for unfocused sentiments. In the beginning, according to the authors, agitators are needed, followed by prophets, and then by administrator-statesmen, although these types are not limited to any one phase. The involvement of leaders varies, as does the response to their differential leadership roles.

> The sporadic fellowship the reformer receives in return
> for his espousal of an unpopular cause rarely compen-
> sates for the rupture of social relations it requires. Of
> all the leaders of social movements, the reformer appears
> the most lonely and therefore the most dedicated to his
> goal.[28]

Smelser discusses leadership as a part of his examination of mobilization for action. Two kinds of leaders are depicted, those formulating beliefs and those mobilizing for action, though it is noted that sometimes the same person can perform both functions. Membership is fleetingly referred to in terms of diversity of motivation and grievances among participants of a movement.

The psychological approach, as typified by Cantril, focuses primarily on membership or followers. This is analyzed in terms of the individual's mental context, motivation, and pursuit of meaning as a participants in a social movement. Hoffer's work is also devoted almost exclusively to the psychological attributes of members or followers and the leaders of social movements. Hoffer contends it is essential for a movement to have a tangible enemy, as well as leadership. He asserts that leadership cannot create the conditions that make the rise of a movement possible; there has to be eagerness to follow and intense dissatisfaction with things as they are before the movement and the leader can make their appearance. Once the stage is set, the presence of an outstanding leader is indispensable, for without him there will be no movement. The types of leadership are related to the phase of the movement:

> The readying of ground for a mass movement is best done by men of words, the hatching of the movement requires the talents of a fanatic, and the final consolidation is largely the work of practical men of action.[29]

At the outset, Hoffer maintains that some peculiarities are common to all mass movements:

> All mass movements generate in their adherents a readiness to die, a proclivity for united action; all breed fanaticism, enthusiasm, fervent hope, hatred and intolerance; all are capable of releasing a powerful flow of activity in certain departments of life; all of them demand blind faith and singlehearted allegiance. . . .
>
> Although all movements differ in doctrine and aspiration they draw their adherents from the same types of humanity and appeal to the same types of mind.[30]

Hoffer's work is chiefly concerned with ". . . the active revivalist phase of mass movements, which is dominated by the true believer— the man of fanatical faith ready to sacrifice his life for a holy cause— everywhere on the march, shaping the world by converting and antagonizing."[31] The obvious fallacy in Hoffer's presentation is his unrealistic conception of social movements as monolithic. It would be rather difficult to place a number of actual social movements into Hoffer's conceptual framework.

Toch devotes considerable attention to the development of members, from indoctrination in childhood, to the consequences of being a member, and finally to the dynamics of disaffection.

In the sociological approach, King considers leadership as part of the organization and status system of a movement, and he categorizes leaders as charismatic or legal, drawing on Max Weber. He maintains that members' motives and acceptance of innovation are the key factors in enabling a movement to survive and flourish.

Killian views the structure of social movements in terms of leadership and following. Three classes of leaders are suggested: charismatic, administrative, and intellectual. The charismatic leader simplifies and symbolizes the values, the administrative leader promotes them and serves as a conservatizing force, and the intellectual leader elaborates and justifies the values. These roles may be combined in one person, but Killian maintains this is unusual.

According to Killian, the two key factors in the strengthening of the values of a movement are the evolution of a hierarchy of leadership and the response of the potential followers. The leader must define ultimate and intermediate objectives to the recruits, and must formulate the strategy in terms of societal manipulation or personal transformation or both.

Cameron divides membership into attitudes toward new members (exclusive, receptive, proselytizing, coercive) and member motivations (interest, fellowship, status, manipulation). The structure and rationale of a social movement is concerned with some theoretical bases of authority, organization (including leadership and policy formation), and unity and continuity (including symbols, creeds, propaganda, and discipline).

Gusfield analyzes leaders in terms of functions—the mobilization function and the articulation function. The first refers to the need to build support within the movement; the second refers to the need to gain acceptance and understanding in the larger society:

> Janus-like, the leader stands in one place, facing two
> different ways. Here he faces inward, toward the goals
> and ideals of the adherents. In the other direction he
> functions as a negotiator and communicator between the
> external environment and the internal one. [32]

More recently, Zald and Ash have also used the charismatic and rational-legal distinction. They see charismatic authority, characteristic of the earliest stages of a movement, as being superseded

by the rational-legal type and they suggest the conditions under which
this will and will not occur. However, they caution against the notion
of a simple and inevitable progression, and suggest that different
kinds of movement organizations make different demands on leaders.

Movement organizations, according to Zald and Ash, can be
differentiated in terms of exclusive or inclusive membership relating
to levels of commitment. The inclusive organization requires minimum
levels of commitment from members, while the exclusive movement
organization (MO) demands maximum commitment, activity, and
participation from members. These two different types of movement
organizations are related to goal types and eventual impact on the
social environment.

The problem of commitment is also examined by John Wilson.
He indicates that the members of a movement are not a monolithic
uniform group, having equal motivations. He suggests that one way
of conceptualizing the personnel of a movement is to imagine them in
an onion-ring formation, in which commitment lessens as the outer
circles are approached. Wilson claims that when an individual joins
a movement he or she does not necessarily make a commitment to
the group, but must be persuaded to do so. Sympathy can be transformed into commitment by participation in tactics. Once commitment
is gained, however, it must be sustained, and this is a chronic difficulty that movements face. One reason for this is that there is
bound to be disappointment over the lack of immediate achievement
of the movement's objectives. Another is that the movement may
operate in a hostile environment that challenges the movement's
right to exist and the integrity of each member in it.

Finally, it has been noted that when a person is ready to join
a movement, it is the movement that gets to him first that will
recruit him.[33] Also important in influencing potential followers is
the extent to which one movement may be more available or accessible
than another. Empirical studies of joiners and followers have shown
that focusing on the characteristics of the participants can tell us
little about the formation of movements, since similar characteristics
have been found in nonjoiners and nonparticipants.[34]

There is, however, statistical evidence that the act of joining
is facilitated by friendship ties between the members of the movement and the potential recruit.[35] So interpersonal contact through
favorable channels is as important as ideological appeal, since people
who join movements do so partly because people in the groups they
already belong to have joined. In the process of becoming a member,
participation in one group facilitates entrance into another.

Ideology and Strategy

Among the collective behaviorists, Turner and Killian discuss
the value-orientations of social movements, stating that the publicly

understood program of a movement is the key to understanding the
movement itself. The ideology of the movement evolves interdependently
with the program (strategy). Both are linked together in values.

The essential aspects of a movement are threefold, according
to Turner and Killian: a program for the reform of society, promotion
of membership gratifications, and the establishment of power
relations favorable to the movement. These depend on the type of
movement; those geared to societal manipulation are contrasted with
those based on personal transformation. Movements are categorized
as to public definition, type of opposition, and means of action. [36]

Lang and Lang consider strategy and tactics as major structural
problems. Tactics are seen by them as the prime sources of the
dramatic success of some social movements, with successful persuasion
cited as most significant in this context.

The ideology of the movement refers to the content of the official
doctrines, and includes a statement of purpose, a doctrine of
defense, an indictment of existing social arrangements, and a general
design for action. Relevant in this context are myths, the promise of
success, heroes and villains, and folk arguments. The existence of
several sets of ideologies simultaneously in the same movement is
recognized, with those of the inner circle and those for popular consumption
differentiated. Unifying forces of a movement are symbols,
esprit de corps, villain-idol stereotypes, and opposition, according
to Lang and Lang. A degree of opposition is believed by these authors
to be needed in order to develop the "zeal and fanaticism necessary
for the success of a movement." [37]

Among those using the psychological approach, Toch defines
ideology as a "set of related beliefs held by a group of persons. The
ideology of a social movement is a statement of what the members of
the movement are trying to achieve together, and what they wish to
affirm jointly." [38] He asserts that the ultimate test of how central a
belief is, is not its position in the logical structure or its objective
importance, but the way it is perceived by the believer.

In the sociological approach, Heberle's analysis of ideologies
of social movements is given extensive treatment and yields some
interesting observations. He sees ideologies as constitutive values
and essential to the movement, forming the spiritual-intellectual
foundation of group cohesion or solidarity. The ideology is "the
principles and action programs on which the members have reached
a general agreement." [39] He notes that publicly proclaimed goals
and ideas are not always the true aims of a movement. Sometimes
these are formulated in a vague way to unite masses of members who
would not agree on more definite formulations. He suggests that
ideas and doctrines are conditioned by their authors' position in the
social stratification of their society and by the historical situation in
which the ideas were conceived.

Ideology is considered by King as one of the critical elements of social movements, which also include goals, group cohesion, organization and status system, and tactics. Goals are categorized as to whether they are explicit or implicit, general or specific, and immediate or ultimate.

Killian notes two common features of social movements: the recognition that people's acts are collective, and the awareness of people's efforts to intervene in the process of change. From these features Killian derives the characteristics of social movements, which he cites as the existence of shared values (goals, ideology), a sense in membership of participation, norms—the shared understanding of how followers should act—definitions and prescribed behavior toward outgroups, and a structure encompassing the division of labor between leaders and followers. [40]

In discussing ideology, Gusfield states that the beliefs of any social movement reflect "the unique situation of the social segments that make up its base." [41] These beliefs represent a model of experience, and this experience is relevant only to the particular segment of society that has experienced it. Thus the ideology seems valid to that segment, and meaningfully specifies discontent, prescribes solutions, and justifies change.

According to Rush and Denisoff, an ideology sets the goals and defines the characteristic nature of a movement. In fact, they refer to movements as ideological organizations, and claim that ideology is interwoven with the type of social change that the members of a movement want. It is, then, a guidepost to the future, as well as being grounded in the past.

John Wilson suggests that an ideology consists of three interrelated aspects: a diagnosis of present problems, a solution for these problems, and a vision of a better world. He sees ideology as a vital bridge between attitude and action, and claims that ultimately it is the ideology that is the carrier of the ideas that mobilize people into action. Action, in social movements, is what is referred to as strategy or program. It is, of course, linked to ideology, and both are necessary to a social movement. Strategy is the general program for achieving the goals of the movement, and tactics refer to the specific ways of carrying out the program or strategy.

Strategic considerations are important, not only for achieving goals, but also for recruiting members and gaining their commitment. Wilson suggests that tactics provide the real meaning of the movement and are the main source of involvement for the followers. For those outside the movement, it is the tactical behavior that gives the movement its identity.

Movements have three primary strategies open to them—persuasion, bargaining, and coercion—but no movement relies solely on any one of these strategies. "Movement leaders must make sure they are not boring their audience (the public, and internal supporters), and thus the popular demand for ever-new tactics places enormous burdens on a movement's leaders."[42]

There is no such thing as the successful tactic—it depends on the movement circumstances, its resources, and the opposition it encounters, according to Wilson. Generally, he suggests that tactics must advance the movement toward its goals and yet sustain the followers as a united group. Specifically, tactics should be comprehensive, simple, and flexible.

Robert Lauer notes that strategies have received little attention in the literature on social movements, though they are of critical importance. He attempts to develop a useful typology of strategies, based on three factors: who implements the change (the movement or the larger society), how much force is required for the change (nonviolent or coercive/violent), and the target of the change (individuals or the social structure). He then suggests how movement ideology and interaction with the larger society relate to the choice of one or more of six different strategies: educative, small-group, bargaining, separatist, disruptive, and revolutionary.[43]

Finally, in considering strategies one must consider not only those of the movement, but also the responding ones of the target group or those in opposition. Three negative responses have been identified as cooptation, suppression, and discreditation. Rush and Denisoff offer prognoses as to which types of movements are most susceptible to each of these responses, and they further relate these to types of society (pluralist or elitist).[44]

Zald and McCarthy have also considered factors outside the movement in the choice of tactics. They refer to tactical dilemmas which are related to five factors that limit strategic choices: the values of the adherents, the values of the public, the relationship to authorities, the activities of the authorities, and the relationship to goals. These authors offer a resource-mobilization perspective on social movements, which is based on organizational use of people, money, and support in the achievement of movement goals. These are linked to the potential for cooperation and conflict between movement organizations.[45]

Types of Movements

The many classifications of types of movements are related to the particular kind of ideology or strategy that characterizes a movement. Thus, movements may differ in goals directed toward changing individuals or society, they may differ in the extent of change sought, and in the means of attaining that change. They may also differ in terms of membership types, leadership types, and other organizational attributes, which in turn may be linked to different phases of development of the movement.

Among the collective behaviorists, Blumer classifies movements as to types of goals: general, specific, expressive. Turner and Killian divide movements into those geared to societal change and those based on personal transformation. They further separate them into type of public definition (revolutionary, reform, or peculiar), type of opposition, and means of action. Smelser divides movements on the basis of whether they are value-oriented or norm-oriented.

Among those using the sociological approach, King classifies movements as revolutionary or reform. Cameron divides movements according to methods of social action: non-violent, quasi-violent, and violent. He categorizes the purposes of social movements as reactionary, conservative, revisionary, and revolutionary. Ash also divides movements into revolutionary or reform, and cautions against the classification into expressive or instrumental, claiming that "all movements have elements of both."[46] Rush and Denisoff describe four types of movements: revolutionary, regressive, reform, and expressive. Roberts and Kloss point out the relationship between reform and revolution, and note its complexity:

> Sometimes reforms are used to prevent revolution; in other cases they have paved the way for deeply radical change. Many. . .have argued that most revolutionary movements, of necessity, shift to reformist goals after a time because of the natural inability of the masses of people to remain mobilized over time.[47]

Process

Logically, process includes the stages of development of a movement, and the consequences or impact of a movement. Each of these is affected by some of the internal aspects of the movement— organizational features previously cited—and some external forces impinging on the movement in its genesis and subsequent development. Zald and Ash state that movement organizations are subject to internal and external pressures affecting their viability, structure and development, and ultimate success in attaining goals.

Among the three approaches, the most substantial theoretical development is found in the more recent literature of the sociological approach, where four models of movement origin are offered. Impact, however, continues to receive little consideration in all three ap-

proaches. Perhaps this is because the concept of success or effectiveness presents such difficulties:

> . . . how is one to distinguish the creative and construc-
> tive elements of social movement(s)? Unless we play gods
> ourselves we cannot finally and definitively hand out the
> prizes at some kind of historical judgement day. [48]

Beginning again with the collective behaviorists, Turner and
Killian see value in studying the development of a social movement in
terms of a life cycle, since this emphasizes process, permits prediction, and allows discovery of the additional conditions needed for
each stage.

In their examination of the endproducts of social movements
the authors confront the stage of institutionalization and equate it
with decline, as has already been noted. Whether a social movement
disappears or becomes a different social form depends on the impact
of the movement on the social order and vice versa. Thus these
authors view the reciprocal interaction between the movement and
the social order an essential part of the study of social movements.
In the stage of institutionalization, further stability is achieved, the
area of activity is diversified, the prestige factor for members is
increased, and the ideologies are modified for acceptability. It is
the success of the movement that leads to its transformation.

Success of a movement, elusive though that concept may be,
is examined by Turner and Killian in terms of meaning, measurement, and prediction. Two meanings of success are offered initially:
an increase in numbers of adherents, and perpetuation of the movement and its objectives. Various criteria of success are found in
every movement, and in the last analysis what is success depends on
the perspective of the observer, according to these authors. A definition of success, as applied to value-oriented movements, is "the
degree to which desired changes are promoted in the larger society."[49]
Somewhat more fruitful is the discussion of the chances of success
for a given movement. The authors suggest that success depends on
a permissive atmosphere, passive sympathy of the masses, flexibility of goals (immediate and ultimate), the linking of movement
values with sacred societal ones, and the presence of a common
enemy.

Even with a decline, Turner and Killian note that a movement
may persist for some time. Loss of power, program, or membership may be followed by transformation, stabilization, and continued
existence. Conditions that keep a movement alive include the desire
of the leadership for maintenance of prestige and the desire of the
membership for continued participation gratifications. Whether

institutionalization and decline is the end result of a movement or not, the conservatizing aspect of movements is seen by the authors as universal. They suggest that any movement arises out of prevailing societal values, and is therefore a conservatizing link to conventional values.

Turner and Killian consider both stability and change as conditions promoted by collective behavior. The new ideas of one period become the old ones of the next; thus, the institutionalization of collective behavior combines man's tendencies toward routinization and toward ideological innovation. The reasoning here suggests an equilibrium theory of society which is not logically consistent with the study of social movements. As illustrations of their concept of the social movement, they cite the Townsend movement, the labor movement, political revolution, and religious movements.

Lang and Lang note three approaches used in the study of social movements: the natural-history method, the cross-sectional method (seen from a variety of perspectives), and the comparative method. They view the development of social movements in terms of the well-known "careers" of Carl Dawson and W. E. Gettys.[50] The career of a social movement is seen as beginning with a period of unrest with the agitator as the typical leader, then a period of popular excitement in which the vision of the prophet or the objective defined by the reformer spreads by contagion. A stage of formal organization follows, headed by an administrator, with the beginnings of a division of labor, formal criteria of membership, and so out. And finally comes the stage of institutionalization, when the movement—now bureaucratized—is represented by a statesman. The style of organization is affected by the degree of opposition, the social position of the followers, the aims of the movement, the cultural ethos of the society, and the type of leadership.

In considering the dynamics of social movements, Lang and Lang view social movements as creators of and responders to changes in social conditions. The heterogeneity of a population sharpens response to change, and social movements are more likely to arise in a society undergoing rapid change. Widespread discontent plus faith in the mission of the movement are seen by these authors as necessary prerequisites for the formation of a movement. Mass communications facilitate the rapid spread of a movement, since shared perspectives are also necessary for the movement's growth.

The authors describe three basic approaches to the study of collective dynamics: one which views it as social progress, one which views it as pathological regression, and one which sees both constructive and regressive aspects through the natural-history approach. Though this is useful in evaluating other works, it must be noted that the natural-history approach might be used equally well with either the progress or regression perspectives. In other words, the use of this method is irrelevent to the value perspective of the user.

Smelser distinguishes the natural-history approach from his value-added approach. The natural-history approach involves an account of one event or situation followed by another, and another, without stating whether the prior stages are necessary conditions for the later stages. The value-added approach, in contrast, does posit a sequence for the empirical establishment of events and situations.

A "map of social action" is offered by Smelser, indicating the main transition points as human resources move "from general unde-fined states to their more specific operative states."[51] His map is systematically presented in terms of "levels of specificity of the com-ponents of social action," and includes values, norms, mobilization for action, and situational facilities.

Development of a movement is very briefly considered by Smelser in terms of three phases: the incipient phase, the phase of enthusiastic mobilization, and the phase of institutionalization and organization. A period of very rapid growth and a period of equally rapid decline is suggested as characteristic of norm-oriented move-ments.

Social control is carefully examined in terms of impact on the movement. General encouragement by political authorities boosts and consolidates the movement. Agencies of social control must permit the expression of grievances, but only within the confines of legiti-macy. They can close off avenues to normative change by the fol-lowing actions: consistently refusing to recognize one or more groups in a community, appearing to vacillate in the face of pressure from the movement, appearing to close off abruptly the avenues for agita-tion, appearing to take sides, and openly encouraging some other kind of collective outburst. Smelser concludes that different kinds of outbursts may be produced by the same kinds of strain if the social structure and social control situations change.

Smelser was among the first to approach a theory of social movements. Some limitations of his analysis, however, should be noted. Although his scheme of the levels of specificity is a tidy one, it is difficult to see how it can be applied to actual situations of collective behavior. Given this neat and orderly sequence of action, one is still at a loss to determine which kind of collective behavior will be produced by which kind of strain or structure or social control situation. Thus the predictability value of this theory is questionable. Also, the line between norm-oriented and value-oriented movements seems a very thin one. Surely values are heavily involved in a situa-tion of normative change, and surely a change in values is likely to have great relevance to changed normative patterns. It is difficult to

accept his careful division, and even more difficult to accept his given
sequence as to norms and values in movements.

The psychological approach to social movements is weakest in
its treatment of development and impact. Cantril offers nothing along
these lines. Hoffer sees a stifling of creativity in active mass movements, and maintains that the way in which the movement begins has
an effect on the duration of its active phase; and that the personality
of the leader plays a crucial role regarding the duration and nature of
the mass movement. This is much in keeping with his general patho-
logical-regression approach to social movements, as described
earlier by Lang and Lang.

Toch does consider briefly the relationship of the social movement to the larger society, and does note the developmental process
of the social movement. He sees evaluation of the movement as an
extremely complex task for the social scientist:

> Different components of a movement have different con-
> sequences—some obviously constructive, others self-
> defeating, and some contingent or uncertain. In certain
> ways a movement may seem to help its members; in other
> ways it may magnify their problems. In some respects it
> may stimulate progress in society, while in other ways it
> may erect barriers to remedial efforts. [52]

For Toch, the main criterion for evaluating a social movement is its
relationship to individual members. The benefit and impact of the
movement on its members are the crucial factors in evaluation, but
he gives no actual directives for making such an assessment.

An award for citing the greatest number of illustrations, of
social movements must surely be given to Toch. From the Anti-Digit
Dialing League, to the American Sunbathing Society, to Alchoholics
Anonymous, the American Humanist Society, the D.A.R., the
Catholic Worker movement, and the Flying Saucer Clubs, to the Nazi
party, the Townsend movement, the civil rights movement, and the
peace movement, he presents innumerable examples, each illustrating
a different aspect of social movements. In retrospect, one is more
confused than ever about the nature of a social movement because of
the very diversity of the actual movements cited. One wonders whether
Toch's work was conceived to illustrate his examples, or whether the
examples were indeed selected to illustrate his concepts.

In any case, the same criticism must be applied to Toch as to
the other representatives of the psychological approach. There is a
singular lack of consideration of the organization and structure of
social movements and of their crucial interrelationship with the
society at large.

Is the <u>sociological approach</u> any better? Heberle sees social movements as related to the general phenomenon of social change, and closely bound to certain social classes and opposed by others. He considers only briefly the impact of social movements, as is revealed in one of his early observations:

> It is true, however, that movements of minor significance which aim at a partial reform in the social order, and even movements limited to a local community, may show traits of general significance in the sociological sense. One can learn from such movements a good deal that is helpful for the understanding of major social movements, and they may therefore contribute to a theory of social movements.[53]

Since he nowhere defines what he means by major or minor significance, it is difficult to relate this to application, but it does indicate his view of the study of social movements as a means of clarifying the general process of social action and social change. The bulk of his work is directed to the analysis of political parties and movements of a totalitarian nature.

King considers the development of a social movement in some detail in terms of "careers." He uses the natural-history approach and suggests four stages of development: social unrest, popularization, formal organization, and institutionalization. Two dimensions of change, suggested as significant, are successive internal alterations and reciprocal relations toward the external society.

There are two principle external influences on growth, according to King, —the general cultural context and the differential receptivity of subgroups. He considers the purposes and consequences of social movements in terms of accidental influences, manifest and latent consequences, and social change in general. Examples cited are the Grange, Christian Science, and the Ku Klux Klan.

King's approach is refreshingly free of the view of social movements and their participants as either destructive or peculiar (the regression approach noted by Lang and Lang earlier). His analysis is straightforward and systematic and seems to lend itself well to application. Of particular interest is his concern with manifest and latent consequences, which seems to offer fruitful possibilities for further study.

Killian views social movements primarily as a process of social and cultural change. He sees the changes that take place as important end products of social movements and also as features of the new setting within which new movements develop. The genesis of social movements stems from the nature of the social order and the socialization process, according to Killian. He notes that the social order is not only satisfying but also frustrating. The socialization process produces unique individuals. Both of these conditions, then, challenge the existing order and stability of the culture. In order for a movement to begin, there must be a vision and organization for the attainment of goals. The values of a movement must be reconciled with those of the larger society, and may be of different types—progressive or reactionary, comprehensive or restricted, explicit or implicit. The values imply the means for achieving the goals.

In considering the consequences of social movements, Killian suggests that some movements leave little mark on society, but even those that die may have a great effect on society. Also the specific movement that fails may leave behind the seeds of another specific movement. Success is not measured in terms of values being actually realized, he contends, since values have something of the nature of myths. One way, however, in which a social movement may contribute to social change is by forcing the established structure of society to come to terms with it and its values. Institutionalization also symbolizes success and may accompany acceptance of values. There is a continuous formulation, revision, and reformulation of values and norms in the process of a movement's development. It is this constant interaction and modification of group structure that produces social change.

Cameron sees no characteristic life cycle of the social movement, but he does consider the development of a theory of social movements. He suggests that it should be interdisciplinary, that it should state how the form of social action is related to the rationale and the purpose, that it should state the circumstances under which a movement may be expected to arise, and that it should state the determinants of the genesis of the movement and its possible success.

Gusfield notes the tendency of movements to generate public controversy as they arise, grow, and become recognized. He, like Smelser, considers the structural conduciveness to the development of a movement: "Dissent may be condoned in one society but so prohibited in another that the movement must take the form of a secret society." In conclusion, he states that ". . .events which are unanticipated and beyond the control or influence of the movement often change the constellation of resisting and supporting forces and thus strongly affect its career."[54]

Four Models of Movement Emergence

Recent structural-Societal explanations of movement origins can be divided into four different models: mass society, collective organization, structural differentiation, and power elite. These are all societal models, dealing with structural differentials. Several status differential models have also been offered, but these are more individualistically oriented and are not included here.[55]

The mass-society model has been advanced by a number of scholars, and is the oldest of these theoretical perspectives.[56] Briefly, this model suggests that the more recent proliferation of social movements in history stems from the social disorganization prevalent in urban-industrial mass societies. Such societies lack social cohesion, are politically fragmented, and have masses that are highly susceptible to the appeals of movements, which are easily spread through mass communication.

Precisely the opposite of mass-society theory is the collective-organization model of Anthony Oberschall.[57] This model suggests that movements emerge out of already existing organizational networks, which may occur in two different types of social structure. The first is organized along traditional lines of kinship or village; the second along modern lines of secondary associations based on special interests. Both of these types of structures (horizontal) produce bonds within the groups, which can be activated for the pursuit of common goals and the formation of protest groups. Along vertical lines, the type of stratification system in the society also affects the mobilization potential. If the system is segmented, there are more bonds between the classes, with less potential for protest group formation. Oberschall's theory suggests that the most organized and cohesive groups will mobilize the most rapidly and effectively to promote their joint interests. It also stresses segmentation as a favorable condition of mobilization. Oberschall offers four hypotheses that expand the theory and offer predictions of movement emergence under varying conditions. Zald and McCarthy have extended this model with their resource-mobilization theory, suggesting how movement organizations can use the environment for their own purposes.[58]

The structural-differentiation model of John Wilson also uses vertical and horizontal dimensions, but in a totally different way. This model describes the way in which societies tend to become differentiated into separate substructures. Horizontal differentiation is a separation of norms and values; vertical differentiation is a separation of specialized institutions. With low horizontal differentiation, any attempt to change behavior is difficult because it is linked to the values. Thus, change is more likely to result in revolution rather than in reform. Similarly, with low vertical differentiation among institutions, any attempt to change one will imply change in all the others, and here too revolutionary movements are more likely than reform. Wilson's model thus suggests not only the potential for movement emergence, but also the type of movement most likely under the structural conditions given.[59]

Ash's power-elite model posits three basic assumptions concerning analytic levels of society (of which there are three), the most important elites of a society (those that control the relations of production), and societal structure (center and periphery). She states that social movements are basically related to the middle level of society—the social-structural level—and are caused by transformations of the material substructure (the production level).

Ash suggests that movements will fail if they try to change ideologies (values) without changing the substructure (norms). She also states that social movements are very likely to change those institutions that are peripheral rather than central to the class structure. The more institutional change in these areas threatens power relations and control of property, the more it will be resisted. The broader the goals of a social movement, the more central its focus; thus the greater its threat to class structure and the less likely it will be to succeed.

Finally, Ash suggests that there are two crucial moments that concern the student of social movements. First is the point at which the individual frees himself from the prevailing ideology, and second is the point at which he acts as a member of a social movement. Ash reminds us that the perception of a problem situation does not necessarily suggest a course of action. What is needed is leadership and organization to channel and sustain popular energies toward constructive change.[60]

Institutionalization

The discussion now returns full-circle to the concept that originally guided this study. As was indicated earlier, much of the literature on social movements includes material on the careers or phases of development of movements, and emphasizes the changes movements undergo as they develop and expand and attempt to establish themselves in society. The final stage of development is referred to as institutionalization.

The idea of social movements having careers is based on two generalizations that prevail in the literature: people in social movements tend to regularize and routinize their affairs as they come to feel the need for order and predictability; and movements typically experience a transformation of mission from general ideological goals to mere survival or self-maintenance. This is referred to as goal displacement, and is usually associated with the increasing bureaucratization of a movement over time. Routinization also leads to the concentration of decision making in a managerial elite, a process referred to as oligarchization.

Centralization in movements develops in two ways, according to Wilson. The first type of growth is centripetal, where coalition of formerly separate groups occurs, merging into one large organization. The second type of growth is centrifugal, where one central group spins off new groups as the movement expands. In both of these situations, routinization tends to lead to the concentration of decision making in a managerial elite.

The central question here is: Does this lead to the decline of the movement qua movement? Or is it possible that despite growth, routinization, centralization, efficiency, and formalization, the movement can continue as a movement—still guided by its original ideology, dedication, and vision? If so, what are the conditions under which this is possible? In any case,

> One thing cannot be denied. Few social movements enjoy the feeling of having completed their mission and contentedly disband. The dream they try to realize can rarely be achieved. Frustration is the fate of all social movements. [61]

SUMMARY

The analysis of the three approaches to the concept of a social movement, in terms of definition, structure, and process, can be briefly summarized.

The psychological approach is inadequate in that it fails to consider the structural aspects of a movement, such as organization and strategy. Especially crucial is its lack of consideration of the development and reciprocal impact of a movement as it relates to the larger society.

There seem to be two primary features that distinguish the collective-behavior approach from the sociological approach. The collective-behavior approach considers the social movement only as a special type of collective behavior—a type that requires more organization than other more elementary types. The collective-behavior approach also presents a much more diffused conception of the social movement, one that encompasses a much wider range of collective activity than is found in the sociological approach. Thus movements that are directed to personal transformation are included in the concept, as well as those oriented to societal change. The sociological approach, on the other hand, seems to limit the social movement to collective action oriented to some form of societal change.

Although both the collective-behavior approach and the sociological approach deal in considerable detail with the definition, structure, and process of a movement, only the more recent works in the sociological approach have moved toward theory construction. This has been primarily in the area of process—the stages of development of a movement, and the accompanying changes within the movement. There is still little theoretical development concerning the impact of movements and their relationship to social change.

In an attempt to develop a synthesis of all three approaches, a social movement is most comprehensively defined as a collectivity acting with some continuity to promote or resist change, extending beyond a local community or single event. The distinguishing features of social movements are change-oriented goals, the use of organization, durability, and geographical scope. Social movements are studied in terms of growth patterns or natural histories or life cycles. External influences are considered significant in the genesis and development of social movements. Internal organizational features such as leadership, membership, ideology, and strategy are of great importance in considering the development of the movement and its ultimate impact. The impact of a movement is viewed in terms of manifest and latent consequences, and the movement itself is regarded as both a product and producer of social change.

The chapters that follow will discuss the longitudinal study of one movement in transition, focusing on the developmental aspects of institutionalization and success as they relate to the open-housing movement. Perhaps in the course of this study, some relationships will be uncovered that will make possible further progress in the development of a theory of social movements within the context of social change.

NOTES

1. Ralph Turner and Lewis Killian, Collective Behavior (Englewood Cliffs, N. J.: Prentice-Hall, 1957), pp. 480-81.

2. Kurt Lang and Gladys Lang, Collective Dynamics (New York: Crowell Collier, 1961), p. 533.

3. Neil Smelser, Theory of Collective Behavior (New York: Free Press, 1963), p. 42.

4. Hans Toch, The Social Psychology of Social Movements (New York: Bobbs-Merrill, 1965), p. 215.

5. C. Wendell King, Social Movements in the U.S. (New York: Random House, 1956), p. 40.

6. Joseph Gusfield, "The Study of Social Movements," in International Encyclopedia of the Social Sciences, ed. David L. Sills (New York: Crowell Collier and Macmillan, 1968), pp. 448.

7. John Wilson, Introduction to Social Movements (New York: Basic Books, 1973), p. 14.

8. Herbert Blumer, "Collective Behavior," in Review of Sociology, ed. B. Gittler (New York: Wiley, 1957); and his "Collective

Behavior," in New Outline of the Principles of Sociology, ed. A. Lee, (New York: Barnes & Noble, 1951), pp. 167-219.

9. Turner and Killian, op. cit., p. 308.

10. Lang and Lang, op. cit., p. 490.

11. Smelser, op. cit., p. 270.

12. Hadley Cantril, The Psychology of Social Movements (New York: Wiley, 1941).

13. Rudolph Heberle, Social Movements (New York: Appleton-Century, 1951), p. 3.

14. Toch, op. cit., p. 5.

15. Heberle, op. cit., p. 3.

16. King, op. cit., p. 27.

17. James VanderZanden, "Resistance and Social Movements," Social Forces, 37 (May 1959): 312-15.

18. Ibid.

19. William Cameron, Modern Social Movements (New York: Random House, 1966), p. 7.

20. Gusfield, op. cit., p. 445.

21. Mayer Zald and Roberta Ash, "Social Movement Organizations: Growth, Decay and Change," Social Forces 44 (March 1966): 329.

22. Gary Rush and R. Serge Denisoff, Social and Political Movements (New York: Appleton-Century-Crofts, 1971).

23. Roberta Ash, Social Movements in America (Chicago: Markham, 1972), p. 1.

24. Wilson, op. cit., p. 8.

25. Max Weber, Theory of Social and Economic Organization, ed. Talcott Parsons, (Glencoe: The Free Press, 1964).

26. Blumer, in New Outline, op. cit.

27. Turner and Killian, op. cit., pp. 480-81.

28. Lang and Lang, op. cit., p. 523.

29. Eric Hoffer, The True Believer (New York: Harper Bros., 1951), pp. 89-129.

30. Ibid., p. xi.

31. Ibid., p. xii.

32. Joseph Gusfield, "Functional Areas of Leadership in Social Movements," Sociological Quarterly Vol. 7, (Spring, 1966): 141.

33. Rush and Denisoff, op. cit., p. 299.

34. Ibid., pp. 121-61.

35. Wilson, op. cit., p. 131-33.

36. Turner and Killian, op. cit., pp. 480-81.

37. Lang and Lang, op. cit., p. 541.

38. Toch, op. cit., p. 21.

39. Heberle, op. cit., ch. 2.

40. Lewis Killian, "Social Movements," in Handbook of Modern Sociology, ed. Robert E. Faris (Chicago: Rand McNally, 1964).

41. Gusfield, "Study of Social Movements," op. cit., p. 447.

42. Wilson, op. cit., p. 232.

43. Robert Lauer, Social Movements and Social Change (Carbondale, Ill.: Southern Illinois University Press, 1976), pp. 85-96.

44. Rush and Denisoff, op. cit., pp. 367-403.

45. Mayer Zald and John McCarthy, "Tactical Considerations in Social Movement Organizations," paper presented at Annual Meeting of American Sociological Association, Montreal, Canada, August 1974; The Trend of Social Movements in America: Professionalization and Resource Mobilization (Morristown, N.J.: General Learning Press, 1973); "Resource Mobilization and Social Movements: A Partial Theory," American Journal of Sociology, Vol. 82, (May 1977): 1212-41.

46. Roberta Ash, Social Movements in America (Chicago: Markham, 1972), pp. 9-10.

47. Ron Roberts and Robert Kloss, Social Movements (St. Louis: Mosby, 1974), p. 39.

48. Paul Wilkinson, Social Movement (New York: Praeger, 1971), p. 152.

49. Turner and Killian, op. cit., p. 335.

50. Carl Dawson and W. E. Getty, Introduction to Sociology (New York: Ronald Press, 1934).

51. Smelser, op. cit., p. 42.

52. Toch, op. cit., p. 235.

53. Heberle, op. cit., p. 7.

54. Gusfield, "Study of Social Movements," p. 447.

55. Status inconsistency, relative deprivation, and status politics models are found in the works of G. Lenski, Benoit-Smullyan, Ringer and Sills, Lipset and Bendix, and others, all discussed in Rush and Denisoff, op. cit., pp. 75-101.

56. William Kornhouser, The Politics of Mass Society (Glencoe, Ill.: Free Press, 1959) is only one example of an extensive literature using this model.

57. Anthony Oberschall, Social Conflict and Social Movements (Englewood Cliffs, N. J.: Prentice-Hall, 1973).

58. Zald and McCarthy, "Resource Mobilization," op. cit., 1977.

59. Wilson, op. cit.

60. Ash, op. cit.

61. Wilson, op. cit., p. 360.

2

OPEN HOUSING AS
A SOCIAL MOVEMENT

PERSPECTIVE

Although open housing may not be regarded as a standard movement, since it lacks a central administrative organization, it nevertheless possesses most of the other cited attributes of a social movement. It has change-oriented goals, it uses organization, it has
durability, and is national in scope.

The open-housing movement is, perhaps, an excellent example
of a grass-roots movement, beginning in a few scattered communities
in the late 1950s and spreading throughout the country to over 2,000
such groups by 1970. A loose alliance of some 51 national organizations formed an open-housing core organization in response to the
growing movement, called the National Committee against Discrimination in Housing (NCDH). Although the NCDH actually has no administrative control over all the open-housing groups on the community
level, the bond has been a strong one, ideological in nature. Many
of the community groups maintain a definitive identity with each other
and with the national organization, which offers information, planning
assistance, and coordination to the community groups throughout
the country.

The specific movement of open housing is seen in this study as
an offshoot of the general civil rights movement, and temporal changes
in each of these are analyzed. On the national level, three aspects
of the movement are examined: the development of the core organization, legislative development, and local community action development.
On the community level, two approaches are used. First, an intensive
case study explores the changing movement in one community over a
13-year period, before and after institutionalization. Second, there
is a comparative analysis of the movement in four other communities;

in addition, 12 brief profiles are presented of ongoing movement organizations across the country. On both the national and community levels, the movement is viewed throughout as a dynamic system of reciprocal influences. Each approach is designed to illustrate a different aspect of this reciprocity relevant to the open housing movement.

James Coleman stated that:

> The relative absence of studies of social movements by sociologists is particularly distressing because of the frequency of such movements in current society. . . . The current neglect leads one to suspect that the whole discipline of sociaology has evolved toward the study of social statics, and becomes impotent in the face of change. Whether this is the case, or whether it is merely that the study of social change, social movements, conflict, collective behavior, and other transient states is simply more difficult, the end result is the same. These are the underdeveloped areas of social research. They are not only backward at present; they are not catching up. [1]

This study may be viewed, then, not only as an exploration of the dynamics of one social movement —the open-housing movement— but also as an attempt to grapple with the methodological difficulties inherent in the study of any social movement.

This research has broad implications, not only for the theory of social movements, but also for the understanding of social change. The relevance and significance of social movements as related to social change is daily called to the attention of all of us— as sociologists, citizens, and human beings. It is hoped that this study may be a small contribution in yielding insight and understanding of the role of the social movement in the processes of change.

EMERGENT PROPOSITIONS

The original focus of this study was on the question of whether the institutionalization of a social movement leads to its decline. Out of this basic research question several others developed: What precise factors account for the success or failure of social movements? Are they internal or external or both? Which are most important? How is the success or failure of a movement measured? These questions are explored through the examination of one specific social movement, open housing. The first observations made in the course of this study are offered as emergent propositions here, gleaned after the first-nine months of field work and three and one-half years of prior participation in the open-housing movement.

1. On both national and community levels, institutionalization of a social movement does not necessarily lead to decline.*

2. On the national level, if a movement does decline after institutionalization, it will be due to external factors.

3. On the community level, if a movement does decline after institutionalization, it will be due to internal rather than external factors.

4. On the community level, after institutionalization, the most important internal factor influencing a movement's success or failure is that of leadership.

5. On the community level, if the leaders of a movement before institutionalization assume initial leadership after institutionalization, the movement will have a greater change of continued growth and success, with fewer strains and tensions.

6. On the community level, the more structured and organized the movement was before institutionalization, the fewer the strains and tensions after institutionalization.

These six emergent propositions are reconsidered after the presentation of the findings.

RESEARCH DESIGN

This study is an attempt to unravel and produce the evidence that led to the formation of the above observations and five additional propositions. It has been noted that the six emergent propositions were developed after nine months of field work. But the total period of observation covered a 13-year period. Since observation is an ongoing process, it is subject to change and reformulation. Thus, the six early observations are reconsidered at the close of the study, with changes noted and explained.

A previous pilot study of organizational analysis applied to three specific social movements, completed by the writer earlier,

---

*At first, this observation was much more emphatic, and stated: Institutionalization does not lead to decline. The automatic assumption of decline due to institutionalization was resisted, contrary to what much of the literature suggested. Then, when it became apparent in the case study that such a decline was indeed occurring, the writer came to see the need for examining the movement in other communities, which had also secured funding for their open housing groups. Thus the idea of some comparative analysis emerged.

revealed weaknesses in the earlier approach. That approach used three elements of organizational analysis in the study of each movement: social and cultural context, structure (consisting of goals and ideology, control and leadership, and membership), and process (viewed in terms of program and strategy, natural history, and consequences and impact.)

The concluding evaluation of this approach as a heuristic device stated:

> The difficulty of working within the confines of this division should now be readily apparent, since process—the dynamic aspect of an organization—intrudes on every other element of analysis. Particularly is this true for the social movement, which is itself a reflector and creator of social change. Thus, structural elements of goals, control, and membership change in response to situational demands, and cannot validly be construed as static, even for purposes of analysis.

> Perhaps a more fruitful approach might have been the analysis of each movement in the context of its overall natural history. This could have allowed the examination of each organizational element in terms of an ongoing process; thus, social and cultural context, goals, control, membership, and strategy would be viewed in terms of dynamic response and modification throughout the career of each movement. [2]

Drawing upon the insight yielded in the earlier study, a natural-history approach is used in this study. This means simply that the movement is studied in terms of phases of development, with the same factors examined in each phase of development. Thus, on both national and community levels, the open-housing movement is studied before and after institutionalization in terms of social and cultural context, goals and ideology, program and strategy, leadership and organization, and impact. On the community level, selected elements of organizational theory and analysis are applied, in conjunction with symbolic interactionism where applicable.

It has already been noted that the author was actively involved in the open-housing movement on the community level since its incipient phase. All past records, news items, minutes of meetings, and correspondence were available over a 13-year period. Continuing participant observation in one community occurred before and during the period of institutionalization, making ongoing study possible at all times. The author's involvement in the national movement also contributes to the broader analysis.

The study is primarily descriptive, qualitative, and inductive. Some salient community and national participants were interviewed, and selected community leaders were surveyed through a questionnaire designed to measure goal and program consensus. Thus the sources of data are manifold: records, minutes of board of directors' meetings, national housing newsletters, local news items, and other documents; participant observation at monthly board of directors' meetings; conversations; interviews; and survey analysis.

It may be helpful to explain the factors explored in the standard terms of variables and indexes, even though this study does not readily lend itself to the use of such terms. The independent variable is institutionalization, defined here as publicly or privately funded and legally sanctioned (federal, state, and/or local open-housing laws). The dependent variable is the success or failure of the movement. This is operationally defined in terms of three factors: goal realization, impact on the public, and internal morale.

Goal realization refers to the extent of growth of equal opportunity in housing. Specific indexes of goal realization in this study are the number of moves of minorities to previously unintegrated areas, the number of discrimination complaints filed with relevant agencies or courts, the number of actions taken to encourage the building of low- and moderate-income homes and/or apartments in unintegrated white areas. Indexes changed after 1971 to include also the number and amounts of monetary damages in legal suits, and number and frequency of initiated audits and subsequent actions. Records and minutes were used to obtain the data for these indexes.

Impact on the public is analyzed through the number of favorable news items printed, the amount and scope of distribution of educational literature, and the number of actions that influenced local decision makers. Data for these indexes were obtained through news items, minutes, records, correspondence, and interviews.

Internal morale can be studied only on the community level, primarily through participant observation. Indexes of morale are the evidence of harmony or discord during and between board meetings, the questionnaire on goal and program consensus, and response to leadership. The intriguing little questionnaire on goals and program consensus was administered to board and staff members in the case study six months after the first funding. It asks for a ranking in importance of goals as they should be, as against a ranking of the same goals in terms of actual program of the funded organization. A mean ranking was obtained, and a rank discrepancy between should and is is presented. In addition, minutes of meetings, conversations, interviews, and a journal kept by the writer furnish the data for the difficult assessment of internal morale.

Because the methods of participant observation and historiography are used so extensively in this study, a brief explanation of each is offered.

Participant Observation

Howard Becker has explained the methodology of participant observation and the problems inherent in this methodology. According to Becker, the participant observer gathers data by participating in the daily life of the group or organization he studies.

> He watches the people he is studying to see what situations they ordinarily meet and how they behave in them. He enters into conversation with some or all of the participants in these situations and discovers their interpretations of the events he has observed.[3]

Becker suggests that sociologists usually use this method when they are especially interested in understanding a particular organization or substantive problem, rather than demonstrating relations between abstractly defined variables. He claims that though participant observation can be used to test a priori hypotheses, this is typically not the case; rather, participant observation seeks to discover hypotheses as well as to test them.

Four stages of analysis in participant observation are distinguished by Becker. Three are conducted in the field, and the fourth is carried on after completion of the field work. The stages are differentiated by the different criteria that are used to assess evidence and to reach conclusions in each stage.

William Foote Whyte has tersely described the participant-observation approach:

> This is a painstaking and time-consuming method. While it does not produce statistics which count all the inhabitants in terms of certain characteristics, it does provide the investigator with a close-up view of the social organization in action.[4]

The term "participant observer" may be a misnomer, however, according to Gideon Sjoberg and Roger Nett. They point out the fact that any scientist must always be able to take the role of his subjects, to participate symbolically, if he is to interpret or impute meaning to the actions of others. Participant observation, as the term is usually employed by sociologists, simply means that the researcher engages in the activities of the group under study.[5]

Sjoberg and Nett also note that whether one engages in casual observation of one's own group or functions as a participant observer in an alien group, certain limitations inhere in the method of direct observation. First, this mode of research has only limited potential outside a relatively small group or subsystem. Second, direct observation must be supplemented by indirect observation, even within a small-group setting.

Finally, Sjoberg and Nett provide a happy link between participant observation and historigraphy:

> . . .and if he is to interpret the "meaning" of social actions, he must place these in terms of some broader whole, particularly in historical context. Even for the person being observed, the meaning of an act in which he engages is usually acquired through its relationship to a set of past actions or events.[6]

Historiography

Historiography may be described as the methodology of the historian. Jacques Barzun has stated that any report is invariably and necessarily historical; insofar as it reports facts, it gives an account of the past. "Only events gone by can disclose the prevailing state of things."[7] He suggests that history is not simply a subject among many others but one of the ways in which people think. "At best, the writing of accurate history calls for all the resources of mind and body that the reported can muster."[8] He notes that the historian must know how to use the results supplied him by others. What he himself contributes is twofold:

> First, he contributes the results of his own original research; that is, facts gathered from sources as yet untouched or possibly ill handled by a previous worker. Second, he contributes the organizing principles and the conclusions or explanations which make of the disconnected facts a "history".
>
> In his first capacity the work of the historian may be likened to a science. In the second, it may be considered an art. Actually, these two functions are not separable except in thought; the historian is an exact reporter working in the realm where the concrete and the imponderable meet.[9]

As Barzun notes, the fashioning of written history requires method. The method makes certain demands and the art obeys certain

rules. It is in reference to this disciplining that the term historiography is best employed. Yet, as he wisely points out, there is such
a close association in one's mind between the event, the account of
it, and the means by which the account is prepared that it is difficult
to separate them. "The ideas overlap and prompt the writer to use
the most general term for the science, the art, and its substance:
History."[10]

The steps in historiography, according to Barzun, are collation
(matching copies with sources), skepticism (sifting out the fitting from
the unfitting), attribution (putting a name to a source), explication
(worming secrets out of manuscripts), disentanglement (unraveling
the snarl of facts), clarification (destroying legends), and identifica-
tion (ascertaining value through authorship).

Barzun cites six virtues of the historical researcher: accuracy,
love of order, logic, honesty, self-awareness (making his standards
of judgment plain to the reader), and imagination (imagine the source
before finding it). He also notes the evidences of history as of three
types—verbal, mute, and written—and cites three categories of
written materials; manuscript and printed, private and public, and
intentional and unpremeditated.

It has been noted that history, when it is written from documents
alone, "is dead stuff and probably more false than true."[11] Thus, if
other men are to enjoy and use the knowledge gathered from records
by the searcher's critical methods, "the breath of life must be in the
product."[12] Otherwise, it is no more than the evidence digested and
collected. Historiography is much more than this, or can be:

> Historiography offers a great storehouse of facts and ideas
> to the sociologist in quest of insight into total social struc-
> tures, their phases of growth, decline, and destruction.
> Only in this way, with one eye on history and one on the
> future, can the sociologist broaden his scope to meet the
> obligations of the contemporary world.[13]

In this study, historiography and participant observation are
used to systematically explore the dynamics of a social movement.
The movement is studied on the national level through historiography,
supplemented by personal interviews with significant leaders. Documents, correspondence, records, and 21 years of specialized newspapers provide the primary sources of information on this level.

On the community level, two approaches are used to study the
movement: an intensive case study of one movement organization, and
a comparative analysis of four other movement organizations in four
different communities. In the case study, involved participant observation is supplemented by historiography. Since the writer was so

involved in the movement before the research began, rapport with the group under study might have been destroyed had the group known of the researcher's new role as participant observer. Thus, since it was not possible to disclose the exact nature of the study to the group under observation, the role of the participant observer in the case study was a covert one during the first period of study.

The comparative analysis of four other movement organizations is conducted through historiography and supplemental field visits. It must be noted that without the experience of the case study, the comparative analysis might not have been viable. It was through the participation in one community that the researcher was able to know what to seek in the other communities.

Thus, the combination of the two methodologies enabled the researcher to develop a systematic approach to the dynamic study of one social movement. This may well be applicable to the study of social movements in general.

SUMMARY

The literature on social movements reveals that a social movement may end because of success as well as failure. If its goals are realized, its raison d'etre is gone, even though other goals are substituted. And if its goals are not achieved, it may disintegrate because of fatigue, discouragement, or internal strife.

This study explores the relationship between institutionalization of a movement and its success or failure, on both national and community levels. Through this study, it is hoped that some contribution will be made toward a theory of social movements within the context of social change. A social movement is a major vehicle of social change; it is not only a reflector of change, but a creator of change.

NOTES

1. James Coleman, "The Methods of Sociology," in A Design for Sociology: Scope, Objectives, and Methods, Annals of the American Academy of Political and Social Science. Monograph 9, April 1969, p. 112.

2. Juliet Saltman, "Organizational Analysis and the Study of Social Movements," Paper presented at Ohio Valley Sociological Society Meetings, Akron, Ohio, May 1, 1970, p. 49.

3. Howard Becker, "Inference and Proof in Participant Observation," American Sociological Review 23, No. 6 (December, 1958); 652-67.

4. William Foote Whyte, "Corner Boys: A Study of Clique Behavior," American Journal of Sociology 46 (March 1941): 647-64.

5. Gideon Sjoberg and Robert Nett, A Methodology for Social Research (New York: Harper & Row, 1968), pp. 160-87.

6. Ibid., p. 162.

7. Jacques Barzun and Henry Graff, The Modern Researcher (New York: Harcourt Brace, 1957), p. 6.

8. Ibid., pp. 14-15.

9. Ibid.

10. Ibid., p. 48.

11. Ibid., p. 49.

12. Ibid., p. 53.

13. Hans Gerth and Saul Landau, "The Relevance of History to the Sociological Ethos," in Readings in Sociology, ed. Edgar Schuler, Thomas Hoult et al. (New York: Crowell, 1967), p. 861.

3

THE NATIONAL LEVEL

INTRODUCTION

Whether a social movement is seen as a social system, or a nest of Chinese boxes, or a series of concentric circles is relatively unimportant. What is important is the fact that a social movement can be fully understood only as a dynamic system of reciprocal influences. One cannot appreciate the significance of events in the history of a movement without considering the total context of those events.

In this study, therefore, the social and cultural context of the general civil rights movement prior to and during the development of the open-housing movement is considered as a crucial element which constantly influenced the course of events in the movement. In the same vein, events in the larger society and the core organization of the national housing movement affected the community levels of the movement.

Social and cultural context is examined in this chapter in three ways. First, the general conditions leading to the development of the modern civil rights movement are briefly considered. Second, events leading to the development of the open-housing movement are noted. Third, each of the four phases of development of the open-housing movement is set against a backdrop of significant events in the larger society.

On the national level, three aspects of the movement are examined: the development of a national organization, legislative development, and local community action development.

SOCIAL AND CULTURAL CONTEXT

In seeking the origins of the general civil rights movement in this country, out of which the specific open-housing movement grew, one could go back to slavery. The slave's protest against bondage and indignity has been echoed, in one form or another, continuously up to the present.

This protest has been focused on relative deprivations rather than on major deprivations inherent in the American social system. Its major thrust has been designed to achieve goals and implement values acknowledged to be implicit in democratic society, and is, thus, a reform movement rather than a revolutionary one. [1]

Since the beginning of the modern civil rights movement in the 1950s, one outstanding characteristic of the protest has been its growing militancy. From 1955 to 1965 the civil rights movement represented a peak of vigor and cohesion. Though separatism as a philosophy has appeared throughout black history, its reappearance in 1966 led to the gradual de-emphasis of the long-sought-after goal of integration by a small, youthful, and vocal minority of the black people.*

It was during the peak of the civil rights movement that the open-housing movement began. An appreciation of the specific conditions that gave rise to it necessitates a consideration of black and white population mobility trends. The impact of these trends and other salient factors have resulted in residential settlement patterns marked by increasing racial segregation throughout the country up to the present time.

One hundred years ago, 95 percent of all blacks in the United States lived in the South. Today, about 50 percent of U.S. blacks are in the South; the other 50 percent have migrated to the North, primarily to the 12 largest metropolitan areas in the country. This has been one of the most dramatic migration streams in the nation's history. It has been interpreted by many scholars in terms of a combination of push and pull factors—that is, "the push of limited social and economic opportunities at the place of origin, and the pull of promised opportunities at the place of destination."[2]

Three major waves of migration brought blacks to urban cores across the country. The third and largest wave took place during and after World War II. Like the other two, it was also a response to economic opportunities and an escape from the social, economic, and political repression of the South.

The settlement patterns of blacks have frequently been compared with those of other migrants to northern urban areas.[3] Foreign

_____

*Reports in Encyclopedia News Annuals of 1966, 1967, and 1968 indicate the changes in the general civil rights movement. See Appendix A pp. 296-97.

migrants, too, settled around the central cores of cities. Such areas were easily accessible to places of employment, to transportation, and to transient and moderate-cost housing. But as soon as some occupational and economic stability was reached, foreign settlers moved away from central city cores as rapidly as possible.

The black migrant inherited the blight left to him by earlier city migrants, and also settled in and around the central cores of cities. But here the parallel ends. The black was not able to leave the blighted areas as readily as the earlier migrants. First of all, he arrived at a later time in history, when occupational skills and training were already beginning to be necessary for economic opportunity and advancement. Second, he had to contend with the past history of slavery as an institution resulting in a slave psychology of majority members, and a continuing inferior status. Third, his visibility precluded any easy assimilation. Whereas the accent of earlier migrants could be lost or modified, and culture patterns could adapt to the dominant culture, the black could not change the color of his skin. Thus technological, historical, and cultural factors, coupled with increasing covert and overt discrimination, have forced blacks to remain primarily in and near the central areas of decay and blight.

These areas of inner-city blight came to be marked for urban renewal and land clearance in the late 1940s, at the very time that blacks were migrating toward them in largest numbers. It has been documented that of three possible reasons for continued black confinement to ghettos—poverty, choice, and discrimination—it has been primarily discrimination that has forced blacks to remain in ghetto areas. [4] Forced by discrimination and lower incomes to seek housing in ever-shrinking ghettos marked by increasing density, the blacks have been shifted from one ghetto area to another.

At about the same time that blacks were migrating in the largest numbers to the urban centers, other factors contrived to encourage whites to move away from those centers. The federal government, through its sins of omission and commission, was largely responsible for this situation. Federal Housing Administration (FHA) building programs and policies regarding new housing construction in suburban areas covertly and overtly excluded minorities from access to such housing. [5] In addition, state courts upheld many discriminatory ordinances passed by local and state governments during these years, making the legacy of discrimination complete. Thus, the resultant past and current patterns of residential segregation are a direct outgrowth of federal malfunctioning.*

---

* Tables indicating residential segregation are in Appendix A.

The sociological implications of the above mobility and settlement patterns have been manifold. Some urban scholars have claimed that the most serious domestic problem of the nation is the social and physical separation of blacks and whites. Segregated housing has led to segregated schools, shopping areas, and recreational facilities, spawning a divided society, with the hostility, mistrust, and discord that characterize such a society.[6] Against such a backdrop, the open-housing movement began.

THE FIRST PHASE: (1950–56)

Context[7]

U. S. Population: 150,697,361; black population: 15,042,286 (10 percent).

1950

- Three Supreme Court decisions undermined legal structure of segregation, June 5. The Court ruled that a student, once admitted, cannot be segregated (McLaurin case); it prohibited "curtains, partitions, and signs" that separated black dining-car patrons from whites (Henderson case); and it held that equality involved more than physical facilities (Sweatt case).

1951

- New York City Council passed bill prohibiting racial discrimination in city-assisted housing developments, February 6.

- University of North Carolina admitted first black student in its 162-year history, April 24.

- Racial segregation in District of Columbia restaurants ruled illegal by Municipal Court of Appeals, May 24.

- NAACP (National Association for the Advancement of Colored People) began attack on segregation and discrimination at elementary and high-school levels. South Carolina court held segregation not discrimination, June 23; Kansas court ruled that separate facilities were equal but said segregation per se had adverse effect on black children.

- Governor Adlai Stevenson called out National Guard to quell rioting in Cicero, Illinois, July 12. Mob of 3500 attempted to prevent black family from moving into all-white city.

- President Truman named committee to supervise compliance with provisions against discrimination in U.S. Government contracts and subcontracts, December 3.

1952

- University of Tennessee admitted first black student, January 12.

1953

- Supreme Court ruled that District of Columbia restaurants could not legally refuse to serve blacks, June 8.

- Bus boycott began in Baton Rouge, Louisiana.

- Movement of black families into Trumbull Park housing project in Chicago precipitated recurring riots lasting three years; required assignment of over 1000 policemen to keep order, August 4.

1954

- Supreme Court ruled racial segregation in public schools unconstitutional, May 17.

- First White Citizens Council unit organized in Indianola, Mississippi, July 11.

- School integration began in Washington, D.C. and Baltimore, September 7-8.

- Defense Department announced complete abolition of black units in armed forces, October 30.

1955

- Supreme Court ordered school integration "with all deliberate speed," May 31.

- Supreme Court banned segregation in public recreational facilities, November 7.

- Interstate Commerce Commission banned segregation in buses and waiting rooms involved in interstate travel, November 25.

- Bus boycott began in Montgomery, Alabama, December 5.

1956

- Home of Martin Luther King, Jr., Montgomery bus boycott leader, bombed, January 30.

- Bus boycott began in Tallahassee, Florida, May 30.

- White mob protested enrollment of black students in Mansfield, Texas, August 30.

- Tennessee National Guard sent to Clinton to quell mobs demonstrating against school integration, September 2.

- Birmingham blacks began mass defiance of bus laws, 21 arrested, December 26.

NCDH Development

In June 1950 the National Committee Against Discrimination in Housing (NCDH) was formed by a group of national organizations concerned with the problems of minorities. It has since played a central role in the national movement toward equal opportunity in housing. Its founders included the principal religious, civic, labor, and civil rights groups of the country, which were dedicated to equal housing opportunity as a basic constitutional and moral right.

NCDH began as an outgrowth of another more localized organization based in New York City.[8] This group, the New York State Committee on Discrimination in Housing, was organized earlier in response to a specific housing struggle in New York City. That struggle began in 1943 and focused on a particular housing development with segregated facilities.*

A national conference in 1949, scheduled by the local group, was the first major public discussion of the role the federal government in fomenting housing discrimination. As a result of statements made by public officials at that conference, the local organization was deluged with requests for information and guidance from all over the country. A volunteer, part-time director was found to handle this. Headquarters were set up in a tiny office (10' x 15') donated by one of the member organizations. A couple of ancient desks, some chairs, and a loaned typewriter were collected, and the work began.

---

*Alarm was generated by the announced plans of the Metropolitan Life Insurance Company to build a $100 million development, Stuyvesant Town, for whites only. This was the first of the mammoth postwar communities to be built under urban redevelopment laws, and it was feared that it might set a disastrous national precedent. A five-year battle ensued, during which legal suit was filed. The court decision paved the way for the action programs that followed, since it stated that discrimination in housing was a matter for legislative action rather than judicial decision.

When pressure mounted for a national organization to spearhead the battle for open housing practices 15 national organizations combined to form the NCDH.* The little office of the state committee with its volunteer staff became the office of NCDH. Both organizations continued to function in this way for ten years.

The purpose of NCDH was to establish nondiscriminatory and nonsegregated housing in the United States.[9] Its initial efforts were directed toward research, education, and consultation, but it became increasingly mobilized toward legislative action on the national level. During its first two years, it drafted model antidiscrimination laws for states and cities, using the nation's foremost experts on housing and race relations as volunteer contributors of their skills.

The NCDH program during this phase focused on federal government agency influence and field consultation and education.[10] One government agency that NCDH successfully influenced was the Housing and Home Finance Agency, under which the FHA operated. As a result of NCDH pressure and impact, FHA directives to builders were changed so as to state contract preference for open-occupancy developments. Another government agency influenced by NCDH was the Public Housing Administration (PHA), which was pressured into giving assurance that all federally owned or operated housing would be tenanted on an open-occupancy basis.

Three major field activities were engaged in by NCDH during its first two years of existence. An examination of each of these field activities will reveal the strategy of NCDH and its focal concerns at the time, as well as the typical housing and race problems in communities across the nation during this period.

In Norfolk, Virginia, NCDH worked closely with the Women's Council for Interracial Cooperation, made up of over 300 representatives of women's church and civic groups. Concerns in this community

---

*An NCDH leaflet, "30,000,000 Americans Need Your Help," (1952) listed the organizations: the American Civil Liberties Union, the American Council on Human Rights, the American Friends Service Committee, the American Jewish Committee, the American Jewish Congress, the American Veterans Committee, the Anti-Defamation League of B'nai B'rith, the Board of Home Missions of the Congregational Christian Churches, the Congress of Industrial Organizations, The Jewish Labor Committee, the Migration Division of the Puerto Rican Department of Labor, the National Association for the Advancement of Colored People, the National Association of Intergroup Relations Officials, the National Council of Negro Women, and the National Council of Churches of Christ Race Relations Department.

related to changing housing patterns and discriminatory practices as a result of increased employment opportunities in Norfolk naval shipyards, and discrimination in urban redevelopment, relocation, and public housing. After a meeting at which the NCDH director spoke, the Women's Council reactivated its housing committee, and made plans to meet with local public officials and private leaders to open new land areas on a nondiscriminatory basis.

In Minneapolis, the primary NCDH activity consisted of education and public speaking at the annual conference of the Council on Human Relations, which had been heavily engaged in studying the local housing problems. Concerns at the time were focused on discrimination in private housing and public housing, urban redevelopment and relocation, and Veterans Administration (VA) loans. At the conference, Charles Abrams of NCDH led a discussion with the Board of Realtors, the Mayor's Council, the Real Property Division of the Bar Association, the Home Builders Association, the Society of Real Estate Appraisers, and the Mortgage Bankers Association. Thus every facet of the housing industry was exposed to NCDH information and views regarding the need for nondiscriminatory and nonsegregated housing practices. TV and radio reinforced these views by carrying them in their broadcasts.

The field work involving the Levittown development in Pennsylvania had the broadest impact. That development, adjacent to the new U.S. Steel Company plant in Bucks County, contained 5,000 homes, none occupied by blacks. NCDH called a meeting of representatives of local and national agencies operating in the surrounding areas. One outcome of the meeting was the formation of the Bucks County Human Relations Council, an interracial group. This group went on to sponsor meetings with local developers, prepared an analysis of the housing situation, and held a large public meeting addressed by an NCDH staff member.

The U.S. Steel Company then initiated two conferences with NCDH and other representatives, at which time housing problems were explored and assurances given that nondiscriminatory employment policies would be followed. NCDH representatives pointed out the company's responsibility to assist nonwhite employees in getting adequate housing. They further recommended that the company make an analysis of the housing picture in Bucks County and surrounding areas, and that it publicly announce its wish to open the housing development to all workers without discrimination. However, the builder, William Levitt, continued to state that he would not sell or rent to blacks in Levittown under any circumstances. An eight-year battle began, and NCDH pressure eventually forced the builder of the development to open his units to minorities. Since the builder became one of the largest in the nation, operating in several eastern geographical areas, this affected thousands of building units in that entire region.

During the next three years NCDH began to expand its program in four areas:[11] development of programs and techniques for opening communities to minorities, through its community advisory service; communication of facts and techniques, and interpretation of legislation and government policies, through its housing information service; planning of conferences, workshops, institutes, forums, and service to educational institutions and community organizations,[12] through its leadership training service; and advice to universities, government agencies and foundations, and independent studies, through its research service.[13]

By the end of the first phase of its development, NCDH was made increasingly aware of the fact that the fight for open housing had to be waged vigorously on the community level in relation to specific programs in specific localities.[14] Field activities were accordingly increased, and a national reporting service (<u>Trends in Housing</u>) was planned, which would review all relevant matters pertaining to housing discrimination and housing patterns.

By this time, despite a constant struggle for funds,* the NCDH had increased its organizational membership to 26 national affiliates, and had conducted its national program with a budget of only $18,000 and a staff of three.

THE SECOND PHASE: (1956-64)

Context[15]

1957

- Southern Christian Leadership Conference organized in New Orleans, with Martin Luther King, Jr. as president, February 14.

- Prayer Pilgrimage, biggest civil rights demonstration ever staged by U.S. blacks, in Washington, May 17.

- Tuskegee boycott of city stores began June 1 in protest against deprivation of voting rights by state legislature.

- Congress passed Civil Rights Act of 1957, August 29—First federal civil rights legislation since 1875.

---

*Repeated NCDH appeals for funds and warnings of financial crisis are contained in Appendix A, pp. 305-07.

- Nashville's new elementary school destroyed by dynamite blast, September 9. Enrollment: 1 black, 388 whites.

- Soldiers of 101st Airborne Division escorted nine black children to high school in Little Rock, Arkansas, September 25.

- New York City became first to legislate against racial or religious discrimination in housing market with Fair Housing Practice Law, December 5.

1958

- Members of NAACP Youth Council began series of sit-ins at Oklahoma City lunch counters, August, 19.

1959

- Prince Edward County, Virginia Board of Supervisors abandoned public school system in attempt to prevent school integration, June 26.

- Citizens of Deerfield, Illinois authorized plan blocking building of interracial housing development, December 21.

1960

U.S. population: 179,323,175. Black population: 18,871,831 (10.5 percent).

- Forty-five college students started sit-in movement at Greensboro, North Carolina in dime store, February 1. By February 10, movement had spread to 15 southern cities in 5 states.

- Race riot, Chattanooga, Tennessee, at sit-in demonstration, February 23.

- One thousand Alabama college students marched on state capitol and held protest meeting, March 1.

- Student Non-Violent Coordinating Committee organized, April 15-17.

- Race riot in Biloxi, Mississippi after wade-in by blacks at local beach, April 24.

- President Eisenhower signed Civil Rights Act of 1960, May 6.

- Elijah Muhammad, black nationalist leader, called for creation of negro state, July 31.

- Several thousand blacks held two mass prayer meetings and marched on business district of Atlanta in protest against segregation and discrimination.

1961

- Riot, University of Georgia, January 11.

- Robert Weaver sworn in as administrator of the Housing and Home Finance Agency, highest federal post ever held by an American black, February 11.

- First group of Freedom Riders had bus burned and bombed by segregationists in Alabama, May 14.

- Attorney General Robert Kennedy sent 400 U.S. marshals to Montgomery to keep order in Freedom Rider situation, May 20.

- Southern Regional Council announced that sit-in movement had affected 20 states and over 100 cities in southern and border states in period from February 1960 to September 1961. 70,000 blacks and whites participated, 3600 were arrested, 141 students and 58 faculty members expelled from colleges.

- Police used tear gas and leashed dogs to quell mass demonstrations by 1,500 blacks in Baton Rouge, Louisiana, December 15.

1962

- Suit accusing New York City Board of Education of using racial quotas filed in U.S. District Court on behalf of black and Puerto Rican children, January 16.

- Sit-in demonstrations and passive resistance movement began in Cairo, Illinois, June 26. Demonstrations against segregation in pools, skating rinks, and other facilities continued for several months.

- Two black churches burned in Georgia, Sept. 9.

- Supreme Court ruled that University of Mississippi must admit James Meredith, black Air Force veteran, whose application for admission had been on file and in courts for 14 months, September 10.

- Eighth black church burned in Georgia.

- 12,000 federal soldiers restored order on University of Mississippi campus after James Meredith was admitted.

- President Kennedy issued executive order barring racial and religious discrimination in federally financed housing, November 20.

1963

- Martin Luther King, Jr. opened antisegregation campaign in Birmingham, April 3. 2000 demonstrators arrested.

- President Kennedy, in TV address, told nation that segregation was morally wrong.

- Medgar Evers, NAACP field secretary, assassinated in front of home in Mississippi, June 12.

- 3,000 students boycotted Boston public schools in protest against de facto segregation, June 18.

- Civil rights groups staged mass demonstrations at Harlem construction sites to protest discrimination in building trades unions, June 12-13.

- 250,000 persons participated in March on Washington, August 28.

- John F. Kennedy, 35th president of the United States, assassinated in Dallas, Texas, Nov. 22.

1964

- U. S. Senate imposed cloture for first time on civil rights measure, ending with civil rights bill with public accomodations and fair-employment sections, passed by Congress and signed by President Johnson, July 2.

- New York police arrested 294 civil rights demonstrators at opening of World's Fair, April 22.

- Race riot started in Harlem, July 18. Spread to ghetto of Bedford-Stuyvesant section of Brooklyn.

- Race riot in Rochester, July 25. National Guard called in.

- Bodies of three civil rights workers found in Mississippi, August 4. Murdered by white segregationists.

NCDH Development

The NCDH program and impact during the next three phases of development are revealed primarily through an examination of Trends in Housing, the national NCDH publication, which began in August

1956 and has continued to the present. The issues of Trends were
analyzed consecutively, with particular emphasis focusing on the
NCDH strategies as they affected and reflected the national open-
housing movement at that time. In addition, since the movement
burgeoned in terms of legislative development and local community
action, these two aspects are examined separately for each phase
of growth.

Recurrent throughout this phase were NCDH public charges in
Senate hearings that federal housing programs were supporting and
reinforcing the spread of residential segregation. [16] Three major
federal housing programs were indicted. Urban renewal critically
reduced the supply of low-rent housing with a net loss of 51,000
homes, forcing nonwhites (who comprised two-thirds of those displaced) into overcrowded ghettos because of a restricted housing
market and high prices. FHA continued to underwrite segregated
housing, with less than 2 percent of the total number of federally
insured new homes made available to minorities. PHA persisted in
utilizing federal funds for segregated housing.

The growing impact of NCDH on the government and the nation
was revealed in three instances during this second phase of development:* positive action taken by federal housing agencies, influence
of the Democratic and Republican election platforms, and the executive order banning discrimination in housing. Three specific positive
actions were taken by government housing agencies as a direct result
of NCDH pressure. First, racial quotas were eliminated by FHA in
relocation housing. Second, FHA ordered that no discrimination be
permitted in the rental or resale of foreclosed housing. [17] Third,
intergroup relations specialists were appointed for each region in
the country by the Urban Renewal Administration. [18]

Both the Democratic and Republican parties were urged by
NCDH to include planks in their 1960 platforms pledging the elimination of discrimination and segregation in the federal government's
own housing programs. Three essential proposals suggested by NCDH
for adoption, were followed by both parties. [19] The first was for an
executive order stating a policy of nondiscrimination and nonsegrega-
tion in all federal housing programs. The second was for the establishment by the president of a committee to develop a program and
timetable for the implementation of the executive order. The third
was for the use of the presidential power of office to bring about an

---

*A letter sent by NCDH to numerous individuals and organiza-
tions in October 1957 reviewed briefly the ten-year achievement
record of NCDH and indicated three major efforts planned for the
future. See Appendix A, p. 305.

end to discrimination and the assurance of equal opportunities in housing.

NCDH presented a proposed executive order to President Kennedy which barred discrimination in all federal housing programs.[20] From 1960 to 1962, when the order was finally issued, a major portion of the NCDH program and strategy was focused on the achievement of this one goal. Even after issuance of the order, NCDH continued to press for expansion of the order, and its more liberal interpretation and enforcement. For example, in July 1963 NCDH planned a three-pronged campaign "for faster and more meaningful action toward ending racial restrictions in federally aided housing," despite the earlier victory of the executive order in November 1962.[21] Trends in Housing, July-August, 1963, p. 1.

Growing NCDH impact on the community level was indicated in three instances during this phase: the successful culmination of the Levittown case, the issuance of the Fair Housing Handbook, and the convening of three major national conferences. When the builder of New Jersey's largest private home development publicly refused to admit blacks to his planned community of 15,000 homes, NCDH mobilized a massive legal and community action program geared to correcting this situation.[22] In 1960, eight years after NCDH began this struggle with the same builder, Levitt announced his intention of opening his communities to minorities.[23]

The Fair Housing Handbook, the first such manual for fair-housing groups, was published in 1963 under the joint sponsorship of NCDH and the American Friends Service Committee. Designed as a practical reference and action guide, it became the prime reference source for most of the mushrooming fair-housing groups across the country. Reciprocal influence of the national organization (NCDH) and local organizations is readily seen here. Growth and increasing influence of the national organization stimulated and reinforced action and growth on the local level. This, in turn prompted further action by the national organization, which then filtered down to the local level. Thus, growth on each level was nurtured by the other. The publication and mass dissemination of the Fair Housing Handbook aided and strengthened the movement on the community level, which thus came under the direct and constant influence of NCDH philosophy and program, thereby strengthening the rationale and program of the NCDH itself.

Three major conferences were held by NCDH during this second phase of development. An examination and analysis of the themes of these conferences indicates the steadfastness of the original goals of the NCDH, and the flexibility of its program and strategy according to situational demands.

The theme of the 1956 annual NCDH meeting was "Rebuilding Our Cities for Everybody." The major topics for panel sessions revolved around three subjects: problems of neighborhood stabilization; management and tenant policies affecting desegregation in public housing; and the roles of builder, lender, broker, and neighbor in the move toward a free market in private housing. At this meeting a major push to enact city and state laws banning discrimination in all housing was called for. The key speakers declared that the total housing market must be open to free competitive bargaining, and the separate-but-equal concept "rejected as thoroughly in housing as it has been in education."[24]

The second conference was held in 1958 in Philadelphia, at which over 300 persons from every section of the country examined "the catastrophic housing problems facing America's increasingly urban society."[25] The theme was "The Open Community—New Concepts for Metropolitan Areas," which was developed in three sessions: "People on the Move—The Significance and Implication of Population Movements"; "Legislation—Its Role in Eliminating Discrimination in Housing"; and "Integration—How to Get It and How to Keep It."

The third conference, in 1963, was particularly noteworthy, since for the first time an entire session was devoted to grass-roots activities. This was indicative of the extent of growth of the movement on the local community level. Almost 400 people from 100 municipalities in 25 states converged in Washington, D.C. to attend the two-day conference on "Equal Opportunity in Housing—Challenge to American Communities." Four workshops were held, all dealing with specific federal activities in housing programs: public housing, FHA and VA, urban renewal, and litigation.[26]

President Kennedy's message to the conference indicates the extent of the recognition NCDH had achieved by this time.

> . . . The NCDH and the many organizations which comprise it have been in the forefront in directing wide attention to the evils of discriminatory practices in housing. . . . Your past vigorous actions in all aspects of this difficult problem provide assurance that you can be counted upon to play a significant role in helping achieve the objectives of the executive order issued last November. . . .[27]

The impact of NCDH was also increased through the assumption by some of its leaders of key positions of power in federal and private organizations outside NCDH.* By the end of the second phase of its

---

*In 1960 Dr. Robert C. Weaver was elected president of NCDH. He subsequently was appointed by Mayor Wagner to serve on New York

development, NCDH had grown to an organization of 37 national member affiliates. Its continuing search for prestige,[28] legitimacy, and funds culminated in a turning point for the organization in 1963.†
At that time tax-exempt status was granted to NCDH making it possible for it to seek foundation funding, and paving the way for the phase of institutionalization that followed. A greatly expanded operation was planned and projected, new offices were obtained, and the first director resigned after ten years of service.

Legislative Development

During the growth of the open-housing movement, legislative development seemed to follow a social-distance scale, proceeding from public-housing coverage to publicly assisted housing to private housing, with increasing resistance encountered in each step. The commitment development of a countermovement also made the task more formidable.

At the beginning of this second phase, only three states had laws prohibiting discrimination in public housing, two had laws forbidding discrimination in public housing and urban redevelopment, and three had laws covering publicly assisted housing. Fourteen cities had laws banning discrimination in public housing, seven covered public housing and urban redevelopment, and only two banned discrimination in all publicly aided housing.[29]

In 1959 the first indications of an organized countermovement appeared, in response to growing legislative efforts toward open housing. The entire August 1, 1959 issue of Economic Council Letter, official publication of Mervin Hart's National Economic Council, Inc., was given over to an article by Robert B. Dresser, outlining his plan of opposition to fair-housing legislation in Rhode Island.‡ The Economic Council Letter states in an introductory foreword:

City's three-man Housing and Redevelopment Board, Eventually he resigned as president of NCDH to accept federal appointment as administrator of the Housing and Home Finance Agency. Also, George Weaver (former NCDH chairman) became special assistant to the U. S. secretary of labor; Chester Bowles (NCDH board member) became undersecretary of state; Eleanor Roosevelt (NCDH Advisory Council) became a member of the U. S. delegation to the United Nations.

†A message from Algernon D. Black, NCDH chairman of the board, to Trends readers in November-December 1963, is reprinted in Appendix A. It indicates the turning point for the NCDH at this time.

‡Dresser was a 78-year-old lawyer, a founder of the America First Committee, and a director of the National Economic Council.

This is one of the most important Council Letters we have
ever published. A liberal combine has set out to take away
the property rights of every American by dictating to the
owner to whom he may rent or sell his property. . . .[30]

Copies of the issue were sent to all members of the New York legislature, as well as to all members of Congress.

Also indicative of the growing countermovement during this
second phase was the survey by the National Association of Home
Builders in 1962. The survey purported to show that building starts
would be adversely affected by a presidential ban on discrimination
in federally aided housing. The report was submitted to the president
and released to the press on July 9, 1962. It should be noted that
59.3 percent of those who responded to the survey said their building
plans would not be affected, would be expanded, or had no opinion;
62 percent of the membership did not answer. More than a third of
the replies came from the South, and more than half of the builders
who said their plans would be adversely affected were from the South.
NCDH urged President Kennedy to recognize as "misleading in its
statements and unfounded in its conclusions" the entire survey report.
NCDH and its 37 member organizations also urged citizens and groups
throughout the country to send letters and telegrams to the president
immediately. [31]

The strengthening of the countermovement was again revealed
in 1963. An article in Trends entitled "Fair Housing and Referendums:
Growing Movement Causes Concern," stated that

. . .in little more than a year, the drive for referendums
to prevent passage of fair housing legislation or to revoke
existing laws has spread from California to Michigan to
Illinois to the State of Washington, and rumblings are
being heard in other areas. [32]

Those who were pushing the referendum movement contended that
fair-housing laws were forced-housing laws; that government inter-
ference with private property rights was wrong; and that their purpose in initiating referendums was to give the people a chance to
vote on an issue of this importance. Those who opposed placing such
issues on the ballot argued that the legislative function should be left
to legislative bodies; that many other large or unpopular issues were
not submitted for approval by popular vote; that moral and constitutional rights were not subject to the popular will; and that issues,
arousing racial or religious prejudice should not be involved in election campaigns.

Despite the growth of the countermovement, by the end of this
phase 26 government jurisdictions had adopted measures affecting

private housing, and 60 cities had laws or resolutions affecting discrimination in housing, both public and private.[33] New York in 1957 was the first city to adopt a law banning discrimination in private housing, with NCDH leadership spearheading the protracted struggle ending in the passage of the law.

Local Community Action Development

At the beginning of this second phase, there was little evidence of local community-action organizations devoted specifically to open housing, although there was considerable action on the local level through other civic, civil rights, and religious organizations.[34] By the end of this phase, however, more than 300 specific fair-housing committees or groups were identified as actively working for open housing.

It is interesting to speculate as to whether the formation of specific fair-housing groups would have occurred without the concurrent development of the NCDH. It is suggested here that local constraints and the force of national events in the civil rights field might have spurred such development on the local level even without a core organization such as the NCDH. However, whether local development would have occurred without NCDH, to the extent that it did, is questionable. There is little doubt, for example, that the publication of Trends in Housing served as a propelling force in the growth of the movement across the country. Mass dissemination of the Fair Housing Handbook also contributed to the reinforcement and strengthening of the movement on the local level.

One growing activity during this phase was the mass signing of "good-neighbor pledges" in local communities throughout the country. By 1958 it was reported that ". . .citizens all over the country are putting themselves on public record to welcome good neighbors to their communities, regardless of race, religion, or nationality."[35] Covenants of open occupancy and welcome statements were used "with dramatic frequency by groups of citizens fighting housing bias in scores of American cities."[36] Sometimes referred to as advertising goodwill, these signing campaigns focused attention on and gained adherents to the open-occupancy movement.

By 1959 there was evidence of the establishment of specific open-housing action groups working across the country. A number of these community organizations were the outgrowth of the welcome-neighbor or open-occupancy covenent campaigns. Trends reported, "And they are contagious! A half dozen or more may be found within the metropolitan expanse of several large cities."[37] Other common characteristics were noted: they operated "squarely at the grassroots"; by and large, they were manned by volunteers; frequently intergroup relations professionals served as advisors.

> Although programs and methods may vary considerably, without exception the groups are committed to the establishment of a community-wide pattern of open occupancy as the only answer to the ghetto.[38]

Among the designations used by these groups were Listing Service, Clearing House, Introduction Service, Housing Registry, or Fair Housing Committee. One committee summed up its program as "Dispersion for Democracy." Another approach was described as the development of a "planned dispersion pattern of nonwhite home ownership in all residential areas throughout a city and its environs."[39]

A typical fair-housing committee program was carried out in San Jose California. In 1956 an informal committee of church and civic group members, augmented by other concerned citizens, embarked on a planned dispersion program. In 24 months, 40 nonwhite families were located in 13 different all-white sections, completely removed from areas of minority concentration. This was accomplished through the following systematic approach. First, the committee did an analysis of the local housing market—that is, the demand for housing, the type desired, the location of houses currently for sale. Secondly, they developed a detailed card file of nonwhite families searching for homes. Next, they located open-minded owners of housing for sale or rent in white neighborhoods, who were willing to make these available to nonwhites, and developed a comprehensive listing of these. In addition to establishing contact between prospective buyers and sellers, the committee searched for and found three sympathetic realtors who would accept referrals on a nondiscriminatory basis; it also assisted in arranging financing, kept a watchful eye out for any neighborhood tensions, and arranged parties to introduce the new residents to their neighbors. A continuous educational campaign to develop a wider base of concerned citizens was carried on.

Another growing type of activity on the local level concerned neighborhood stabilization of already integrated areas. By 1960 Trends noted the growth of stabilization groups in an article called "The Challenge of the Changing Neighborhood."[40] It was reported that voluntary community groups had formed in cities across the country in an attempt to develop democratic residential patterns, to stop exploitation by unscrupulous real estate dealers, and to maintain high neighborhood standards.

Some sources have indicated that such stabilization groups preceded open-housing groups, and indeed provided the impetus for

their formation. It is a fact that stabilization of one area cannot be
effective unless there is an open housing market in the entire community. But it is equally true that an open-housing group cannot work
effectively unless stabilization of integrated areas occurs. Thus they
are two sides of the same coin, and regardless of which type of group
forms first, each soon comes to recognize the necessity of the other.

By 1961 it was noted that "grassroots fair housing committees
have been springing up over the nation at a sharply increased rate
during the past two years. This contagious movement has spread
from town to town, cutting across economic lines."[41] These committees were not confined to suburban communities but were forming
in neighborhoods in many cities. They worked for the enactment and
implementation of fair-housing legislation. They actively promoted
residential integration, whether fair-housing laws applied to their
community or not.

> They are committed to the proposition that integrated
> communities are socially healthy, politically desirable,
> and economically sound. Typically called Fair Housing
> Committees, they are a spontaneous sign of the times.
> Most of them are not chapters of any national or state
> organization. They start in various ways: some are
> related to religious organizations; some grow out of
> discussion or study groups; some are initiated by the
> action of an individual. . . [42]

Activities of the local groups varied considerably. Some conducted surveys, studies, workshops, speaker bureaus, pledge campaigns, stabilization programs, or home-listing services. Other
supplied white checkers for nonwhite applicants who faced discrimination. Some were able to locate cooperative real estate agents; others
faced a solid wall of resistance from the industry.

Those groups that operated listing services attempted to facilitate direct communication between the home seeker and the owner or
landlord, bypassing the restrictions imposed by discriminatory real
estate practices. They did not serve as brokers, and they accepted
no fees. Their aim was to bring together willing buyers and willing
sellers. The listing-service operation was described as complex and
often discouraging. Supply exceeded demand in many groups, with
more homes available than prospective buyers.

Despite complexities, success stories were numerous. Riverdale,
New York, almost totally white two years earlier, had become inte-
grated through an intergroup relations housing committee. Great Neck,
New York became integrated through the efforts of the Great Neck
Commission on Human Rights housing committee. Levittown, New

Jersey became integrated through the Burlington County Human Relations Council. Similar gains were made in Boston, New Haven, Washington, Chicago, San Francisco, and other urban areas over the country.

Toward the end of this second phase, federation of local groups was noted as a growing trend, and direct action became the focus of attention in many local housing groups. Trends noted in 1962 that

> . . . housing is the latest area in civil rights to be tackled by non-violent direct action. Sit-ins, sleep-ins, equality vigils, picketing protest marches, sympathy demonstrations, and "operation windowshop" are being used increasingly to further open occupancy in many sections of the country. [43]

As has already been noted, by the time NCDH held its third major conference during this phase of development, it was necessary to hold a special session on grass-roots activities. At this time, in 1963, NCDH indicated that there were almost 300 identifiable voluntary, unaffiliated, fair-housing committees working in many sections of the country for integration in their own communities.

The closing speech of the conference, given by NCDH Vice-President Loren Miller, noted that recent developments had heightened the need for voluntary citizens' action. With increasing urgency, he said, it was necessary to continue pressing government—local, state, and federal—to meet its responsibility, to bring more and more buyers and sellers together, and smooth the way for the newcomers; to formulate effective appeals to blacks to move into the mainstream of housing; and to support programs and organizations seeking to increase the supply of middle- and low-income housing. The time was seen as a "moment of crisis—a time when a task done or left undone may well shape the future for a long time to come."[44]

THE THIRD PHASE (1964-70)

Context[45]

1965

● Malcolm X, leader of Black Nationalists, assassinated while addressing gathering, New York City, February 21.

● Blacks marched from Selma to Montgomery. Police used gas and clubs, March.

- Five hundred blacks marched in Bogalusa, La., protesting KKK violence, April.

- King led 18,000 marchers in Boston, protesting school segregation, April.

- Six days of racial violence and rioting in Watts section of Los Angeles, August. 34 dead, 898 injured, 4,000 arrested, $45 million damage.

- Voting Rights Act of 1965 signed. Abolished literacy tests, attached penalties for intimidating anyone trying to vote.

- OEO expanded operation, September. Senate approved bill for over $1.75 billion for second year of War on Poverty.

- All-white jury acquitted white killer of civil rights workers, October.

1966

- Vietnam divided country.

- New phrase: Black Power. White "liberals" withdrew support from CORE and other more militant civil rights groups.

- Whites rioted in Chicago suburbs, in response to King-led demonstrations against discrimination in housing.

- Black children stoned when school integration began in Grenada, Mississippi.

- Summer riots in Atlanta, Omaha, Detroit, Los Angeles, San Francisco, Chicago, Cleveland, and Milwaukee.

1967

- Riots in Newark, Detroit, Jersey City, Houston, Tampa, East Harlem, Rochester, Plainfield, Pontiac, Jackson, Cincinnati, Providence, Nashville, Hartford, and Toledo. One hundred killed, 2,000 wounded, 11,000 arrested in 31 cities.

- H. Rap Brown succeeded Stokeley Carmichael as head of Student Non-violent Coordinating Committee. Stressed racial separation. Floyd McKissick moved CORE toward greater militancy. Wilkins, Young, and King dissociated themselves with Black Power movement and violence.

- Civil rights movement divided.

1968

- Martin Luther King assassinated in Memphis, April 4.

- Congress passed civil rights bill eliminating discrimination in housing in 80 percent of nation's housing. Stiff penalities for persons guilty of intimidating civil rights workers, April 10. Interstate riot amendment.

- Supreme Court decision upholding constitutionality of 1866 Civil Rights Act barring discrimination in housing based on race, June 18.

- Black mayors elected in Cleveland and Gary.

- Report of National Advisory Commission on Civil Disorders released, March. Conclusion: "U.S. a racist society, with white majority deeply implicated in the conditions of ghetto life that caused the riots."

- Poor People's March on Washington, May. Solidarity Day, June 1; 50,000 supporters.

- Robert Kennedy assassinated, June.

1969-70

- Richard Nixon elected president, November.

- Campus riots

- Antiwar demonstrations proliferated.

- Antipollution campaigns.

- Black Panthers harrassed by police in several cities.

- War on Poverty continued, with some services shifted to other government agencies.

- War in Vietnam continued.

- Moynihan, adviser to President Nixon, proposed "benign neglect" of race issues, March 1970.

NCDH Development

It may be said that the stage of institutionalization was reached during this third phase of development. Because of increased budget, staff, legitimacy, and scope and impact of its program, NCDH came to be recognized as "a desirable or unavoidable adjunct to existing institutionalized arrangements."[46]

With private foundations contributing to a greatly increased budget of some $200,000, the NCDH program was able to expand its national role as stimulant, catalytic agent, and clearing house.* During the third phase NCDH convened 12 national regional conferences, contrasted with only three during the previous eight year phase. In addition, NCDH was able to greatly increase its impact on local communities through its new advisory Center for Fair Housing and its change to monthly issuance of Trends in Housing.

Four direct impact of NCDH on local communities were indicated in its role in the struggle against Proposition 14 in California, its influence regarding the Weston, Illinois atomic energy site, its impact on the Louisville, Kentucky Model Cities funding, and in its pressure in the Greenburgh, New York urban renewal controversy.

Proposition 14 in California symbolized the growth of the referendum countermovement. In less than two years, real estate interests, with the strong support of the National Association of Real Estate Boards (NAREB), had successfully promoted local anti-fair-housing referendums in the cities of Berkeley, Seattle, Tacoma, Detroit, and Akron, Ohio.

> The showpiece of this grand design to persuade voters across the country to legalize housing segregation and discrimination was the skillful campaign which resulted in the adoption of 'Proposition 14' by an overwhelming majority of the California electorate. . .on November 3, 1964.[47]

In rapid succession, NCDH took the following actions: It convened an emergency meeting of directors and key staff members of all state and local commissions administering nondiscriminatory laws; representatives of these agencies from all over the country met to examine the legal implications of anti-fair-housing referendums. It issued and publicized an appeal to NAREB to halt its divisive and disruptive movement to kill fair-housing legislation. It mobilized nation-wide support for the federal government's action in withholding

---

*The break between the second and third phase was, in fact, a sharp and tangible one. After the November-December 1963 issue of Trends in Housing, there were no more issues until September-October 1964, at which time the entire issue was devoted to the launching of NCDH's expanded program, with its new leadership.

federal financing for urban renewal projects in California, following adoption of Proposition 14. It planned and convened a national conference to bring together lawyers and legal scholars from across the nation to examine the legal aspects of anti-fair-housing referendums, and to stimulate both long- and short-range additional legal study and exploration. And it submitted to the Supreme Court an amicus curiae brief in an appeal on the constitutionality of Proposition 14.

In 1967 an all-white suburban area of Chicago (Weston, Illinois) was chosen for the site of the world's largest atomic accelerator by the U.S. Atomic Energy Commission (AEC). The commission had made an open housing market a major criterior for selection of the site. In a letter Chairman Glenn Seaborg and NCDH executive heads, Edward Rutledge and Jack Wood, urged the AEC to use the selected site as an opportunity to build a new town in Weston "which would be a truly integrated community and would open the entire surrounding area."[48] The Weston, Illinois situation was followed closely by NCDH, and culminated in testimony given by NCDH before the Joint Committee on Atomic Energy, urging that congressional approval of the Weston site for an atom smasher be withheld until specific action was taken to "open the job and housing market on a metropolitan basis."[49]

In a similar action involving a locality with national implications, NCDH aided Louisville civil rights forces in Kentucky in demanding that model Cities funding be withheld by the Department of Housing and Urban Development (HUD) until the city assured equal opportunity in housing for all its citizens. NCDH executive heads Rutledge and Wood were in Louisville at the invitation of local civil rights leaders, and wired HUD Secretary Weaver urging denial of Model Cities funds and a cut-off of funds for urban renewal, housing, community facilities and related planning, since such funds might be used to promote increased segregation in housing.

Greenburgh, New York's $8.7 million urban renewal program, was the subject of raging controversy, resulting from the Greenburgh Housing Authority's plan to build low-rent public housing for relocatees in or near areas of black concentration. At the request of community leadership, NCDH and the National Association for the Advancement of Colored People (NAACP) jointly filed a formal protest with federal and New York State officials, demanding full-scale investigations of the Greenburgh authority, since the issue involved both the federal and state responsibility to insure that local housing authorities and urban renewal agencies stopped using public funds to entrench and extend segregation.

Of the 12 national and regional housing conferences convened by NCDH during this phase, five may be considered as especially significant, in view of subsequent developments in the movement. The

first conference of particular significance was the country's first
national legal conference on equal opportunity in housing, held in
February 1965.* Its purpose was to launch a multipronged, nation-
wide drive to combat the growing referendum movement spearheaded
by a countermovement opposing fair-housing laws. This was a direct
outgrowth of the struggle concerning Proposition 14.

The Capahosic Conference in May 1965 included representatives
from a number of private foundations, as well as government, the
housing industry, and intergroup relations practitioners.† One principal feature of this conference was an in-depth analysis of the program
activities of a demonstration project initiated earlier by NCDH, Operation Open City in New York, which pointed up the potential of a metro-
based fair-housing operation. Another major feature of the conference
was a special session devoted to the role and responsibility of foundations, as well as government and industry, in expanding the scope and
effectiveness of local community fair-housing programs. In view of
the enlarged financial support of NCDH itself, and the subsequent trend
of local fair-housing groups to secure funding, this entire conference
was especially significant. It revealed the role of the NCDH is prolif-
erating funding possibilities for the community level of the movement.
And, in effect, it placed the local groups in competition with each
other, as well as with NCDH itself, in the eventual scramble for
scarce funding sources.

A third conference of significance was the Chicago Conference
in October 1965, which confronted a weakness of the fair-housing
movement, publicly noted there as its middle-class and upper-class
orientation.‡ It was emphatically emphasized at this conference that
any meaningful effort to achieve integration must cut across all economic levels, with its major thrust beamed toward low- and moderate-
income families.

---

*This was held at the University of California in Berkeley on
February 5 and 6, 1965, and was jointly sponsored by the university's
School of Law. It brought together 48 of the nation's outstanding law
professors and attorneys concerned with civil rights.

†This was held in Capakosic, Virginia, on May 26-28, 1965 and
was jointly sponsored by the Phelps-Stokes Fund and NCDH.

‡This conference was held on October 21-23, 1965 and was
attended by over 300, representing the fair-housing movement in every
section of the country. Titled "How to Break Up the Ghetto," it was
here that NCDH Executive Director Rutledge said, "The youthful fair
housing committee movement is coming of age."

The fourth conference of significance was the National Housing Conference for Community Action Program (antipoverty) Directors in April 1966, held in conjunction with OEO.* This conference represented the culmination of a special project NCDH had been conducting for eight months under contract with OEO. A prime objective of the demonstration, conducted in four pilot cities,† was the development of guidelines for local programs to expand housing opportunities for poverty-stricken families. This alliance with OEO heralded the subsequent funding of other local fair-housing organizations, with occasional disastrous results, such as in Akron. The abortive funding by OEO of the New York and Los Angeles open-housing efforts also suggests some negative results of this alliance.

The fifth significant conference had as its theme "Model Cities and Metropolitan Desegregation."‡ The conference, which drew 500 representatives from all sections of the country, focused on "Model Cities: Promise or Threat?" It featured four major workshops; on government housing programs, revitalization of the racial ghetto, forces of community power, and metropolitan fair-housing centers. The significance of this conference lay in two of its workshops. The one devoted to the revitalization of the racial ghetto was a clear indicator of NCDH response to changes in the general civil rights movement emphasizing black power and separatism. The other, devoted to metropolitan fair-housing centers, foreshadowed the subsequent trend of local fair-housing groups to secure funding, clearly in response to NCDH emphasis.

Continuing growth and legitimacy of NCDH during this phase was indicated by presidential communication to NCDH[50] and involvement of NCDH in the planning of a massive White House conference, held in June 1966. Other indications of the increased impact of NCDH were seen in an agreement between national religious leaders and NCDH,** in national radio commentator recognition,[51] and in the continuing outreach of NCDH leadership to key positions in other relevant organizations of influence.†† One additional indicator of impact was the

-----

*Held April 27-29, 1966, at West Point, New York with top officials of antipoverty boards from 36 cities.

† This was held in New York on April 13, 1967, and was combined with an Annual Awards dinner honoring Charles Abrams and Loren Miller (president and vice-president).

‡Atlanta, Providence, Denver, and Rochester, New York.

**After a meeting on March 28, 1966, the religious leaders joined NCDH in a program dealing with the ghettos of urban America.

††U.S. Commission on Civil Rights, Police Review Board of New York City, Senate Judiciary Committee on Constitutional Rights (testimony).

Ford Foundation grant to the National Urban League for a three-year open-housing, funded demonstration project involving eight cities. This project was to be conducted in collaboration with NCDH, which had itself recently received funding from the foundation for the enlargement of its program on the local community level.

The U. S. Government was labeled a "ghetto builder" in February 1967 when NCDH released a 32-page manifesto charging the federal government with primary responsibility for "undergirding a ghetto system that dominates, distorts, and espoils every aspect of life in the U.S. today."[52] The indictment was issued at a Washington press conference on February 8, and was called by news media over the country one of the most serious by any civil rights organization. It was based on a bill of particulars prepared and submitted by NCDH to the White House almost a year earlier, setting forth 17 specific charges against federal agencies for policies and practices that perpetuated and extended racial segregation.

By the end of the third phase NCDH had enlarged its membership to 51 leading national organizations, had moved its offices to a new prestigious location, increased the cost of a Trends subscription by one dollar a year, opened two new regional offices in Washington, D. C. and San Francisco, and had received almost one million dollars in funding from HUD, the Carnegie Corporation, and private foundations.

By this time, too, fair housing was the law of the land, with the adoption of the 1968 Civil Rights Act and the Supreme Court decision upholding the constitutionality of the 1866 Civil Rights Act. For NCDH this became the beginning of a new program and a new focus. The program was to be a translation of open housing from stated policy and legal right into a fact of life for all citizens. The focus was to be the link between jobs and housing, with land-use bias in zoning restrictions as the target for action.

The job/housing link deserves special mention here, as it indicates the magnitude of the problem confronting fair-housing forces, now that open-housing laws were secured, and that portion of the struggle won. It can also be seen that the second focus, on land-use bias and zoning restrictions, is directly related to jobs and housing.

In a special report issued by NCDH the findings of the first year's study of the New York Metropolitan tri-state region (financed by the Carnegie Corporation) were publicized as an interim report. The conclusions reached by NCDH, at midpoint, about minority access to jobs and housing in the three states, were that development policies were irrational and rooted in institutional racial and economic discrimination. Only a radical restructuring of suburban home and job relationships for minority workers could make the region livable.

The report, "Jobs and Housing," also indicated that there were no
counterforces currently operating which were capable of blunting the
impact of current trends. Separation by income and race on a regional
scale was an unprecedented and qualitatively new phenomenon. Massive ghettos with hundreds of thousands of blacks were one to two
hours' travel time from jobs in suburban areas, which had massive
concentrations of whites who did not work there. Suburban labor
shortages reflected the abnormality of labor force distribution due to
separation by income and race. And finally, "concentration of housing
may be essential for environmental preservation."[53] Yet high density
housing is antithetical to present suburban zoning patterns. Large-lot
zoning, on the increase, most often results in waste of land and multi-
plication of sewage disposal problems; higher density, on the other hand,
permits economical treatment of sewage, solid-waste incineration, and
smoke control. The report concluded that:

> The movement of minority households to non-ghetto areas
> in sufficient numbers to halt expansion of the ghetto and
> provide free choice of residence to all minority families
> will require massive efforts involving government at all
> levels and private corporations.[54]

What would be required, according to the report, was not only
more efficient enforcement of open-housing laws, not only a greater
supply of housing geared to the earnings of minority workers, not
only fair employment practices and training programs designed to
tap the full potential of the minority labor force, but actually a
national committment to do all of this, comparable to "World War II's
commitment to victory; in the words of William James, 'the moral
equivalent of war'."[55]

Impact of Changing Civil Rights Movement on NCDH

In spite of seeming imperviousness in the Trends publication,
changes in the general civil rights movement did affect NCDH. Three
overt responses to such changes occurred. In February 1968 NCDH
joined with the Metropolitan Applied Research Center, Inc. (MARC)
in a formal cooperation agreement. At that time, Kenneth Clark,
president of MARC, and Rutledge and Wood of NCDH said: "We reject
the idea that full equal status for any group can be achieved within the
framework of racial segregation or separatism"[56]
Further evidence reflecting the national changes in the civil
rights movement at this time was indicated in the March 1968 annual

report of NCDH which sharply attacked separatist theory, and suggested ways of alleviating racial crisis.

Additional evidence of the effect of the changing civil rights movement on NCDH was seen in October, 1968. NCDH sponsored a meeting in Denver on "Housing and the Urban Crisis," drawing over 500 delegates. The Metropolitan Denver Fair Housing Center (funded with NCDH assistance) was both the host and subject for the meeting. NCDH President Robert Carter, in a keynote speech, warned of defeatist attitudes and gilding the ghettos.[57]

Covert responses to the changing civil rights movement were found by a closer analysis of Trends, revealing several subtle indications of the effects of such changes on NCDH. One subtle indicator was the change in the types of surveys reported, shifting from white attitudes to black attitudes.* Another was the almost sudden growth of emphasis on revitalization of the ghetto. This was followed first by ambivalent response to and interpretation of this concept, then by a reversion to the earlier concept of ghetto elimination, and finally by a modification of the concept to include improvement of the ghetto along with the efforts toward its elimination.[58] A third indicator of the effect of changes in the national civil rights movement on NCDH was the decrease in the use of the term integration in Trends during its 14 years of publication, from an average of 37 times per issue in 1956 to twice in 1970.

A final indicator of the impact of the changing civil rights movement on NCDH was revealed in two personal interviews with leading administrators of NCDH. In August 1969, NCDH Executive Director Rutledge frankly acknowledged to the writer his exasperation with some aspects of the open-housing movement as it then existed.[59] In answer to the question: How do you feel about the current status of the open housing movement?, Rutledge replied, "I think we're raising a monster." When pressed for an explanation, he said that fair-housing groups were "becoming part of the establishment and were not resolving any major problems. They should be a catalytic agent in each community. The one-to-one approach is dead. They should be using litigation to open housing opportunities." He also referred with some bitterness to the fact that some fair-housing groups would not be in existence if it hadn't been for NCDH. Yet this

---

*From 1956 through 1966, seven national opinion surveys were reported in Trends. All but one of these were primarily concerned with white attitudes toward integration or results of integration. Only one survey was reported after 1966, in the Fall-Winter issue of 1968. That survey was of black attitudes.

was apparently not acknowledged by those groups and they wanted the full glory for their achievements and didn't "consider or consult NCDH any more." His final remark was, "All the volunteer fair housing groups want to be funded. The volunteer movement is suffering and dwindling."

Rutledge also expressed some dissatisfaction with the name NCDH. When asked what he would suggest instead, he said: "National Committee for Urban Opportunities in Jobs, Housing, and Education." This seemed to indicate a view of the need for more public emphasis on the interrelationship of housing opportunities with other vital aspects of urban life. It might also appeal even to the separatists?

An interview with Margaret Fisher, almost one year later in April 1970, did not produce as frank a response. She spoke freely of all aspects of NCDH's early and subsequent development, but seemed less willing to comment on the state of the fair-housing movement today. Yet, even though veiled, some very revealing expressions of dissatisfaction came through. She did, for example, say that "the separatist movement has hurt the whole civil rights movement," and expressed her view that "it was totally unrealistic—people can't learn to live together by living apart." She also stated that we were in a period of retrogression, and that maybe this would unite the civil rights movement.

Finally, she commented that in spite of gains, "we still haven't scratched the surface because of the magnitude of the problem—all this plagues the open-housing movement."[60] In a most revealing statement she indicated her preference for the use of the term "open" rather than "fair" in relation to the housing movement. She felt that this really conveyed more adequately the concept of options—freedom of choice rather than just integration. Again, freedom of choice might be thought to be more palatable to separatists and militants than integration per se.

Despite response to the changing civil rights movement, the growing emphasis on black power, and the disenchantment among some militants with the concept of integration, it must be noted that NCDH clung stubbornly throughout its 20-year existence to its avowed goal of an open integrated society, ghetto-free, with full equality of opportunity in housing for all. Yet it occasionally modified its public statements in response to situational demands.

Legislative Development

The general trend of legislative development during the third phase was the continuation of the social-distance-scale model indicated earlier. The culmination of this trend was reached with the

1968 Civil Rights act and the Supreme Court decision upholding the
constitutionality of the 1866 Civil Rights Act. Thus it took 102 years
to merely reaffirm man's basic right to shelter. During this phase
several local and state actions barring fair-housing laws through
referendum were declared unconstitutional by state and federal
supreme courts. NCDH was active in this entire effort, submitting
amicus curiae briefs in several such cases, notably California's
Proposition 14 case and the 1866 case.

When the Senate passed the 1968 fair-housing bill, which was
to cover 80 percent of the nation's housing by January 1970, the total
number of fair-housing laws in the country numbered 153, and covered
23 states and 129 cities, towns, and counties. In June 1968 the
Supreme Court upheld the constitutionality of the 1866 Civil Rights
Act, and declared it to be in effect, thus opening up all housing with
no delays and no exemptions. NCDH directors commented:

> Thus, action by the three branches of the National Govern-
> ment converged to outlaw racism in housing: the Executive,
> by proposing legislation; the Congress by enacting it; and
> the Supreme Court by upholding a basic constitutional free-
> dom guaranteed by a 102 year old statute.
>
> The sweeping decision of the Court goes far beyond
> the concept of a mere prohibition of racial discrimination
> in the sale or rental of all real property. The Court said
> that the herding of people into racial ghettos because of
> their color is in fact a relic of slavery. . . . This declara-
> tion is central to the position long espoused by NCDH, and
> we are proud to have played a leading role in this historic
> case. . . . [61]

In a period of three months after the passage of the Fair
Housing Act of 1968, the total number of local fair-housing laws
increased by 100. By the end of the third phase in 1970, there were
229 state and local fair-housing laws. Figure 1 indicates total legislative development.

The National Association of Real Estate Boards, long recognized as the most powerful and effective organization opposing fair-
housing legislation, called on its 85,000 members to comply with
the Supreme Court's decision upholding the 1866 law.[62] In an article
published in NAREB's official publication, its vice-president said
"those who have opposed open housing laws should now understand
that their position is forever negated."[63]

Though the battle for a national open-housing law was won, the
struggle for open housing as a reality was not. NCDH shifted its
legislative attack to zoning restrictions in urban and suburban areas,

FIGURE 1

Legislative Development, 1956–70

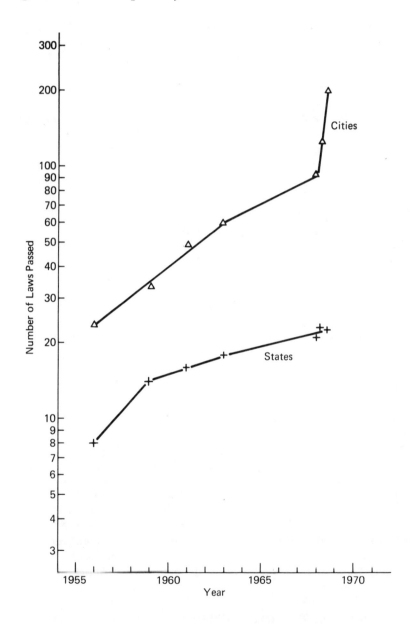

Source: Compiled by the author based on data from Trends in Housing, 1955–1970.

and advocated replacement of the one-by-one discrimination complaint process to the broader pattern or practice approach.

Local Community Action Development

Local community action during the third phase was marked by three trends: continuing proliferation, funding, and increased emphasis on low-income housing. The extent of proliferation is revealed by the fact that at the beginning of the phase, 300 local community groups had been identified as fair-housing organizations while at the end of the phase there were 2000 local fair-housing groups across the country.[64] Figure 2 indicates the geometric progression that occurred up to 1966. Growth continued after that time, but not at the same rate. There are several possible explanations for this growth pattern. Events in the general civic rights movement may have been responsible, such as separatist philosophy and splintering of traditional groups. Funding may have weakened the volunteer movement. Or, funding may have consolidated some voluntary groups, with a resulting decline in overall numbers. Perhaps a combination of these factors offers a valid explanation. In any case, the overall trend of proliferation was marked during this phase.

The second trend, funding, was evident in 1967. By this time NCDH was heavily involved with the national antipoverty program (OEO), and was publicly committed to the concept of the Metropolitan Fair Housing Center, a funded, professionally staffed operation. In April 1967, one of the major workshops at the NCDH Model Cities Conference was devoted to metropolitan fair-housing centers.

It therefore came as no surprise that Denver won OEO funding, aided by NCDH, in July 1967, to open its Metro Fair Housing Center. The grant of $172,460 was considered by NCDH to have special national significance as the first such major federal agency action to provide substantial investment in a fair-housing center. NCDH executives told OEO Director Shriver that the Denver funding ". . . sustains and promises to expand a vigorous attack on the root cause of poverty, the housing deprivation which sustains every other facet of poverty."[65]

At this time, other local fair-housing groups began to search for funding in order to expand their scope and impact. Fifteen cities across the nation secured funding for local fair-housing organizations, formerly voluntary.* Many of these indicated a new emphasis on low-

---

*Baltimore, Providence, Chicago, Los Angeles, Wichita, Buffalo, Akron, Long Beach, Dallas, Louisville, Washington, Kansas City, Boston, St. Louis, and Seattle.

FIGURE 2

Local Community Action Development 1956-70

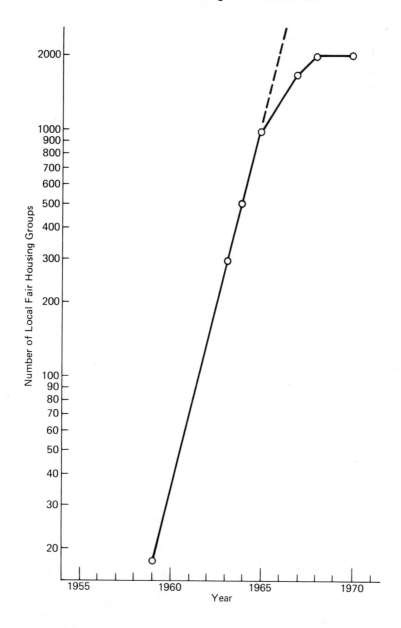

income housing, either through rehabilitation efforts or the expansion of the supply of low-cost housing through the building of new units.

One significant indicator of the increased impact of the movement on the local level is revealed in the announcement that the League of Women Voters included open housing as part of their national agenda in January 1969.[66] No item is included in the national agenda unless it has been studied—usually over a period of years—and consensus has been reached in every branch in the country. The League at that time had some 1000 branches with 160,000 members.

The three trends of proliferation, funding, and emphasis on low-income housing are unmistakable during this phase, and their underlying causes are also clear. The heavy emphasis of NCDH on funding as a requisite for effective action programs on a metropolitan basis has already been noted. Not only was wide publicity given to this concept in Trends and in conferences, but the success of a few voluntary groups in securing funding encouraged others.

NCDH's growing emphasis on increasing the supply and dispersion of low-cost housing also permeated Trends and national and regional conferences, and filtered down to the local groups. But all of this must also be seen as a reflection of the general national emphasis on the War on Poverty, which affected and was affected by the civil rights movement, which also affected the NCDH and eventually the local housing groups.

THE FOURTH PHASE (1970-77)

Context[67]

1970

- Vietnam war continues.

- U. S. Supreme Court set February 1, 1970 as deadline for school desegregation in six states.

- Governors of four southern states met in Mobile, Alabama, to discuss strategy against court-ordered school desegregation plans.

- U. S. Senate voted to cut off federal funds to all school districts where residential patterns resulted in de facto school segregation.

- Florida Governor Kirk capitulated to a federal district court, ending his week-long defiance of orders to desegregate Manatee County public schools.

- Four students killed at Kent State and nine wounded when National Guard fired into group of antiwar demonstrators on May 4.

- Two black students killed when police fired into crowd outside women's dorm at Jackson, Mississippi State college, May 15.

- Civil rights marchers rallied in Atlanta, Georgia at end of 110-mile "march against repression," May 23.

- U. S. Government announced federal budget deficit of $2.9 billion for fiscal year ending June 30, 1970.

- Desegregated classes began for first time in more than 200 school districts across the southern U.S., August 31.

- U. S. Civil Rights Commission reported major breakdown in enforcement of civil rights legislation, October 12.

1971

- U. S. Supreme Court issued four unanimous decisions supporting school desegregation, April 20.

- U. S. death toll in combat in Vietnam reported above 45,000 men.

- President Nixon issued major policy statement supporting existing bans on racial discrimination in housing, June 11.

- Emergency Employment Act signed by President Nixon to provide 150,000 government jobs, July 12.

- U. S. Vice-President Agnew said at African news conference that "querulous U. S. blacks could learn from African leaders."

- U. S. Senator Edward Muskie said that having a black as vice-presidential candidate would defeat the Democratic ticket.

- U. S. jets staged massive raid inside North Vietnam, September 21.

1972

- U. S. Federal judge ordered black schools of Richmond, Virginia to merge with white schools of two suburbs, January 10.

- First national black convention in Gary, Indiana set up permanent body to provide leadership for black political and social action.

- President Nixon asked Congress for legislation denying courts power to order busing of elementary school children to achieve racial integration, and concentrating federal aid to education in poor districts, March 17.

- U. S. Senate and House conference committee agreed on provisions of education bill including antibusing provision, May 17.

- U. S. Court of Appeals reversed lower court order that would have merged school systems of Richmond and two suburbs, June 6.

- U. S. Congress cleared higher education bill with three antibusing provisions, June 8.

- U. S. District Court ordered most massive busing program to date to integrate schools in Detroit and 53 suburban districts.

- Five men seized while trying to install eavesdropping equipment in Democratic National Headquarters in Washington, D.C., June 17.

- President Nixon, in press conference, criticized court-ordered busing of Detroit area school children.

- U. S. Labor Department announced cost of living had risen .4 percent, price of meat rose in July 2.89 percent and was 10.1 percent higher than a year earlier.

- U. S. Court of Appeals panel issued indefinite stay of massive busing program ordered for Detroit area schools, August 24.

- President Nixon signed revenue-sharing bill, October 20.

- President Nixon reelected in 49 states, November 7.

- U. S. B-52 bombers conducted heaviest raid of war in North Vietnam.

1973

- Cease-fire agreement signed, January 27.

- President Nixon submitted 1974 budget calling for drastic cuts and elimination of over 100 antipoverty and aid-to-education programs.

- U. S. Supreme Court upheld appellate court ruling that merger of black Richmond, Virginia schools with two white suburbs was unconstitutional, May 21.

- U. S. Supreme Court stated in Denver, Colorado school case that segregation would be treated the same in northern and southern schools.

- U. S. Supreme Court agreed to review federal district court plan ordering integration of black Detroit schools with white suburban schools, November 19.

1974

- President Nixon refuses to comply with subpoenas for tapes, January 4.

- Inflationary trend continues.

- Watergate indictments, March 1.

- Watergate transcripts published, May 1.

- Formal impeachment hearings open, May 9.

- Nixon announces intention to resign, August 8.

- Gerald Ford sworn in as president, August 9.

- Stock market hits four-year low.

- Court-ordered busing leads to violence in Boston, September 12.

- National Guard mobilized in Boston, October 15.

- Ford said United States faced three challenges: inflation, recession, and energy crisis, December 2.

- Layoffs increase in United States.

1975

- War in Cambodia ends, April 17.

- Teachers' strikes and busing disrupt U. S. schools (New York City and Louisville, Kentucky), September 10.

- Ford vetoes funds to save bankrupt New York City, October 29.

1976

- Violence in northern Ireland.

- U. N. debates Israeli occupation, May 4.

- Blacks riot in South Africa, June 16.

- U. S. economy slows down, October 19.

- Carter wins presidency, November 2.

- Carter's church integrated (Plains, Georgia), 11-year ban on blacks dropped, November 2.

- Amy Carter to attend public school predominantly black, December 28.

NCDH Development

Just as there was a sharp tangible break between the second and third phases of NCDH's development, so also was there such a break between the third and fourth phases. During 1970, Trends appeared irregularly. After the year-end report of 1970, which did not arrive until well into 1971, there were no more issues of Trends until the summer of 1972. What happened? NCDH fell upon hard times, and all the good sources in the literature on social movements appeared to be right after all about institutionalization leading to decline.

Hard Times. Soon after its twentieth anniversary, NCDH faced the loss of its Ford Foundation support and its HUD funding. Its local networks were discontented and it was in imminent danger of bankruptcy—financial, organizational, and spiritual. This was set against a national backdrop of presidential disavowals of forced integration of the suburbs, bitterly resisted and challenged by NCDH and other civil rights organizations throughout the country. The entire year-end Trends issue of 1970 was devoted to this subject, with the lead article captioned, "NCDH Demands U.S. Fair Housing Action: Law Enforcement the Issue; Not 'Forced' Integration." In that issue were individual supportive statements from 13 metropolitan fair-housing groups around the nation. Also in that issue was an NCDH plea to Trends readers for funds, an increase to $5 for the subscription price, and notice of removal of free mailing list and nonrenewals.

After this no issues appeared for more than a year. In the interim a serious financial deficit and organizational discontent contributed to doubts about refunding on the part of the Ford Foundation. Local fair-housing organizations had voiced marked discontent with NCDH at the February 1971 national open-housing conference in Chicago. Representatives from local groups were vocal and forthright in their expression of the need for better communication with NCDH. Some said that NCDH was more concerned with its own funding, glory, and survival than with the growth and development of the local movement organizations. At that time NCDH defended itself by accusing local groups of neglecting to feed information to the national organization, thus robbing NCDH of vital continuing data on the movement. "How can we write or know about you if you don't tell us what you're doing?"

Rival Organization. During this time, also, the appearance of a rival national organization—National Neighbors (NN)—shook the firm support for NCDH, and added to the growing uncertainty as to its efficacy and worth. The doubts and discontent with NCDH were exacerbated by the obvious contrast in style and organizational format of the new rival organization. National Neighbors was grass-roots-oriented and led, and thus appealed to those with strong objections to the elitist organizational structure of NCDH. Morevoer, NN's focus was on neighborhood stabilization, which was also appealing to those who yearned for greater participation and control on the local level. NCDH's increasing stress on funded, metropolitan, staffed fair-housing centers offered no place for struggling volunteer fair-housing groups that wanted to be affiliated with a national movement but found themselves overlooked and ignored precisely because they were small and struggling. National Neighbors, on the other hand, welcomed as members or associates anyone who agreed with its principles and could pay $10. This, of course, was not enough to sustain it, and it soon sought funding from the Ford Foundation—the main source of foundation funding for NCDH.

Intrusive Movement Organization. What was happening here was clearly an example of an "intrusive movement organization," so aptly described by Harold Nelson. [68] An intrusive movement organization, according to Nelson, may compete with an existing movement organization (MO) on three dimensions: ideological, power-prestige, and resource. Though NN was not competing ideologically with NDCH, since its focus was not open housing but neighborhood stabilization after integration, it nevertheless was competing for power-prestige and resources.

Nelson suggests that MOs may intrude on the established movement structure in two ways, by sponsorship or by competition. Sponsorship refers to the impetus for intrusion arising within the movement; competition refers to the unwillingness of the established MO to accept the intruder. Each of these was at work in the NCDH/NN situation. Some of the discontented open-housing supporters were the leaders of the new organization, making it sponsored. According to Nelson; "sponsorship indicates a conclusion that in terms of appeal. . . strategy. . .or resources, the existent movement is somehow deficient. It is perceived as filling a gap or providing a valued service of some kind to the movement." NN was certainly not sponsored by NCDH, though there were attempts by NCDH to establish friendly relations. These were never actualized, and the treading by NN on NCDH's turf remained a problem for the first six years of NN's existence.* Since neighborhood stabilization depends on an open

---

*This problem was discussed openly at the 1975 National Neighbors Great Lakes Regional Conference. There, a special workshop

housing market, the issue of open housing quickly became a major focus for many of the stabilization groups and their national organization, National Neighbors. Open housing, on the other hand, needs to be able to show that integration can work. So neighborhood stabilization is critical for the success of the open-housing movement. Each needs the other in order to succeed. Yet the administrative leaders of both organizations claimed that they had tried to work things out with the others without success. This uneasy coexistence and semi-rivalry continued, while each national organization met its different sets of problems internally and externally over the next few years.

Organizational Change. All of this led to an organizational shake-up of NCDH, mandated by the Ford Foundation as a condition for refunding. (It later funded NN also.) The NCDH board of directors changed from an organization of organizations to 35 individuals elected annually (one-third each year) for three year terms, meeting quarterly. Most significantly, the director and co-director left NCDH, and were replaced by a new director, Ed Holmgren, who had been executive director of Chicago's open-housing group* for ten years, and before that of Baltimore Neighbors, Inc. (one of the few combined open-housing and neighborhood-stabilization groups in the country). Holmgren had previously served as housing director of the Chicago Urban League and director of an American Friends Service Committee regional housing opportunity program. He was also an NCDH board member for many years. So he brought many years of active involvement and knowledge to his new position. NCDH President Robert L. Carter stated:

> The personal commitment being made of a professional
> of Mr. Holmgren's experience to NCDH is particularly
> significant in the fact of overwhelming statistical, emo-
> tional, and public policy evidence of the deepening failure
> of the national will to pursue equal rights for all citizens.[70]

Holmgren assumed the directorship of NCDH with a $200,000 deficit, which he promised to make up through a responsible and cautious fiscal management and strong administration.

---

dealt with the issue, and leaders of both national organizations were present and participated in the discussion.[69]

    *Leadership Council for Metropolitan Open Communities, pro-filed in Chapter 4.

Image Restoration. In the next five years, NCDH struggled to restore itself and its image. By 1977 it had re-established itself as the only national organization representing solely the open-housing movement. (During this period, NN went through its own shake-up and internal disasters and complete reorganization. In January 1978 it moved its offices to Washington, almost next door to NCDH!) NCDH's reorganization was done first through moving its national office from New York to Washington, on September 1, 1972. Three primary reasons were given for the move: the opportunity to secure funds for expansion of NCDH's legal services program if based in Washington, which would allow increased emphasis on NCDH's exclusionary zoning litigation; closer liaison with related Washington-based national organizations and institutions, with a mutually beneficial exchange of information, ideas, and resources; and the essential need to provide more intensive guidance and impact on HUD and other agencies in the formulation and implementation of federal policies and programs, to interpret federal activities to the field, and to mobilize action. NCDH retained an eastern field office in New York (until November 1974) and a western one in San Francisco until its HUD project there was completed (April 1974). These were both eventually closed because of budget tightening.

During the five-year period after Holmgren took over as director, NCDH held ten regional conferences, litigated 15 major suits, prepared and mailed Trends 25 times (five per year) to 14,000 readers, gave major testimony at countless congressional and government hearings, wrote and distributed numerous policy statements, research monographs, and research papers, helped to organize a nation-wide protest against the Nixon housing moratorium, and finally in 1976-77 directed a HUD-funded nation-wide $1 million audit covering forty metropolitan areas across the country. Except for the audit (which will be discussed separately), all this was accomplished with a modest, gradually acquired staff of five lawyers, two research analysts, one field services director, six secretaries, several student interns, one special researcher for special projects, and a few consultants as needed. NCDH's sources of funding were mostly the Ford Foundation and two other New York-based foundations, individual contributions, and occasional HUD contracts. In 1976 its annual budget was $800,000.

Conferences. The ten regional conferences convened by NCDH during this phase reflected some ongoing concerns of the movement and some new ones generated by national events and developments in housing and related issues. These, in turn, reflected local community developments in the movement and then generated new activities on the local level.

Four regional conferences in 1973-74 were designed to provide maximum participation of those attending and in-depth discussion of the current crisis in federal housing policy (moratorium), the lawsuit against the moratorium, other current legislation, metropolitan planning (fair-share plans), revenue sharing, A-95 review, pattern and practice suits, state licensing power for compliance, and monitoring. The primary focus was on ways in which the housing/civil rights movement could expand and improve its influence and effectiveness. The first conference was held in Atlanta (October 15-16), co-sponsored with the Southern Regional Council; it drew 175 delegates. In Chicago (January 29-30), also with 175 people attending, the conference had two major themes: strategies to increase the supply of housing, and strategies to expand equal access to housing. Topics, in addition to the ones noted above, covered controlled, exclusionary zoning, auditing and testing, and redlining.

A San Francisco conference on March 8 and 9 added the following topics: the San Francisco HUD demonstration project, and the use of new tools, for example, housing allowances—employer services, neighborhood housing, and regional approaches to housing needs. A northeastern conference October 24 and 25 in New York focused on the impact of the 1974 Housing and Community Development Act (HCD) and its implications for the movement.

Again in 1976 four regional conferences were announced for Minnesota, New Orleans, Philadelphia, and Los Angeles. Issues discussed included redlining, block-grant citizen participation, housing litigation, and housing assistance plans.

In addition to these conferences, NCDH convened a panel of housing and ecology experts in 1972 to meet in on-going sessions for clarification of the issues relevant to both fields of interest. Also convened by NCDH during this period was a nation-wide legal conference in Washington, on November 14 and 15, 1974, with 55 experts from all over the country meeting to discuss land-use litigation trends. "Frustrations abound" was the phrase that came out of that conference. Noted there was the fact that in the past 46 years, only one zoning case had ever gone up to the Supreme Court. By 1974 NCDH's attorneys were heavily involved in a significant number of zoning cases, and were setting some major legal precedents. But the legal decisions coming from the courts were conflicting and confusing; what has been called the tango of civil rights (one step forward, two steps backward) is well applied here.[71]

Housing and Community Development Act of 1974. The passage of the Act of 1974 prompted the organization of a new major NCDH program of massive proportions and impact. In late October 1974 NCDH launched a nation-wide program aimed at stimulating immediate action by citizen fair-housing advocacy groups to safeguard equal opportunity objectives of the $11.3 billion act. The critical and urgent need for local citizen action was stressed by NCDH in its warning that the new federal system of funding housing and community assistance by block grants to local government represents "a crossroads that will determine racial and economic patterns of residence for decades to come."[72]

While the new legislation reaffirmed the nation's commitment to adequate shelter and equal opportunity for all citizens, it marked a radical change in the method of distributing federal monies for housing and community assistance. With increased emphasis on planning and decision making by local governments, the danger was seen that HUD might interpret the new act as sanctioning a transfer of authority from the federal to the local level. Thus, the role of citizen groups as effective forces in determining how federal dollars would be spent was viewed by NCDH as critical.

To assist local groups in their efforts to become more effective participants, NCDH launched a six-point program. A Handbook for Citizens Fair-Housing Advocacy under the HCD Act of 1974 to be prepared and made available for distribution on request; consultative services were to be provided by NCDH staff for local groups; housing and community development progress were to be monitored in selected cities with periodic status reports issued; NCDH officers and staff would support local advocacy efforts with representations to HUD; legal staff would investigate civil rights abuses by local and state governments and initiate legal action where feasible; and periodic information bulletins would keep the field informed on pertinent developments and possible opportunities for influencing local plans and projects.

Concerning the new HCD Act, NCDH President Robert Weaver said in a keynote address at one of NCDH's conferences, "On the plus side, the Act's primary objective is the development of viable urban community that provides decent housing and a suitable living environment particularly for low and moderate income people."[73] He praised the act's objectives of reducing isolation of income groups, of increasing diversity of neighborhoods, and of deconcentrating housing opportunities for the poor. But beyond the promising rhetoric, Weaver saw serious threats in the "new federalism" approach: the decision-making power of local governments over federal monies; the extent to which HUD would enforce the requirements of the law; the near-total reliance on leased housing and virtual abandonment of other subsidy programs; the effect on credit and production. By the fall of 1976 NCDH was among those charging that HUD's administration of the Community Development Block Grant (CDBG) program was a failure, and recommended 15 steps for strengthening the program.[74]

School and Housing Desegregation. Another major concern of NCDH was reflected in an important policy statement adopted by the board of directors in October 1975—the relationship of school desegregation to housing desegregation. Speaking at a time when the school desegregation issue was marked by increasing confusion and tension,* the board of NCDH noted with concern a growing tendency among opponents of busing to claim that housing desegregation was the preferable means of achieving school desegregation:

> Busing and open housing should not, and logically cannot, be counterposed because they are <u>both</u> means of ending segregation in the schools. As open housing increases, the need for busing diminishes, but until truly open housing is achieved, busing will be necessary. . . . [A]lthough open housing must be viewed as the long range solution to school segregation, busing results in an immediate rearrangement of enrollments by race. Those who sincerely desire equal opportunities in education for children of minority races can, and should, give their strong support to <u>both</u> open housing and to busing where necessary.[75]

New-found supporters of open housing in the anti-busing groups were challenged in the statement to join in organized efforts to expand minority access to housing throughout metropolitan regions. The statement cited as a model for local action the rational and comprehensive fair-housing proposals issued by the Kentucky Commission on Human Rights (See Chapter 4; Across the Country.)

<u>Government Inconsistency</u>. The NCDH policy statement noted the inconsistency, and consequent danger, in the federal government's civil rights posture. It pointed out that at the very time Congress was considering legislation to terminate or limit busing, the HCD Act of 1974 was curtailing opportunities for minorities to move from central-city areas with the highest concentration of racially segregated schools to suburban areas where schools were predominantly white. In the view of the NCDH board, enactment of federal antibusing legislation "would constitute a major setback in the struggle for equal opportunity."[76] The Kentucky commission cited federal policy conflicts in another way: "It is unfair to the people. . .to allow HUD to support . . .housing. . .which is segregated, while other branches of the Federal Government require desegregation of schools."[77]

---

*See the Context section for this fourth phase.

Despite these active NCDH efforts to reach out to local groups, Holmgren felt in July 1976 that NCDH still had a long way to go: "We've not really reestablished the link with local groups enough."[78] But by the end of 1977 that link had been strengthened considerably by NCDH's direction of the nation-wide audit, which brought funding and a discrimination investigation technique to forty fair-housing groups and advocates in metropolitan areas throughout the nation. The audit will be discussed later in this chapter.

Legislative and Legal Action Development

Legislative action during the first three phases of NCDH's development was primarily focused on the passage of a federal fair-housing law, which was achieved with Title VIII of the 1968 Civil Rights Act. The fourth phase of NCDH's development was accompanied by extensive legal action brought to implement Title VIII. That act, it should be noted, was to be phased in over a three-year period, so that only by January 1, 1970 did it begin to cover fully all available housing. On that date, coverage under the last stage of the federal fair-housing act was extended to some 34 million privately owned single-family homes. By 1970, 927 legal cases had already been filed charging violations of the act.

Legal action was a new tool in 1970 for open housing, and its efficacy has grown and developed since then. As in many areas of the law, attorneys at first moved cautiously, and judges showed reluctance to expand the law. Each case was a prod to create new precedent and better remedies. As the remedies became publicized, more and more minority home seekers looked for legal advice and the help of the courts. The courts, in turn, came to recognize the need for prompt and effective relief, and granted restraining orders and temporary injunctions (which froze the property in question until the case was settled). Plaintiffs were able to obtain the housing of their choice and began pressing for damages, costs, and attorney's fees. Small amounts were awarded at first, but increased as the importance of monetary relief came to be recognized.

Damages. In 1970 a precedent was set when a record-breaking $2500 was awarded to two complainants in a housing discrimination case of the New Jersey Division of Civil Rights. The division director, James H. Blair (who later became the head of the Equal Opportunity Division of (HUD), claimed this "the largest sum ever awarded as damages for humiliation, mental pain, and suffering anywhere in the U.S. in a case connected with Civil Rights."[79] Eventually, judges and courts began to award some of the money to the fair-housing groups that had gathered the data, spurring them on to gather more data and file more cases, in a repeating cycle. By 1977, claimed damages of $1 million were not unusual.

Consent Decrees. The first federal suit against a multiple listing service (MLS) under the 1968 open-housing act was brought by the Department of Justice, using data compiled by Chicago's Leadership Council for Metropolitan Open Communities (LCMOC). The suit, against a suburban Chicago area MLS and ten member real estate firms was settled under a consent decree filed in Chicago. The federal complaint charged a pattern of racial discrimination in property sales and rentals by the West Suburban Board of Realtors and ten of its members.

Under the decree, the board and brokers admitted no wrong-doing but were ordered by the court to refrain from discrimination because of race, religion, or national origin in all sales and rentals and related advertising, and from denying real estate brokers admission to realty board membership and participation in the multiple listing services because of race, religion, or national origin. The court also ordered the board and brokers to permit federal inspection of appropriate records at six-month intervals for the next two years in order to assure compliance. This case set a precedent for hundreds of subsequent suits brought by the Department of Justice in the next seven years. Consent decrees were obtained all over the country, requiring extensive affirmative action as part of the agreement.

Fair-housing groups provided the data needed for such Department of Justice action. This was in direct response to the request by Frank Schwelb, chief of the department's housing and civil rights section for open-housing and allied groups in local communities to notify Department of Justice officials of situations where racial discrimination in housing seemed to be a pattern in their communities. "A letter is sufficient", said Mr. Schwelb.[80] However, it was soon learned that a letter was not sufficient for legal action to ensue, and this prompted a wave of community auditing that followed in the next seven years (reported under community action development.)

Zoning Challenges. Challenges by NCDH to exclusionary land-use controls and zoning continued and were taken up by sever of its organizational affiliates, such as NAACP, the League of Women Voters (LWV), and the American Jewish Congress. In 1970 NAACP initiated its challenge in Oyster Bay, Long Island, an area where multifamily units were prohibited. In the same year LWV published Local Zoning Ordinances and Housing for Lower Income Families— Goals in Conflict?;[81] and the American Jewish Congress published "Housing for the Other America, a Fifty-state Strategy, a manual to stimulate citizen action for expanding the housing supply, and calling for "fair housing through full housing."[82] NAACP's legal defense fund asked the Supreme Court in 1970 to review a decision in a Lansing, Michigan case involving exclusionary zoning.

In the next seven years the bulk of nationally noted legal suits focusing on housing (18) involved the issue of exclusionary zoning or land-use control. This issue seemed to peak in 1976, and then during 1977 was overshadowed by two other related fair-housing issues that had been drawing increasing attention: redlining, and compliance with block-grant provisions under the HCD Act of 1974.

The SASSO case in California and the Lawton, Oklahoma case, were among the most significant zoning challenger. SASSO was the Southern Alameda Spanish-Speaking Organization, a nonprofit corporation, which wanted to build a 280-unit subsidized housing development in Union City, California, in response to a critical need among Mexican American residents. Union City's zoning laws were typical of those in most communities; that is, they favored single-unit housing, but exceptions were occasionally made for apartments and other large projects. After SASSO obtained an option to buy a 23-acre tract of land in Union City, the city council passed an ordinance, at SASSO's request, to rezone the area to permit construction of the project. Then Anglo residents used California's referendum laws to submit the rezoning ordinance to the voters, who voted against it. This was the first time a referendum of any kind had ever been held in Union City. After six years of court challenges, voting referendums, and appeals, in April 1973 the struggling SASSO finally won its right to build. By this time, however, the federal moratorium was in effect, which curtailed the subsidies, and part of the site had been sold to pay the massive legal expenses of the suit.

The Lawton, Oklahoma case was one of the first in which a federal court ruled that local communities which attempt to zone out housing for the poor and minority citizens must prove a specific nondiscriminatory reason for such zoning. The decision on May 1, 1970 was the first federal appellate decision compelling specific local rezoning for lower-income, integrated housing. It confirmed a lower court decision requiring rezoning by Lawton officials to permit construction of a 65-unit, federally subsidized low- and moderate-income housing development. NCDH's attorneys represented Mrs. Willie Mae Dailey, a low-income, black Lawton resident and potential tenant of the development, and Columbia Square, Inc., the development's nonprofit sponsor. In the next seven years, exclusionary zoning and land-use cases were fought in Cleveland, Toledo, and Parma in Ohio; Belle Terre, Long Island; Delrey Beach and Palm Coast, Florida; Middlesex County, New Jersey (23 suburbs); Chicago; Horseheads, Huron, and Penfield, New York; Mt. Laurel, New Jersey; Philadelphia, Pennsylvania; and other communities across the country.

Moratorium. Several other monumental legal cases and legislative
actions were significant for the open-housing movement between
1970 and 1977. On January 8, 1973 an indefinite moratorium on
federally subsidized housing and community development programs
was announced by the Nixon administration. Every type of locality
was affected: cities, suburbs, and rural areas. Immediately halted
by the freeze were such programs as public housing (conventional,
turnkey, leasing); Section 235 (moderate-income home ownership);
Section 236 (moderate-income rental); and rent supplements. Also
halted were commitments for water and sewer grants, open space
grants, and public facility loans. The moratorium was to be extended
to the Model Cities and New Communities programs, and urban renewal
on July 1, 1973. The 1974 budget called for much additional curtail-
ment; more than 100 social and economic programs were to be abolished or sharply curtailed, affecting millions of impoverished and
disadvantaged Americans. Impounded were $991 million for housing
and community development programs.

On February 1, 1973 NCDH Director Ed Holmgren issued a call
to open-housing proponents everywhere in the nation to exert immediate and maximum leadership in reversing the administration's
moratorium. The NCDH policy statement charged that the administration's action would deprive "blacks and other minorities of the
supports needed to close the gaps between them and the white majority
in income, jobs, housing, education, health and community environment."[83] The moratorium dashed the hopes and aspirations of vast
numbers of people in desperate need, as well as denying housing opportunities. NCDH called on the president to do four things: rescind the
moratorium on federal housing subsidies; release all impounded funds
already appropriated by Congress for housing and other social and
economic programs; recall his Budget Message and cooperate with
Congressional leaders in developing laws and budget allocations which
would give priority to meeting human needs; and act to insure that all
federal programs were used affirmatively to achieve equal opportunities,
as mandated by federal law and executive orders.

The moratorium resulted in immediate suspension of all pre-
construction work on developments throughout the country, cutbacks in
employment, and cessation of future planning. On May 21, 1973 NCDH,
the state of Pennsylvania, the Maine State Housing Authority, and a
number of nonprofit housing sponsors and community groups filed suit
against the secretary of HUD. The suit, which had been in preparation
since January, within days after the freeze was announced, charged
that the administration's action halting housing subsidies nullified
congressional enactments, was an illegal exercise of executive power,
and violated the 1968 Fair Housing Act as well as portions of the
National Housing Acts. Two months later (July 23), a federal court

lifted the moratorium. Holmgren of NCDH hailed the court's decision as "a victory for the entire civil rights/ housing movement," under-scoring "once more the key role of a national center for fair housing and open communities and the importance of NCDH's research and legal capability, which enabled this challenge to be made."[84]

The jubilation, however, was short-lived. On October 1 the administration's housing act of 1973 was introduced in Congress. Holmgren commented:

> The Administration's housing and community development package halts the nation's feeble and belated efforts to expand housing and related opportunities for minorities and lower income Americans. It places its stamp of approv-al on the metropolitan status quo—a society divided along racial, economic, and city/suburban lines. It is morally untenable, socially dangerous, and economically unwork-able.[85]

Two Critical Legal Cases. During this period, two legal cases had critical implications for the open-housing movement. Trafficante v. Metropolitan Life Insurance Co. was filed December 7, 1972, and was won in the Supreme Court four months later (February 1973). This case grew out of complaints filed with HUD by two tenants—one black, one white—of an apartment development in San Francisco (Parkmerced), with 8200 residents. The tenants charged the owner had discriminated against nonwhite rental applicants by such tactics as manipulating waiting lists, delaying action on applications, and using discriminatory acceptance standards. When HUD did not secure relief within 30 days, as provided in the 1968 Fair Housing Act, the tenants went to court. They claimed they had been injured by loss of the social and economic benefits of living in an integrated community, and by being stigmatized as residents of a "white ghetto." Two lower courts ruled the tenants had no standing to sue. The Supreme Court reversed those rulings and returned the case to the district court for trial, where the evidence was introduced. The Supreme Court ruled unanimously that the tenants did have standing to sue: "any person who claims to have been injured by a discriminatory housing prac-tice" could be applied to all in the same housing unit who were injured by racial discrimination in the management of those facilities. The significance of this for the movement was the extension and broadening of the right to sue.

Another significant case for the movement involved the legiti-macy of the use of testers to determine compliance with fair-housing laws. This court action (October 1973) arose from an ordinance adopted by Upper Arlington, a suburb of Columbus, Ohio, in January

1973. The ordinance prohibited discrimination in housing, employment, and public accomodations, but also prohibited the use of testers
or checkers. NCDH and NAACP joined with LWV, NN, Housing
Opportunities Center (HOC) of Columbus, and several black and white
individuals, as plaintiffs. They argued that testing had been found a
legitimate method of securing evidence of discriminatory practices
by the courts at all levels, and was routinely used by official agencies
in enforcing the law.

The Department of Justice intervened, and Assistant Attorney
General Stanley Pottinger stated that federal efforts to assure equal
housing opportunity would be substantially impaired if checking and
testing were eliminated. Pottinger noted that many black home
seekers had no way to determine whether a "no vacancy" response
to an application for an apartment was the truth, or whether credit
standards were being fairly applied, unless white checkers made
application at the same time. The Ohio Civil Rights Commission later
entered as a plaintiff to the suit. The case was won six months later
(April 1974), and the court ordered Upper Arlington to delete the ban
on testers, affirming the validity of this investigative technique.

Fair-Share Plans. During this fourth phase, the development of fair-
share housing allocation plans also had an impact on the movement.
Such plans are designed to disperse low- and moderate-income housing
equitably throughout metropolitan areas, through the voluntary cooperation of suburban governments and jurisdictions.

One rationale for such plans is the fact that between 1960 and
1970, for each new job in the central city nearly three new jobs were
created in the suburbs of major cities.[86] Both white-collar and blue-
collar employment expanded in the suburbs during this time. But the
known inadequacy of housing opportunities near these jobs deprived
inner-city workers of access to them, except by costly and time-
consuming travel. These facts were used as an economic rationale
to plan housing near such employment opportunities.

The Dayton, Ohio, metropolitan area was the first to adopt a
fair-share plan, largely through the dynamic leadership of Dale
Bertsch, director of the Miami Valley Regional Planning Commission.
In the five years since the Dayton plan was initiated, over 25 other
metropolitan areas undertook housing allocation planning, with about
half of those officially adopted, and more in preparation. Despite the
years of haggling and negotiation required to achieve this, "rarely
has a new concept in planning spread so widely and so swiftly."[87]

The implications for the open-housing movement are seen in
the Dayton Area, where nearly half of the proposed 14,000 housing
units have been built and dispersed throughout the five-county area
in sections that previously had never had minority or moderate-

income residents. Some suburbs obtained their first public-housing complexes under the plan. However, the success of such plans is linked to political and economic considerations, which have posed enormous obstacles in other communities, and have prevented their ability to significantly affect housing patterns in the direction of open housing.

Local Community Action Development

During this fourth phase of development, there was a growing emphasis on neighborhoods around the country, resulting in significant grass-roots pressures against redlining.* At this time also occurred the proliferation of National Neighbors stabilization groups, noted earlier. One of the consequences of intrusive movement organizations is that they "increase the ideological or strategic breadth of the movement."[88] It may well be that NCDH's growing and renewed emphasis on the local movement organizations was partly in response to the contrasting organizational style of National Neighbors and other organizations focusing on grass-roots participation. In any case, movement activity on the local level continued during this phase, despite legislative setbacks and dire national economic and international conditions plus compelling national political concerns. (See Context section of this chapter.)

Four increasing aspects of local fair-housing group activity were evident during this phase. First, there was a pronounced increase in the use of systematic auditing of housing availability, which led finally to the HUD national audit in 1976-77. Second, there was a marked increase in the amount of legal action to implement the federal open-housing law. Third, there was an increase in local citizen participation in the A-95 review process and the Community Development Block Grant application and monitoring process. Fourth, and perhaps most significant for the entire movement, there was a marked proliferation in the funding of metropolitan fair-housing centers, allowing for full-time staff to operate and coordinate the local fair-housing programs. As of this writing, there may be no more voluntary fair-housing groups left in the movement!

Each of these aspects will be briefly reviewed in order, and it will be seen that they formed an additive and circular process. Each trend and activity led to the next and culminated in the final one—that

---

*Redlining efforts were spearheaded by Chicago's National Information and Training Center, led by Gale Cincotta.

of funding. The reciprocal impact of the external national situation and the national organization on the local groups and on each other is clearly evident.

Auditing and Legal Action

In 1967 Hubert Blalock wrote: "Discrimination must be measured indirectly—necessitating theoretical assumptions—which will be untestable."[89] He then raised the question, "How does one know that two people are in fact equal in all respects except that of race?" His answer was that this was not possible to know, and that was why it was not possible to measure discrimination directly. He was wrong. The audit does measure discrimination directly, using matched pairs of black and white home seekers. The use of the audit as a technique for achieving open housing is itself a mini-movement within the larger movement. It must be noted that audits were also widely publicized and used in many neighborhood stabilization groups, through emphasis by their national organizations, National Neighbors. Most stabilization groups conducting audits were eager to learn the extent of racial "steering" to their integrated neighborhoods, which was seen as contributing to the resegregation of such neighborhoods. Steering is the illegal practice (under Title VIII) of discouraging white home audit was the 1969 study conducted by the Greater St. Louis Committee versely discouraging minority home seekers and attracting whites to white areas. It is the principal tool used by real estate agents to implement the transfer of interracial areas to the minority market, while maintaining the white areas as white.

By the time Trends, in 1973, devoted a special feature to auditing, the practice had been under way for several years. An audit is a survey of actual housing availability for minorities. Upon completion there is usually disclosure of the findings to the community and relevant housing industry and law enforcement agencies. The survey is conducted with trained matched pairs of black and white home seekers (one black and one white to each pair), who attempt to secure identical available housing, at different controlled times and sequences. A careful comparative analysis of their written report forms provides the basis for determining the extent of equality of opportunity in housing for minorities in a given community. Since all relevant factors have been controlled except that of race, any difference in treatment that is negative for the black person must be assumed to be due to racial discrimination. An audit is a field experiment conducted with careful controls. Each audit takes from 6 to 12 months to plan, execute, analyze, summarize, present to the public, and pursue individually for affirmative action. In view of the time taken to complete an audit, it is remarkable that so many of these have been conducted by volunteer groups.

The audit can be successfully used to bring about constructive change on the local level.

St. Louis. The first nationally publicized report of a fair-housing audit was the 1969 study conducted by the Greater St. Louis Committee for the Freedom of Residence. Its report, "Patterns of Discrimination," describes the group's investigation of practices in 15 real estate companies in that city. The study took eight months, involved 13 black and 13 white testers, and culminated in a legal suit filed in March 1970 against four of the companies audited. The case was scheduled for trial in St. Louis Federal Court on June 14, 1971, but just prior to that date the Department of Justice entered into negotiations with the four companies for a possible consent decree. After several months of negotiations, a fair-housing agreement was negotiated and agreed to by the Justice Department and the four companies on December 15, 1971. A separate agreement was also reached by the Justice Department and the Metropolitan St. Louis Real Estate Board, consisting of 509 member firms, 740 brokers, and 3300 sales personnel. This was the first time such an agreement was reached between the Department of Justice and a metropolitan real estate board. The agreement consisted of an affirmative action program of compliance to be effected by all realtors and associates of the metropolitan board within 60 days. This was first reported in Trends, May 1970, and it awakened eager local groups around the country.

Palo Alto. The second report of an audit came from Palo Alto, California, in 1971. At an NCDH conference in Chicago in 1971, the Mid-Peninsula Citizens for Fair Housing (MCFH) described rental audits they had conducted in the previous year. Using black and white teams drawn from a pool of 75 volunteer testers, MCFH audited apartment complexes in 7 out of 13 surrounding suburbs, and found discrimination in over half of them. MCFH first used their findings to communicate with the housing establishment to encourage voluntary corrective action in eliminating racial discrimination. They then initiated hearings with the Palo Alto City Council, leading to the adoption in 1973 of new legislation on apartment licensing. Finally, their audit findings were sent to the U. S. Department of Justice, which filed a pattern-and-practice suit against the owner of 11 apartment complexes in the Palo Alto area (United States v. Youritan Construction Co.) on February 8, 1973 in Federal District Court.
When the suit was filed by the Justice Department, only 14 (1.2 percent) of a total of 1133 units were occupied by blacks, and 11 of the 14 were in buildings near the East Palo Alto ghetto. Six of the buildings had no nonwhite residents. These statistics alone, the court emphasized, constituted a prima facie case of racial dis-

crimination which it was up to the owner to disprove. In addition,
however, substantial evidence of racial discrimination was indicated
by rental agents and managers in inequitable application procedures,
misrepresentation of availability of units, delaying tactics, and other
devices to discourage minority occupancy.

An injunction was issued, and the owner was ordered to institute affirmative action, including: an educational program to inform
all employers of their duties in compliance with federal fair-housing
law; installation of uniform application procedures at all apartment
complexes; maintenance and prominent posting of current and upcoming
vacancy lists at the central rental office and at each apartment complex; and submission of detailed reports to the Justice Department for
a three-year period, giving the name, address and race of each applicant, and a chronological account of each step taken in processing
each application.

The court decision called the MCFH's testing activities "a
reasonable means by which citizens may ascertain the compliance
status of landlords with fair housing laws" and found the evidence
compiled appropriate "in a proceeding of this nature."

Akron. Akron was next, with its longitudinal auditing in that community with successive feedback and wide publicity.

Baltimore. Studies conducted in 1972 by Baltimore Neighborhoods,
Inc. (BNI) found that almost two-thirds of Baltimore's black families
could afford to buy homes or rent apartments in suburban areas, but
were consistently discriminated against by real estate brokers and
rental agents. The studies had two primary objectives: to evaluate
compliance with state and federal fair-housing laws, and to challenge
the common belief that "the main reason few blacks live in suburbia is
because they can't afford to." The economic analysis was based on
1970 Census data and the Multiple Listing Sales Report for a six-
month period.

The discrimination study was an audit of 93 apartment complexes
by 45 biracial teams of testers, who found evidence of racial discrimination 45 to 55 percent of the time, even prior to making an
application. The audit used the "sandwich" method of sending a team
of a white, black, and another white to all buildings. Their written
reports were then examined and compared for evidence of racial
discrimination.

After the release of its findings, BNI initiated overtures to
housing industry representatives. It proposed and secured an agreement for the development of an affirmative marketing program to
eliminate discrimination and promote equal housing opportunities.
Funds were sought from HUD to implement the program, and two

years later such funds were granted (October 1975). The program
consisted of a demonstration and analysis of an affirmative marketing
plan operated by a consortium of the real estate industry and BNI.
The affirmative marketing plan was to cover public education as well
as internal practices in the real estate companies, including employment practices. The two-year project was budgeted for a total cost
of $323,417 of which HUD was to pay $250,000.

Audits of BNI also resulted in a $200,000 lawsuit filed by tenants
against the owner and manager of a 295-unit apartment complex in a
suburb of Baltimore. The tenants have charged the landlord with
assigning blacks and whites to separate areas of the complex, and
failing to provide blacks with equal maintenance. They have asked for
an injunction against the alleged practices and actual and punitive
damages. The Justice Department has also filed suit against the same
owner and manager for discriminatory practices in violation of
federal fair-housing law.

Chicago. The Leadership Council for Metropolitan Open Communities
(LCMOC) conducted a one-year auditing program in the suburbs of
Chicago. LCMOC used the findings to file suit against nine real estate
firms, charging racial steering and other practices of racial discrimination in violation of federal law. Actual and punitive damages
sought were close to one million dollars. An injunction was sought to
halt the alleged discriminatory practices of the firms and to enjoin
them from any efforts to illegally influence the choices of prospective
homeseekers on a racial basis.

Cleveland Heights. Eighteen months of auditing by 17 teams of black
and white volunteers resulted in new legislation and a $1 million law-
suit filed by Heights Community Congress (HCC) against a real estate
company owned by the president of the Cleveland Area Board of
Realtors. Two major types of discriminatory practices found in the
audit were racial steering and negative neighborhood reference.
Steering occurred at 70 percent of the companies audited; whites were
not shown homes in already integrated areas, and blacks were directed
to such areas and not to all-white areas. Negative neighborhood
references about integrated neighborhoods were made to white home
seekers by 50 percent of the agencies.

The findings were publicized at suburban city council meetings,
which culminated in antisteering legislation in 1973. The lawsuit
was filed in 1975 after various cooperative educational approaches to
the real estate industry proved unsuccessful.

Strategy for Change. It can be seen that each of these local groups
used audit findings as a strategy for reducing discrimination. Their

findings, remarkably consistent, document the continued existence of racial discrimination in housing. They reveal from 7 to 44 different techniques of denying freedom of choice in housing to home seekers.

Each movement organization has used its findings in different ways as strategy for change; some have used multiple action approaches. The use of audit findings may be categorized into four major types: legislation, negotiation, remuneration, and litigation.

The legislation approach involves the use of audit data as a basis for obtaining new community legislation, such as an antisteering law, or an antisolicitation law. These are designed to supplement and/or reinforce existing federal and state open-housing legislation.

The negotiation approach involves direct communication with all those audited in the housing establishment—real estate company presidents, brokers, agents, rental managers, owners, and so forth. Private meetings are arranged with those audited, and the pertinent data are revealed to them in order to obtain a corrective affirmative action or voluntary compliance agreement. This, of course, is made feasible only by the existence of open-housing laws and the knowledge of the possiblity of legal action against racial discrimination in housing. (See Appendix C for sample affirmative action memo.)

The remuneration approach involves the use of audit data to secure funding from private or public sources for the operation of a metropolitan open-housing organization, since the data establish the need for a staffed, full-time program. Funding enables such an organization to implement the law through monitoring, and to secure compliance through constant staffed activity involving community education.

The litigation approach involves two options: filing a lawsuit against discriminating companies and/or individuals, and sending the audit data to the U.S. Department of Justice for their investigation and possible litigation. In addition, other relevant enforcement agencies may be informed of audit results in order to initiate additional investigation and official action to bring about compliance with the law.

All four approaches are generally preceded by a public hearing or meeting, at which the audit data are revealed to the public for the first time, with media and area organizational representatives invited to be present. Each of the four types of action approaches was illustrated in the previous accounts of audits conducted by six movement organizations.

Citizen Participation: A-95 Review

The increase of citizen participation in the A-95 review process was stimulated by NCDH in Trends, research publications, and regional conferences, and was a direct outgrowth of the NCDH/HUD San Francisco Bay pilot program. In its lead article of the November-December

1973 Trends, the NCDH headline was "Civil Rights and A-95 Review."
A-95* is a procedure for analyzing and evaluating applications for
federal financial assistance before funding. The evaluation is based
on determining from the application and other knowledge of the
applicant any possible adverse or beneficial effects of the proposed
project. Though originally related to environmental impact, A-95 was
amended in March 1972 to permit evaluation and comment on the
civil rights implications of proposed projects. The determination can
be made by any local or state groups or agencies involved in programs relevant to the one proposed. These comments are gathered
by an area agency designated as a clearinghouse, —a regional planning commission, a council of goverments, or the like. Though comments attached in the A-95 review process are not binding on any
federal funding agency, the agency must take them into consideration
in making its decision on funding.

More than 100 federal aid programs and planning grants for
community development are covered by the A-95 review process,
ranging from HUD's mortgage insurance programs to law enforcement assistance, flood control, mass transit, and construction of
educational and health facilities. Agencies and groups are notified in
advance of the applications to be considered by the clearinghouse.
Thus, the review process can serve as an early-warning system to
alert public agencies and private groups as to which applications
should be supported and which opposed in an effort to prevent misuse
of federal moneys.

Immediately after the civil rights amendment was added to the
A-95 regulation in March 1972, NCDH arranged to develop guidelines
and analysis of the review process, using California's Bay Area as a
pilot program. Two program tools were developed to guide this
analysis: a Civil Rights Impact Questionnaire, and a Flow Chart on
Methodology. Though the pilot program evaluated the A-95 process in
only 11 proposals for federally funded projects in the Bay Area, it
had some positive results. Out of the effort was developed the Greater
Vallejo Minority Coalition representing black, chicano, and Filipino
communities in that area, which wielded considerable influence on later
area policies. In addition, the A-95 review process was an effective
instrument in bringing the Oakland Chinese community together for
the first time to create a citizen participation mechanism in the
Chinatown urban renewal area. Finally, a brochure, "Civil Rights
and the A-95 Review Process," was written and widely distributed
to local groups on request.

---

*The name comes from Circular A-95, Office of Management
and Budget, 1969, which outlined the regulations for this procedure.

Participants in the pilot program concluded that effectiveness of the review process hinged on four factors: the strength of the A-95 directive itself, affirmative compliance by federal funding agencies, the commitment and efficiency of the civil rights agency performing review and comment functions, and the active and determined participation of citizens' groups. Seven recommendations for strengthening the procedure evolved from the NCDH pilot program, some of which were later considered by government agencies for adoption.

Block Grants Monitoring. Under the HCD Act of 1974, citizen participation was mandated. Citizens were to be involved in preparing the application for city funding and its accompanying plans and programs. NCDH immediately prepared a Handbook for Citizen Fair Housing Advocacy under the Housing and Community Development Act of 1974, which was widely publicized and distributed across the country. Five major topics were covered in the 46-page booklet: the need for citizen participation; how fair-housing advocates can be effective in influencing local applications and required plans; fair-housing objectives to be pursued in reviewing local applications and plans; what fair-housing advocates should know about block grants for community development; and what fair-housing advocates should know about subsidized housing programs. For each of the five topics, detailed information was provided to enable local fair-housing groups to take maximum advantage of the citizen participation provisions so as to guide, direct, and ensure equal housing opportunities for minorities and lower-income persons.

One of the main activities encouraged by NCDH at this time was the formation of coalitions for block-grant compliance. This was done through conferences, Trends, publications, and field assistance. NCDH played a significant role in the creation of such local coalitions in Hempstead, Long Island; Haverford, Pennsylvania; East Hartford, Connecticut; Parma, Ohio; and Livonia, Michigan. In each of these communities there were active citizen groups formed for the purpose of monitoring community development applications, to ensure compliance with fair-housing and equal eopportunity provisions. Some groups were successful in blocking CD money from those municipalities that had not complied with the equal-opportunity stipulations of the act.

Subsidized Housing. The last topic of the NCDH Handbook is important, since subsidized housing programs have come to have considerable negative impact on open-housing goals and neighborhood stabilization objectives. The Section 8 program of housing subsidies for low- and moderate-income families, for example, was perceived at first as an avenue to expanded housing opportunities for minorities and the poor. Even NCDH leaders believed this to be true. As late as July 1976 Holmgren said, "Suburban areas have rental units, subsidized, which are available for low- and moderate-income families,"[90] though the acknowledged that financing arrangements did not make this attractive to builders.

The fact is that despite the HCD Act's provisions, clearly stating "deconcentration and neighborhood diversity" as a prime objective, there is nothing in the act that provides for any implementation or enforcement of this. New construction is covered with enforcement in site selection policies, but existing housing is not. What has happened to housing allowances and subsidies for the poor has thus created the usual pattern of resegregation. This is so partially because HUD's own fair-market rents are placed too low to allow any deconcentration, and partially because the act itself has no provisions for enforcing its own objectives. If the objectives were requirements, the results might be more positive. Without such requirements, federal money is again being used to promote ghettos, segregation, and resegregation.

HUD Manual

In addition to NCDH's publication on citizen participation, and added emphasis in Trends and regional conferences, other events and influences outside NCDH reinforced fair-housing groups' attention to the HCD Act, and the roles of fair-housing groups in response to that act. In April 1975 HUD's Office of Equal Opportunity held a national fair-housing conference which culminated in a 251-page manual titled, Fair Housing and Funding: A Local Strategy, published in March 1976. The manual, based on the conference, was organized to provide basic necessary information for fair-housing organizations to seek and obtain funding. The preface, written by OEO Director James H. Blair, stated:

> The Department of Housing and Urban Development
> is committed to the enforcement of fair housing stan-
> dards prescribed by law. Whether these standards are
> applied with full force and effectiveness depends, in
> large measure, on the creation and operation of viable
> fair housing organizations and on the ways in which these
> organizations interact with local planning groups.[91]

Seven topics were covered in the manual: a review of the national fair-housing conference; an overview of fair-housing groups; fund-raising—why it's done is more important than how it's done; relation-ships of fair-housing groups to local governments; public resources applicable to fair-housing groups; private resources available to fair-housing groups; and grantsmanship—is it important? (yes).

Funding Possibilities

The fourth chapter of the manual was the most significant one for the open-housing movement organizations, as it identified the HCD Act and revenue-sharing funds as the most substantive sources of potential financial support for fair-housing groups. This was the primary focus of the conference, and included information about the specific titles and sections of the act that were applicable to fair-housing groups in relation to funding. For example, one reference was to Section 8 programs as "requiring and utilizing fair housing information and assistance. All or part of these responsibilities may be contracted by the housing agency to a fair housing group."[92] This was a highly significant how-to chapter for struggling fair-housing groups, eager to have staffed operations.

Comprehensive Agencies. The second chapter of the manual was also important for the fair-housing movement, and may have had some negative consequences. Presumably, after getting funding, the group would want to have some kind of effective program. Chapter 2 offered some unfortunate models. Case studies were offered of five fair-housing groups which had successfully obtained funding, but not a single one of these groups could be considered as operating a concentrated fair-housing program. They were, instead, broad comprehensive programs.

In short, this fair-housing conference manual paved the way for comprehensive fair-housing agencies rather than concentrated ones by suggesting;

> Comprehensive housing services is a new approach for
> fair housing groups. . . . The program differs from the
> traditional work program of most fair housing groups:
> it offers an array of services, it has much more of a
> client focus, and the emphasis is on safe and sanitary
> housing for every individual rather than just integration
> and open housing for middle and upper class minorities.[93]

If one did not know the year was 1976, one would surely think this was 1969 with the words coming right out of the antipoverty agency that funded Akron in its earlier disastrous experience! Moreover, long before 1977 the open-housing movement had clearly established its position that freedom of choice in housing was the goal for all income levels—certainly not for just middle- and upper-class minorities. This was a serious misstatement, followed by others.

The manual continues:

> The services which comprehensive housing agencies offer,
> like the HOC of Columbus, Ohio are aimed at fulfilling
> 3 basic objectives: 1) to help eliminate discrimination in
> the rental and sale of housing, 2) to assist citizens in
> improving their housing conditions, 3) to stimulate public
> awareness of rights and responsibilities in regard to
> housing law and general housing conditions. Some fair
> housing groups are quickly becoming leaders in the
> emerging field of comprehensive housing services. . . .
> [T]he reasons are simply that the services are needed
> by the community, the funding possibilities are much
> greater, the program expansion is not too difficult. . .
> and the larger the scope of services offered. . .the
> greater and more effective the clout and influence that the
> organization has in the community. [94]

Following this is a list of the scope of services offered by HOC
in Columbus: discrimination complaints ("all the traditional services"),
housing placement, especially on an emergency basis, landlord/tenant
counseling, housing counseling (foreclosures, home maintenance),
emergency housing assistance (relocation, utility shutoffs, and so on).

Hypothesis. The more comprehensive the program of a fair-housing
organization, the lower the probability that open-housing goals will
be achieved in the local community. Conversely, the more concentrated the program of a fair-housing program, the higher the probability that open-housing goals will be achieved in the local community. (This is expanded in Chapter 5.)

What is suggested here is that an open-housing program will
be greatly diluted in a comprehensive agency, though all the above
reasons for operating a comprehensive agency are no doubt true.
The services are needed by the community (but they do not all have
to be offered in one agency, and in fact should not, in a fair-housing
organization). The funding possibilities are much greater. (Indeed,
this seems to be the prime reason for some wanting to become more
comprehensive) Program expansion is not too difficult (easiest thing
in the world to hire more staff, and assign each one a different
program aspect). And the larger the scope of services, the greater
the clout the organization has in the community? Perhaps—but what
kind of clout, and representing what point of view, and for what purpose? It may well be argued that far greater clout would ensue from
the single-minded, concentrated organization, which devotes 100
percent of its time and energy and thought and action to the one goal

of equal access to housing for all. This is not to say that other
housing services should not be offered, but rather, that other organizations can and should offer those services, leaving the open-housing
task to those that care about it the most.

Manual Inconsistency. The manual is inconsistent with its own promotion of comprehensive agencies when it states that "as the problem
of discrimination becomes more complex and the strategies to overcome this become more involved and require more expertise, the
staff of fair housing groups will respond accordingly."[95] This would
surely suggest specialization rather than the diversification of a comprehensive agency.

One of the new programs suggested in the manual for fair-
housing groups is housing conservation and neighborhood stabilization.
Again, these services and programs surely are necessary, but why
all in one organization? And why in a fair-housing organization? What
might be done is to have the fair-housing group begin a neighborhood
stabilization group, and then back off to let it run itself. In Akron
the two became sister organizations, complementing each other, but
each with its own board and program. In fact, it might be deeply
resented and resisted if metropolitan fair-housing groups were to
actively begin organizing neighborhood stabilization groups and make
this an ongoing part of their program. Baltimore Neighborhoods, Inc.
is the only known metropolitan organization that combines both fair
housing and neighborhood stabilization. In most other communities
the two functions have remained very related, but separately directed,
with neighborhood groups led and run by their own residents and leaders.

The manual's Appendix tells the tale. Six civil rights organizations are listed as having received funding from Community Development Block Grants for fiscal year 1975. By October 1977—15 months
later—the list had grown to 12, with more reported each day since.

Wave of Funding. Why has this happened? Was the 1975 HUD conference and manual responsible for this wave of funding? Was it NCDH's
influence through Trends and regional conferences? Perhaps both of
these factors played some part in the funding. More likely, though,
is the fact that some HUD Equal Opportunity Offices at the regional
level are utilizing the equal-opportunity provisions of the NCD Act
to demand a fair-housing component of every locality that wants
block grants.

The net effect of this can be seen, for example, in states like
Ohio, where suddenly within a year and a half news items have
appeared advertising for fair-housing directors in Alliance, Massillon,
and Canton, all within short distances of each other in Stark County.
In addition, an ad appeared for a fair-housing director for Stark

County. One can imagine what this proliferation of services might do for the achievement of open housing in that lucky county. With proper staff training and orientation, and wise and skillful coordination of effort, this could evolve into an effective county-wide program. On the other hand, lacking these conditions, the cities involved and the county may simply have fulfilled the requirement for funding and may have no further interest in achieving an effective open-housing program. Or, what is even more tragic, they may not even know what an effective program consists of, and may be totally unable to evaluate the services rendered.

Toward that end, with the great increase of funding under the HCD Act, the HUD Equal Opportunity Division convened a working conference on November 29, 1977 in Columbus, Ohio, to develop an evaluation guideline for the entire country. This will be used to monitor and assess fair-housing programs receiving block grants under the act. It is to be hoped those guidelines do not appear too late.*

The Nation-wide HUD/NCDH Audit

It is appropriate to end this chapter with a brief account of the nation-wide HUD/NCDH audit, for it is an excellent example of the reciprocal influences operative in this movement. That reciprocity exists between the national core organization, NCDH, and the federal government agency most influential in the open housing movement, HUD. It exists also and simultaneously between NCDH and all the fair-housing groups on the local level. In fact, one reason NCDH received the million-dollar contract to direct the audit was undoubtedly because it had the capability of utilizing so many local fair-housing groups to conduct the audit.

This interplay on three levels is further seen in the fact that the nation-wide audit was an outgrowth of eight previous years of audits conducted and publicized by local groups in more than 20 different communities across the nation. These were conducted to test the extent of compliance with the federal fair-housing law, which was passed at the end of a 20-year effort by NCDH. So the intertwining of these three levels of national government, national core organization, and local fair-housing groups is responsible for an integral part of the nation-wide audit.

Request For Proposals. The wave of local audits from 1969 to 1976 constituted a mini-movement in itself, as suggested earlier. This is not surprising to sociologists, who refer to the dissemination of new

---

* Sample guidelines developed by author are in Appendix D.

ideas as cultural diffusion—one of the principal elements of social change. But what was surprising is that suddenly in the early summer of 1976 there appeared in the Department of Commerce Bulletin a request for proposals (RFP H-2551) from HUD for a ($1 million) nation-wide Audit, sponsored and funded by HUD's Policy Development and Research Division. Several large professional research agencies responded to the request, including the Rand Corporation and Abt Associates. Also responding was NCDH, which submitted on July 21 a 202-page proposal, 112 pages of which were design and 90 were the capability statement.

Several weeks later the contest had narrowed to two contenders: the Abt Associates and NCDH. NCDH was asked by HUD to revise several portions of its proposal, and on August 12 submitted 48 pages of revisions. In mid-September the awarding of the contract to NCDH was announced, with much jubilation among staff and open-housing supporters everywhere. From October 1976 until the following August, NCDH was involved in the implementation of the audit, under the direction of George Schermer, urban affairs consultant and one of the writers of the proposal, who became the project manager.

Audit Design. The project was called by HUD, "Contract H-2551, to Evaluate the Impact of Civil Rights Enforcement Activity," named the Housing Market Practices Survey (HMPS) by NCDH. Where and when the actual audit was to take place was strictly confidential; even the consultants who designed it (this author among them) did not know all the areas where the audit was to occur, though they did know the time period. The NCDH design was as follows: The country was to be divided into six regions, with six to eight metropolitan areas (SMSAs) within each region to be audited under the direction of regional coordinators, selected and trained by NCDH.* A total of 40 metropolitan areas were to be audited, selected randomly from all those having at least 100,000 residents and 11 percent black population. Ninety-three percent of all blacks in the country live in those areas.)

Of the 40 metropolitan areas, five were designated "in-depth," requiring 200 site visits, and the rest (35) were "surface" areas, requiring from 60 to 80 site visits, depending on the size of the SMSA. In all, over 3000 site visits were made to real estate companies and apartment complexes across the country. The entire audit had to be conducted in May and June and completed by July 1. A three-day intensive training period was required for supervisors for each metropolitan area, and later for the auditors of each area.

---

*The author became one of these, after the design was completed.

Subcontractors were local fair-housing groups, where these existed, and other organizations where there were no fair-housing groups. Other subcontractors included urban leagues, civic organizations (LWV), academic research groups, and so forth. More than 800 persons participated. Subcontractors received stipends of $9,000-25,000 depending on the number of site visits to be made and the number of auditors and staff required.

Before the actual audit took place, there was to be a pilot audit in one SMSA. And before the pilot audit took place, there had to be the writing and preparation of manuals of instruction (for regional coordinators, supervisors, and auditors) and forms (for sales visits and rental visits). In addition, a thorough reassessment and decision regarding methods of sampling within each SMSA was necessary. Finally, after much deliberation and discussion, news ads—randomly selected from a specified date in each SMSA—were agreed on for the sampling of the real estate offices and apartment complexes to be audited. The news ad date was to precede the audit by no more than two weeks.

Timeline. The timeline was a very tight one, with minimal lead time for the actual audit. Much of the time between October 1 and December 3 was spent in writing and preparing the manuals and forms, and in weighing alternative sampling procedures. This was done by the small team of consultants (9) hired as a design team by the project manager for NCDH. On December 3, the completely revised design package, including all forms and instruction manuals, was delivered to HUD. The pilot audit was conducted in Cincinnati in January, selected logically because it was not too far from Washington, had an active fair-housing group Housing Opportunities Made Equal, or (HOME), and was thought to be not too cold in January. (That was the winter that Cincinnati was buried under ten inches of snow during the pilot audit period! The only people out on the streets were the auditors.) In February there was an evaluation and revision of all materials, based on the pilot audit experience. In March, regional coordinators began their work in preparation for the actual audit in June (some areas began slightly earlier, toward the end of May.)

Hypotheses. The national audit tested 33 hypotheses. The dependent variable was, of course, discrimination (the absence of it). The independent variables were divided into three categories: 8 dealt with fair-housing program variables—for example, housing accessibility for blacks is positively correlated with the existence and effectiveness of local civil rights organizations, with the existence and effectiveness of private litigation, with the existence of Department of Justice Title VIII enforcement, and with the existence of local fair-housing ordinance; eighteen independent variables dealt with housing market and demographic factors—for example, an excess supply of housing, socioeconomic status of homeseeker versus neighborhood, degree of racial integration of neighborhood or complex, and so on; and 7 variables dealt with industry awareness and attitude, obtained through surveys conducted after the audits were completed (by a separate research firm, under subcontract).

Rigorous bookkeeping and records were mandated. All materials were to be inventoried and shipped back to NCDH at a designated time, and NCDH was then to spend weeks checking the results, before transferring data to computer tapes and delivering these to HUD.

Rigorous Controls. The controls during the actual audit were necessarily rigid because of the standardization required across the country. For example, a daily intensive review of the completed forms of each pair of auditors were mandated. A rigorous call-back system from the auditors in the field was instituted: for example, black phones supervisor right after visiting apartment; white phones supervisor within one hour, right before going out to same apartment. This was to ensure proper timing and sequence and avoidance of problems at the site visits (no one there, office closed, and so on).

This was the first time that a single, standardized auditing technique was used for the entire country. It was the first time that a nation-wide measure of housing discrimination was obtained, with an analysis of its forms, extent, and the effectiveness of enforcement programs designed to alleviate the problem. Though HUD's analysis of the delivered tapes will not be completed till late 1978, NCDH reported that the survey revealed that "[d]iscrimination in housing still persists in the U.S., in most of the housing markets audited. It is quite overt in many cases and more subtle in others. [96]

Early Conclusions. Two of the early conclusions were that none of the areas surveyed was without evidence of racial discrimination, and that none presented a solid wall of exclusion—that is, there were some agents that seemed to treat black and white home seekers equally. An early preliminary analysis of the mid-central region's audit results reinforced these conclusions. That region, coordinated by the writer, included eight SMSAs: five in Ohio—Akron, Canton, Cincinnati, Columbus, and Dayton; two in Kentucky—Lexington and Louisville; and one in Tennessee—Nashville (all randomly selected by computer.) The levels of racial discrimination in that entire region ranged from 33 to 90 percent in rentals and from 38 to 93 percent in sales. These results, however, were hand-tabulated and based on local supervisors' comparative analyses of completed paired reports. It will be interesting to compare these results with those of the computer, when HUD produces these.*

The National Association of Real Estate Boards knew an audit was going to take place from the public announcement of the HUD/NCDH contract. In their June 1977 national newsletter The Executive Officer, they had this to say about the national audit, which by then was completed—but which they thought had not yet begun:

> Obviously the process of racial testing is highly subjective and of questionable utility in gathering realiable informa- tion. There is no guarantee that both teams will ask the same questions or state the same housing needs. . . . Anyone watching will find that Realtors offer equal pro- fessional services to all people and do not discriminate on the basis of race. . . .[97]

One objective of the rigorous intensive training of supervisors and auditors was to remove subjectivity as much as possible from this audit. Another objective was to offer to local groups a valuable investigative technique which they could continue to use long after the audit was over. It is too early to tell whether local groups have utilized the methodology of the national audit in subsequent open- housing monitoring on the local level.

Need for Ongoing Auditing. The general technique of auditing, how- ever, is one that local fair-housing groups would have to use con- tinuously in order to measure trends in discrimination. One early

----

*On April 17, 1978 (as this book was going into production) HUD revealed some partial results of the national audit at a fair-housing conference in Washington, D. C., cosponsored with NCDH. On the basis of the partial data analysis, HUD estimated that blacks in this country are likely to encounter discrimination in housing 75 per- cent when seeking apartments, and 62 percent of the time when seeking to buy homes. This announcement was made by HUD Secre- tary Patricia Harris and was a major news release to all news- papers across the country. It should be noted that this projection is based on partial data which did not include any analysis of steering. When subsequent data is released over the next six to eight months, the more inclusive figures on racial discrimination will no doubt be higher.

conclusion reached in the mid-central region, for example, was that not only is housing availability positively correlated with previous auditing in the area, but also the recency of the auditing is a significant factor. As NCDH said in its initial training sessions, "The single most effective deterrent to racial discrimination is repeated auditing."

What was observed in the mid-central region was that an area that had not conducted audits recently showed an increase in the level of discrimination. Clearly, the more auditing done, and the more feedback and followup in the community, the greater the likelihood that discrimination will decrease. This is why the single-minded fair-housing groups have a greater chance of achieving open housing in their local communities—they will undoubtedly make use of the audit technique in their concentrated program. A comprehensive agency, on the other hand, will rarely have time or staff or inclination to devote to continual audits.

SUMMARY

A social movement can be fully understood only as a dynamic system of reciprocal influence. The social and cultural context of the general civil rights movement prior to and during the development of the open-housing movement was considered a crucial element.

Each of the three aspects of the open-housing movement on the national level were examined: the development of a national core organization (NCDH), legislative development, and local community action development. Each of the three phases of development of the movement was set against a backdrop of significant events in the larger society related to the general civil rights movement.

First Phase (1950-56)

The national core organization (NCDH), formed as an outgrowth of another localized organization concerned with a local situation of constraint, was organized in response to country-wide demand for a national organization to direct and coordinate the struggle for open housing. As an organization of organizations, its purpose was to establish nondiscriminatory and nonsegregated housing in the United States. Its program during the first phase was focused primarily on influencing federal government agency influence and field activities. Two government agencies influenced by NCDH during the first phase were the Housing and Home Finance Administration and the Public Housing Authority. Three major field activities were engaged in, of which the Levittown development had the broadest eventual impact.

A national reporting service (Trends in Housing) was inaugurated toward the end of the phase, increasing NCDH impact on the local level. The core organization grew from 15 to 26 member organizations during this phase, and changed from a volunteer group to an organization with a staff of three and a budget of $18,000.

Second Phase (1956-64)

During the second phase, three major federal housing programs were indicted by NCDH in recurrent public testimony: Urban Renewal, FHA, and Public Housing. Growing impact of NCDH was indicated in three instances: successful culmination of the Levittown case, the issuance of the Fair Housing Handbook, and the convening of three major national conferences. The third conference had an entire session devoted to grass-roots activities for the first time, indicating the extent of growth of the movement on the community level. The NCDH grew from 26 to 37 organizational affiliates and achieved tax-exemption, which allowed it to seek foundation funding and paved the way for the phase of institutionalization that followed.

At the beginning of the second phase, only 3 states and 14 cities had laws prohibiting discrimination in public housing. By the end of the phase, 26 governmental jurisidctions and 60 cities had laws affecting discriminatory housing. Legislative development generally seemed to follow a social-distance scale model.

There was little evidence of local community action organizations devoted specifically to open housing at the beginning of the second phase. By the end of the phase, 300 specific fair-housing committees were identified as working solely for open housing.

Third Phase (1964-70)

With a greatly increased budget, NCDH was able during the third phase to expand its program and impact considerably, as was demonstrated in the struggle against Proposition 14 in California, the development of the Weston, (Illinois) atomic energy site, the Louisville (Kentucky) Model Cities funding, and the Greenburgh (New York) urban renewal controversy.

Of 12 national and regional housing conferences convened by NCDH, five were considered especially significant, in view of subsequent developments in the movement. The five conferences were concerned with combating the growing countermovement's referendums, foundation and government financial support of community fair-housing programs, emphasis on low- and moderate-income families in open-housing efforts, the alliance with OEO and the focus on metropolitan fair-housing centers.

By the end of the third phase, NCDH had grown from 37 to 51 national organizational affiliates, had moved its offices and opened two new regional offices, and had received almost one million dollars in funding from government and private sources. When fair housing became the law of the land, NCDH shifted its focus immediately to the link between jobs and housing, with land-use bias in zoning restrictions as the new target for action.

During the third phase, legislative development culminated in the passage of the 1968 Civil Rights Act and the Supreme Court decision upholding the constitutionality of the 1866 Civil Rights Act, thus opening all housing immediately to minorities. By the end of the third phase, there were 229 state and local open-housing laws, of which 100 were passed in the three-month period following federal law passage.

At the beginning of the third phase, 300 local groups had been identified as working specifically for open housing. By the end of the phase, there were over 2,000 such groups. Local community action during this phase was marked by three trends: continuing proliferation, funding, and increased emphasis on low-income housing. The trends were traced to NCDH influence.

Changes in the general civil rights movement were seen as having a persistent and pervasive effect on the open-housing movement, as reflected in responses of the core organization. Yet, though it modified its public statements in response to situational demand, NCDH clung stubbornly throughout its 20-year existence to its avowed goal of nondiscriminatory and nonsegregated housing in the United States.

Fourth Phase (1970-77)

Between 1970 and 1972, NCDH faced financial, organizational and spiritual bankruptcy—almost validating all the theories of institutionalization. NCDH's major source of foundation funding mandated several organizational changes, which resulted in new administrative and board leadership, new structural arrangements for board representation, new location for national headquarters, new caution concerning fiscal management, and renewed program emphasis on reciprocal relationships with local movement organizations.

In the next five years, NDCH struggled to restore itself and its image, against a backdrop of national and international economic, military, and political crises. The appearance of a rival national organization may also have spurred the intense efforts toward restoration. Under new leadership, NCDH held ten regional conferences,

litigated 15 major lawsuits, organized and influenced numerous government policy decisions, led and assisted local organizations in effectively using the Housing and Community Development Act of 1974 to
achieve open-housing goals, and directed a nation-wide audit of
racial discrimination in housing. At the end of the fourth phase,
NCDH had succeeded in reestablishing the link with many fair-housing
groups at the local level.

Legislative development and legal action during the fourth phase
was focused on the implementation of Title VIII of the Civil Rights
Act of 1968, which became fully effective only in 1971. Monetary
damages were increasingly awarded by the courts as open-housing
law developed and expanded. Each ease was a prod to create new
precedent and better remedies. These, in turn, spurred the local
movement organizations to gather more data and file more cases. Two
critical cases for the movement were the Trafficante case (won in
1973) and the Upper Arlington case (won in 1974). These broadened
the right to sue and legitimated the use of testers, both critical for
the open-housing movement. In addition, exclusionary zoning and
land-use control were the focus of 18 nationally noted legal suits,
fought with NCDH involvement.

The Department of Justice was helpful to the movement by
obtaining consent decrees in hundreds of suits brought by them across
the country. These suits charged patterns of racial discrimination in
the real estate industry, and were based on data collected and provided
by local movement organizations. The consent decrees required
extensive affirmative action as part of the agreement with those engaged
in discriminatory practices.

In 1973, an indefinite housing moratorium was announced by the
Nixon administration, prompting immediate distressed response and
nation-wide mobilization by NCDH. Though the moratorium was
finally lifted, the 1973 Housing Act was enacted which sharply curtailed housing opportunities for minorities and low- and moderate-
income families throughout the nation. Fair-share allocation plans,
however, were developed during this phase, and the concept quickly
spread to many metropolitan areas, though actual implementation
was not easily obtained anywhere because of political and economic
considerations and complexities.

Local community action development was marked by four trends
during the fourth phase: a pronounced increase in the use of systematic
auditing by movement organizations, a marked increase in the amount
of legal action to implement federal open-housing laws, an increase
in local citizen participation under the HCD Act of 1974—particularly
in the A-95 review process and block-grant compliance process—
and a great proliferation of funding for metropolitan fair-housing
centers, under the HCD Act. These trends and activities formed an

additive and circular process. The reciprocal impact of the triple levels of government, NCDH, and local movement organizations is clearly evident throughout the fourth phase, culminating in the HUD/NCDH nation-wide audit of 1976-77.

Other events and influences outside NCDH affected the local movement organizations. One such influence, a HUD-sponsored manual on funding, offered encouragement for the development of comprehensive housing agencies by movement organizations. This may have had some serious negative consequences for the ultimate achievement of open-housing goals on the local level.

NOTES

1. Some scholars have seen the black protest as an endorsement of the "American Creed" and a reaffirmation of faith in the essential goodness of the individual. See Daniel Thompson, "The Rise of the Negro Protest," The Annals, 357 (January 1965): 20.

2. Karl E. Taeuber and Alma F. Taeuber, Negroes in Cities (Chicago: Aldine, 1965), p. 12.

3. Oscar Handlin, The Newcomers (Cambridge, Mass.: Harvard University Press, 1959); Philip M. Hauser, Population Perspectives (New Brunswick, N. J.: Rutgers University Press, 1960); and Charles E. Silberman, Crisis in Black and White (New York: Random House, 1964).

4. Karl E. Taeuber, "Residential Segregation," Scientific American, 219 (August 1965): 12-19.

5. Restrictive covenants and policies deliberately excluding minorities from new housing developments were promulgated and encouraged by the FHA. See Charles Abrams, The City Is The Frontier (New York: Harper & Row, 1965), pp. 61-62.

6. Loren Miller, "The Protest Against Housing Segregation," The Annals, 357 (January 1965): 73-79.

7. Adapted from Lerone Bennet, Jr., Before the Mayflower (Baltimore: Penguin Books, 1966 ed.) pp. 398-403.

8. NCDH, "Toward Democracy in Housing," New York, July 1960; and personal interview with Margaret Fisher, April 22, 1970.

9. NCDH, "Statement of Principles," New York, 1950(?).

10. NCDH, Director's Action Report, 1952.

11. NCDH, "Opening a New Frontier," New York, 1954(?). Though the leaflet was not dated, it mentioned the "recent" Supreme Court decision on desegregation, thus providing a clue as to the time period.

12. Letter signed by George Weaver, acting chairman of NCDH, indicating a series of conferences planned by NCDH, June 14, 1955.

13. NCDH, "Ghettoes—The Last Barrier," New York, 1955(?).

14. NCDH, Executive Director's Report, May 1956.

15. Lerone Bennet, op cit.

16. NCDH, Trends in Housing, August 1956, April–May 1957, June–July 1958.

17. Trends in Housing, November–December 1959, p. 1.

18. Ibid., March–April 1960, p. 7.

19. Ibid., July–August 1960, p. 1.

20. Ibid., November–December 1960, p. 1.

21. Trends in Housing, July–August 1963, p. 1.

22. Trends in Housing, June–July 1958, pp. 1-3.

23. Ibid., January–February 1960, p. 1.

24. Ibid., October 1956, pp. 1-3.

25. Ibid., January–February 1959, p. 3.

26. Ibid., March–April 1963, p. 1.

27. Ibid.

28. In April 1960 an NCDH advisory group was formed, comprising "a group of the country's most distinguished citizens. . .to support and extend the work and objectives of the NCDH," Trends in Housing March–April 1960, p. 8.

29. Trends in Housing, August 1956. See Appendix A for tables indicating growth of legal coverage.

30. Economic Council Letter, August 1, 1959.

31. Trends in Housing, May–June, 1962, pp. 1-2.

32. Ibid., November–December, 1963, p. 4.

33. Ibid., September–October 1963, pp. 1-8.

34. Ibid., August 1956, p. 5.

35. Ibid., March–April 1958, p. 5.

36. Ibid., August–September 1958, p. 5.

37. Ibid., September–October 1959, p. 5.

38. Ibid.

39. Ibid.

40. Ibid., January–February 1960, pp. 4-5.

41. Ibid., November–December 1961, p. 5.

42. Ibid.

43. Ibid., July–August 1962, p. 5.

44. Ibid., March–April 1963, p. 6.

45. Associated Press, The World in 1965, New York, 1966; Encyclopedia News Annual (New York: Year, Inc.), 1967, 1968, 1969.

46. This is the working definition for this study.

47. Trends in Housing, January–February 1965, p. 7.

48. Ibid., January 1967, p. 1.

49. Ibid., February 1967, p. 1.

50. Trends in Housing, September–October 1965, p. 8.

51. Edward P. Morgan referred to NCDH programs and leaders on the national ABC network twice within a two-week period: March 24, and April 6, 1966.

52. NCDH, "How the Federal Government Builds Ghettos," New York, 1967.

53. Trends in Housing, July 1970, p. 1-2.

54. Ibid.

55. Ibid.

56. Trends in Housing, February 1968, p. 1.

57. Ibid., October 1968, p. 3.

58. Found in conference workshop in May 1967, keynote speech in November 1967, NCDH report in 1969, and brochure in 1969. Cf. "NCDH: A Descriptive Overview of Its Organization and Activities," NCDH, 1969, p. 8 (mimeographed); also, "The Essentials," NCDH, 1969, p. 5.

59. Interview with Edward Rutledge, San Francisco, August 27, 1969.

60. Interview with Margaret Fisher, New York City, April 22, 1970.

61. Trends in Housing, May-July, 1968, p. 1.

62. Earlier shifts in policies among realtors in the counter-movement were indicated in February 1966 by the Wisconsin Realtors Association, the Fort Wayne Board of Realtors, and the Greater Baltimore Board of Realtors, as reported in Trends in Housing, January-February 1966, pp. 1-3.

63. Trends in Housing, May-July 1968, p. 1.

64. NCDH, "The Essentials," op. cit., p. 22.

65. Trends in Housing, June-July 1967, p. 1.

66. Trends in Housing, January 1969, p. 5.

67. Encyclopedia Brittanica Book of The Year, 1971-1977 (Chicago: Encyclopedia Britanica, Inc.)

68. Harold Nelson, "Intrusive Movement Organizations: A Preliminary Inquiry," Paper presented at the Annual Meetings of the American Sociological Association, Montreal, Canada, August 1974.

69. Juliet Saltman, ed., Integrated Neighborhoods in Action (Washington, D.C.: National Neighbors, 1978), p. 250-305.

70. Trends in Housing, Summer 1972, p. 1.

71. Some examples of conflicting zoning decisions are discussed in Juliet Saltman, "Three Strategies for Reducing Involuntary Segregation," Journal of Sociology and Social Welfare 4, No. 5 (May 1977): 806-21.

72. Trends in Housing, November-December 1974, p. 1.

73. Ibid., p. 2.

74. Ibid., Fall 1976, p. 1.

75. Ibid., October-December 1975, p. 1.

76. Ibid.

77. Ibid.

78. Interview, July 1, 1976, Washington, D. C.

79. Trends, June-July 1970, p. 1.

80. Ibid., p. 2.

81. Trends in Housing, Winter 1970, pp. 1, 7.

82. Ibid.

83. Ibid., January-February, 1973, p. 1.

84. Ibid., July-August, 1973, p. 1.

85. Ibid., September-October, 1973, p. 1.

86. Among the many sources citing this fact are Ernest Erber, "Housing Allocation Plans: A National Overview." (Washington, D.C.: NCDH, 1974); Louis Massotti and Jeffrey Hadden, The Urbanization of the Suburbs (Beverly Hills, California: Sage, 1973); John Palen, The Urban World (New York: McGraw-Hill, 1975).

87. Erber, op. cit., p. 3.

88. Nelson, op. cit., p. 3.

89. Herbert Blalock, Toward a Theory of Minority Group Relations (New York: Wiley, 1967), pp. 15-16.

90. Interview, July 1, 1976, Washington, D. C.

91. Fair Housing and Funding (Washington, D. C.: HUD, 1976), p. i.

92. Ibid., p. iii.

93. Ibid., p. 23-25.

94. Ibid., p. 24.

95. Ibid., p. 20.

96. Trends in Housing, Fall 1977, p. 1.

97. NAR, "The Executive Officer," p. 1. Chicago, Illinois, 1977.

4

THE COMMUNITY LEVEL:
AKRON, A CASE STUDY

INTRODUCTION

Herbert Blumer has suggested that "scholarly study or analysis of organization cannot afford to ignore the process of interaction between people that is responsible for sustaining organization as well as for affecting it in other ways."[1] The point of view of symbolic interactionism, which Blumer advocates, is that organization "has to be seen, studied, and explained in terms of the process of interpretation engaged in by the acting participants as they handle the situations at their respective positions in the organization."[2] Such studies, according to Blumer, would illuminate a host of matters of concern to the organizational theorist or to the system analyst—problems such as poor morale, blockage in effective communication, cliquishness, the disintegration of the organization, or the need for infusion of new vigor into the organization.

In chiding organizational theorists and system analysts for their formulation of principles and research, Blumer points to their neglect of a crucial historical factor: joint action temporally linked with previous joint action.

It is not surprising to find some of the same elements of analysis in the literature on both social movement and organizations, for a social movement is a form of voluntary association which is, in turn, a type of organization. Even the definitions of each exhibit some similarities. Amitai Etzioni, for example, defines the organization as a social unit deliberately constructed to seek specific goals.[3] Warren Bennis defines the organization as a goal-seeking unit that must maintain its internal system as well as adapt to and shape the external environment.[4] Peter Blau and W. Richard Scott define the organization as being established for a specific purpose and having goals, rules, and status structures.[5] Talcott Parsons defines the organization as a collectivity with shared and collective specific goals.[6] Recalling the earlier ideal-type definition and explanation of a social movement, goals and the use of organization were cited as two distinguishing features of a social movement. Thus elements of analysis used in the study of organizations are also applicable to the study of social movements. These elements may be examined in terms of Robert Merton's paradigm on functional analysis.[7]

The environmental setting is referred to as a significant factor in organizational analysis, and this may be viewed as relating to Merton's "Structural Context or Constraint." Bennis, Parsons, Scott, and Etzioni concur in the importance of this as a feature of the organization. Scott, for example, in his discussion of organizations and their environment, contends that the degree of receptivity or hostility of the environment, plus the effectiveness of leadership in dealing with it, determines whether goals will be reached or whether they will be displaced. The effectiveness of an organization is dependent on some autonomy from the environment.[8]

Goals are included in every above definition and component of organizations, and may be equated to Merton's "Subjective Dispositions." Etzioni specifically cites goals as a desired state of affairs which the organization attempts to realize. The functions of goals are cited in several ways. In depicting a future desired state of affairs, they set guidelines for the organizational activity; they are a source of justification for the activity and existence of the organization; they provide standards for success measurement, that is, effectiveness and efficiency. In addition, they are affected by the goals of the component units of the organization and are determined by consultation or the power play of the subunits, and are to be examined in terms of real versus stated goals. Etzioni also notes that new goals are sought when old ones are realized, or when the old ones are unsuccessful.[9]

Scott maintains that the goals pursued will determine the characteristics of the structure of an organization. He further examines the concept of goals in terms of specificity and implementation. Specificity focuses on organization differentials as to multiple or single goals, clarity, need for consensus, amount of consensus, and professed and operative goals (similar to stated versus real goals, as in Etzioni). Goal implementation for Scott is problematic and is concerned with whether the aims of the subunits are directed toward the purposes of the larger organization. He notes that much organizational energy must be devoted to such nongoal activities as sheer preservation. The choice of dominant goals depends on which elite gains control, which in turn is dependent on the stage of development and type of activity of the organization.[10]

Herbert Simon refers to organization goals as inducements for participants in an organization. Less tangible goals are seen as creating greater controversy concerning means of attainment. Applying the concept to specific types of organizations, he refers to the volunteer organization as one that uses goals as direct inducements for the services of its members, as well as one that is subject to conflicting interpretations regarding goals. [11]

The authority structure is another significant element of organizations. This would correspond to Merton's "Statuses and social interrelations of those involved," as well as to "Mechanisms through which functional requirements are fulfilled." Max Weber was concerned with the distribution of power among organizational positions. His typology of authority was based on the sources and types of legitimation: Traditional, legal, and charismatic. It can be applied on three levels: societal, subsocietal, and intra-organizational. Weber distinguished between power and authority by noting that power refers to the probability that an actor within a social relationship can carry out his own will despite resistance. Authority, on the other hand, refers to the probability that certain commands from a given source will be obeyed by a given group of persons. [12]

Scott, in discussing the authority structure, notes that Weber's concept of control by consent ignores conflicts of interest. [13] Alvin Gouldner cites conflicts between new and old organizational elites, and the conflict between the need for loyalty and the need for expertise. He considers such conflicts a principal source of organizational tensions. [14]

The career of organizations could be equated with Merton's "Dynamics and change" in his paradigm. Sometimes referred to as the natural history of an organization (as in the study of social movements), this aspect frequently focuses on the consideration and evaluation of success. Merton also refers to this as "Consequences" (manifest and latent), and it may be viewed as consequences for the participants (internal) and for the environment (external).

It is in this aspect of organizational analysis that one is faced with the most difficult problems of examination and interpretation, for success of an organization is traditionally measured in terms of goal realization, and goals themselves are often vague and diffused, as well as being both professed and operative. A number of organizational analyses refer to effectiveness and efficiency, but these likewise are difficult to operationalize and even more difficult to interpret.

Etzioni distinguishes between effectiveness and efficiency by defining effectiveness as the degree to which goals are realized, and efficiency as the amount of resources used to produce a unit of output. These are not always concomitant, he notes, and advises using several measures of success. Stressing the features closest to the organizational goal, in addition, is likely to reduce some of the analytic problems inherent in these concepts, Etzioni suggests. He further advocates comparative analysis as a fruitful approach in analyzing success. Here he suggests comparing performances in relation to those of similar organizations, rather than in terms of an ideal for the prototype of that organization. This recognizes other problems besides goal attainment, and might include such indexes of success as productivity, strain absence, and flexibility.

Thus the study of social movements and the study of organizations are marked by similar elements of analysis. This study examines the actual process involved in the development of a specific movement organization as it responded to a changing situation, which will be done through the use of symbolic interactionism as an analytic tool. The case study is approached with the hope that the fusion of organizational analysis with symbolic interactionism will lead to greater understanding of the social movement as a reflector and creator of change.

This case study is an attempt to understand the intricacies and complexities of one open-housing movement organization as it developed in one community over a 13-year period. It illustrates the reciprocal impact of the larger society and national organization upon the local movement organization, and the impact of the human participants in the movement organization upon each other as they individually and collectively met the situations that confronted them.

SOCIAL, CULTURAL, AND ECOLOGICAL CONTEXT

The name Akron, from the Greek word Akros, meaning high place, describes the city's location, lying across a ridge 950 feet above sea level in northeastern Ohio. Akron is the largest rubber-manufacturing center in the world, and serves as the home of four of the world's largest tire and tube manufacturing plants. The community maintains an art institute, a symphony orchestra, an extensive public library system, and a university of some 20,000 students. The population of Akron is 290,351, making it the fifth largest city in the state. After 1900, the rapid growth of the rubber industry attracted workers from the South, as well as from Europe. More than half the present population consists of people from southern states, especially West Virginia, Kentucky, the Carolinas, Tennessee, and Alabama. The black population is 18 percent of the total.

During the period 1940-60, the nonwhite population of Akron increased from 12,309 to 37,636, or 208 percent. During the same time period, the white population of Akron increased from 232,482

to 254,457 or 9 percent. For the same period the black population of
Summit County increased from 13,938 to 41,667, and its white population from 325,467 to 471,902. Of the 15,746 total gain in Akron's
population between 1950 and 1960, 14,012 were nonwhite, but of the
total gain of 103,537 for Summit County, only 15,138 were nonwhite,
of which 14,012 was Akron's gain. Thus the city has absorbed almost
all of Summit County's nonwhite population increase since 1950. As
of 1960, there were seven whites to one black in Akron, and 58
whites to one black in Summit County. [15]

Akron typifies most northern urban communities in this demographic growth pattern, and is also typical of such communities in
its segregation pattern. The index of segregation used by Karl and
Alma Taeuber[16] reveals that residential segregation in Akron increased between 1940 and 1950, and that there was a further increase
between 1950 and 1960 (Tables 1 and 2). Akron City Planning Department maps indicate that in 1940 there were no tracts containing 800
or more dwellings occupied by nonwhites, but that in 1960 there were
four. Out of a total of 58 census tracts, blacks occupied 7. Despite
a population increase of 208 percent in the 20-year period from 1940
to 1960, blacks moved into only two additional census tracts during
that time. The census tracts occupied by blacks contained the most
blighted areas of the city.

As with most northern urban communities, the period from
1940 to 1960 was marked in Akron by a surge of urban renewal. The
expansion of the University of Akron, the construction of an inner-
belt expressway system, the enlargement of Akron General Hospital,
the expansion of B. F. Goodrich Company, and the land clearance in
Opportunity Park were but some of the urban renewal projects that
affected the black population, forcing them to vacate areas designated
for urban renewal.

Akron's Community Improvement Program in 1964 established
its priorities for improvement projects over a ten-year span. Redevelopment, rehabilitation, and a combination of the two were the
three proposed categories of action. Upon the completion of this
action program, 24,000 nonwhites would have been affected, because
their homes were "either moderately deteriorated or deteriorated so
far below standard as to render rehabilitation not economically
feasible."[17]

An analysis of the Akron metropolitan area housing market
as of April, 1965, prepared by the Federal Housing Administration,
reports that 2,875 housing units were removed from the housing
inventory from January 1, 1960 through March 31, 1965, an average
of 550 units per year. Nearly three-fourths of the demolition has
taken place in the city of Akron, largely the result of urban renewal
activity (900 units), and clearance for the interstate highway system

TABLE 1

Changing Black–White Ratios, Akron and Summit County

	Akron				Summit County			
	White		Nonwhite		White		Nonwhite	
	Number	Percent	Number	Percent	Number	Percent	Number	Percent
1940	232,482	95.0	12,309	5.0	92,985	98.3	1,629	1.7
1950	250,727	91.2	23,878	8.8	132,776	98.1	2,651	1.9
1960	252,457	87.0	37,894	13.0	219,445	98.3	3,773	1.7

Note: In 1960 the black–white ratio in Akron was 1 to 7; in Summit County, 1 to 58.

Source: U. S. Department of Commerce, Bureau of the Census, Census of Housing, 1940, 1950, 1960.

121

TABLE 2

Index of Segregation, Akron and
15 Southern Cities, 1960

City	Index
Akron	88.1
Bessemer, Alabama	87.9
Huntsville, Alabama	87.9
Covington, Kentucky	87.8
Alexandria, Virginia	87.8
Spartanburg, South Carolina	87.5
Lexington, Kentucky	87.0
New Orleans, Louisiana	86.3
Hampton, Virginia	85.8
Lynchburg, Virginia	84.0
Macon, Georgia	83.7
Galveston, Texas	82.9
Springfield, Missouri	81.2
Washington, D. C.	79.7
Charleston, South Carolina	79.5
Charleston, West Virginia	79.0

Note: The index represents the percentage of nonwhites that would have to move in order to effect segregated distribution; that is, 100 indicates a totally segregated area.

Source: Karl E. and Alma F. Taeuber, Negroes in Cities (Chicago; Aldine, 1965), pp. 32-34.

(800 units). "It is estimated that demolitions in the Akron Housing Market Area will total 700 units during the April 1, 1965 to April 1, 1967 forecast period."[18] Since 1960, 5000 units have been demolished.

In view of the great increase in nonwhite population in the last 25 years and the reduction of the housing supply through demolitions, the decline in housing construction further compounded the housing shortage for minorities. Between 1955 and 1959 an average of 1,430 houses were built per year; in 1960, 1,313 houses; in 1961, 1,300; in 1962, 1,255; in 1963, 1,215; in 1964, 1,129. It is the city, not the entire metropolitan area, that experienced this reduction in housing supply. Especially serious is the shortage of low- and moderate-cost homes. The FHA report mentioned above stated that few new homes were available for less than $17,500, and that most new homes were in the $20,000-30,000 price range. Since 1960 there has been a sharp increase in rental-unit construction in the Akron area, but the rental rates make them unavailable to those most likely to be displaced by urban renewal.

The extreme disadvantage to which Akron blacks were put is illustrated by a comparative analysis of Census Tracts F8 and F9. These adjacent tracts are separated only by an imaginary line assigned by the census takers. Yet according to the 1960 census, F8 contained 3,532 blacks, or 75 percent of the total population, and F9 had only 22 blacks, or .6 percent. F8 was overcrowded by 16 percent, compared to 5 percent in F9. There was 40 percent dilapidation in F8, and 20 percent in F9. The average rent paid in F8 was two dollars more per month than that paid in F9: $63 in F8; $61 in F9. It would appear that the races were separated by unnatural barriers, and that blacks paid more money for less housing.

Civil rights organizations and black groups protested Akron's housing situation on numerous occasions.[19] In 1962 a new organization was formed as a study group concerned with the elimination of discrimination in housing. This was the Council on Housing Opportunities Made Equal in Summit County (HOMES), which subsequently formed an ad hoc committee to gather and present data to the Akron City Council in support of a proposed fair-housing ordinance.

Several months of hearings, at which the presentation of testimony in favor of the ordinance was organized by the ad hoc committee, led to the passage on July 14, 1964, of an emergency fair-housing ordinance, by a vote of 11 to 2. The Akron Beacon Journal called this the City Council's finest hour.

Immediately thereafter, real estate interests led by the Akron Area Board of Realtors organized to petition for a referendum on question of the fair-housing ordinance. When a sufficient number of signatures was obtained, the issue was placed on the November 1964 ballot, and an ad hoc citizens' committee was formed to work for the retention of the fair-housing law. In that election, the fair-housing ordinance, less than five months old, was overturned by the voters of Akron by a vote of some 60,000 to 40,000. Local and national attorneys for the NAACP began a five-year court battle testing the constitutionality of the referendum, which was finally won in 1969.

Following the election, a black organization, led by churches, announced a boycott of the Akron Board of Realtors in reprisal for their role in defeating the fair housing law.[20] At a mass meeting held two months after the election, in January 1965, concerned citizens recommended unanimously that a subcommittee be established to investigate the possibility of forming a listing service in Akron, to be run by volunteers.

On the advice of NCDH the subcommittee sought and received information from other communities that had such listing services. When a substantial amount of information had been accumulated, the subcommittee called a meeting with 32 representatives from civic, religious, labor, and civil rights organizations in Akron and surrounding communities. This meeting resulted in a decision to establish a local listing service to be known as the Fair Housing Contact Sercie (FHCS).

Thus coming into existence in May 1965, during the third phase of development of the national movement, FHCS announced itself dedicated to providing equal opportunity in housing for minorities through a double program of education and actual housing assistance.

DEVELOPMENT AS A VOLUNTEER MOVEMENT

A 21-member executive board of directors was elected to carry on the operations of the new organization, with the assistance of a corps of volunteers. The composition of the membership and its leaders was biracial and interfaith. All former members of previous ad hoc committees and the Council on HOMES became associated with FHCS. A volunteer telephone secretary was recruited, who would be on call at all times,* a post office box was secured for receipt of mail, and the organization was ready to begin its work.

Goals

As Charles Perrow and others have indicated, the types of goals most relevant to understanding organizational behavior are not the official goals, but those that are embedded in major operating policies and daily decisions of the personnel involved.[21] In the study of FHCS, it must be noted at the outset that the operating policies and decisions of the organization were remarkably consistent with the stated goals of the organization throughout the entire three-and-a-half year voluntary phase of its existence. In Perrow's terms, the stated official goals and the operative goals were the same.

From its inception the stated goal of FHCS was equal opportunity in housing, revealed in its constitution, its stationery, all of its educational literature, and its bimonthly newsletters. For exam-

---

*She was bedridden, which explained her availablity.

ple, the first mailing sent out by the fledgling group was a mimeographed sheet announcing a new voluntary nonprofit organization, the FHCS, dedicated to Providing Equal Opportunities in Housing.* The earliest printed brochure followed the flyer within several months, repeated the goal of equality of opportunity in housing, and included a brief credo:

> We believe in encouraging freedom of residence so that all persons, regardless of race, religion, or nationality, can secure the housing they want and can afford, in the neighborhood of their choice.

> We believe it to be in the best interest of our community and our country that all persons of good will take an active role in bringing about this freedom and equality of opportunity in housing.[22]

However, it was the operative goal of the organization that captured the attention of the community, largely because of newspaper emphasis. Of the 80 news articles and items on FHCS that appeared in Akron's only newspaper (the Akron Beacon Journal) during the three-and-a-half-year voluntary phase, only three referred to the stated goal of the organization as equal opportunity in housing. All others referred to the operative goal of the organization, specifically, its housing assistance program. For example, the first news article in May 1965 describing the newly formed organization stated that "Akron civil rights leaders Monday night formed an organization designed to bring Negroes who want to buy homes in contact with whites who have homes to sell in all-white neighborhoods."[23] This was repeated in a second article the following day, and in most subsequent articles during the next three and a half years, with variations in wording and emphasis. Some variations were: "the objective of the service is to make it possible for anyone to obtain housing in a neighborhood of his choice"; "a volunteer organization that brings together white property owners and Negroes who want to buy or rent in white neighborhoods"; "an organization which attempts to place renters and home-buyers in a non-discriminatory manner"; and "a Summit-County-wide organization fighting for an end to discrimination in housing."[24] Thus, the diffuse and rather vaguely stated goal of equal opportunity in housing was bypassed in the community for the more specific operative goal referring to the housing assistance

---

*First announcement, FHCS, May 1965; see Appendix B.

program. However, even the operative goal of the organization was
stated only partially correctly in newspaper coverage, since almost
no references were made to the educational aspects of the program,
which actually comprised at least half of the total effort.

Program and Impact

For purposes of analysis the program is separated into housing
assistance and education, though the two were constantly intertwined,
as will be seen.

The housing assistance program was a free listing service combined with a compliance service to combat discrimination in housing.
At the first board of directors meeting policies were established to
provide its guidelines.[25] A composite of policies used in other fair-
housing groups throughout the country served as a basis for comparison in the formulation of the new FHCS policies. The policies of
the Akron organization were explicit and detailed in their directive
to assist housing moves to nontraditional areas only. All other requests
for housing aid were to be referred to normal channels of housing
service. These policies remained in effect throughout the entire voluntary phase.

The housing assistance program necessitated a recruitment of
property owners, home seekers, and volunteers, which was accomplished chiefly through public relations and educational means. All
educational literature developed and distributed by the organization
contained clip-out forms recruiting the three needed categories of
owners, seekers, and volunteers.

However, one major source of recruitment other than the
FHCS literature itself, was the newspaper coverage of the organization. Every time an article appeared about FHCS, there was an upsurge of requests for assistance, offers of housing, offers of volunteer help, and occasionally a small financial contribution. Though
some of the FHCS leaders had personal rapport with some of the news
staff, it was the novelty and pluck of the organization's efforts that
stirred the imagination of the news writers and prompted the steady
and positive coverage of the organization during its voluntary phase.

When the first news article appeared in May 1965, announcing
the formation of the organization, there were 19 immediate responses
requesting the use of the new service. By the second month this had
increased to 34, including 30 owners and four minority home seekers.
However, not all owners had property that met the policy requirements of the organization in terms of area, and many were referred
to other sources. Shortly after the first year ended, FHCS had
received over 300 phone calls for information or materials, had provided actual assistance for 20 owners and 33 home seekers, had

utilized 12 volunteer escorts, and had successfully assisted 7 minority families in moving to 7 different all-white neighborhoods.

During the entire first voluntary phase, FHCS provided housing assistance to more than 300 families. In this period, 117 properties were offered by owners, 65 volunteers were utilized, and 18 complaints of discrimination were filed with relevant agencies. Forty successful moves were made to 40 different neighborhoods. Most of these were to all-white neighborhoods, but some were for stabilization—that is, whites moved to integrated neighborhoods.

These figures may be better understood in terms of comparisons with other fair-housing volunteer groups across the country. Before the FHCS was organized, materials from other fair-housing groups indicated that a successful move might not take place at all during the first two years of operation. At the most, one or two such moves might be expected to occur with a new fair-housing organization. The sense of excitement and accomplishment may be understood, then, when it is noted that the first move-in took place during the third month of FHCS's existence. The second move-in followed one month later. The resultant joy abated somewhat, however, when a seven-month period elapsed between the second and third move-ins.

The difficulties of achieving success in housing moves stemmed from two factors. First was the voluntary nature of the program itself. It has been ascertained that the average home seeker generally views from 10 to 20 homes before making a choice. With a volunteer staff involved, the time span involved in making all necessary arrangements is necessarily greater. With rental home seekers, another difficulty arises. When the vacancy rate for apartments is low, the demand is very high. This necessitates immediate viewing of any vacancies. Volunteers are not always available when needed, and thus apartments are quickly taken by others who are not dependent on volunteer assistance.

Second, the inadequacies of the law created difficulties. Only some portions of the housing market (20 percent) were covered by state law at the time FHCS came into existence. There was no local law, and federal provisions were no broader than the state law at the time. In addition, the enforcement provisions of the state law were extremely weak. The only recourse in cases of suspected discrimination was the Ohio Civil Rights Commission, which was notoriously slow in processing complaints. There was no injunctive procedure, and no penalty. The ultimate negative sanction was a public hearing, and a ruling by the state commission forcing the discriminator to comply. This meant that the quest for housing covered by law was extremely limited and cumbersome.

A natural consequence of this was the reliance on offers of housing by friendly owners, but these were never sufficient to provide adequate bases of comparisons for the home seekers. Other fair-housing groups had indicated that an adequate fair-housing organization provided ten homes for every home seeker. The FHCS seldom had more than one to three homes at a time that met the needs and price range of each home seeker.

It became apparent to the fledgling organization that only in housing not offered by friendly owners would discrimination be revealed. Thus the volunteers and home seekers were encouraged to view housing covered by law, which at the time included new unoccupied homes, multiple dwellings which contained more than two units, individual houses which were not owner-occupied, and vacant land. Since 80 per-cent of the housing in Ohio was individual-owner-occupied, this severely limited the possibilities. Public housing and FHA- and VA-repossessed homes were also covered by the law at that time.

Whether or not provisions of the law were known to the general community, the fact is that in almost every instance of attempted home seeking, discrimination was encountered by the FHCS. In every such case, the procedures involved in confronting and combating the dis-crimination were extremely cumbersome and protracted. Often by the time a discrimination case was successfully concluded—from four to eight months was usual—the home seeker had long since lost interest in the unit and had found other housing, usually in traditional areas for minorities.

An examination of some of the cases of discrimination encoun-tered by FHCS in the housing assistance program reveals the widely divergent tactics of evasion and infraction of the law practiced by owners, real estate agents, managers, builders, and, indeed, all facets of the housing industry. This account also indicates the frustra-tions and obstacles met by the developing FHCS, and yields some under-standing of the reason there was not a greater number of successful moves. It also affords some insight as to the sense of achievement the organization experienced with whatever it was able to accomplish. In addition, this account of selected cases of discrimination reveals the changing tactics of the FHCS in testing the efficacy of various ap-proaches used in combating discrimination.

Cases of Discrimination. Taken directly from the complaints filed with the Ohio Civil Rights Commission are the following testimonies of FHCS home seekers:

Case of Charles B——.

On Sunday, July 30, I answered an ad in the Akron Beacon Journal concerning lots for sale. I made an appointment for

11:45 that day, with the owner. When I met the owner at H—— Rd. he informed me that he would not sell to a Negro, because then he would not be able to sell the other lots. He also said that the only way he would sell to me was if he were forced to do it. He indicated that he knew this was in violation of the state law.

A volunteer with the FHCS, Mr. B. R., had made an appointment to follow mine at 12 noon. He was told by the owner that he could have any lots of his choice.

The owner's name and address and phone no. are ——.

Case of Mrs. Robert N.

I, Mrs. R. N., a Negro, went to see the home at —— on Thursday, September 14, at 10 a.m. It had been advertised in the Goodyear Newspaper, and I had been informed of this by the FHCS, who provided an escort for me, Mrs. M. K. The appointment had been made and confirmed on Tuesday. The owner had been informed that the home seeker would come on Thursday.

When we arrived, the owner met us at the front door and informed us that the house had been rented on Monday night to an acquaintance of hers. She apologized for not having telephoned us of this, but said she had not known how to reach me. She also suggested that I look for housing in the Negro residential section nearby.

That afternoon, at 4:45, a checker from FHCS, Mrs. M. M. (address, phone no.), called the owner and inquired about the ad in the Goodyear news. The owner invited her to come to see the home, and said it was still available.

(Owner's name and phone no.)

Case of W. R.

On Wedensday, Sept. 27, my wife and I went to see the lots at ——. We arrived at 6:45 p.m., and met Mrs. Ritchie (agent for S—— Realty) in one of the model homes at the development. Mrs. Ritchie said, when she saw us, there were no lots available at this time. Her boss had said that afternoon that the lots were no longer available for sale since they would have model homes built on them and they were to be used for display purposes only.

On Thursday, Sept. 28, a checker from FHCS (Mrs. J. K.) called and then visited the allotment at 7 p.m. She was shown 7 lots and given her choice of any of them by the same agent.

Case of Miss C. M.

I, C. M., age 21, and a Negro, answered an ad in the Beacon Journal pertaining to an apartment for rent at ——. I called the given phone number and made an appointment for 3 p.m. on Sunday, June 4, 1967.

Accompanying me was Mrs. S. of the FHCS. When we arrived at the house, Mrs. S. went in alone. She met the owners, Mr. & Mrs. P. M., who showed her the apartment. She told them that the apartment seemed very suitable for a friend (me), and asked if she could bring the friend up to see it, since the friend was in the car. They agreed.

When I came up, I looked around the apartment, and said I would like to rent it. I asked how much of a deposit was necessary. They said it was up to me. I suggested the entire first month's rent, but Mrs. S. suggested that a 25 dollar deposit would be sufficient. When Mrs. S. asked how soon I could move in, they said they wanted to show the apartment to other people for two more weeks at least, and then would decide on the most suitable tenant. When we asked why I was not a suitable tenant, being a college graduate, employed, and of quiet habits, they became angry and said that it had nothing to do with my color, but that they had wanted a middle-aged person. When Mrs. S. said that she did not think a middle-aged person would want to climb up three flights of stairs, they said that they thought they had the right to decide who should rent their apartment.

They suggested that I destroy the check, since they did not want to take the deposit. I wrote my name and phone no. on the back of a copy of the Ohio Fair Housing Law, and gave it to them, suggesting that they reconsider, and call me by 10 p.m. that night. They did not call.

Of these cases, only the third, the case of W. R., ever culminated in a public hearing, which received wide notoriety when the prominent real estate company involved was found guilty of discrimination. This hearing took place 13 months after the incident actually occurred. By this time, the W. R.s were so weary from the prolonged investigation that they no longer wanted the lots that were finally offered to them, reluctantly, by the discriminatory real estate company. Won: the case, and two lots. Lost: one home seeker.

The education program was directed toward both the white and black communities. In the white community, the education was designed to increase awareness and understanding of the harmful effect of discrimination, and to dispel common myths and fears regarding desegregated living. In the black community, the education was primarily a publicity program, to acquaint potential black home seekers with the nature of the free service, and to encourage them to make use of such a service. Education was conducted through every available medium—printed materials, newsletters, mass media, open meetings, a speaker's bureau, and special campaigns.

Three major educational campaigns had significant impact on the community. Two were planned, with positive manifest consequences; one was only partially planned, with pervading negative latent consequences. The first planned campaign, held in 1965 during the first year of the organization's existence, involved a pledge-signing drive culminating in the appearance of a full-page newspaper advertisement paid for by the signers. Such a campaign had never been conducted in the entire geographical region, though it was rather outdated across the nation by this time. Because of its novelty and appeal, it elicited a powerful positive response, not only from the community itself, but also from many surrounding communities. A number of these surrounding communities went on to form voluntary fair-housing groups of their own, counseled by the Akron group.

The second planned campaign was conducted during the third year of the voluntary phase of the organization, and consisted of a series of newspaper educational advertisements, appearing consecutively during Brotherhood Week. The funding for the advertisements was solicited from business, industry, and churches, as well as individual supporters and other organizations. The second campaign was actually an extension of the earlier pledge drive, since it began with a full-page newspaper reproduction of a map of the area showing the location of all previous pledge signers. A clip-out form reproducing the pledge for potential new signers was included in each advertisement. In addition, a narrative contained facts about race and housing in the Akron area, and information about the FHCS. The general response was positive, tangible, and immediate.

The third campaign had perhaps the most far-reaching and pervasive effects. The sequence of events was largely unplanned and unanticipated in its development and consequences. During its second year, FHCS responded to a request from NCDH to secure petition signatures calling on heads of federal, state, and local governments for increased activity toward equal opportunity in housing. A surprisingly large number of signatures were secured and duly sent to relevant heads of governments. This created an image of FHCS as a powerful mobilizer and pressure group, to the delight of the organization itself,

which was surprised at its own ease in securing such large-scale
support for these petitions.

Proposal for Funding. During this entire period, the FHCS had been
engaged in the writing of a proposal for a fair-housing center, involving
large funding possibilities, an effort that has been greatly encouraged
and promulgated by NCDH. However, when the proposal was sent to
NCDH for suggestive evaluation, their response was negative because
of the insufficient supply of low-cost housing in the Akron area, as
documented by facts contained in the proposal itself.

The April 17 board of directors meeting of FHCS contained a
main agenda item that concerned the response of the NCDH to the
funding proposal. The minutes reported that

> . . . a phone call was received from Neil Gold of NDCH,
> noting his very favorable impression of the written propo-
> sal. However, Mr. Gold stated that he did not see how we
> could have a Center with the terribly inadequate total sup-
> ply of low-income housing in Akron, as shown by the data
> in our own Proposal. He said, "How can you have Fair
> Housing when you really don't have enough units and vacan-
> cies?" He indicated that a number of other cities have
> been denied funds for Urban Renewal which had better
> housing situations than did Akron. . .[26]

The board's dismay upon learning of this response can be understood, since it had taken seven months to gather the data and write
the proposal for funding. Moreover, widespread support in the community had been sought and secured for the concept of a funded fair-
housing center, involving many meetings, speeches, presentations,
and preparations with and for other organizations and groups. In
addition, there had been extensive newspaper coverage of the FHCS
proposal for a funded center. But most of all, the disappointment with
NCDH response stemmed from the fact that the board had developed
a genuine feeling of need and affection for the idea of a funded center
during the long months of the development of the proposal. It was as
if, in the fashioning of the plan for a staffed center, the plan became
a reality and acquired an identity all its own. Board members were
extremely reluctant to part with this creation, and out of this felt
need for a center, the board evolved a plan of action:

> Intense and lengthy discussion followed, culminating in
> the following motion: We are in favor of requesting of the
> city of Akron by a specified date a public commitment of
> a plan for expanding the supply of low-income housing on

scattered sites for persons displaced from urban renewal.
Motion passed unanimously.[27]

Plan for Action. It was decided that the board would request an initial
meeting with the mayor, who would be given two weeks to formulate
a plan for increasing the supply of low-rent housing. It was further
agreed that if the city did not respond within the time limit, a formal
complaint would be filed with HUD, requesting temporary cessation of
urban renewal funds for the city until the city developed a plan for such
housing. The mayor was to be warned of this possible action.

The board was actually reluctant to take this final drastic action,
and met not once, but twice with the mayor and mobilized a dozen other
leading civic and civil rights organizations to support its request. But
it was not until June 19, one month after the deadline, that the minutes
contained the following significant item:

> On the basis of data contained in our Proposal, the local
> chapter of CORE has lodged a complaint with Secretary
> Weaver of HUD, calling for a temporary cessation of urban
> renewal funds for Akron, until the city develops a plan for
> expanding the supply of low-rent housing units. . . .[28]

What the minutes did not reveal was that FHCS arranged for
CORE to take this step, rather than FHCS itself, because of fear of
jeopardizing the possibility of the funding of a fair-housing center. The
letter sent to Weaver and signed by the CORE president was actually
written by the FHCS secretary, with the prior approval of the entire
board. (This was facilitated by the fact that the president of CORE
was on the FHCS board.)

No one on the board was prepared for the swift sequence of
events that then occurred. Nine news article headlines appearing in
the Akron Beacon Journal in rapid succession from June 24 to July 19
(1967) reveal the enormous impact of FHCS action: June 22, "Core
Asks Pause in Urban Renewal"; June 24, "Orders HUD Report on
Housing Charge"; June 26, "11 Akron Units Join Push for Housing";
June 29, "To Discuss Low-Cost Housing"; June 30, "City Feels
Pressure." This last headline was followed by an article which stated:

> There are growing indications Akron officials may have a
> real fight on their hands trying to show that work on urban
> renewal here should not be stopped. A group representing
> at least a dozen civic, civil rights, and religious organi-
> zations is insisting that a plan to provide more low-income
> housing throughout the city be produced.[29]

Results. And finally came the victory: July 1, "Scattered Housing for Poor Proposed"; July 7, "Step in Public Housing"; July 18, "City to Ask Federal Rent Aid for Needy"; and July 19, Editorial, "Help in Housing."

The July 7 article indicated that Akron's Metropolitan Housing Authority (MHA) would apply to HUD for funds for 500 scattered-site homes to accomodate from 2,000 to 3,000 poor persons, and stated that a letter from the mayor would accompany the application. Indeed, it was the mayor who, under pressure, was forced to demand of the Metropolitan Housing Authority that it take such action.

The significance of this entire sequence of events can best be understood in the light of past action concerning public housing in Akron. No public housing had been built in the city for the past 20 years. Moreover, such public housing as did exist was almost totally segregated.

As a result of FHCS action, the Akron public housing agency was completely shaken by the publicity given to its inaction over a 20-year period, and an administrative turnover resulted. The new administrator, in response to mayoral demand, proceeded with a vigorous acquisition of funding for low-cost housing.* A massive building and leasing program ensued in the next three-year period, totalling $30 million of funding from HUD and resulting in 4900 additional units of housing for low-income families.

FHCS board members expressed early fears that the location of the new public-housing units might be in areas already integrated or ghettoized. In a meeting with the new public-housing director. FHCS made known its position on desegregation and on the meaning of scattered sites ("We don't mean scattered along Wooster Avenue," referring to the heart of the ghetto).

Despite assurances from the new public-housing director that goals of FHCS would be considered in the new scattered-site housing program, early fears were soon justified. Within a few months, reports began to drift in with increasing rapidity indicating that a number of homes in ghetto and already integrated areas had been bought or leased by the MHA for its new program. In addition, new building programs of MHA were announced, primarily in two wards which were already segregated.

---

*The new director of MHA was 43, white, a former president of a large supermarket located in the ghetto, and the owner of a considerable amount of ghetto property. He did not endear himself to the black community, despite the fact that the regarded himself as "the black man's best friend."

Many meetings, marked by tension and frustration, were held with and without other community organizations to attempt to deal with the situation. Despite repeated attempts by FHCS and other organizations to secure information, MHA refused to divulge the exact locations of its acquired properties, and refused to reveal the racial composition of the occupants of the leased homes, saying that these facts were not available. MHA was thus added to the list of "enemies" of FHCS, joining the realtors and the urban renewal relocation authorities. Complaints were lodged with HUD, to no avail.

Latent Consequence. The irony of the situation was that FHCS itself had created this monster. The tragic latent consequence was that MHA created new patterns of housing segregation, as well as reinforcing and perpetuating existing residential segregation patterns. This, of course, compounded the difficulties of the FHCS in its efforts to desegregate the community, and made its task even more insurmountable than when it began.

Nevertheless, three annual reports of the FHCS indicate tremendous zeal, productivity, and vigor in its total program during its first voluntary phase.* The scope and impcat of the FHCS program was enormous, and reached far beyond the community itself. Recognition of this is indicated in the fact that two national awards and two local awards were received by the organization for outstanding volunteer service.† The entire program was achieved with no office, no staff, and a budget of $300 a year.

Morale

It is recognized that morale is an extremely elusive concept. In attempting to assess its nature as it exists in any one group, one must examine the type and quality of interaction among its members. It is the network of social relations between individuals that finds expression in their interaction.

In the study of the FHCS, one must understand the flow of authority and response as it affected decision making in the group. This, in turn, entails an exploration of the background, orientations, and roles of the various board members, since it was the board that conducted all the activities of the organization.

---

*See Appendix B.

†Awards were: Akron Urban League, 1966; Akron NAACP, 1967; Freedom of Residence, 1968; Lane Bryant, 1968.

The composition of the board of directors closely reflected the composition of the general membership, and was described in the earliest FHCS brochure under "Who It Is."

> Members of the FHCS are all who have subscribed to the ideals and principles of the organization. . . .
>
> The FHCS bi-racial membership represents the entire community with:
> > Clergy of all faiths
> > Men and women of various professions and occupations
> > Housewives
> > Students
> and Organizations such as:
> > Church groups
> > Civic organizations
> > Fraternal clubs
>
> A 21-member Executive Board carries out the program of FHCS. [30]

The board membership remained primarily the same during its first two years of existence, with changes occurring each year thereafter. Generally, the board could be characterized as predominantly middle-class and professional, though low-income representation was always maintained. For example, the first board contained 19 members, 7 women and 12 men. Of the men, five were black; of the women, one was black. Five of the men were ministers, one of them black. Of the other men, one was a white businessman, one an Urban League director (black), one was a teacher (black), one was a college professor (white), two were attorneys (white), and one was a doctor (black) who was prominent in NAACP and other civil rights activities. Of the women, the secretary—the author—was a college professor (white), one was a teacher (white), four were housewives (white)—one of whom was very active in local civic and political affairs—and one was a real estate agent (black). In the second year, a woman social worker (black) was added, and other women (white and black) gradually replaced some of the men who left the board.

The president was a white businessman, who retained the office for four years, as did the secretary. The doctor was the research chairman for four years, and remained on the board for its first five years as did one of the attorneys.

Each board member knew a majority of the other members prior to the formal organization of the board, acquaintances gained largely through participation in earlier legislative action or civil rights organizational work. Five of the board members were personal friends and social gatherings among them were quite standard, with occasional inclusion of other board members at such functions.

During the first three-and-a-half-year voluntary phase, the president served as titular head of the organization, with frank and total recognition on the part of all board members and volunteers that it was the secretary who actually led the organization, and on whom the major responsibilities fell for the organization and execution of all tasks. Thus the secretary had great influence but limited authority, while the president had full authority but lacked influence because of his inadequacy as a taskmaster. In addition, because the secretary (who had been the founder of the organization) also had the most relevant professional knowledge she was acknowledged as the most competent spokesman for the organization. Accorded great respect, also, were the doctor because of his knowledge and influence in the community, and the director of the local Urban League because of his authority and power in the community.

Robert Bales has described status, role, and interaction elements in his analysis of small-group behavior. He refers to the frequency of three factors occurring in group self-evaluations, which seem to represent underlying dimensions in the evaluations persons make of each other in small groups: (1) individual prominence and achievement—behaviors of the individual related to his efforts to stand out from others and individually achieve various personal goals; (2) aiding attainment by the group—behaviors of the individual related to his efforts to assist the group in achieving goals toward which the group is oriented; and (3) sociability—behaviors of the individual related to his efforts to establish and maintain cordial and socially satisfying relations with other group members. Bales delineates these as "activity," "task ability," and "likeability" factors, and suggests that they are not mutually exclusive, nor mutually supportive, but tend to be uncorrelated. He notes that the fact that they are uncorrelated does not mean that there are no dynamic relationships among the phenomena represented by the factors.[31]

Small-group Analysis. If we consider these three factors in the analysis of the FHCS board during its first three-and-one-half years of operation, it may be said that this group might have evaluated itself as strong in factors (2) and (3)—task and sociability—with a minimum of emphasis on factor (1)—personal gain or achievement. Occasionally there were indications that some residents of the community were mildly suspicious of the motives of the leadership in terms of factor (1), but this did not appear to be the case within the board itself.

Small-group analysis factors (2) and (3) are similar to two factors noted in social-system analysis by Talcott Parsons[32] and George Homans.[33] The social system is seen by both scholars as an

organization of the interaction of units which endures through time.
The system is related to its environment and its units are related.
to each other. Two types of member units are recognized: individuals
and groups of individuals—which in turn are made up of roles enacted
with interaction. There are external and internal patterns of interaction. The external patterns refer to task, the internal patterns to
maintenance, according to Homans. Parsons offers a similar analysis,
and suggests the external pattern as an instrumental one and the
internal pattern as an expressive one.

Applying this to the FHCS board, we may say that it was strongly
task-oriented with positive maintenance of morale throughout its
voluntary phase; or, that it had great strength in both instrumental
and expressive patterns. It is suggested here that the strength of the
task orientation was responsible for the maintenance of high morale,
for it was the achievement of success in its program that created the
sense of excitement and hope that pervaded the group. The growing
awareness of its own power in influencing local decision makers further contributed to its high morale. But although productivity (as
revealed in program) is an empirical indicator of morale, it does not
of itself reveal its full extent, nor does it indicate the reciprocal relationship between task (program) and morale.

An examination of the minutes of board meetings during the
entire first voluntary phase reveals little evidence of discord or major
disagreement regarding policies or program. Even during the first
year, when so many small and large decisions were necessitated,
there was remarkable cohesion, harmony, and unanimity on the board,
despite the presence of two chronic negative reactors.

Bale's delineations of interaction categories are helpful in this
respect.[34]

Area A	Interaction Category
Positive reactions	Shows solidarity
	Shows tension release
	Shows agreement
Area B	
Problem-solving attempts	Gives suggestion
	Gives opinion
	Gives orientation
Area C	
Questions	Asks orientation
	Asks opinion
	Asks suggestion

Area D	Interaction category
Negative reactions	Shows disagreement
	Shows tension increase
	Shows antagonism

The board during its first voluntary phase was characterized by an extremely high number of interactions in the first two areas, some in the third area, and almost none in the fourth area.

The format of board meetings was generally the same during this phase. The group assembled gradually, with friendly and often enthusiastic exchanges among those who had not interacted between board meetings. The minutes were approved as mailed, the treasurer's report was given, and committee reports were made. The housing assistance program and special educational efforts were usually regarded as the major agenda items. The secretary's report was usually last, and was the most time-consuming. It included reports on all incoming and outgoing correspondence, relevant community activity, meetings attended, educational work accomplished, and usually ended with requests for decision making on several key items. Old and new business were considered last on the agenda, but frequently were brought up during the meeting when considered relevant. The atmosphere was very informal, and most decision making was done through consensus. There is only one indication of a formal vote during the entire first year. This concerned a matter of constitutional amendment, which was raised at the last meeting of the year.

During the second year, four votes were taken. At the first board meeting (June 20, 1966), a vote was taken to establish a committee to explore the possibility of an OEO-funded fair-housing center. At a special board meeting on September 13 with the NCDH representative, a second vote was taken to write the proposal for funding. A third vote came at the January 1967 meeting on a proposal for the executive board to act in the name of the entire organization regarding NCDH petitions. A fourth vote was held on April 17 and concerned the action requesting the city to publicly specify a plan for expanding the supply of low-income housing on scattered sites. All votes were unanimously in the affirmative.

In the third year of its operation, 12 new board members were elected and 11 were reelected. Twelve votes were taken during this year, reflecting heightened activity, an increase in formality, and new board membership. Again during this period, all proposals were passed unanimously and there was little evidence of even minor disagreements.

Other indications of the positive interrelationships on the board and the general buoyancy of spirit among members are revealed in the minutes, where informality, intimacy, warmth, and humor are evident.

Since so much of the work of the organization was channeled through the secretary, her contact with board members and volunteers was constant. Her assessment of their response to task divisions was one of ready willingness to do work for the organization and an enthusiasm and dedication to the organization and its goals.

There was a growing effort made by the secretary during the third year to further divide the tasks, so that a greater portion of the involvement and responsibility would be shared by a number of different individual board members. There were also several repeated attempts to broaden the base of board decision making. Generally, the entire first voluntary phase was marked by strong board involvement and participation in the FHCS program.

Effects of Separatism. The third annual meeting of the FHCS on May 27, 1968 was significant in that it signaled a public change in attitude on the part of one important black leader of the organization, the doctor and research chairman, Dr. F. He had been one of the founders of the organization, and had worked very closely with the secretary and other leaders in the organization and planning of the program and policies of the FHCS. Long a leader in the local NAACP, and chairman of its Education Committee, he was considered a militant in his day. He was now confronted with the national change in the civil rights movement, as well as the local manifestations of growing militancy in portions of the black community. Also significant was the fact that his oldest son was a student at the local university and a leader of the newly formed militant Black United Students (BUS).

At this third annual meeting, Dr. F. was the moderator of a panel of four local black leaders who were asked to discuss the 30-minute film, "Segregation, Northern Style" (a CBS documentary), after its presentation to the audience. The meeting itself was held in a branch library in the heart of the ghetto, and was attended by over 150 people. The panelists were the one black city councilman, the president of the local NAACP, the assistant regional director of the Urban League, and the director of employment at the local Urban League. The news article which later described the meeting, and featured Dr. F.'s picture, stated:[35]

> E. D. [the city councilman] said segregation is worse in Akron than it was 10, 15, and 20 years ago and it is getting worse. . . .
>
> Members of the panel agreed that progress in fair housing is now up to the white community. The only alternative is a divided nation, white and black, they said. . . .

Dr. F. said: I feel the white community has no intention
of living up to its commitment. Therefore, black power
makes sense. . . .

If integration is not accepted by the white community
swiftly, the drift to black power and black communities
is inevitable, the panelists said. . . .

Dr. L. N., an obstetrician, put the matter in the strongest
terms when he told the audience: These guys have had it.
Because, as I see it, the black people don't desire integration any more . . . the day of blazing trails is over
for the Negro. It's up to whites now, and whatever comes
out of it, you've done it. . . . I think it's clear all over the
country, the young (Negro) people are not interested in being
bothered with the whites. . . .

E. D. warned: I believe the time is short. We are on a
collision course.

It should be noted that Dr. L. N. shared an office with Dr. F.,
and the two were considered best friends. When Dr. F. agreed that
black people were not interested in integration any more, some members of the FHCS board were visibly shaken. The discussion period
which followed included private whispered discussions among several
members and board members concerning Dr. F's remarks. The tenor
of the sotto voce comments was that Dr. F. had every right to his
opinions, which were highly understandable in view of the frustrations
of the times, but as a public representative of FHCS, at its annual
meeting, it was felt that he had breached an unwritten unspoken code
of ethics; that is, one did not publicly make statements damaging to
the goals of the organization.

At the next board meeting on June 17 (1968), which included
eight new members, the usual election of officers was held. Dr. F.
was not present—one of the few board meetings he had ever missed
in three years. When the secretary suggested Dr. F. for vice-president, there were murmurs of disapproval from some original board
members. He was not nominated for any office.

At the next board meeting on July 15 Dr. F. presented a suggestion which was not well received by the group. Although this incident was not manifestly significant at the time, it was later revealed
as such. As research chairman, Dr. F. "raised the issue of whether
we would want to sponsor a research study of ghetto resident needs
in possible cooperation with the University of Akron Sociology Department." He offered as one rationale for this suggestion the fact that,
in his opinion, the image of FHCS was not favorable in the black community at that time. He suggested that such a study would at least

convince the black community that "we were considering more relevant issues." The minutes reported:

> After considerable discussion about this, Dr. F. was
> encouraged to look further into the possibilities of this,
> as well as into what studies had already been done by
> the Center for Urban Studies. It was pointed out by K.R.
> that students can not do such studies as part of their
> curriculum, as a rule. The secretary noted that we were
> engaged to capacity at present with our current programs,
> and although such a study would be meaningful, we might
> not be the best group at this time to sponsor it.[36]

Although it was not readily apparent at this meeting, Dr. F. was
quite wounded by the responses to his suggestion. Many times during
subsequent meetings, he referred to the incident with some bitterness.
He seemed especially hurt that the secretary had not supported his
view. She, in turn, was irritated at the idea of more work being added
to the ongoing FHCS activities, since the existent programs were
already absorbing her every waking moment, and utilizing to the fullest
extent every available board member and volunteer. On the other hand,
she was torn between sense of being overburdened with work and empa-
thy with her good friend Dr. F. and compassion and understanding of
his role as a "marginal man" in the civil rights struggle. It is interesting to note that in succeeding months Dr. F. referred to this period
in the organization's history as one of "least productivity," while it
was the general impression of a majority of other board members and
the community at large that this was the peak of activity of FHCS. Empirical indicators confirm the latter view. (See Annual Reports,
Appendix B).

Ghetto riots occurred in Akron in August 1968—the first of such
magnitude in the community, though among the last to occur in the
nation during this period. Seven days of unrest resulted in a city-wide
curfew and requests for National Guardsmen, who patrolled the area.

It was against this backdrop that the surprise announcement
came, early in August 1968, that the FHCS had been granted $59,726
by OEO to administer a fair-housing center, to open October 1.

INSTANT FUNDING: THE TRANSITION

The news article publicizing the funding was headed "Fair
Housing Unit To Step Up Work" and stated:

> After three years of part time, out-of-pocket operations,
> the Fair Housing Contract Service happily is looking for
> a home of its own. . . .

The Service, formed to fight discrimination in housing in Akron, has received a $59,726 federal grant. . . .

The grant, effective Oct. 1, will allow the Service to transform itself from a strictly volunteer agency to a full-time unit headed by professionals. . . .

The Board of directors will meet Monday night and form committees to find office space and to interview applicants for a full-time director, assistant director, field coordinator, and secretary. . . .

The Center will concentrate efforts on finding more low-income housing for the poor, but will concern itself with "every facet of minority group housing," the secretary said. "We'll continue our present duties, and we'll also have a new focus on administering to the needs of the poor."

The special memo sent to all board members prior to the August 19 board meeting read as follows:

SPECIAL MEMO ! ! ! ! !

WE HAVE BEEN FUNDED BY THE FEDERAL GOVERN-
MENT, THROUGH THE ANTI-POVERTY PROGRAM,
TO RUN A FAIR HOUSING CENTER. URGENT THAT
YOU ATTEND THE AUGUST BOARD MEETING. PLEASE
COME PREPARED WITH ANSWERS OR SUGGESTIONS
FOR THE FOLLOWING QUESTIONS:

1. We need a director and a secretary immediately. Who is qualified and available?
2. What kind of office would be best? Location? Type (store, house, church rooms)?
3. What special emphases should we add to our program?

The first board meeting after the funding announcement was devoted primarily to discussion on how to proceed. Members were excited and exhilarated and somewhat frightened by the tremendous occurrence. A brief reexplanation of the center proposal was given by the secretary, who read portions outlining philosophy and goals. It was again stated that the existing program was to be continued, with an additional program related to the housing needs of the poor. There was uncertainty as to whether the director should be hired prior to the other staff, so that he or she could help in the staff selection. It was pointed out that the director might be much more difficult to find (and might take much longer) than the rest of the staff, thus suggesting the possibility of hiring a skeleton staff first, while the search for the director continued. Finally, this was resolved by a motion, unanimously passed, that the president appoint a personnel committee to interview staff and making recommendations to the board at the September meeting, with emphasis on the director, if possible.

Also significant at this meeting was the secretary's brief statement to the board indicating her feeling that a change in leadership at this time would be healthy for the organization. She expressed a preference for a black director, who could relate well to all facets of the community regarding open housing.

At the next board meeting on September 16, discussion of office rental, the hiring of the director, and budget revisions foreshadowed the types and contents of board meetings which were to follow for the next two years. At this meeting, the Personnel Committee chairman unanimously recommended the hiring of a man from Cleveland as the new director of the Center. Indicative of the poor business sense of the board, as well as its naive trust, was the fact that they agreed to hire the man for a larger salary than that provided for in the OEO budget:

> It was the unanimous recommendation of the committee that Carl G. be hired. However, he will not consider the job for a salary of less than $13,500/yr, and our budget only allows for $11,000 for this position.

> W. T. personally guaranteed the provision of the extra money needed for the salary of Carl G. If OEO budget could not be revised by Chicago, W. T. will raise the money. [37]

What the board did not know, and could not have known at that time, was that OEO rarely expands budgets—it usually decreases them. And people like W. T. could withdraw from a promise of "guaranteed provisions" for money raising, despite the fact that it was he who said "Akron needs Carl G.—let's hire him."

At a special board meeting on September 29, the new director was introduced to the entire board, and further business relative to the new center was discussed. Since the appearance, personality, and character of the new director are discussed at length in the subsequent section on morale, these will not be considered here. Center business focused on the prepartation of the newly acquired suite of offices, telephone installation, furniture acquisition, outdoor office sign, insurance, and the hiring of the new assistant director.

The Fair Housing Center opened on October 15, after a tremendous frenzy of activity during the prior three weeks. The offices

were cleaned, repaired, and painted by a volunteer youth group; files
were turned over to the new offices by volunteers; the director was
sent to a national housing conference in Denver; and constant instructions were received from the local antipoverty agency which was
administering the funding. Because of Personnel Committee delays,
the newly hired secretary was unavailable during the first two weeks
after the Center opened. In addition, the furniture ordered did not
arrive until five weeks later, and the staff had to use makeshift
arrangements for the first month of its operation.

At the first board meeting after the Center opened, on October
21, the first sign of board difficulty appeared:

> Dr. F. suggested a program development committee to
> work with Carl G. in planning our Center program. No
> Board action was taken on this. However, S. P. and
> D. C. offered to accompany Dr. F. to meet with Carl
> to discuss program. The secretary offered to be pre-
> sent also, though she suggested that such a committee
> was premature and also unnecessary since our Proposal
> is very explicit about program. [38]

This represented an initial difference of opinion on board functioning in its new role in relation to the Center. The secretary and
some other board members were fearful of loss of interest and
involvement of the board. They felt that the program of the Center
should be discussed at each board meeting, with policy-making decisions made by the entire board. To place the responsibility for the
program in a subcommittee would weaken board involvement and
interest, according to this view.

It may be conjectured that Dr. F. and some others feared that
the secretary would herself carry too much responsibility for program
planning and heavy involvement with the Center, and wished to shift
this responsibility to another group on the board. In actuality, they
could not have known the secretary's intense relief at transferring
most of her responsibilities to the Center staff. Yet, with this relief,
there was also an anxiety regarding the Center's successful operation.
The secretary had, then, a grave sense of responsibility in making
the transition an effective and competent one, with adequate orientation for the new staff. With this, she also thought it wise and necessary to allow the Center staff ample time to make its own way without
overdirection.

It should be noted that the Center and the FHCS, as its sponsor,
continued to retain separate identities throughout the funded period.
FHCS retained its post office box for mail, and its name. At first,
this seemed less disruptive in terms of public relations and tax-

exemption considerations. Also the uncertainty of funding made it seem reasonable to retain the identity of the older parent organization. However, the separation proved to be a constant source of confusion in the community, though the FHCS was openly acknowledged as the delegate agency sponsoring the Center.

DEVELOPMENT AFTER INSTITUTIONALIZATION

Goals

Whereas in the previous three-and-a-half year voluntary phase the stated goals of FHCS were completely consistent with the operative goals, this was not the case during the two-year phase of institutionalization. In this second phase, the original stated goals were the same during the first year, while the operative goals (program) changed quite rapidly—in fact, almost immediately. Moreover, there came to be differing interpretations among board and staff members of even the original stated goals. During the second year of institutionalization, the stated goals changed and became more consistent with the actual operative goals and program at the Center, though this was not representative of general board opinion.

The proposal for a fair-housing center, originally submitted in 1967 and resubmitted, unchanged, in 1968, was clear. "The goal of the Fair Housing Center will be to accomplish, by a variety of means, equal opportunity in housing in Akron and Summit County.[39] In addition, three major means of achieving this goal were clearly outlined:

1. Making dispersed housing available to minority groups.

2. Establishing a community-wide educational program aimed at (a) creating general acceptance of the need for dispersal of minority families, and (b) stabilizing existing integrated neighborhoods.

3. Cooperating with public officials and civic groups in the solution of area-wide housing problems, particularly as they affect low-income and minority families.[40]

Each of these three major means of achieving the overall goal was further explained in terms of exact, detailed delineations of specific program items to be implemented. The proposal also contained a rationale that further elaborated on the goals and functions of the proposed center. Thus the intent and specific program details were clearly outlined in the original proposal for funding.

Content Analysis. An examination of news articles appearing during the two-year funded phase of the FHCS reveals the changing stated and operative goals of the organization. The first news article (quoted on pp. 140-41), describing the funding of the Center, reflected the views of the volunteer organization and reinforced the original stated and operative goals, adding a new focus on meeting the housing needs of the poor. An article on October 15, 1968 was devoted to an interview with the newly hired director of the Center, and indicates his initial, publicly stated views on open housing.

> Akron has demonstrated to me that it has the climate to bring about a change in attitudes. The Fair Housing board here has operated rather successfully for several years without funds. They have had enough success with untrained individuals working part-time to give evidence that concentrated effort by trained individuals can be quite fruitful. . . .
>
> Integration of schools and the upgrading of the ghetto black in employment can only come through total integration—where people live, work, and relax together. [41]

On November 29 another article exposed the director's position and program regarding discrimination in housing:

> . . .a former Harlem Globetrotter in the 1940's. . . G. believes he can change people's attitudes to sell and rent their homes without regard to the buyer's race. . . . In his office, G. heads a staff of caseworkers who help everyone—black and white—find housing. . . .
>
> The Center, which evolved from the volunteer FHCS, is funded through a one-year Federal grant of $59,726. "When discrimination is found, we sit down and talk the problem over. . . ."[42]

This article caused some consternation among board members, according to the minutes of December 16. In particular, the term "caseworker" was judged invalid, since no staff member had such training. And the wording "evolved from" was questioned, since it implied that the FHCS was no longer in existence. There was also some wry resentment of the reference to untrained individuals in the preceding article, since no staff member had any special training in housing techniques, whereas board members had acquired considerable knowledge in this area.

A news editorial on December 28 was headed "Steps Toward Open Housing," and was primarily concerned with federal and local legal possibilities for open housing. A reference to the Fair Housing Center indicates the general early view of the function of the Center:

> . . . there is the accelerated program now being under-
> taken by the Fair Housing Contact Service under a . . .
> grant from the Office of Economic Opportunity. . . .
>
> With a full-time paid staff and office, the work which
> formerly had been carried on by volunteers can be greatly
> expanded. Specifically, the organization's goal is "expan-
> sion of equal opportunities in housing, so as to provide
> maximum freedom of choice for Negro home seekers."[43]

But on February 17, 1969 an article appeared with the heading "There's More Than One 'Fair Housing' Meaning":

> Fair housing does not always mean finding decent housing
> for blacks in predominantly or all-white neighborhoods. . . .
> Occasionally, the phrase means finding decent housing
> for whites. . . .[44]

An article on May 22 quoted from a public talk given by the Center's field coordinator at the local university. It indicated further changes:

> On open housing, C. said the goal is to provide for
> blacks the opportunity to live anywhere they want —
> in decent housing. . . . "People think blacks are dying
> to move into all white neighborhoods. They are not."[45]

What the article did not reveal was the open skirmish regarding the goals of the Center, between a board member attending the above occasion and the field coordinator. The board member later reported that she had had to openly correct C's statement concerning the goal of the Fair Housing Center. In response to a question from the floor, "Would you say the goal of the Center is no longer integration?", C. had replied, "Yes, I would." Whereupon the board member (female, black) had stood and publicly corrected this, stating that the policy and goal of the FHCS had not changed, and noting that it was the board of directors that set policy for the Center.

On August 11, less than one year after the Center opened, a news article explained the imminent possibility of no refunding for the Center, because of a negative decision of the local antipoverty executive committee. The article noted that

Fair Housing Center officials say they have helped a total
of 1,841 persons find suitable homes to buy or rent. Of
these, 1,589 were officially classified as "poor"—with
incomes less than $3500 annually. . . .

CAC [local antipoverty agency] president W. M. said,
'The basic concept of Fair Housing is integration. We
feel that the real problem of poor people is substandard
housing. . . ."

B. [Center Director] denies this, citing the 15 eviction
cases the center is handling. "We're trying to help these
people, all of them poor, find new places to live. There's
no one else in the city who does this kind of a job."[46]

An editorial on August 20, headed "Akron Still Has Real Need
for Fair Housing Center," demonstrates the change in reference to
the goals and functions of the Center:

Some of the CAC people feel that the Center has primarily
sought integration of housing for middle class Negroes.
This is less important, they feel, than spending money
for economic development with the hope of creating more
jobs for poor people. . . .Housing Center officials counter
by saying that they have helped families in the poverty
class to find homes, including some who have suffered
eviction for non-payment of rent. . . .

To allow the Fair Housing Center to close its doors would
be to say that Akron has no interest in the idea of helping
poor people and black people find homes.[47]

Goal Changes. Thus, in less than one year, the Center came to be
known as an agency that secured "suitable" or "decent" housing for
poor blacks, rather than one openly dedicated to "equal opportunity
in housing for all minorities," or one "seeking homes outside ghetto
areas for minorities," or one "opening non-traditional areas for
minorities by fighting discrimination in housing," as earlier newspaper
references stated.
    The change in stated goals is also clearly reflected in the second
and third proposals submitted to OEO for refunding. These proposals
were prepared by the staff and were not discussed or evaluated by
the board before submission; thus they reflect staff opinion rather than
board opinion. The second proposal stated that the purpose of the Fair
Housing Center would be to solve ten problems.[48] Of these, only one
was clearly related to the original goal of the FHCS. Under Program,
in answer to the question, "What activities will be carried out in the

work program?" 13 activities were listed, of which one was related to the organization's original goal. In answer to the question, "What major steps will be taken to carry out the work program?" ten steps were outlined, of which two were related to the original goal.

The third proposal submitted to OEO for refunding was almost identical to the second, except that it was shorter.[49] Only six problems were cited under Purpose, of which one was related to the original goal. Only nine problems were named under Program, of which one was in keeping with the original goal. Two of the steps under the work program related to the original goal. Thus, both the stated and operative goals changed in the course of the two years of funding, despite the fact that they were clearly and specifically delineated in the original proposal.

Program and Impact

It is extremely difficult, if not impossible, to separate program from morale at this point in the study, for changes in morale were in part reflections of changes in program. However, for purposes of orderly analysis, the attempt will be made to maintain this distinction. Impact, then, will refer here to the external impact of the program on the general community. Morale will follow in the next section, and will refer to the internal impact of the program and other factors on the board and staff members.

It has already been noted that the program of the new Center was intended to be an extension and expansion of the former volunteer program, with an added new emphasis on meeting the housing needs of the poor. Actually, the housing needs of the poor quickly came to be the primary focus of the entire program, with all other aspects of the program relegated to a position of minor importance.

What was not recognized by anyone for some months was that the new focus, as it was implemented, was in direct conflict with the original goals and policies of the organization. Even with the growing recognition of this fact, there was confusion and division among the board members as to how to cope with the situation, and indeed, whether to cope with it at all.

The negative impact of the Center on the community during its first funded year was indicated by community responses to three specific situations promulgated by the Center director and his staff, and by newspaper articles reflecting a negative image of events involving the Center. In addition, the annual report of the Center provoked immediate negative community response, when it revealed publicly the vast extent of Center placement of minority families in racially concentrated or already integrated areas, in direct violation of stated organizational policies.

The second report to the board on December 16, 1968—two months after the Center opened—contained the first clues as to change of policy in the Center's program. This report indicated that 12 rental seekers had moved with Center aid, but only two of these had moved into all-white areas. This meant that ten had been helped to moved into all-white areas. This meant that ten had been helped to move into already concentrated or integrated areas. The report also corporation, and had received $1,300 in pledges for that endeavor.

This last item, though not directly discussed at the board meeting, became the focus of considerable attention in the next two months. The new venture, called Akro-Met, led to open conflict between the staff and some of the board and created public confusion in the community at large.

The minutes of the next board meeting, on January 20, 1969, reflect some of the rising tensions.* The secretary's report noted the following items:

> . . .a meeting on December 27 of the Executive Com-
> mittee and Director concerning budget revisions, field
> program, and Akro-Met; summary of concerned inqui-
> ries from members and supporters about Akro-Met.
> The inquiries were directed to two concerns: is it
> needed, and is it in the best interest of the Center to
> have its staff involved in the formation of it? . . .

> The following action was taken by the Board: further
> discussion of Akro-Met was tabled until written goals
> of Akro-Met are available for consideration.[50]

The Center's program reports to the board in January and February continued to reflect changed program and policy, with minority placements in already segregated and integrated areas. The February report also revealed the growth of other types of housing aid, peripheral or unrelated to the major goal. It was by this time known by the board that such other aid included fixing toilets, repairing heaters, replacing hot-water tanks, and the like.

A partial summary of the first seven-and-one-half months of the Center's program was given by the director at the FHCS annual meeting:

> 680 families or individuals sought aid, of whom 218
> were home seekers. 132 move-ins were made, of which

---

*See Appendix B for community questions about Akro-Met.

117 were rentals; 15 were purchases. Of these, 22 moved
into all white areas, 110 into integrated or concentrated
areas.[51]

Thus the movement of minority families into nontraditional areas
was but a fraction of the total number of move-ins, and roughly
equalled the number that had been placed during the last year of the
voluntary phase of the organization.

The impact of this report on those in attendance at the annual
meeting is only partially revealed by these items from the minutes:

Discussion and questions from the floor followed for a
short time. Some of the questions and comments were:
What is your rationale for placing minority families
in concentrated areas? (Carl G., the Director, stated
there were emergency cases requiring this, and also
OEO said we have to serve the poor.) Another question
was raised concerning placement of black families into
already integrated areas. . . .

V. O. [director of local Urban League] commented that
he thought a Fair Housing group should be concerned with
desegregation. He suggested that we not listen to every
call for separatism that comes our way, since this type
of philosophy has always existed. . . .

G. R. [Board member] stated that we had to serve the
poor. E. D. [black city councilman] called for economic
integration in addition to racial integration.[52]

Actually, the secretary was deluged with phone calls from concerned
members and supporters who did not understand the change in program, and did not understand why the board permitted it to continue.
The newspaper article that reported the statistics presented at the
meeting also drew a barrage of criticism from members and supporters.

Negative Impact. In addition to the Center's report of its program and
the Akro-Met real estate venture already described, two other aspects
of the program had a negative impact on portions of the community
at large during the first year of funding. One concerned the unethical
mortgage counselor engaged by the Center director; the other concerned the rent strike coordinated by the Center staff.

The mortgage counselor was secured by the director three
months after the Center opened, to provide lending assistance to
Center registrants. He came from Cleveland, as did the director,

and worked one or two days a week in the Center office with the home seekers from the Center files. The January report contained the first reference to the matter:

> Arrangements have been made with a Mortgage Broker, by the Director, to take care of Center applicants needing mortgage money for home improvements, second mortgages, so houses would not be forfeited. This service was made available to 4 persons unable to obtain loans through local sources. [53]

What was not known until several months later was that this broker was charging unusually high fees. The situation was exposed four months later at the May 19, 1969 board meeting. Just prior to the meeting, an item in the weekly bulletin of the Akron Area Board of Realtors had been called to the attention of the president, who asked the director for an explanation. The item stated, in part:

ATTENTION ALL MEMBERS

> Recently a Cleveland broker by the name of N. S. . . . placed an ad in the Akron paper as follows:

>> Join our rent-option-lease; your way to home ownership. Maybe the 1968 housing law will help you. Yes, it provides for low income, ADC, welfare. It depends on you plus you can use your labor as funds necessary. Application fee $85. Guaranteed satisfactory or application fee returned. Contact Mr. Mason, Midtown Motel.

> One of our broker members was approached by a prospect who was shown a number of homes. When the prospect found one of interest, the salesperson was told to contact the Fair Housing Center, whereupon Mr. Mason was brought into the transaction as the financing agent. He then endeavored to inject himself into the transaction as a co-broker, but the broker-member refused to accept him other than as the financing agent. . . . [54]

The director's explanation was that the mortgage broker had been engaged only because similar local sources were not available at the time. He then noted that such local sources had finally been obtained, and that the broker's services would no longer be needed. When asked about the fees paid by some 30 Center home seekers, the director replied that these would be returned to the people involved.

However, the enormous negative impact of the news item could not be reversed. It must be recalled that to the FHCS and its supporters the Akron Board of Realtors was the arch-villain. Moreover, the FHCS had strived for three-and-one-half years to project itself as a group with the highest integrity, and had earned and maintained this image. This event, then, not only damaged its reputation in the community, but caused it to appear ridiculous in the eyes of its arch-enemy.

The rent-strike stiuation concerned a blighted building in the heart of the ghetto, where tenants had been encouraged by Center staff to withold rent from the owner until repairs were made. The rent money was held in escrow by the Center director, who turned over the money to the owner before the repairs were made. The local NAACP and some other community organizations were angered by this action, which was reported to them by ghetto residents. The FHCS board did not know of the matter until after it had appeared in the newspaper, and until after the other organizations complained to some board members. Their representatives were encouraged to come to the May 19 board meeting to state their views before the entire board.

NAACP's presentation to the board called for clarification of the roles of the Center and the FHCS, as revealed in the minutes by these four questions and two comments:

What is the role of the Fair Housing Center in relation to the FHCS?

Who sets policy?

Does OEO funding ever conflict with FHCS philosophy and policy?

Can't we work together with FHCS on relocating minority families from blighted areas? NAACP Housing committee believes we all should be working to integrate people outside of concentrated areas.

There is a lack of communication between the Center and other relevant organizations. This was evident in the rent strike situation.

NAACP Housing committee objected to the Center handling the rent strike on Crosier St. They do not believe the building can be rehabilitated; instead they believe it should be demolished. [55]

At this meeting, another board member objected to the wording and tone of the Center report, which contained a very defensive account of the rent-strike stiuation and a hostile reference to "other groups and glory seekers" who wanted to get in on the act." The board member also said he had received many angry complaints about the handling of the recent rent strike. He felt that the Center had alienated a number of people in the community.

The newspaper carried two articles on the rent strike, the first on March 25, 1969, explaining the nature of the strike and the Center's involvement in it. The second article appeared on April 30, and cited 11 local pressure groups "loaded for bear," who were angered by the Center's handling of the situation.* Especially painful for the board was the recognition of many of these groups as former allies and cooperators during its entire voluntary phase.

The rent strike culminated in all tenants moving out of the building, which was condemned by city authorities as unfit for human habitation, and referred to in the newspaper as a "crumbling moldy building that City inspectors have repeatedly cited for 30 years."[56] The strike had been publicized on two television shows, and by four radio stations in addition to the two news articles already cited. Its negative impact in the community regarding the image of the Fair Housing Center was immeasurable.

Content Analysis. During the two years of funded operation, news articles about the Fair Housing Center numbered 36 the first year, and 18 the second year. Of the 36 articles printed in the first year, six had to do with the possible demise of the Center because of the local antipoverty agency dispute over refunding, two with the ill-fated rent strike, one with a case of eviction from a roach-ridden apartment which the Fair Housing Center had found for the tenant, one with a fund-raising dinner dance with keynote speaker Congressman Lou Stokes publicized, one with the nonappearance of Stokes at the same event, and two with the resignation of the director at the close of the year and his immediate hiring by the Public Housing Authority. Thus, almost one-third of the articles that appeared during the first year in the city's only newspaper might be considered somewhat negative with reference to the image of the Fair Housing Center.

Consultants' Critique. At the end of the first year of funding, the board of directors (after considerable and prolonged discussion)

---

*NAACP, Community Action Council, Christians for Commitment, Unitarian Church, Intergroup Ministry, Poor Peoples Headquarters, Urban League, Coalition for Action, Concerned Citizens, Land Improvement Association, and the New Politics League.

engaged a consultant from NCDH to evaluate the Center program.
The consultant's report included the following:

> The reports of progress (Center Reports) show no sub-
> stantial and sustained success at placing black families
> in formerly all white areas, white they show much work
> with general housing services totally unrelated to broad
> changes in the housing patterns. . . .

> A typical report (Aug. 18, 1969) discloses the dismal
> nature of "progress". Of 289 renter carryovers from the
> previous month, only seven were placed in formerly white
> areas. Of 56 buyers, none were placed in previously white
> areas and one found a home in a rapidly changing area. . . .

> Conclusion: Whatever else may be said about the status
> of program and structure, it is abundantly clear that the
> singular goal of promoting unrestricted access to other
> than ghetto housing for Akron's black citizens has not
> been significantly approached. . . .

> Finding housing in "black areas" for every black family
> who has not yet acquired the nerve to break out of the
> latter day plantations or who are too poor to do so, may
> on the surface seem rather humanitarian, but in fact is
> diversionary and self-deceiving. . . .

> One must acknowledge that groups engaged in fair housing
> operations are operating all alone, while there are multi-
> tudes of agencies and organizations who are involved in
> finding housing for poor destitute emergency cases. . . .

> Whatever is not done in "fair housing" by legitimate fair
> housing groups is not done at all by anyone. Fair housing
> specialists who leave the field in an attempt to supplement
> traditional welfare services leave the whole ghetto at the
> mercy of discriminatory forces, and in the end they do
> very little to correct welfare deficiencies. . . .

> Therefore, officers and administrators of fair housing
> operations must be ruthlessly single-minded in their dedi-
> cation to continually open up new housing opportunities
> outside the ghetto, and do this in such a fashion as not to
> be diverted even for one hour by one or a hundred situa-
> tions which should be answered by some other group.[57]

After the board received this sobering and very negative evaluation, a program committee was appointed to develop recommendations

for the second year of activity. Immediately after the board approved a new sweeping program recommendation of the committee, new constraints were imposed on the board and the Center by revised OEO regulations and local antipoverty agency directives.

New Constraints. In effect, there were two restraints: OEO directed that 90 percent of all those served in its programs had to be "poor" by government specification ($3,600 for a family of four); and the local antipoverty agency director ordered that the board could not use the OEO money "for integration," but only to serve the housing needs of the poor, regardless of area.[58]

Board response to these communications is considered in the next section on morale. But it is important to note here that the second year of funding began with these newly imposed restraints which seriously affected program planning, and in fact nullified the new recommendations for program which the board had approved.

In addition to these two restraints imposed on the FHCS program, it is important to note the organizational changes that occurred in the second year of funding, which also affected the program. In the first year the $59,726 budget allowed for a director, an assistant director, a field coordinator, a housing counselor, a secretary, and five field representatives. The second year's operation was allocated only $30,000 by the local antipoverty agency, the Community Action Council (CAC), which allowed for a director, a secretary, and a housing counselor. The first director and the housing counselor left after the first year, leaving the assistant director in charge as acting director. A new housing counselor was hired. The acting director left after six months, and a new acting director was hired to complete the second year. These staff changes necessitated constant searches by the board, and adjustment and readjustment of staff and board. There was, in fact, little time to even consider program or housing or the very reason for their existence.

Thus, the annual report at the end of the second year was a dismal continuation of the trend set during the first year. At the end of the second year of Center operation, 654 additional families had received service. Of these, 36 families moved in white areas, 181 in already integrated or ghetto areas. Housing complaints numbered 437, of which 30 were discrimination complaints.[59]

In an effort to retrieve its image, the board during the second year of funding undertook a community-wide educational campaign. This educational effort consisted of a combined area-wide educational and fund-raising campaign, conducted by the public relations committee set up by the board. The campaign was carried out entirely by volunteers over a three-month period. Fifty thousand pieces of new educational literature and 2000 posters were distributed throughout the metropolitan area. Five giant billboards were rented for one month. Despite the positive impact of this educational effort, the simultaneous efforts of the fund-raising committee did not produce tangible results. Less than $1,000 was raised, falling short of the $28,000 hoped for and needed to maintain an independent office and staff, which would have enabled the FHCS to give up the OEO funding.

At the end of the second year of funding, eight new board members joined the group, the Center was still maintained under OEO funding, a proposal was submitted to OEO for refunding, and the dual uneasy organization continued.

Morale

The responses to events of the first year of funding conditioned the responses during the second year. In seeking to understand the series of incidents and events that affected morale during the first year of funding, one must first understand the "actors" involved, their roles, and their interaction patterns and responses.

The Staff. The two staff members most involved with the board of directors of FHCS were the director and the assistant director. The Director had previously been employed as assistant director of the Aims-Jobs program in Cleveland, an equal-opportunity employment service for minorities. He was a Harlem Globe-Trotter in his younger days, and had been a physical education major at San Francisco State in the 1940s. He continued to live in Cleveland during his period of employment with the Fair Housing Center.

The director gave his age as 48; he was tall, black, and made an excellent appearance. In addition, he had a very deep, mellow voice and spoke well. The Personnel Committee, after interviewing five other applicants for the job, recommended him unanimously to the board. One committee member, a white attorney who had been on the board since its inception, offered to make up the difference in salary if the federal budget could not meet the director's financial demands.

The director was described during the first year in various ways that changed as time passed. At first, he was considered very charming, and possessed of a great personality; it was said that he could get people to do anything just by asking them, and that he was charismatic, and "just lovely." By the end of the first year he was described as arrogant, a rotten administrator, a phony, a manipulator, a liar, and a con man. These epithets were used by some black residents in the community, some board members, and some organizational supporters. His staff remained loyal to him throughout the first year. Few others who had had extensive contact with him remained neutral.

The assistant director (upper middle-class, in her mid-forties, white), was well known to a majority of the board, since she had been a former board member during its first year, a co-chairperson for the housing assistance program. She was a personal friend of three of the board members and was hired primarily because of her prior acquaintance with the goals and program of the organization. Whe was pleasant and likable, though quiet and reserved; and her only previous work experience had been in merchandising. It was thought she could function competently if strong direction were provided by her superior.

Though some board members had reservations about her adequacy in the new position, none were openly voiced at the time of the Personnel Committee's recommendation. She had a personal problem concerning her chronically ill husband, who was hospitalized at the time of her application for the position, and this was also an underlying factor in the recommendation of the Personnel Committee. She needed and wanted the job, and had the sympathy of the entire committee, as well as of her personal friends on the board.

Two other staff members were the field coordinator and the housing counselor, who interacted only peripherally with the board. The field coordinator was a young man in his late twenties, black, with some college education and some community experience with low-income families. The housing counselor hired by the director, was white, had no college education, and no community experience; she was extremely attractive and very pleasant. She had been a secretary and a supporter of the organization. All other staff members were black, including the secretary of the Center and the five part-time field representatives.

The board of directors, has already been described as consisting of eight new members, eight remaining from the previous year (who had been new at that time), and five of the original members, including the president, the secretary, Dr. F. (as research chairman), the social worker (female, black), and another attorney (white, and not the one who offered to pay the salary difference for the director).

Changing Authority Patterns. The pattern of authority and response during the volunteer phase had been characterized by presidential weakness, strong board participation and direction, and secretarial execution. When the funding began, this pattern was no longer operable, though it continued briefly into the funded period.

An example of the difficulties of changing the pattern or authority is revealed in the following incident, which produced the

first staff-board misunderstanding. During the entire funded operation of the Center, the secretary rarely visited the office, for two
reasons. She thought it would be wiser to assume a minor role, and
also she was involved in a venture which necessitated several days
of commuting out of town, leaving her little time. When the new
offices were ready, the secretary turned over to the new staff all
files and documents on the day of opening. At this time, she discussed policies of the organization, and some current minority
housing problems in the community. After the first month of operation, the secretary had little direct contact with the staff outside of
board meetings. Thus, this first visit constituted the major orientation provided by the secretary for the new staff.

However, during the first month of operation the local CAC
was in constant communication with the secretary regarding rules,
regulations, forms, budgets, and so on, pertaining to the Center.
Thus, contrary to her expectations and wishes, the secretary was
placed in the role of middle man, requiring her to pass on these
communications to the president and/or the director of the Center,
as needed. Since the president assumed his former role of passing
all responsibilities on to the secretary, she resorted to sending
memos to the new director in order to transact necessary business.
It was also extremely difficult to reach the Center by phone, since
the instruments were in constant use, and the director was there only
intermittently.

At the end of the first month, when it became known that personnel policies and staff attendance at board meetings were to be
discussed at the next directors' meeting, the CAC advisor suggested
to the secretary that the entire staff not be present when such policies were to be discussed. The memo sent by the secretary to the
director repeated this suggestion, not mentioning its source. This
was responded to negatively by the director, who showed the memo
to the doctor, who called the president, who immediately hurried
over to visit the secretary to discuss the matter.

Though the situation was soon clarified, and the secretary
wrote a note of apology to the director, it indicated an underlying
authority pattern that the staff did not regard the secretary as having
legitimate authority; and the president, who did have the authority,
had not prepared the staff for his earlier typical direction to the
secretary: "Take care of everything." This had worked very well
during the voluntary phase, but obviously was not workable in the
new, funded phase.

Authority has been defined by Max Weber as "the probability
that a certain command from a given source will be obeyed by a
given group of persons."[60] Chester B. Barnard has suggested that

a person will accept a communication as authoritative only when four conditions are met:"he understands it, he believes it is not inconsistent with organizational purposes, he believes it compatible with his personal interest, and is mentally and physically able to comply with it."[61] In the above instance, the director was evolving a pattern of authority of his own as it related to his staff, and he believed the communication of the secretary to be incompatible with his own interest since it interfered with his autonomy.

After board discussion, the matter of staff attendance at meetings was left to the discretion of the director. In keeping with his efforts to promote staff cohesion and unity from the very beginning ("we are a team"), he was accompanied to all board meetings by the assistant director and frequently by one or more other staff persons. It was his practice to attend other community meetings with a similar entourage. While this was felt by some board members to be an admirable display of unity and group harmony, others began to wonder who was running the Center office and program while all the major staff members were attending meetings.

The immediate consequence of constant staff attendance at board meetings was that the members no longer felt free to discuss controversial matters of program and policy at the meetings, which were the only open forums for such discussion. The net result was that some members spoke more frequently with each other outside of meetings, with two cliques eventually forming: those who supported the staff and Center, and those who did not. Some board members were ambivalent, and did not identify with either clique.

Analysis of Organizational Change. Herbert Simon has noted two types of individual response to organizational change.[62] Individuals loyal to the objectives of the organization will resist modification of them and may refuse to continue to participate if the objectives are modified too radically. On the other hand, individuals loyal to the organization will support changes in the objectives if those changes are thought to promote survival and growth. Using this framework, it is suggested here that the board members who came to find fault with the Center operation were more loyal to the objectives of the FHCS than those who supported the Center operation. The Center' supporters were either more loyal to the staff, personally, or to the organization itself, and perceived the funded operation as essential to survival and growth.

In probing further as to why the board seemed unable to engage in open discussion after funding, three factors may be significant: the implicit sociability norm, role uncertainty, and goal ambiguity and eventual conflict.

L. F. Carter has described the sociability factor as behaviors
of the individual related to his efforts to establish and maintain cordial and socially satisfying relations with other group members.[63]
This is one of the three factors cited by Bales in his study of interaction in small groups.[64] It has already been established that the
pattern of board interaction during the volunteer phase was characterized by congeniality and harmony. The rare incidents of differences
of opinion that did occur were resolved amicably through frank inter-
change. The implicit norm, then, was one of maintenance of harmony
leading to compromise and consensus. This norm persisted throughout
the funded period even when it became apparent to all that undercur-
rents of rage, tension, and conflict existed within the board and
between some board and staff members.

The prevailing attitude among most board members seemed
to be that any discussion of matters that might lead to conflict or
might hurt someone's feelings was a violation of the norm. Particularly was this true of the president, who chaired the board meetings.
Thus, even a question about the Center reports was usually received
with anxiety and tension, and disposed of as quickly as possible. A
few board members sincerely believed that the staff and program were
completely above reproach, and others felt that the staff was human
and therefore capable of error. But most believed that they should
be protected from any criticism. Thus the implicit norm persisted,
and though outward harmony was for a time maintained, the underlying disharmony grew.

The second factor, role uncertainty, refers to the fact that the
board had no clear perception of its role as a board in relation to the
operation of the Center. Though it was nominally accepted, according
to the proposal, that the board was to set policy and advise on program,
the boundaries between external policy making and internal administrative decisions were not clear to the board. This was apparent
in the very first board meeting six days after the Center opened. The
minutes of that meeting have already been cited, noting that Dr. F.
suggested a program development committee to work with the director
in planning the Center program. The secretary and some board members opposed this, believing that the program of the Center should be
discussed at each board meeting, with policy-making decisions made
by the entire board, rather than relegated to a subcommittee. This
represented a basic difference of opinion on the board's new role in
relations to the Center. Theoretically, the entire board should have
been responsible for planning program and setting policy. But with
the sociability norm operative, this would have been misconstrued
by some as an admission of inadequacy of staff, and thus could not
be condoned, and thus was not done.

Continuing Role Uncertainty. Role uncertainty and the implicit sociability norm were also apparent in subsequent incidents that took
place during the first year. After the matter of Akro-Met (real estate
company) was raised at the January 20 board meeting (three months
after the Center opened), the first executive committee meeting ever
held by FHCS took place—requested by the secretary, ostensibly to
discuss matters that required decision making between meetings.
Actually, it was for the purpose of engaging in open discussion about
the board-center relationship.

The five original board members were on the Executive Committee, as were two members who had served on the board the previous year. At this meeting, the president was delegated to meet
with the Center director to discuss engaging an NCDH consultant for
program evaluation. In addition, a three-person committee to represent the Executive Committee was approved for the purpose of meeting
with the staff of the Center as needed to discuss policy and program
evaluation. These recommendations were made to the board at its
next meeting in February 1969, and were approved by the board.
However, the president typically exhibited role uncertainty and the
sociability norm in his delegated meeting with the Center director.
In broaching the subject of the consultant, the president later reported
that he had simply asked the director how he felt about the idea of the
board engaging a consultant. The director replied that he did not
think it necessary. There the matter ended.

Though the first year's budget provided $600 for consultation,
the board was unable to function in engaging such professional help,
because the director did not like the idea, and because the board did
not want to offend him by doing it without his consent. It was only at
the end of the first chaotic funded year, after the director had
announced his intention of leaving, that the board finally approved the
hiring of a consultant.

One droll indication of anxiety is seen in the fact that periodi-
cally, when confusion and tensions surfaced, the president appointed
a committee to reexamine the FHCS constitution and make recommendations for revision. (Each time this was done, the committee
reported back that there seemed to be no need for revision. This
seemed to reveal a pathetic attempt by the president to seek concrete
cause of difficulty, which could be altered to ameliorate the situation.)

Almost five months after funding began, the board of directors
had a special meeting to develop Center policies. By this time, enough
board members had communicated their frustrations privately to the
secretary and the president so that such a meeting was perceived as
necessary and crucial by the Executive Committee. The most important question in holding such a meeting was how to exclude the staff

members, so that open discussion could take place. Accordingly, the meeting was held on a Sunday afternoon in a new meeting place.

A list of six topics commonly included under "organizational policies" was distributed to the board members: prior board approval for new action programs, reference to sponsoring group and to outside interests in public relations activity, hiring of consultants, use of office and staff, program priorities, and channels of communication. For each topic the group was to consider whether it should be included in a policy statement; what might be the consequences if it were not included; how it should be stated if it were to be included; and whether any other aspects should be considered.

Of these six, only two were acted on—channels of communication and public relations—representing the least controversial items in relation to the sociability norm, role uncertainty, and goal ambiguity. The lion's effort produced a mouse of a memo, immediately dispatched to the Center staff after the meeting (See Appendix B).

The policies on these two items, stated in the memo, were never observed by either the staff or the board in subsequent months. The one tangible result was the standardization of the Center report forms. However, what remains significant about the policy-making meeting is the nature of the discussion that took place. For the first time in the five months after funding, the board was frank, and the comments about the Center program were made heatedly and openly. Response was equally heated and open.

Negative comments about the Center operation referred to its lack of emphasis on open housing and overemphasis on other housing problems that were considered trivial. "Are we in the business of fixing toilets or are we supposed to be doing something about open housing?" "Are we just a tool of the CAC, running their housing service program?" Comments defending the Center operation generally referred to the source of funding as justification for program. "Since we're funded by OEO, we have to serve the needs of the poor." Some defensive comments also referred to the belief that blacks were no longer interested in integration. "If these people don't care about open housing and moving out of the ghetto, why should we force it on them?" Thus, goal ambiguity and conflict were evident. But role uncertainty and the implicit norm continued to prevent the board from resolving its dilemmas.

Goals and Program Questionnaire. The depth and extent of the board's dilemmas were clearly and dramatically indicated in the answers to a questionnaire sent to all board and staff members by the author on April 2, 1969, six months after funding. The results of the questionnaire are extremely significant in that they reveal a marked perception by the respondents of the disparity between the

goals and the program of their funded operation—a further major
indicator of the three operative factors previously cited which continued to paralyze the board into inaction.

The letter accompanying the questionnaire asked for help in
private research the author was conducting as part of her graduate
work (see Appendix C). This research was actually the dissertation,
though this could not have been stated, due to the covert participant
observer role the writer played. The board knew the author was
doing a dissertation on open housing as a social movement, but they
did not know that one portion of that study was the case study involving
themselves. Thus the stated purpose of the questionnaire was modified.

The respondents were asked to rank six goals in order of importance, in answer to the question, "What do you think the goal of the
Fair Housing Center should be?" The goals listed were:

a.   Helping the poor with day-to-day housing problems
     (evictions, tenant-landlord complaints, repairs,
     etc.)

b.   Increasing the supply of housing units for the poor.

c.   Educating the community about open housing.

d.   Influencing local decision-making to further our goal.

e.   Fighting discrimination.

f.   Ending segregation by making housing available on
     a dispersed basis.

g.   Other (please specify)

In addition, they were asked to rank the same six goals, in
order of emphasis, in answer to the question, "Which goals do you
think the Fair Housing Center is now emphasizing?" One more question was open-ended, relating to the perception of problems in the
Center-board situation.

Of 25 questionnaires sent, 20 were returned. Of the 20 returned,
the four staff members and one board member did not rank either
question, (that is, they ranked all items as 1, the top rank); and one
board member returned the questionnaire unanswered, with a note
of explanation. Thus, 14 board members ranked the goals. For each
item, a mean rank was obtained. The items were then rearranged to
correspond to the total mean ranking. The discrepancy of the mean
ranks was noted, with items a and f yielding the greatest discrepan-
cies. The results are reproduced in Table 3.

TABLE 3

Rank Discrepancy of Goals and Program

What should the goal of the Fair Housing Center be?		Which goal is the Center now emphasizing?	
Item	Rank	Item	Rank
f	1.69	a	1.60
c	2.66	c	2.92
d	3.13	e	3.14
e	3.61	d	3.53
a	3.86	f	3.61
b	4.28	b	4.38

Source: Compiled by the author.

Item a referred to helping the poor with day-to-day problems. Item f referred to ending segregation by making housing available on a dispersed basis. Thus, it was perceived by those who responded that goal f was the most desirable goal of the Center, while goal a was one of the least desirable goals for the Center to pursue. As for the actual Center emphasis, goal a was perceived as receiving the greatest emphasis by the Center, while goal f was receiving almost the least emphasis by the Center.

Of the 14 respondents who ranked goals, ten checked "yes" in answer to the open-ended question, "Do you think there are any problems that exist in the present Center-FHCS situation?" Of those who did not rank goals, the three staff members checked "no" in response to the open-ended question, as did the one board member who also did not rank. One staff member left the question unanswered.

Thus, those that responded and ranked were most aware of staff-board problems, or most willing to reveal such awareness. Those that responded and did not rank were either unaware or unwilling to reveal their awareness of the existence of problems. It is hardly conceivable that at that time, six months after funding, anyone on the staff or board could have been unaware of the deep conflicts that pervaded the group. It must be assumed that, either by personal inclination or by direction, the staff was unwilling to

---

The author is grateful to Marie Haug Case Western Reserve University for suggesting this method of analysis.

TABLE 4

Perception of Staff-Board Problems

Respondents	Yes	Uncertain	No	No Answer	Total
Rankers	10	4	0	0	14
Non Rankers	0	0	4	2	6
Total	10	4	4	2	20

Source: Compiled by the author.

rank and admit the existence of problems. It is also significant that two board members who did not return the questionnaire were open admirers of the director, and the one board nonranker was a personal friend of the assistant director.

No significant response pattern was ascertained between old and new board members. Of the 14 who responded, six had been on the board for three or four years, four were members in their second year, and four were new. Of those who did not return the questionnaire, one was new and three were old. However, it was confirmed, in a follow-up phone call, that only one old board member, Dr. F., and the one new member consciously failed to return the questionnaire. For the two others, it was an oversight. The phone conversation with Dr. F. was noted in the writer's journal:

Routine check of non-returners of goal questionnaire: Dr. F. said, "I had some question about this. I thought it might get back to the Center and reopen old wounds. . . . If it's for pure research, that's one thing, but that's what I wasn't sure of. . . . Neither was another Board member (referring to "new" non-returner, an admirer of the Center). . . the Center is just beginning to get settled. . . it would be a shame to start any trouble with these results."

Note: It seems that he must think the results will be negative—or else why would he fear their impact on the Center? General mistrust of my motives too—though he said, "You know I love you, you're my friend, I can tell you anything, though we've had words. . . ."[65]

The journal entry was revealing not only in reference to awareness and anxiety about the Center-board relationship, but also in its indication of the extreme difficulties involved in participant-observation research, particularly when the role of the observer is a covert one.

The open-ended answers to the question regarding Center-board problems also indicated awareness and anxiety about the organization's problems. Three major problem areas were indicated: staff-board relations, program, and source of funding. Staff-board relations were commented on most frequently (ten times), program next (six), and funding least (five). The respondents were instructed, "If you checked YES, please describe briefly any problems as you see them, and indicate (if possible) any suggestions you have for reducing these."

Comment #11:
  (1) Need for better communication; I think we are on the way
       to correcting this.
  (2) Need for funds from two or more sources (which we are
       seeking). We need "poverty funds" to help the poor, and
       other funds for our broader task.

Comment #8:
  Misunderstanding and apparent lack of trust among Board
  members and staff members.

Comment #5:
  Problem of transfer of authority from the FHCS which was
  spearhead-spokesman before formation of Center which serves
  in the public view as the present spokesman for "Fair Housing"
  in the community. In terms of the possible change in emphasis
  from desegregation to aid for low-income minority groups,
  perhaps Center would more aptly be called "Adequate Housing
  Center."

Comment #27:
  Poor communication between Board and staff.
  Weak Board leadership.
  Confusion and misunderstanding concerning goals of Center
       and Functions of Board.
  Poor staff administration.
  Uncertainty of funding.

Comment #10:
  I think the staff has a big heart, but I feel there are agencies
  already in existence to do a. (helping the poor with day-to-day
  problems), and the staff should properly refer their clients
  to these agencies, or themselves call the appropriate agency
  and get assurance that they will help. Seems to me this would
  be the best compromise.

If we are forced by OEO to have goals in line with OEO, we will have to dilute our original effort. I would like to see us divorced from OEO, but I know I'm dreamin'.

Comment #1:

How to relate to other agencies, government and private in the city, that have similar goals—how best cooperate and work together. Think main goals should be to help blacks move in to all-white areas.

Comment #19:

(1) Center needs assurance of added financing.
(2) Center should be blended into FHCS.
(3) The problem in making the Center effective in desegregating housing is involved in the source of funds. Presumably, adequate funding from other sources would allow renewed interest in integration.
     However, the idea of handling day-by-day housing complaints is not a bad one, since no other agency exists to coordinate housing complaints, even if some of these problems can be cleared by one group or another.

Goal Conflicts. Program priorities were finally considered by the board, but only indirectly, at a special board, but only indirectly, at a special board meeting on April 29, 1969. A second proposal for funding had been prepared by the proposal committee, and the meeting was called to consider and evaluate this proposal, which was to be submitted to sources other than OEO (Ford Foundation, HUD, other foundations, and so on). The minutes of this meeting reflect serious division of opinion as to the meanings of the stated and operative goals. The meeting is also significant in that it marks the first open board discussion, with staff present, on a controversial matter:

There was discussion of the goals stated in the Proposal, as reflected in the proposed program of the Center. One point raised was whether we are violating the principles of the fair housing movement by placing twice as many black families in black areas as in white areas. Should we be doing this at all, or should such placement be referred to other sources, i.e., real estate agents, etc.

Discussion of the meaning of fair housing followed. One explanation made was that the meaning is quite specific and standardized nationally and is: the opening of new neighborhoods to minority families. The question of freedom of choice was raised: what about black families who don't want to leave the ghetto?

One response was that there can be no true freedom of
choice until there is an open community—and shouldn't
our prime task be the opening of the community (in
order to make real freedom of choice possible), and
are we any different from Urban Renewal Relocation and
Metropolitan Housing Authority, both of whom we've
been objecting to for years?

The questions were not resolved.[66]

Though the questions were unresolved, some attempt to grapple
with the problem was made in the final draft of the second proposal
for funding (from sources other than OEO). This proposal again
reiterated equity in housing as the prime goal, and gave top priority
to the objective of "making dispersed housing available to minority
groups." This was submitted in May to HUD and various foundations,
all of which refused funding.

Shortly after the special board meeting on goals, another
Executive Committee meeting was held on May 4, 1969. This was
the second that year. Following is the agenda for that meeting.

During the past week, the following complaints about
the Center have been received:

1. Fee Splitting: It is believed that the real estate
   agent employed by the Center (3/4 time) plans to
   split her commissions with the staff.

2. Placements: The Center is placing twice as many
   black families in concentrated areas as in white areas.

3. Tenant strike escrow fund: It is considered a violation of trust for the Center Director to have returned the rent escrow fund to the landlord. There
   is dissatisfaction with the way the strike was planned
   and executed.

4. Budget changes in Proposal: Though a 20 percent
   salary increase was proposed for all other staff,
   A. C.'s [field coordinator] proposed salary was
   decreased.

5. Disorganization re hours: The two top staff members repeatedly come in late; the secretary is sometimes unable to eat lunch; sometimes no other staff
   members are present, etc.

6. Nature of association with builders, etc.: The
Center Director seems to promote a few "favorites"
and has been criticized for this and other handling
of land acquisition matters.

Of the six items, four were agreed upon as requiring immediate attention (#1, 3, 5, 6) and a three member committee was
delegated to discuss them with the director on May 9, over lunch.
It is most significant that the crucial item #2, relating to goals and
program was not referred for discussion. Thus, several internal
administrative matters were perceived as soluble and within the
boundary of the board's role. But the grave policy matter was not
perceived as soluble, though clearly within the boundary of the
board's role, and thus was left unresolved.

Each of the three members of the Executive Committee delegation later reported to the secretary the results of the meeting
with the director. Each had a different, though characteristic, response to the confrontation. The president cheerfully noted that the
matters had been discussed, and that he thought everything would
be fine. He expressed his disapproval of the attorney's open angry
remarks to the director, and expressed his approval for the tactful
handling of the director by Dr. F. Dr. F., in turn, noted soberly
that the meeting had taken place, but that the director gave little
evidence of taking heed of it. And the attorney said darkly that the
whole meeting was a waste of time, and the director would go on
doing as he pleased. Each referred to matters that had been discussed, — all different. The one tangible result was that the real
estate agent on the staff was asked to resign, and the fee-splitting
item was resolved. No other situation was changed.

It was at the next board meeting, on May 19, that the angry
community delegation appeared before the board with its charges.
In addition to the Board of Realtors' complaint regarding the mortgage
counselor, and the NAACP complaints about the handling of the rent
strike, one long-time supporter and volunteer and well-known community member asked, "Why didn't anyone come to see my house
when I listed it with the Center? It is moderately priced ($13,000)
and in a white neighborhood. Has your policy changed? Don't you
deal with middle-income people any more?" The board was quite
stunned by this barrage of criticism, and the implicit sociability
norm was shattered in the face of such confrontation.

The fourth annual meeting of the FHCS, was held on June 2,
1969. The board secretary's final report indicates another desperate
attempt to clarify issues:

The secretary's final report concerned thoughts about
Fair Housing, and included a clarification of the relationship between the Fair Housing Contact Service and
the Center. She raised the question of the meaning of
Fair Housing, equal opportunity in housing, and especially freedom of choice in housing. She cited the conditions that first gave rise to our beginning a fair housing
group in Akron: steady growth of segregation due to massive continuing discrimination. She noted the consequences
of segregation, and stated that those conditions were just
as rampant today as they were then, which made our purpose just as vital and meaningful as when we began.

She noted that real freedom of choice in housing is
impossible until there is an open community; thus, our
prime task is still the opening of new neighborhoods to
minority groups, to provide a living demonstration of
real freedom of choice.

She suggested that since billions have been spent on
segregation and discrimination, it was time to spend
some on desegregation. She challenged any fair housing
group (including the Center staff) to ask each day what it
could do to change the system. [67]

At this time, board leadership changed, with Dr. F. assuming
the presidency. He was generally thought to be the only one who could
adequately handle Center problems, especially the director. Dr. F.
quickly reasserted the implicit sociability norm at the July 21 board
meeting when he said, "This is not the year for controversy - we
want no more 'falling-outs'."

The Doleful Dance. Immediately a controversy arose over the question of the director's salary. The attorney, who had originally offered to make up the difference between the director's promised
salary and the amount in the federal budget, stated his intention of
not meeting this obligation unless the board made an attempt to raise
the money ($2,700). Thereupon, a fund-raising committee was set
up, and its chairman announced at the public fourth annual meeting
(before this was approved by the board) that a fund-raising dinner-
dance would be held. Few on the board were receptive to the thought
of this gala festivity, in view of past constant frustrations and current
heated tempers. The minutes did not fully reflect the disgust some
Board members felt about the dinner-dance:

The announcement of a dinner-dance to be held in the
fall touched off a turbulent discussion as to purposes

of money to be raised, and of the (suggested) obligation
of the board to reimburse W. T. (attorney) for assuming
the responsibility of a portion of the Center Director's
salary.

There was some question about community support for
such a venture.

This whole venture engendered enormous ill-will on the board—
especially since no public mention could be made of the real purpose
of the event—to pay the director. It was simply publicized as a fund-
raising event to provide for operating expenses of the Center. Since
by this time there was little support on the board for the director,
the work for the dinner-dance was done largely by two members who
had consistently supported and admired him, by the attorney who had
promised to make up the difference, and by the staff of the Center—
especially the director.

The event itself was a doleful one, at best. The widely touted
keynote speaker failed to arrive. Only 100 people appeared in the
huge ballroom, the food was not consistent with the $10 fee, and by
the time the huge orchestra struck up the music, only a handful of
people remained to dance. One joyful moment occurred when the
Director publicly intimated that he was leaving.

Exit Director. Soon after this, he did indeed announce his resignation
"to save the Center," which was interpreted in several ways by
members of the board and members at large. The news announcement
of his departure stated:

FAIR HOUSING DIRECTOR QUITS

Fair Housing Center Director [Carl G.] has submitted
his resignation, saying this is "the only way to save the
Center". . . . [G's] resignation comes in the wake of
futile efforts by the center's board of directors to find
new funding for the upcoming year. . . . The CAC's executive committee cut back the FHC's budget to $31,000,
which board members feel is not enough to operate a
meaningful program. . . . After CAC's decision to make
the 70 pct. cutback in FHC's funds, the center's officers
and board members tried to obtain financing from HUD,
local sources, and the Ford Foundation. So far, all of
these efforts have failed to bear fruit. . . .[68]

Shortly after, one additional news article about the ex-director
appeared:

[C. G.] JOINS STAFF OF AMHA

[C. G.], head of the Fair Housing Center until it withered
from financial malnutrition, has joined the staff of the
Akron Metropolitan Housing Authority. . . as administrative assistant to the AMHA director. . . . When the Fair
Housing Center's funds were slashed from $59,726 to
$31,000, he resigned "to save the center."[69]

This had been foretold by a number of board members for some
months before, since the director had worked very closely during
the entire year with the arch-enemy of the FHCS, the director of the
MHA. The housing counselor soon followed the director to the MHA.

Board-Staff Interplay. The interplay between the old leader (the
volunteer secretary) and the new administrator (the director) throughout the first year of funding merits consideration here. It has been
noted that the secretary was greatly relieved at shifting her heavy
responsibilities to the Center staff. When the director was first
hired, the secretary regarded him as something of a messiah, as
did many other board members. The initial relationship between
the secretary and the new director was one of warm cordiality and
mutual admiration.

This quickly changed when the secretary became aware of the
ineptness and malfunctioning of the director and his staff. She attempted for some time to keep to herself the growing accumulation of
distasteful episodes and community criticism, but finally shared these
with the Executive Committee of the board and then the board itself.
The first community criticisms of the proposed real estate venture
(Akro-Met) were communicated to the secretary, still regarded in
the community as the leader of the organization. In her normal role,
these criticisms were routinely transmitted to the board. The director was extremely upset by this public acknowledgement of criticism
of his venture, and reacted with defensive hostility. The relationship
between the secretary and director was never the same after this,
moving from the initial warm admiration to veiled indifference to
latent hostility to open hostility by the end of the year.

The director was in the difficult position of replacing a leader
whose presence and influence continued to be evident. Moreover, she
was a woman, and white. Though her physical presence was evident
only at board meetings, her previous role as leader kept pursuing
the new director at every turn. When the Center office opened, the
first phone calls were for her. Some callers refused to talk to the
new director and insisted on speaking only to her. Wherever the
director went and in every new community situation, he found himself

confronting references to the former leader. Thus, this constant reminder of the leader he replaced must have been awkward and painful for him. He thought it important to have her approval of his activities, but at the same time he did not want to appear inadequate by seeking her advice.

It was, thus, an especially tense situation when the first criticisms of his new venture were brought to the board by the former leader. The ensuing hostility was understandable from both viewpoints: his, because her presence annoyed him and made him feel inadequate and especially because she presented the first criticisms of his program; hers, because he was incompetent and was hurting the program which she had begun and had worked so hard to implement, and she was bitterly disappointed in him and the entire operation.

Second Funded Year. Thus the second year of funding began with the director gone, the weak assistant director elevated to acting director, a new president of the board—Dr. F.—and half a budget for the Center. Its image in the community was shattered, all major issues were unresolved, and a new one had been added: If the program had been a dismal failure with a staff of ten and a $59,725 budget, how could there be an effective program with a three-member staff and a $31,000 budget? Though the ex-secretary (now the public relations chairman) made repeated attempts to persuade the board to search for a new, top-notch director, the board and the new president were unconvinced that this course of action should be taken, and the issue was unresolved.

The Letter. The fundamental problem of the year was the letter sent to the board by the local antipoverty agency director, noted earlier, addressed to the president of the board. It informed the board that the OEO-allocated money was not to be used for purposes of integration, but rather to meet the housing needs of the poor:

> At your last Board meeting, there was some discussion
> centering around using the money which is delegated to
> the FHCS to operate the Fair Housing Center, and not
> following OEO guidelines. I MUST WARN NOT ONLY
> THE BOARD OF DIRECTORS OF FHCS, BUT ALSO THE
> STAFF OF THE FAIR HOUSING CENTER, THAT ANY
> VIOLATION OF THE CURRENT CONTRACT UNDER
> WHICH YOU OPERATE, WILL BE CAUSE FOR MY
> OFFICE TO EXERCISE THE OPTION TO CANCEL. In
> order to make myself quite clear, the Fair Housing Cen-
> ter is to serve poor people in helping them to obtain

suitable and decent homes, apartments, and whatever other areas of assistance is required in housing.

This Office will not tolerate the use of OEO funds for any other purpose. If some of the people on the Board of Directors feel that the direction of the Fair Housing Center should be in the area of integrated housing, then I will advise them to conduct this type of activity on a volunteer basis.

It is my hope that the FHCS's Board of Directors will not continue to misunderstand the intentions of the Community Action Council. [70]

The tragic element of this letter was that it came just after the board had engaged a consultant and had reached consensus on a new program for the year, refocusing on the original goals of the organization. The minutes barely indicate the deep despair and frustration of the entire board during the discussion of the letter: [71]

First order of business was discussion of a letter from the Director of CAC, concerning our proposed use of OEO monies. It was moved and seconded that the question of continuation of Center funding with OEO be considered at the next Board meeting. Motion carried.

There was much discussion as to whether the Contact Service should disassociate itself from the Center, but due to the absence of so many Board members, it was moved and seconded that the question of continuation of our association with the Center be delayed. Motion carried.

K. R. gave the report of the personnel committee. Recommendations: 1) That we begin immediately to search for a director for the Center. 2) That Item 4 of the Program recommendations (area involvement) be implemented as soon as possible by the Contact Committee.

These recommendations brought on more questions concerning our future involvement with the Center. J. S. moved that we reconsider the earlier motion as to dissociation from the Center. Motion seconded and carried.

After a long and frustrating discussion concerning availability of monies with which to hire new personnel, time elements involved, CAC opinions of whatever decisions are made, D. moved that present staff be retained, that we insist that the Center live up to CAC regulations, and that the FHCS implement all other parts of its program through a vigorous volunteer organization. Motion was seconded and carried, with four abstentions.

The author's journal entry on the same meeting is somewhat more revealing:[72]

A new low in chaos and division and confusion, resulting from F's letter. Meeting began with Phil (attorney) calling for action to give back the OEO money. I seconded. (This was unnecessary since meeting had not even been called to order yet! Dr. F. immediately said if we gave up the Center he would resign. Phil said if we didn't, he might resign. Impasse. Much endless commenting on the letter. Dr. F. dragged out old grievance about being rebuffed 1 1/2 years ago re poor people survey. Phil finally said he would postpone his motion to the next meeting if it were placed on agenda for discussion - (after Judy pointed out that 9 people shouldn't make such a basic decision). This was later reconsidered, after a straw vote showed only Phil and me voting to give back funds. Personnel committee recommendations were made haltingly by K. R. Board passed the one concerning implementation of area involvement program. They talked around and around the other re hiring a Director—and finally Dottie's motion passed: that we retain present staff and reactivate volunteer program separately and with full speed. I pointed out that a permanent commitment to staff for the rest of the year meant that we could not hire a Director at all. At 11 p.m. this dreadful decision was made. . . only 7 of us remained.

And I am convinced now that there is absolutely no hope for an effective program without a Director, and certainly none with the present staff operation. So I may as well resign myself to this—I would so much like to resign from the whole thing. Only the field research keeps me in it—very weary and discouraged by it all.

How odd that Dr. F. said it was "dishonest and vicious" for us to even consider giving up the Center. Seemed to think we had an obligation to CAC to carry through. I believe it is truly dishonest for us to continue under present circumstances—because we are supposed to be working for desegregation and are really ghettoizing poor people as well as hurting stabilization efforts.

I wonder if I'm really right in thinking that Dr. F. does not want a Director because he has much more power without one. No action taken on a meeting with CAC director to clarify CAC's exact meaning in the letter. Very unsatisfying all around. Dr. F.: a marginal man. As leader, he reflects the ambiguities of his situation with ambivalent reactions.

Board Despair. This journal entry not only indicates the author's deep involvement and concern with the situation, both mirroring and influencing other board members' responses, but also contains a revealing item of significance. The fact that no action was taken on the drastic letter is itself a profound indicator of the board's state of morale at that time.

The logical expected response to such a letter would have been a fight, a challenge, an action plan to contest it, a confrontation with OEO, or at least a meeting with the sender of the letter requesting clarification or modification. Though the ex-secretary suggested such a meeting, the board response was immediate and final in its rejection: "What good would it do?"

Thus, the board's despair was evident in its total submission to this final destroyer of its goal and program. It was noted at the outset that the board's responses to the events of the first year of funding conditioned its responses in the second year. The first year began with great hope for what the Center could be. The growing and finally overpowering disillusionment during the first year stemmed from the negative impact of the Center's activities in the community, as well as from its own inability to cope with the entire situation. This group, which had had such pride in its image of integrity and vigorous productivity, was shattered in the face of what it had become during the first year of funding. Then, after torturous self-searching, it had finally achieved consensus on resolving its goal conflicts. Having renewed so recently its hope in what it might again become, the letter—coming when it did—broke the spirit of the group. This was why no action was taken.

The Final Blows. The next series of small but persistently troublesome events were merely the final blows. The Center had to move its offices (to the basement of the CAC building, which was the only free space found, since OEO refused to pay rent any longer); the Center acting director and field coordinator could not work together; the acting director fired the field director; the acting director resigned, and a new acting director was found; the Center had to move its offices again (because the CAC building was condemned as unfit); the ex-field director filed grievance complaints against the FHCS for illegal firing; the new acting director submitted to OEO another proposal for refunding, which only the president (Dr. F.) and one attorney saw; the new acting director had personnel problems with the housing counselor.

A New Start. At the fifth annual meeting of FHCS, a new president was elected (attorney Phil R.), and eight new board members joined 11 who were reelected. Both former presidents left the board, leaving only two of the original founding members of the organization: the new president, and the former secretary. The new president immediately reactivated all volunteer committees, which responded with renewed—though cautious—hope for a better future.

The final four journal entries of the writer indicate a gentle upsurge in morale as the group prepared itself for renewed task orientation, having finally abandoned all hope of having an effective funded operation.

> First Board meeting with new people and new President. Very informal, very friendly. Set up committees. Public Relations committee to work with new Board people expanding volunteer operation. Will spin off into separate committees when stable and expanded sufficiently. This might work. Underlying dilemma re Center mentioned. Phil said, "Let's just use the office as best we can for our own purposes". Seemed to think we would not be refunded. Everything in flux as usual. [73]

> Met with Public Relations committee. Divided tasks. Maybe this will work. One new member queried, "Has anyone thought of questioning OEO as to their views of our purpose, and as to lifting some constraints?" Suggested she raise this at Board meeting. [74]

> Board meeting very cozy, friendly, relaxed. Report on expanding volunteer committees well received. In car, going home K. R. said, "This meeting made me feel better than I have in months. For the first time I feel as though something positive may happen. Things might work out."[75]

> Matter of Proposal raised. The one submitted was almost identical to the one submitted last year, and is most certainly not a strong statement of our principles and goals. It was only seen by outgoing President and outgoing attorney. New President raised question as to what to do about this. Decided to copy exerpts of Proposal, send to each Board

member for study, and come to next meeting (September 21) prepared to make final decision as to whether we want to continue our alliance with CAC (local anti-poverty agency), or give up the funding.[76]

Crucial Item. On September 21, 1970 the board voted unanimously to give up the funding and resume its former totally volunteer status.

RETURN TO VOLUNTEER STATUS, 1970-74

After one glaring headline* announcing the dramatic return of the funding, all was quiet. The board of directors was already doing all the volunteer work for fair housing through its newly reorganized committees, so the transition back to the total volunteer status was not a traumatic one. In fact, there was a shared, open sense of relief and freedom as the directors slowly took hold of the destiny of the organization. The former volunteer telephone secretary was reactivated to receive phone calls, and the old post office box was again secured for the receipt of mail.

Searching for a specific new program focus at its next meeting, the board heard a report from J. S., the public relations chairperson (former board secretary and founder) concerning an audit of housing discrimination that had been conducted in St. Louis some months earlier. Mrs. S. was urged by the board to send away for the written report of the audit, for presentation at the next board meeting. At that time, she offered it to the board as an idea for a new program activity for FHCS to undertake in its newly freed status. The board somewhat timidly agreed, if Mrs. S. would assume the responsibility of organizing and implementing the project. So began an activity that was to have profound implications and repercussions, not only in Akron—for the FHCS itself and the entire community—but also across the country, where the news of audits eventually reached other groups and affected the whole open-housing movement.

In the next four years, there were three things that affected the destiny of FHCS: the audits (three successive ones covering 5000 rental units and 40 real estate companies from 1971 to 1974), the winning of the National Volunteer Award (a $5000 prize awarded in Washington, D. C. in 1973), and the HUD-funded summer Demonstration Project in 1973. Each of these three events will be described,

---

*Actually, it was the funding for a third year that was not accepted. The news article describing this is in Appendix B.

and it will be seen that a snowball effect was produced, catapulting FHCS toward success and eventual refunding at the end of the four-year period.

The Audits

Setting. The federal open-housing law (Title VIII of the 1968 Civil Rights Act became fully effective only in 1971, and little research had been done to test its impact when FHCS began its audits. In Akron, the black population increased between 1960 and 1970 from 13 percent to 17.5 percent. In the suburbs it declined from 1.6 percent to 1.2 percent during that time. The white population in the city declined during the same period, and increased in the suburbs during that time, following the general pattern throughout the country of increasingly black cities surrounded by white suburbs.[77] The audits were designed to measure the extent of equality of opportunity in housing for blacks. Each audit will be described as to method, findings, and results.

Audit I; Real Estate Companies

The first audit was a survey of attitudes and practices in the real estate industry relating to open housing. There were two phases of the study: the first examined awareness of open-housing legislation among executives of real estate companies; the second examined the actual practices in the housing industry regarding equal housing access for blacks, and the second phase that was patterned after a similar survey conducted by the Greater St. Louis Committee For Freedom of Residence.

Phase I. The first phase of the audit was conducted in January, 1971 by eight trained, white volunteers who interviewed the presidents of 24 of the largest and most prestigious real estate companies in the Akron metropolitan area. The stated purpose of the interview was to gather data on the housing market in the area. The open-ended questions were designed to reveal progressively four types of infor-mation: the types, price ranges, and geographical areas of housing handled by the specific company; the usual procedures of buying or renting housing through the company; the extent of service to black home seekers; and awareness of open-housing legislation. Each volunteer was instructed to keep written records of all responses, verbal and nonverbal. Volunteers were trained in one orientation session, and received both verbal and written instructions.

Of the 24 companies, only two refused to participate, and one was unavailable, making a total of 21 surveyed companies. Sixty-two

percent of these indicated that an employment and/or income check
and credit check were standard procedures followed before housing
service was rendered to clients seeking housing. Seventy six percent
of the companies indicated specific knowledge and awareness of open-
housing laws.

The key question (Number 7) was worded: "Sometimes people
don't want to sell or rent to Negroes. How do real estate companies
handle such a situation?" Forty two percent of the executives indicated
that they would not deal with a seller who wanted to discriminate
against blacks; 14 percent stated they would merely inform the client
this was against the law: and 7 percent stated there was no such problem possible, since "no one engaged in discrimination any more."
Two executives stated that they showed homes to all though they recognized "the right of the owner to refuse." One company president
stated that he did not deal with black home seekers, "I turn them
away," since they are "not educated enough and too much trouble."

The key question evoked noticeable anxiety responses in some
of the company executives. Such responses were noted in the volunteer reports as follows: "Slightly wary after Number 7"; "Suspicious,
but seemed to answer all questions except Number 7 quickly and
openly"; "Company president said after Number 7, " 'I would rather
not elaborate further on this item at this time' '; "Very cooperative
until Number 7, then wouldn't comment— he said 'You are getting too
far afield'." Several other executives became very talkative with
Number 7, often about extraneous matters. One executive refused to
answer any other questions after Number 7 (there were a total of
ten questions).

One question specifically asked if there were any recent laws
that affected real estate companies, and 76 percent of the company
presidents referred to open-housing legislation. This majority
response indicated great awareness of the existence and implications
of the new federal open-housing law, which by now was fully effective
in coverage.

Phase II. In the second phase of the audit, six pairs of trained black
and white volunteers contacted 13 of the above real estate companies
for actual housing assistance, between February and June 1971. Each
black and white pair was matched as to age, family composition, and
income level, so as to achieve close similarity in all respects except
that of race. Each pair contacted the same real estate companies
(at different times, with black preceding white), requesting the identical type of housing unit (that is, with regard to number of bedrooms,
price range, rental or purchase). All volunteers received verbal and
written instructions, and kept written accounts of their experiences,
which provided the basis for the final analysis of results.

<u>Findings</u>. Twelve out of the 13 companies indicated discrimination in one or more of the following seven categories: locations offered, forms required, access to units, access to listings, price differentials, courtesy, and racial remarks. Discrimination was defined as any difference in treatment on the basis of race. The one company in which discrimination was not indicated was one for which one partner of a pair of auditors did not turn in a report; thus, there was no basis for comparison with the other partner's report, and no evidence of discrimination.

Table C.1 indicates that a total of 29 counts of discrimination were found, reflecting one count each in five different companies, two counts each in two companies, three counts in two other companies, four counts each in two additional companies, and six counts in one company. The types of discrimination the black volunteers encountered were in terms of locations offered, price differentials, access to units, access to listing, forms required, and courtesy. The types of discrimination the white volunteers encountered were in terms of locations offered, access to listings, and racial remarks. Examples of each of these types of discrimination follow.

Concerning locations offered, whites were not offered housing in integrated areas unless they specifically requested it. Blacks, on the other hand, were consistently offered housing in integrated areas or black areas even though they did not request it. In addition, they were not readily offered housing in some all-white areas, but had to insist on such areas. In some instances, such areas were not made available to them, even upon request. This is "steering" and violates the Fair Housing Laws.

With regard to forms required, in one company the black volunteer was told he had to quality for a Master Charge credit card at a bank before he could file an application for housing. His white partner was given no requirements at all. In another company, the black volunteer was told she would have to fill out an application, which would be kept on file. The white partner was not required to do this.

Concerning access to units, in one company the black volunteer was told that no agents were available on weekends or evenings, which was the only time the volunteer was able to see housing. The white volunteer was told that the names and phone numbers of various building superintendants would be furnished on request, so that weekend or evening arrangements could be made.

As for price differentials, in one company the black volunteer was consistently offered housing in the $40,000-$50,000 price range, when he had asked for housing in the $20,000-$30,000 price range. In another company, the black volunteer was offered housing priced considerably lower than the $25,000 he said he was willing to pay.

Concerning courtesy, in one company the black volunteer had to make five times as many phone calls and visits as the white volunteer in order to receive comparable housing assistance. In another company, the black volunteer was never asked his name or asked to be seated during his visit.

With regard to racial remarks, in one company the agent referred to an integrated area as "becoming a mixed area—and the houses have already suffered somewhat as a result of it." She also said to the white volunteer, "I'm not prejudiced—I just wouldn't want to put you where you would be uncomfortable." Except for courtesy, all of these actions were against the law.

Public Presentation. Three steps were involved in presenting the results of Audit I to the community. First a public meeting was held under the auspices of the mayor's Human Relations Commission. Many area organizations were invited to send representatives, including the Board of Realtors and the press. Second, each real estate company involved in the audit was notified if there was an indication of discrimination in the company. Each company was also given an opportunity to meet individually with FHCS representatives to learn the exact details of the findings in the company. Third, the audit report and summary, plus original documents, were sent to the Department of Justice in Washington, D.C. for further investigation, and the possible filing of a pattern-and-practice suit in the federal courts.

At the public meeting, only the results of the second phase of the audit were presented. Actual companies audited were referred to by number only, not by name. At the close of the presentation, it was announced by FHCS that audits would continue as an ongoing activity, with different phases of the housing industry under investigation at different times.

Results. Two months after the public audit presentation, the press revealed that the audit results had been sent to the United States Department of Justice. Immediately thereafter, the Board of Realtors established its Human Relations Committee of 33 members "to do something about the problem of minority housing." Next, its newly elected president requested a meeting with open-housing leaders. This marked the first time in the seven-year history of the FHCS that such a meeting had ever been initiated by the Board of Realtors. Only one of the 12 discriminating companies responded to the offer to meet privately with FHCS leaders to discuss the findings of the audit in that company. Ten months later, the Board of Realtors issued a brochure on equal opportunities in housing under law, which it distributed to all its members (over 200 companies) and their agents.

One month after this publication was distributed, the FHCS revealed to the president of the Board of Realtors for the first time the names of all the companies which had been audited, with detailed summaries of the findings for each. The board president called a special meeting of the companies involved to discuss the specific findings of the audit with them, and notified the FHCS of this action. Several weeks later, the Board of Realtors invited the president of the FHCS (this author) to be a keynote speaker at an evening dinner-meeting, attended by over 300 real estate brokers and agents. The subject of the talk was "Open Housing Under Law." One and one-half hours of questions followed the talk, most of the questions directed toward gaining additional information about open-housing legislation and how it affected real estate practices.

The Department of Justice response to the audit was immediate. It sent an attorney to meet with FHCS leaders to discuss the audit and the feasibility of filing a pattern and practice suit. An investigation, was conducted using the local FBI. Subsequently, the FBI proved to have been poorly trained for this type of inquiry; for example, they met with the presidents of the real estate companies to find out if discrimination had been taking place! A second attorney from the Justice Department was assigned to the audit case after the investigation was completed. By this time, Audit II had been conducted and publicly presented, and its results were requested by the Justice Department in order to continue and combine its investigation of housing discrimination in Akron.

Audit II: Apartment Discrimination

Method. This audit period covered the three months from November 1971 through January 1972. Five teams of trained auditors visited 30 apartment complexes, covering a total of 3,110 units. The apartment complexes were selected on the basis of size (over 20 units), known vacancies (as advertised in the press), and geographical scope.

Each audit team consisted of one black person and one white person, with matching family compositions and income qualifications. Each auditor independently visited the assigned complexes, after telephoning to ascertain 1- or 2-bedroom vacancies and to arrange appointments for viewing them. Team members visited a given complex within a few hours of each other, the black auditor preceding the white auditor. Each auditor filled out a form designed to record his experience at each complex, and these written reports provided the data for the summary reports and analyses. Auditors were instructed to proceed up to the point of deposit.

Findings. Of the 3,110 units audited, 2,075 (67 percent of the total) clearly indicated outright discrimination. Of the 30 complexes audited,

19 (or 63 percent of the total number of complexes) indicated discrimination. An apartment complex was considered to indicate discrimination only if the evidence obtained appeared conclusive. Discrimination was defined as any difference in treatment on the basis of race.

Seven types of discrimination were indicated in Audit II. These concerned differentials in access to units, locations offered, quality of units, prices, information requested, courtesy, and racial remarks. Table C.2 indicates types of discrimination by number of units.

The types of discrimination encountered by the Audit II teams are illustrated in the following accounts of two of the teams.

Team 1 audited eight complexes covering 944 units. Of these, four complexes (50 percent), representing 420 units, indicated discrimination. In the first complex (214 units), the black auditor was told there were no two-bedroom units available; the white auditor was told they were available. The manager told the white auditor that there were no blacks in the complex, and that they were "screened." He also referred negatively to the prior visit of the black auditor. The black auditor was shown a 3-bedroom unit for $370/month. The white auditor was show a 2-bedroom unit for $250, which was what both had asked for in the telephone call preceding the visit.

In the second complex indicating discrimination (96 units), the black auditor was show a 2-bedroom unit in a building different from the one shown to the white auditor. The white auditor was told by the manager that some buildings in the complex were reserved for whites, others were mixed. The manager stated: "That is the way the company wants it." The "whiteness" of the complex shown to the white auditor was pointed out by the manager three times during the visit.

In the third complex (24 units), the black auditor was told no unit was available; the white auditor was shown an available unit. In the fourth complex (86 units), the black auditor was told there were no vacancies, despite having been told on the phone that three or four vacancies existed. The white auditor was shown two units, both immediately available. The manager told the white auditor that if apartments were scarce, she would tell any blacks that none were available.

Team 2 audited eight complexes, covering 919 units. Of these, 660 units (72 percent) in four, or half, of the complexes indicated discrimination.

In the first complex indicating discrimination (120 units), the black application was taken. The white auditor was shown an apartment and was told it was immediately available.

In the second complex (500 units), the black auditor was told there were no units available, and was shown none, despite having been told on the phone that several vacancies existed. The white auditor was offered two units—and a $25/month reduction in rent if she would take a unit instead of the black, who was still there at the time. The white auditor was urged to take a unit and not to indicate to the black that any units were available. The reduction in rent was offered "for being a good sport." The two vacant units were shown to the white auditor after the black auditor left.

In the third complex (20 units), the black auditor reported that a credit check was required. The white auditor reported that it was not required. The same apartment was shown to both auditors.

In the fourth complex (20 units), the black auditor visited and saw the vacant unit one day. When he called the owner back the next day to say he wanted the apartment, he was told it was no longer available. The white auditor phoned one-half hour later and was told the apartment was available.

Public Presentation. In May 1972, Audit II results were revealed to the community for the first time at a city council, public protest hearing concerning the relocation difficulties of 453 black families to be displaced by an inner-belt highway. The hearing was called at the request of FHCS and another community organization, West Side Neighbors.

The audit was used to show that adequate open housing to relocate the families was not available, contrary to the allegations of the city's Urban Renewal Department. A request was made to halt further construction of the inner-belt until the city provided adequate open housing. Four additional public hearings followed in the next two months and culminated in a series of recommendations, made at the city's request by FHCS and its companion organization.

In addition to filing the complete summary report and original documents with the Department of Justice, five additional agencies received the complete results of Audit II: the HUD Equal Opportunities Division in Columbus, which controls urban renewal funding in the Akron area; the Department of Commerce of Ohio, which controls real estate licensing in the state; the Community Relations Division of the Department of Justice of Cleveland, which investigates community unrest; and the Akron Commission on Equal Opportunities in Housing, which was formed to hear complaints of housing discrimination. In addition, the Ohio Civil Rights Commission local office requested and received reports on one apartment complex, where they were investigating an actual complaint of discrimination.

Results. The most immediate and positive response was made by the
HUD Equal Opportunities Division in Columbus, which began a series
of meetings with Akron's urban renewal and city planning officials.
HUD informed them that further urban renewal funding would be withheld if the city did not produce a workable plan to open housing opportunities for blacks in the area. At stake was $3.4 million for a Model
Cities neighborhood development program, which had already been
promised. The city officials then initiated meetings with FHCS to
discuss the possibility of a service contract with it to expand housing
opportunities for minorities.

Four months after the public presentation of Audit II, at a joint
meeting of HUD representatives, city officials, and FHCS leaders,
the specific details of such a contract were discussed and agreed
upon. The contract was to furnish funding for the FHCS to perform
two open-housing services for the city: immediate checking on all
complaints of discrimination in housing, with swift referral for legal
injunctions or other legal assistance; and research (on-going auditing)
on the availability of housing for minorities in the metropolitan area.

Though the city planning and renewal officials were receptive
to this, the mayor rejected the proposal, publicly claiming he would
rather give up the $3.4 million than be forced by HUD into such a
contract. The following week a tremendous negative reaction to the
mayor's position, stemming from both the black and white communities appeared in the press. The mayor maintained his position for
several months, by which time federal revenues were impounded,
leaving HUD with little real power to negotiate with the city, and leaving
the city without the $3.4 million.

As an outgrowth of Audit II, the Board of Realtors cooperated
with FHCS in a series of joint sales-training sessions for agents,
stressing open-housing laws. In addition, resolutions were directed
to the city council and school authorities of Akron requesting plans
to end racial isolation in the schools. These resolutions were supported by a coalition of organizations recruited by FHCS and its sister
organization, West Side Neighbors. The link between segregated
housing and segregated schools was readily perceived, but the solutions were not forthcoming without continued bitter struggle, which
still continues as of this writing.* Also as an outgrowth of the presentation of the findings of Audit II, legislation was passed by the

---

*Suit was filed by the American Civil Liberties Union against
school and government authorities on January 13, 1978. The suit
charged both housing segregation and school segregation, each reinforcing the other.

city council temporarily banning solicitation and for-sale signs in
the integrated area of West Side Neighbors, which was fighting
valiantly to prevent the resegregation of its 200-block area. This,
however, was short-lived and was revoked within a year, involving
one legal action along the way.

Ongoing Program. During all this time, the·regular FHCS program
continued, with 55 discrimination complaints investigated, and 28
of these subsequently filed with relevant agencies of attorneys for
legal redress. In addition, business and industry contacts were begun,
seeking cooperation from businesses in referring minority employees
to the FHCS for housing assistance, as well as distribution of FHCS
educational literature at industrial sites. Also, in January 1972,
FHCS began to share a small church office with West Side Neighbors
in a predominantly black neighborhood on the west side of Akron.
Three volunteer student interns came from Kent State University for
several successive quarters to assist the FHCS board of directors
in carrying on its program. They worked 20 hours a week, under
board members' supervision. The coordination of all of these volunteers, however, was a formidable task which took an increasing
amount of the president's time. The president, by this time was the
former board secretary and founder.*
     In February 1973, FHCS received national acclaim and recog-
nition by winning the National Volunteer Award of 1972—a $5,000
prize awarded in Washington, D.C. for excellence in community
volunteer activity. Two months later, HUD arranged through a regional agency that one of its final small grants be given to the FHCS to
conduct a county-wide open-housing program with a full-time staff
from July through October 1973.

Audit III: Company and Apartment Discrimination

Method. This audit period covered the four months from July 1973
through October 1973, and was conducted by board volunteers,
separately from the HUD-funded project which occurred during the
same period. Five trained auditors visited 43 assigned apartment
complexes with a total of 2,343 units. In addition, they visited seven
real estate companies in an effort to purchase homes in the $25,000-
$35,000 price range. The two principal auditors were actually in
the market for housing at the time of the audit.

---

*The president (this author) was the founder and fifth president of
FHCS, elected in 1972 as the first woman president of the organization.

All apartment complexes had known vacancies, ascertained from newspaper advertisements and phone calls. Auditors sought 1- or 2-bedroom units, renting for up to $280/ month and were instructed to proceed up to the point of deposit. Visits were made by trained matched pairs of anditors, using the same methods as for Audits I and II. Some complexes and companies were also revisited by other auditors, to confirm information previously gathered. As before, the auditors' written reports and summaries provided the basis for the final analysis.

Of the 43 apartment complexes audited, 29 (67 percent) indicated discrimination on the basis of race. A total of 53 different acts of racial discrimination were encountered in those 29 apartment complexes. Eighteen of the audited complexes were in suburban locations; 15 (83 percent) indicated racial discrimination. Twenty-five complexes were in Akron; 14 (59 percent) indicated racial discrimination. (See Tables C.4 and Figures C.1, C.2, and C.3.) Of the seven real estate companies audited, six indicated racial discrimination (85 percent) in a total of 13 different acts. (Two of those companies had also indicated racial discrimination in Audit I.)

Types of Discrimination. Discrimination was defined as any difference in treatment on the basis of race. Six different types of discrimination were indicated in Audit III:

1. Unequal Treatment Regarding Availability of Units. Blacks were told nothing was available, either at present or in the near future; whites were told one or more units were or would shortly be available. In real estate companies, blacks were not given access to listings; whites were given such access. Of the 29 apartment complexes where discrimination was found, 20 (62 percent) indicated racial discrimination regarding availability of units. Of the six real estate companies where discrimination was found, one (16 percent) indicated racial discrimination regarding availability of housing.

2. Unequal Treatment Regarding Prices. Blacks were quoted different prices or security deposit costs as compared to whites. Of the 29 complexes where discrimination was found, 11 (37 percent) indicated racial discrimination regarding prices. Of the six real estate companies where discrimination was found, two (33 percent) indicated racial discrimination regarding prices.

3. Unequal Treatment Regarding Requirements. Blacks were told credit checks or applications or a second interview

were required; whites were not asked for these. In addition, blacks were asked for personal information not required of whites. Of the 29 complexes where discrimination was found, 11 (37 percent) indicated racial discrimination regarding requirements. No real estate companies indicated this type of discrimination.

4.   Discrimination in Racial Remarks. Negative and disparaging remarks about blacks were made to white auditors, or remarks were made concerning the racial composition of the neighborhood or complex. Of the 29 complexes where discrimination was found, six (20 percent) made discriminatory racial remarks. Of the six real estate companies where discrimination was found, four (66 percent) made discriminatory racial remarks.

5.   Unequal Treatment Regarding Locations. Locations of available units differed for blacks and whites, either within the same complex or in separate geographical areas. Of the 29 complexes where discrimination was found, three (10 percent) offered different locations to blacks and whites. Of the six real estate companies where discrimination was found, three (50 percent) offered different locations to blacks and whites. (Note: this is termed steering, and is in violation of the federal fair-housing law.)

6.   Unequal Treatment in Courtesy. Blacks were told to drive themselves out to see various suggested properties, or were not escorted to rental units, or were not asked to be seated during office visits, or received poor or no response to their phone messages. Of the 29 complexes where discrimination was found, one (3 percent) indicated discourtesy in one or more of these respects. Of the six companies where discrimination was found, three (50 percent) indicated such discourtesy.

Public Presentation. As with Audit I, three steps were involved in presenting the results of Audit III to the community: a public meeting, notifications sent to all those audited, and summary reports sent to relevant agencies.

In March 1974 the results of Audit III were publicly presented in city council chambers, under the cosponsorship of the Human Relations Commission and the County Council of Governments. At this time, results of the previous two audits were compared with the third audit, revealing that racial discrimination in housing continued to be a pervasive and crucial problem in the metropolitan area. No names of actual discriminators were revealed at the public meeting, but it was announced that letters were on their way to all those audited, and that reports would be sent to relevant government agencies, after those audited had had ample opportunity to respond.

At the public presentation, three sets of specific recommendations were made to the Akron Area Real Estate Board, the Goals for Greater Akron Committee (a blue-ribbon group newly appointed by the mayor to propose long-range goals for the area), and to elected city and county officials. The recommendations included funding an area-wide open-housing program to implement the laws, and indicated the nature and scope of such a program.

The presentation contained the following statements:

> It is particularly significant that the amount of racial discrimination in suburban areas is substantially higher than within the city. The implications of this for future metropolitan growth and development are extremely serious, and gravely reminiscent of the Kerner Commissions' Report that we are "a divided society—separate and unequal. . . .

> There are only three basic human commodities: food, clothing, and shelter (housing). Most people would think it incredible to find food and clothing offered selectively on the basis of race, with dual markets, prices, qualities, and locations for each—according to race. Yet we seem to calmly accept the fact that housing continues to be the only basic human commodity not offered on the open market, without regard to race. . . .

> The findings of our studies do not and can not reveal the actual extent of personal humiliation, disrespect for law, and human injustice which are implicit in these results. Our findings cry out for action by area-wide public bodies and citizen groups. We call on all concerned officials, organizations and citizens to respond with prompt affirmative action to correct these inequities. Specifically, we recommend the following. . . .

> Both the city and the county should take immediate steps to see that such a program (open housing) is funded well enough to move this area forward in the direction of real freedom of choice in housing for all minorities, and true equality of opportunity in that basic human commodity of housing. The time has come for community leaders to respond to this Audit report. . .with a new sense of responsibility and urgency, calling for prompt, meaningful affirmative action.[78]

At the public meeting, the FHCS presented for the first time an Equal Opportunity Award, recognizing two real estate agents in one company who practiced fair housing during the time of the audit. Immediately following the public meeting, letters were sent to the presidents of all audited real estate companies and to the owners of all audited apartment complexes (see Appendix C). The letters informed the recipients that their company or complex had been audited by the FHCS, and that racial discrimination had or had not been found. The letters also cited pertinent sections of federal and state open-housing laws. If discrimination was not indicated in Audit III, the recipient was encouraged to continue observance of the laws. If discrimination was indicated, the recipient was invited to meet with the leaders of FHCS to learn the specific details pertaining to that company or complex.

After some weeks had passed, allowing sufficient time for discriminating auditees to respond, the summary audit reports were sent to government agencies. Included with the reports were the names of discriminators and notations as to which of those had responded to the invitation to meet privately with FHCS, and which had made commitments to take corrective action. Government agencies receiving these reports included the Department of Justice (Civil Rights Division) in Washington, D.C., the HUD Equal Opportunity Division in Chicago and Columbus, the Ohio Civil Rights Commission, and the Ohio Department of Commerce (which controls real estate licensing). In addition, 35 copies of the audit report (with no names of discriminators included) were sent to selected national and area organizations, agencies, elected officials, and the media.

Results. The response of the community was swift and positive. The area newspaper (Akron Beacon Journal) give extensive front-page coverage to the audit results, followed by a powerful lead editorial (March 25, 1974) headed "Akron Area Housing Bias Cries for Stronger Action." The editorial ended with these statements:

> It will take a concerted effort both within and without government to change the pattern of racial discrimination in housing. But the FHCS audit report presents a powerful indictment of the area in allowing such an intolerable situation to persist. . . . As serious as it is, the indictment should be enough to move community leaders to make the effort necessary to break down the racial barriers.[79]

Of the six real estate companies found practicing discrimination, the presidents of four responded immediately by setting appointments with FHCS leaders to discuss the specific findings pertaining to their companies. All made a commitment to take corrective action with their employees. The Board of Realtors had an emergency meeting to discuss the audit findings. Of the 29 apartment complexes where discrimination was found, nine owners responded with personal meetings and commitments for corrective action.

All government agencies responded to the audit report, with the Department of Justice and the Department of Commerce avowing their intention to begin their own investigations. The Department of Justice did an intensive investigation of the housing discrimination reported in Audit III. However, again using FBI investigators to conduct their inquiries, the Department of Justice never took definitive action beyond the initial investigation.

On the national level, the FHCS was named one of 15 open-housing groups across the country (the only totally voluntary one) to receive a small HUD federal grant to implement equal housing opportunities, called the Jaclyn project.* On the local level, perhaps the most significant and gratifying response was the incorporation of the explicitly stated goal of equal opportunity in housing in three recent official documents concerned with metropolitan planning: the County Council of Governments Housing Development Plan, the Little Hoover Commission Report, and the Goals for Greater Akron Summary Statement. All included quotations from FHCS audit reports, all acknowledged serious awareness of the problem of racial discrimination in housing, and all called for the implementation of equal-housing opportunities through a funded area-wide open-housing program.

The repetition and reinforcement of these concepts by three separate official bodies was the culmination of all of the nine previous years of constant effort of the FHCS to call attention to the problem of housing discrimination and to increase the level of awareness, in the hope of bringing about constructive social change. The fact that the goals of FHCS were incorporated publicly by three other official groups indicated that a significant measure of change had already occurred.

Summary of Audits

Thus, three years after the passage of federal open-housing legislation, which was the culmination of a protracted 20-year struggle, these three audits were conducted successively by FHCS

---

*This grant was finally received, three years after it had been applied for, in 1975. It was the first FHCS experience with contract research; their new staff was ill-prepared to cope with it.

in Akron, Ohio. The audits were designed to indicate the effect of the open-housing legislation on actual black housing access in the Akron area. Putting this another way, the audits were a measure of the extent of racial discrimination in housing in the area. The result of the audits, with repeated feedback to the community each time, was an increased level of community awareness of the problem, leading to constructive change in attitudes and actions.

It can be seen that the most significant aspect of conducting an audit is the sharing of the results with the community, the housing establishment and industry, and law enforcement agencies, so as to move toward constructive change. Each audit involved many months of planning, execution, analysis, written summarization, public presentation, and subsequent efforts to attain affirmative action. With only volunteers responsible for this mammoth undertaking, one full year was the average length of time for a complete audit—from the planning stage all the way to the follow-up individual meetings with those found discriminatory, and the actual attainment of affirmative action.

Two types of affirmative action were sought by FHCS leaders from those found discriminating. One was an affirmative action memo (see Appendix C) to be circulated among all employees of the company (including telephone operators and maintenance people!). The memo indicated knowledge of the provisions of fair-housing law, and acknowledgement that any personal violation of that law would result in dismissal. The memo was to be signed and dated by each employee, and was to be circulated by the company president (or apartment complex owner and manager.) The other type of affirmative action was the inclusion of a slogan or symbol indicating equal housing opportunity or equal opportunity realtor in all subsequent advertising of the company or complex. Both of these actions were suggested as preferable to a lawsuit. Most company executives agreed and complied, after they were confronted privately with the evidence obtained in the audit.

In addition to increasing awareness of and potential for open housing in the Akron metropolitan area, the Akron audit has led other communities to take an interest in the audit as a device for implementing existing open-housing legislation. Cleveland requested a presentation of Akron's audit and completed its own audit of real estate practices. Columbus requested and received the same presentation, and began to audit in that area. A National Neighbors conference in Baltimore featured the Akron audits in its two-day meetings, and communities from across the country responded enthusiastically to the presentation. The city of Tulsa requested the Akron FHCS to serve as consultant in setting up an audit in that area, and the state of West Virginia also requested assistance from the Akron group in implementing open-housing legislation. Eventually, all of the auditing activity culminated in the nationwide HUD audit of 1977.

The National Volunteer Award

In the spring of 1972, after Audit II had been presented publicly, FHCS routinely answered a bid from the National Center for Voluntary Action in Washington, D.C. for nominations for a National Volunteer Award. These awards had formerly been given by the Lane Bryant Foundation, and FHCS had received citations twice before. These were then locally publicized as part of the public relations work of the organization. This time, however, the prize was to be a monetary one of $5,000.

Believing that periodic citations were beneficial to the morale of a volunteer group such as FHCS, the public relations chairperson wrote the 400-word summary of the organization's activities, obtained several friends' signatures as references and nominators, prepared a supporting packet of newsclips and educational materials of the organization, and sent it all off to Washington in time to meet the deadline of mid-April. The only thought behind this was to secure another citation, a certificate, to hang on the wall of the little church office, and to then have this publicized in the local newspaper—all for the morale of the group, as a reward for its labors.

In the past, out of hundreds of nominations, FHCS had been among the 70 or 80 semifinalists who received citations. So when the letter was received in August, announcing that FHCS was again one of the 74 semifinalists, this was routinely passed on to the board, and was included in a small item in the FHCS newsletter. A fleeting thought was given to where the certificate would be hung in the office, and then the matter was promptly forgotten in the flurry of on-going program activities.

In the next few months, FHCS was one of the groups featured on a major TV network in an hour-long documentary on housing, "The Right to Live—the Freedom to Choose." Also, FHCS was featured in NCDH's Trends in its series of articles on audits. The FHCS Newsletter of October-November, 1972 reveals the state of its affairs at that time with these headlines: "FHCS on TV Dec. 9"; "Next Issue of Trends Features FHCS' Audits"; "Requests for Help from East, West, and South U.S."; "Four Court Cases Pending"; "All Audit Reports Filed"; "Membership Drive Continues" (joy over 45 new memberships!); "Thank You, St. Phillips Church" (for mimeographing the Newsletter), and "Thank You, Adventures Unlimited" (to a youth group for assembling the Newsletter and preparing it for mailing).

It was a complete surprise when one day in December, four months later, the FHCS president received a letter from Washington, informing her that FHCS was one of the eight finalists in the country for the grand award, four of which were individuals, and four were groups. The letter said they should prepare to send two delegates to Washington on February 14, all expenses paid, when the final winners would be announced. Great jubilation prevailed, and a local event of recognition was arranged by the director of the local Center for Voluntary Action.

Shortly after, the National Center for Voluntary Action sent a movie company to Akron to film FHCS and its members in action. The company stayed two days, putting together a six-minute color film which was to be shown at the time the final awards were announced.

Late in January 1973, only a few weeks before the Washington event was to take place, the FHCS president received a phone call from Washington, informing her that FHCS had won the final grand award of $5000 as the top volunteer group in the country!

In Washington, the award was presented by Governor Romney at an evening banquet held in the Kennedy Performing Arts Center. The presentation of the $5,000 check and plaque followed a showing of the six-minute color film about Akron's FHCS. The next morning at 7 a.m., several million people across the country saw the National Volunteer Award winners on the Today Show, where an appearance had been unexpectedly arranged. The FHCS Newsletter of February-March 1973 ended its report with, "It was wonderful, we loved it, and we love sharing it with you—our readers—for without your cooperation and support none of this would have been possible. We can't exist without you—hang in there, please!"

The 700 nominations for the National Volunteer Award were evaluated by a panel of five nationally known judges: Elliott Richardson (then secretary of defense, formerly secretary of HEW), Roy Wilkins (NAACP director), Bess Myerson (then New York's consumer affairs director), James Michener (author), and James Roche (corporation executive). The award was given on the basis of seven criteria: merit, community need, scope, use of resources, means used, obstacles encountered and overcome, and innovation.

Though FHCS was not really very different from the other voluntary fair-housing groups across the country—all operating valiantly—it may have been their renunciation of the funding that impressed the judges as an act of singular courage. Perhaps that was the most important factor considered in obstacles encountered and overcome, along with the repeated audits and community feedback indicative of innovation and positive means used. The award to FHCS, in any case, was a morale booster for the entire open-housing

movement. NCDHs <u>Trends</u> reported on it in the January-February
1973 issue, "Top Award to Akron FH," noting:

> "More than two years ago, the Akron group "went volun-
> teer" when it turned back OEO funding rather than bow to
> controls which would have violated its open housing policy.
> With dynamic volunteer leadership, FHCS has maintained
> an office and continued a broad range effort to insure equal
> access to housing. . . . Its highly systematized "audit"
> program. . . has been a model for open housing centers
> across the country. . . . NCDH congratulates its friends
> and colleagues in Akron. [80]

Letters of congratulation continued to pour in from around the country,
including one from the president (then Nixon) and one from Elliot
Richardson.

The HUD Demonstration Project

<u>Setting.</u> The eighth annual meeting of FHCS had NCDH's director
Ed Holmgren as the keynote speaker, and featured the showing of the
six-minute award film, seen in Akron for the first time. The June-
July 1973 <u>Newsletter</u> reported the event, and its headlines indicated
the current concerns of the organization: "Announcement of Publisher's
Equal Housing Opportunity Notice, to Appear Regularly in Sunday
Paper"; "Schools Resolution Filed with HEW" (referring to complaint
on racially isolated Akron schools); "Support for Sign and Solicitation
Ban"; "New Board and Officers" (9 new members, 19 re-elected,
2 new officers, 2 reelected, indicating stability of the organization);
"Board members in the News" (recognized individual board members
for varying achievements, indicating the high calibre of the board at
that time). The <u>Newsletter</u> ended with the familiar: "May We Remind
You?—June 1 is the start of our new fiscal year—your dues and/or
contributions are our only means of support and enable us to continue
working toward our goal of equal opportunity in housing for minorities."

<u>The Summer Open Housing Program.</u> Very soon after the annual
meeting, FHCS learned on July 5 that it had received a $22,500 grant
from the regional HUD Equal Opportunity office to conduct a three-
month demonstration open-housing project. This was actually a subcontract from Operation Equality (Cleveland Urban League open-
housing program), as part of a total contract with NOACA/HUD for

the NOACA* region (7 counties), funded under Section 701 of the
1954 Housing Act.

FHCS's subcontract was confined to one county (Summit), and
called on FHCS to do three things, which they were already doing as
volunteers: investigate and verify all complaints of racial discrimination in housing in Summit County; councel minority home seekers who
had encountered discrimination, inform them of their options under
law, assist them in filing complaints with the proper agencies, and
refer them to relevant agencies and/or legal counsels; and expand
community education on open housing, with particular emphasis on
the black community as to minority rights to housing provided by
federal, state and local laws.

Immediately, the FHCS board went into frantic action. They
hired a director six days later, and by July 16 had a five-member
staff operating out of the little church office, and one adjoining room
and full basement. The staff consisted of one office manager and four
field representatives, plus the director. The director worked very
closely with the FHCS president. Very early he asked her, "What are
your dreams and hopes—what would you like to see us do in this brief
concentrated period of time (three and a half months)?"

Out of those dreams and hopes, fashioned over the past nine
years, and reflecting cross-country observation as well as the bitter
earlier funding experience, came the swiftly developed crash open-
housing program. It was an outstanding program, one, that some
open-housing groups do not accomplish in a year—or ever. Undoubtedly the short-term contract was a spur to tremendous activity, precisely because there was so little time and the group was so eager to
show what it could do under optimum conditions: plenty of money, an
excellent staff that knew how to utilize dedicated, experienced volunteers, and expert experienced board leadership and involvement, plus
a contract that called for all the things that meant the most to the
organization!

Summer Achievements. Expansion of community education and awareness was accomplished primarily through distribution of literature
(over 50,000 pieces), bulk mailings (over 6,000), billboards (12
located on arterial highways at strategic points), workshops (legal,
volunteer, suburban: 10), radio-TV programs (11), business and
industry personal contacts (18), community meetings (56), formation

---

*Northeast Ohio Area Coordinating Agency, a regional body
that allocated government funding to a seven-county area, which at
that time included Summit County, containing Akron.

of voluntary affirmative action groups in suburbs (11), and advertising through constant notices in newspapers and periodicals and radio public-service spot announcements.

This intensive public-relations blitz campaign resulted in more discrimination calls coming in to the office during the three-and-one-half-month period than had occurred during the entire previous year. In fact, more investigations of housing discrimination (23) were handled by the staff during the summer than were handled by the state Civil Rights Commission during the whole previous year. In addition, there was an increase in the volume of requests for general housing information, requests for speakers, and requests for literature. Specifically, the telephone calls increased from one per day at the start of the project to over ten per day at the end of the project. Over 1,000 volunteer hours were contributed to the project, in addition to the staff time. Many additional contributions were made in printing, space, media time, equipment, and so on, by various groups and individuals throughout the metropolitan area.

One example of the innovative and creative approach to community education in the summer project was the mobile van. The van was staffed by volunteers and carried in it a volunteer rock "soul" band; the van toured the summer playgrounds and parks in black neighborhoods, attracting young people who received cardboard Fair-Housing sunglasses, a Fair Housing Fun Book, and brochures to be taken home. Another example of the creativity of the summer staff was the slogan used on the 12 giant billboards, with the FHCS equal opportunity logo prominently displayed: "housing Discrimination is a Social Disease. . .For free check-up, call 434-8380."

The three-and-a-half-month demonstration program had great impact on the entire metropolitan area, and was an excellent indicator of what FHCS could do with the right funding source and an effective staff on a full-time basis. The HUD project was extremely valuable for several reasons. It served as a model for an effective, staffed open-housing program; it offered eivdence that funding need not be a disastrous experience; it demonstrated that excellent administrative leadership could obtain maximum cooperation and positive working relationships with volunteers and staff; and it generally invalidated all the theories that have equated institutionalization with decline—almost. It is soberly recognized here that this was a very short-term project; had it continued, more problems would no doubt have appeared. As it was, the three-and-one-half-months were, for the most part, a wonderful experience for board, staff, and volunteers—mostly due to the excellence of direction and leadership from all three sources.

Conclusions. Several important conclusions were reached at the close of the project, and summarized as a basis for future action research programs on open housing in that metropolitan area:

1. Housing discrimination in Summit County cannot be dealt with as a separate entity. Discrimination in surrounding counties must be considered. Residential growth patterns and industrial development force boundary overlapping into these neighboring counties.

2. Many white persons, particularly in the suburbs, do not believe that housing discrimination exists to any large extent, and are still relatively unaware of open housing laws, the social and economic bases of them, and the possible legal consequences of violating them.

3. Many minority persons are unable to recognize racial discrimination in housing when it occurs, or are unsure of how to seek aid if they encounter clearcut discrimination. Still, they seek housing in non-traditional areas because of better living and school conditions.

4. Area legal assistance for housing discrimination is not well developed in terms of knowledge of specific relevant laws, cases, and procedures involved in obtaining redress.

5. There is a growing awareness on the part of business and industry of the negative economic and social effects of racial discrimination in housing, both on the individual minority employee, and on the business itself.

6. Much of the housing delivery system (real estate companies, builders, lending institutions) is increasingly aware of the open housing laws, and state their willingness to comply with them. However, they have difficulty understanding how their existing practices continue to reinforce and perpetuate racial discrimination in housing.

7. Racial discrimination in housing persists daily, despite the passage of federal, state and local open housing laws.

Back to Total Volunteers. The contract expired on October 31, 1973 and was not renewed.* The next FHCS Newsletter ended with the

_____

*There was a bitter political struggle at that time concerning the jurisdiction of NOACA, contested by the Akron delegation. FHCS was a victim of that power struggle, and was not granted a renewal

usual reminder about dues and contributions: "Now that we're poor
again, how about it?" It was during the period of the summer HUD
program that FHCS conducted Audit III, independently of the HUD
program and directed by volunteer board members. Much work
remained to be done on that audit, and this occupied the months until
the public presentation of the Audit III findings in March 1974. This
presentation resulted in the strong outcry for action in the local
newspaper, and prompted three separate regional planning organizations to name equal-housing opportunity as a major goal and called
for a funded county-wide effort for open housing. But it was the cuma-
lative effect of all the previous ten years of work, the two previous
audits, the National Volunteer Award, and the summer HUD project
that led eventually to the resumption of funding in 1975.

Change and Transition

    In June 1974, shortly after the public presentation of Audit III,
the founder and immediate past president of FHCS left the board
after ten years of service, and moved to an honorary position on the
advisory council. She had prepared the board for some months for
this action, and gave several reasons for leaving: "(1) I believe it is
healthy to rotate the leadership of an organization. (2) This Board is
very capable, bright and conscientious—I think they know what needs
to be done, and I feel confident they will do it. And (3) the things I
do best can be done in an advisory capacity. . . ."
    In a tearful farewell talk to the board before the public announce-
ment at the annual meeting, the founder shared some final reflections
with the group and reminded them of their prime reason for existence: ". . .because racial discrimination in housing exists!. . .
there's no point in having that law without citizen groups like ours
which can implement it and make it a reality. . . .remember, though,
no one will call us if they don't know we're available. . . ." Finally,
let me end this by saying that our work is at times exasperating and
frustrating—but also beautiful. . .because in it is a dream of a better
community and a better world. I'm sure you'll help to bring this about
by carrying on with the organization. And I'll be cheering you on,

------

of the contract. Shortly after, NOACA's jurisdiction was cut to four
counties, not including Summit County, which then became part of
a new four-county administrative agency: NEFCO (Northeast Four
County Coordinating Agency).

ready to help in any way whenever you need me." What she did not know was that most of the board would be gone within a year.

The new president worked closely with the past president in the next year, which was one of transition. FHCS moved its office in November 1974 and hired one staff person as program coordinator, using some of the award money to pay the small rent and salary. In addition, it received from the city of Akron a $4,000 contract to provide fair-housing counseling for the urban renewal relocation program. Another small contract of $2,000 from the National Association of Social Workers (Northeast Ohio chapter) provided for continuation and expansion of the Metropolitan Outreach program in the suburbs.

During this year of change, the new program coordinator (who received intensive orientation from the past president) handled 41 investigations of discrimination complaints, resulting in 10 filed with relevant agencies or attorneys for legal redress. Monetary damages were awarded in three: $3,750, $1,000, $2,250. (The program coordinator later became an attorney.) Also during this year, 30 presentations were made to community organizations, and eight workshops were conducted for volunteers and lawyers, Media coverage included six TV and four radio programs. Over 5,000 pieces of educational literature were distributed.

Funding Proposal. Most significantly, the program coordinator and FHCS board prepared a proposal for funding under the Community Development Act of 1974, and contacted the relevant individuals and groups needed to gain political support for the funding. This activity was undertaken against an uneasy backdrop of board-staff discontent, revealed in minutes of meetings and personal interviews. The old familiar troubles arose concerning the role of the board in relation to the staff (one person), and the relations of board members to each other and to their leaders—now functioning through an executive committee, which met to conduct business between board meetings.* Some board members felt that the executive committee was now running the organization, and they felt left out. Others complained that the staff member was not well organized and should be doing a more professional job. Still others felt that the whole board was disorganized and did not know where it wanted to go in terms of program.

---

*The past president had a different leadership style, using the entire board as an executive committee. This produced greater involvement with all details—large and small (and also resulted in longer board meetings).

Some of this is reflected in the proposal for funding submitted to the city. The proposal listed nine programs it would implement with the funding of $40,000 from the city and $10,000 from the county:

1. Educate white persons about housing discrimination, its effects, and fair-housing laws.

2. Educate minority persons concerning fair-housing laws and their rights; recourse available when discrimination occurs; housing available in non-traditional areas.

3. Educate and aid real estate and building industries and financial institutions in fair-housing laws and what these laws mean to them.

4. Help train appropriate city employees in fair-housing laws.

5. Investigate housing discrimination complaints and counsel and assist person discriminated against.

6. Conduct on-going research into availability and accessibility of housing for minority persons within the city.

7. Cooperate with existing groups and agencies on discrimination problems.

8. Work with builders, contractors, lending institutions, and landlords to insure compliance with fair-housing laws and HUD requirements in financing advertising and rental of subsidized units.

9. Encourage a supportive climate for the establishment of integrated housing patterns.

It is not clear why these nine programs were expanded from the original ones of education, housing assistance, and research, but they were so general that it almost does not matter. The proposal did not offer specific methods of attaining those objectives. More seriously, it did not offer a timeline indicating which tasks would be done when, and in what sequence. Neither the city nor the county seemed to require anything more detailed. This need not have been a problem for a well-seasoned staff and board, but there was neither when FHCS opened its new offices on October 1, 1975 with a full-time staff of four.

After ten years of primarily volunteer effort, the two local governments recognized the legitimacy of the organization by funding it for a county-wide open-housing program—but what they funded was quite a different organization from the one that had won the National Volunteer Award five years earlier.

SECOND FUNDED PERIOD, 1975—

Now into the third year of funding, the board and staff have completely changed. The program has changed, too.[*] FHCS is now, of course, a different organization from the one that existed for the prior ten years of voluntary effort. It is not even an organization any more; it is now an "advocate agency," in the words of the new director. The following very brief review of its program is based on minutes of board meetings, analysis of funding proposals, quarterly and annual reports, newsletters, interviews with board and staff members, taped radio presentations, and occasional attendance at board meetings.

Of the four staff members who opened the new offices under the newly funded program, only one had been involved with the organization before—the program coordinator, who had been holding the program together part-time during the previous year. The director (public relations training), and her assistant (urban studies background), and the office manager (age 22) were brand new and had no previous association with the organization or any other fair-housing program. There was a long learning period, apparently made awkward by the fact that the program coordinator and board president had to inform the new staff about numerous policies, procedures, and minute details for some time—yet the new staff (understandably) wanted to assume authority very quickly. The quickest way of doing this was to institute a number of changes, for which they asked board approval. Since the board itself by this time was greatly changed in membership, most having resigned by the end of the previous year,[†]

---

[*]The 1976-77 proposal for funding streamlined the program into an even vaguer list of nine elements, three months after the new director took charge: affirmative action and marketing, evaluation of the housing delivery system, complaint investigation, relocation assistance, metropolitan outreach public education and community relations, inter-agency coalition, referral and exchange, and home seekers contact. In 1978, FHCS added a tenant/landlord counseling program to its overburdened, evershifting staff, which by then had relegated racial discrimination to a very low priority in its actual time, energy, and budget allocation.

[†]There was great dissatisfaction with the organization the year after the founder left the board, and even greater discontent when the new director took charge. Those who were unhappy left, no longer willing to struggle to maintain the original goals of the organization.

this was not difficult—few realized the extent of the changes, and those that did were reluctant to challenge the new staff so soon.

Under the best of circumstances, an orientation and settling-in period would be needed for a newly funded organization—how long a period is difficult to judge. In this case, it took about a year. But by this time, the staff had shifted again, as had almost the entire board, and again newcomers and readjustments made for great instability of the funded operation. The second year of funding was even more fluid than the first, and by this time all ties with the past program and organization had been broken. Because of these serious administrative problems, it is extremely difficult to assess the program. It would, in fact, be quite unfair to do so, since the only persons who remained from the previous year were the director* and a few board members, who were having an anxious time coping with the constant turnover.

Early Trouble Signs. Some clues as to the new director's priorities and attitudes are found in immediate references to FHCS as "an agency," the choice of downtown office location with no free parking, the designation of the office manager (age 22) as the coordinator of discrimination complaints, the slashing of the mailing list from 1400 to barely 200, the growing incompatibility between the director and the staff and some board members, and the reluctance to turn to the past president and founder for any advice on policy or program.

Some other signs of trouble are found in irregular newsletters, loss of volunteers (from 65 down to virtually a handful), dwindling memberships (only 78 paid-up members as of March 1977), and decreased quantity of news items referring to the organization in the newspaper.†

As for program, no new audits have been initiated by the board or staff since the founder left the board. The number of discrimination complaints is about the same or even less than before funding

---

This left the least committed as remaining members. Soon even these left. The 1978 board has only four out of 21 members in any way identified with the original goals and purposes of the organization.

*As of this writing, the Director has resigned, as has the Board president—both leaving the city, and leaving the organization in its usual state of flux.

†The number of local news items about FHCS followed this sequence: in unfunded years—19 in 1971, 43 in 1972, 54 in 1973, 29 in 1974, a transition year; in the funded period, as a staffed agency —26 in 1975, 16 in 1976, 12 in 1977.

(three or four a month). During the whole second year of funding,
the agency handled 31 discrimination complaints, of which only two
resulted in legal suits with damages. And the newest program focus
is none other than tenant-landlord counseling, for which the agency
has received an additional $40,000 for the third year of funding.

Yet the program continues, and the funding is larger than ever
(now $133,000/year). As one board member put it, "At least it's
still alive." Another member said wryly, "The goal seems to be to
get bigger and richer." The philosophical perspective of the new
director and most of the executive committee is clearly one that
uses a comprehensive housing agency as a model, such as is found
in the Columbus Housing Opportunity Center (HOC—formerly a Model
Cities program.) In such a model, the program is a diffused comprehensive one, with racial discrimination only one of many pursuits.
The perspective of the earlier FHCS and its leaders was one of a
highly concentrated program, with top priority going to racial discrimination and the systemic, vigorous combating of it. The older
organization had been based on exclusive membership; the newer
funded one is inclusive in nature. [81] The older one was based on
internal resources, the newer one on external resources. [82] Or, as
Jo Freeman would say, the older one used intangible resources,
while the newer one uses tangible resources. [83]

When these attributes are assembled, it is evident that the
older group was a movement organization and the newer one is no
longer that. It is an agency in the fullest sense of the word, and
the director is correct to refer to it in that way. In social-movement
theory and terminology, it might qualify perhaps as an interest
group, or service agency although even that designation is questionable. The sense of commitment and the existence of the following seem
to be the missing elements; yet, when the earlier definition of a social
movement is recalled, there was nothing in it about dedication or
commitment or even a following. Only scope, durability, organization,
and an orientation to social change were listed in that definition. Does
the definition need revision? Or does one continue to call this funded
agency a movement organization? (And does any of this matter?)

Whether history is uneasily repeating in Akron cannot be stated
here—it may be too soon to judge. Perhaps if the sands stop shifting
in that organization, an effective program could develop. One thing
seems certain: FHCS could never return to a volunteer organization.
Those times may be gone for this entire movement. The new concern
must therefore be how to make the funded program truly effective in
achieving an open community. It may be quite unimportant whether
the organization is a movement or an interest group or a service
agency, which it now appears to be. Conceivably, an interest group
could be immensely effective, even though not a movement organiza-

tion. Some conclusions about this are reached in the last chapter, after the movement in other communities across the nation is examined.

SUMMARY

The Fair Housing Contact Service was a local manifestation of the open-housing movement, which came into existence as a result of local constraints and inaction. An immediate crisis provided the actual impetus for the formation of the organization.

The reciprocal impact of NCDH and the FHCS was evident in five specific instances: (1) in the founding of the organization, NCDH provided information and educational materials which directly aided the initial organization of the local group; (2) in the funding of the organization, NCDH provided the initial encouragement for FHCS to seek funding through OEO; (3) in the development of FHCS as a legitimate and powerful pressure group, when NCDH requested local aid in securing signatures to petitions, FHCS found itself able to organize other groups in securing such support; (4) in the expansion of the local supply of low-income housing units, when NCDH rejected the FHCS proposal because of an inadequate supply of low-income units, FHCS applied organized pressure to local decision makers, resulting in a massive expansion of public housing units (latent consequence: the hardening of existent patterns of residential segregation and the creation of new patterns of segregation); and (5) in the renewed recognition and clarification of open-housing goals, the NCDH consultant provided a framework for FHCS to re-examine itself after funding had produced goal ambiguity and conflict.

FHCS, during its first voluntary phase, maintained consistency between its stated and operative goals. Its program, both actual housing assistance and education, had enormous impact on the local community and surrounding areas. It received two national awards for outstanding volunteer service, as well as two local awards for distinguished achievement in equal opportunities in housing. Its internal morale during the voluntary phase was extremely high in both task and maintenance, or instrumental and expressive patterns. It has been suggested that the strength of its task productivity was a prime factor in the maintenence of high morale. The entire first year voluntary phase was characterized by strong involvement and participation toward a clearly specified goal.

After the FHCS was first funded, both the stated and operative goals changed. There was extremely slow recognition of the fact that the change in operative goals, as implemented, was in direct conflict with the original goals of the organization. Two types of individual response to organizational change were noted. It was suggested that those who were critical of the funded operation were more loyal to the original objectives of the organization. Those who supported the funded operation were more loyal to the organization itself, and perceived the funded operation as essential to survival and growth.

The board of directors' inability to cope with the situation was seen as stemming from three factors: the implicit sociability norm, role uncertainty, and goal ambiguity and conflict. Interaction patterns came to be marked by tension, anxiety, and open hostility. Morale was finally shattered when a new powerful constraint imposed by the funding agency made any implementation of the original goal impossible. Even then, the board was unable to take action to resolve this problem.

Only when all hope was abandoned of having an effective funded operation was the board able slowly to moblize itself toward a reactivation of its volunteer effort. Such renewed task orientation provided tension release and led gradually to increased morale, though all other basic problems remained unresolved.

A subtle but omnipresent contextual factor affecting the development of the organization and its participants during its first five years was the change in the national civil rights movement in the direction of increasing black separatism.

After much internal division and soul searching, FHCS gave up the OEO funding with which it had struggled for two years. Reverting to its volunteer status, the board slowly took hold of the organization's destiny and embarked on a four-year phase of program growth, impact, and achievement that culminated in national recognition, local legitimacy, and eventual refunding. Three events affected the development of the movement organization in Akron: the audits, the winning of the National Volunteer Award, and the HUD summer demonstration project. These, in fact, were all outgrowths in some way of the earlier act of relinquishing the funding.

The three audits covered over 5000 rental units and 40 major real estate companies. They resulted in increased awareness of open-housing laws and the issue of racial discrimination in the real estate industry, government, law enforcement agencies, and the community. On the local level, after the third audit and community feedback, three separate official bodies incorporated equal-housing opportunity as an explicitly stated goal in their official documents. They also recommended a county-wide funded open-housing program to reduce discrimination. The manifest result of the audits was constructive change in attitudes and actions regarding equal access to housing.

The latent result was the winning of the National Volunteer Award in 1973, which led to heightened prestige, legitimacy, and influence on the local level. The seven criteria for winning the award included obstacles encountered and overcome. One of those obstacles was the OEO funding and its renunciation; another was the refusal of the local mayor to fund the organization after HUD's intervention following the public presentation of Audit II.

The HUD summer demonstration project was fashioned out of nine years of hopes and dreams, and reflected cross-country observation and analysis of other movement organizations as well as the bitter earlier funding experience. The achievements of the crash program were outstanding, and demonstrated what an open-housing organization could accomplish in a short period of time under optimum funding conditions: clear, concentrated objectives; ample funds; and excellent leadership and cooperation among staff, board, and volunteers. This experience offered evidence that funding need not be a disastrous situation. It also served as a model for an effective staffed open-housing program.

When the founder of FHCS left the board in 1974, after ten years of constant service, the board quickly developed a proposal for funding under the HCD Act of 1974. In 1975, FHCS became one of the first open-housing groups in the country to receive funding under this act. The funding came from the city and county, and was the cumulative effect of all the previous ten years of work. The organization that was funded, however, was not the same as the one that existed before.

Analysis of this latest funded program is difficult because of heavy board and staff turnover. This in itself is symptomatic of difficulties in board-staff and staff-staff relations. It is also symptomatic of weaknesses in HCD funding arrangements for open-housing groups. There are no clearly defined goals and objectives, and above all no mechanisms for the evaluation of open-housing programs. A general assessment of the latest FHCS funded program indicates the use of a comprehensive agency model, with racial discrimination only one of many other pursuits. Because the organization is not vigorously combating systemic racial discrimination, the current FHCS may no longer be considered a movement organization by some observers. The critical issue is how to make funded open-housing programs truly effective in achieving open communities.

NOTES

1. Herbert Blumer, Symbolic Interactionism (Englewood Cliffs, N.J.: Prentice-Hall, 1969), p. 59.
2. Ibid., p. 58.
3. Amitai Etzioni, Modern Organizations (Englewood Cliffs, N.J.: Prentice-Hall, 1964).

4. Warren G. Bennis, Changing Organizations (New York: McGraw-Hill, 1966).

5. Peter Blau and W. Richard Scott, Formal Organizations (San Francisco: Chandler, 1962).

6. Talcott Parsons, Structure and Process in Modern Societies (Glencoe, Ill.: The Free Press, 1957).

7. Robert Merton, Social Theory and Social Structure (Glencoe, Ill.: The Free Press, 1957), pp. 50–60.

8. W. Richard Scott, "Theory of Organizations," in Handbook of Modern Sociology, ed. Robert E. Faris (Chicago,: Rand McNally, 1964), pp. 485–529.

9. Etzioni, op. cit.

10. Scott, op. cit.

11. Herbert Simon, "Inducements and Incentives in Bureaucracy," in Reader in Bureaucracy, ed. Robert Merton et al. (New York: The Free Press, 1952), pp. 327–34.

12. Max Weber, Theory of Social and Economic Organization, ed. Talcott Parsons (Glencoe: Free Press, 1964).

13. Scott, op. cit.

14. Alvin Gouldner, "Organizational Analysis," in Sociology Today, ed. Robert Merton, Leonard Broom, and F. Cottrell (New York: Basic Books, 1959), pp. 400–28.

15. U.S. Census, 1960.

16. Karl Taeuber and Alma Taeuber, Negroes in Cities (Chicago: Aldine, 1965), pp. 32, 39.

17. Community Improvement Program, Department of Planning and Urban Renewal, Akron, Ohio, 1964, p. 19.

18. "Akron Area Housing Market," Federal Housing Administration, April, 1965.

19. NAACP (Akron Branch), Civil Rights Committee, "The Status of Civil Rights in Akron," 1961, p. 2; Akron Community Service Center and Urban League, brief on urban renewal, March 1961, p. 1; Report of the Mayor's Task Force on Human Relations, Akron, Ohio, September 1, 1962, pp. 84–85.

20. Akron Beacon Journal, January 2, 1965, p. a–9.

21. Charles Perrow, "The Analysis of Goals in Complex Organizations," American Sociological Review 26, No. 6, (December 1961): 854–66.

22. Brochure, FHCS, December 1965, pp. 2–3.

23. Akron Beacon Journal, May 13, 1965.

24. Ibid., May 1965–September 1970.

25. Minutes, board of directors meeting, FIICS, May 17, 1965.

26. Ibid., April 17, 1967.

27. Ibid.

28. Ibid., June 19, 1967.

29. Akron Beacon Journal, June 30, 1967.

30. Brochure, op. cit.

31. Robert F. Bales, "Task Roles and Social Roles in Problem-Solving Groups," in Readings in Social Psychology, 3rd ed., ed. Eleanor E. Macoby, Theodore M. Newcomb, Eugene Hartley (New York: Holt, Rinehart and Winston, 1958).

32. Talcott Parsons, Toward a General Theory of Action (Cambridge, Mass: Harvard University Press, 1951).

33. George Homans, The Human Group (New York: Harcourt, Brace and World, 1950).

34. Bales, op. cit.

35. Akron Beacon Journal, May 28, 1968.

36. Minutes, board of directors meeting, FHCS, July 15, 1968.

37. Minutes, Board of Directors meeting, FHCS, September 16, 1968.

38. Ibid., October 21, 1968.

39. Proposal for a Fair Housing Center, FHCS, 1967, pp. 1-2.

40. Ibid.

41. Akron Beacon Journal, October 15, 1968.

42. Ibid., November 29, 1968.

43. Ibid., December 28, 1968.

44. Ibid., February 17, 1969.

45. Ibid., May 22, 1969.

46. Ibid., August 11, 1969.

47. Ibid., August 20, 1969.

48. Second proposal to OEO, FHCS, 1969, pp. 1-4.

49. Third proposal to OEO, FHCS, 1970, pp. 1-3.

50. Minutes, board of directors meeting, January 20, 1969.

51. Fair Housing Center Report, 4th Annual Meeting, FHCS, June 1969.

52. Minutes of 4th Annual Meeting, FHCS, June 1969.

53. Fair Housing Center Report, FHCS, January 20, 1969.

54. Akron Area Board of Realtors, Akron Realtor, May 7, 1969, p. 1.

55. Minutes of board of directors meeting, FHCS, May 19, 1969.

56. Akron Beacon Journal, March 25, 1969; April 30, 1969.

57. Clarence Funnyl, "A Directional Critique of the Akron Fair Housing Center," NCDH, October 19, 1969. Mimeographed.

58. Letter from Jordan Miller, Community Action Council director, October 27, 1969.

59. Fair Housing Center Annual Report, June 1970.

60. Weber, op. cit.

61. Chester B. Barnard, "A Definition of Authority," in Merton et al., op. cit., pp. 18-185.

62. Herbert A. Simon, "Inducements and Incentives in Bureaucracy", in ibid., pp. 327-334.

63. L. F. Carter, "Recording and Evaluating the Performance of Individuals as Members of Small Groups," Personnel Psychology 7 (1954): 477-84.

64. Bales, op. cit.

65. Juliet Saltman, Journal, April 15; 1969.

66. Minutes, Special Board Meeting, FHCS, April 29, 1969.

67. Minutes, 4th Annual Meeting, FHCS, June 2, 1969.

68. Akron Beacon Journal, September 20, 1969.

69. Ibid., October 8, 1969.

70. Letter from Jordan Miller, op. cit.

71. Minutes, board of directos meeting, FHCS, November 18, 1969.

72. Juliet Saltman, Journal, November 18, 1969.

73. Juliet Saltman, Journal, June 15, 1970.

74. Ibid., June 30, 1970.

75. Ibid., July 20, 1970.

76. Ibid., August 17, 1970.

77. U.S. Census, 1960, 1970. See Appendix B.

78. Based on FACS News History files, 1965-1977.

79. Akron Beacon Journal, editorial, "Akron Area Housing Bias Cries for Stronger Action," March 25, 1974.

80. Trends in Housing, NCDH, January-February, 1973.

81. Mayer Zald and Roberta Ash, "Social Movement Organizations," Social Forces, 44 (1966): 327-341.

82. Mayer Zald and John McCarthy, "The Trend of Social Movements" (Morristown, N.J.: General Learning Press, 1973).

83. Jo Freeman, "Resource Mobilization and Strategy—A Model for Analyzing Social Movement Organizations." Paper presented at Social Movements Symposium, Vanderbilt University, Nashville, Tenn., March 17, 1977.

5

THE COMMUNITY LEVEL:
MOVEMENT ORGANIZATIONS,
A COMPARATIVE ANALYSIS

INTRODUCTION

Etzioni has been cited as advocating a comparative analysis of organizations in evaluating organizational success. This approach he delineates as a "system model" in contrast to the more traditional "goal model."[1]

The goal-model approach defines success as a complete or substantial realization of the organizational goal. Two weaknesses in this approach are noted by Etzioni. First, the goal model tends to impart a tone of social criticism rather than scientific analysis. Since most organizations do not usually attain their goals in any final sense, and are low in effectiveness, the organization can invariably be reported to be a failure. Etzioni admits to the validity of this approach rather reluctantly, but notes that it is valid only from the particular viewpoint chosen by the researcher. (Is this not true of all research?)

The system model, on the other hand, assesses performances in relation to one another rather than comparing existing organizations to ideals of what they might be. The system model recognizes that the organization solves certain problems other than those directly involved in the achievement of the goal. It also allows one to conclude that there may be overallocation as well as underallocation of resources to meet the goals of the organization.

Two subtypes of system models are noted by Etzioni. One is referred to as a survival model—that is, a set of requirements which, if fulfilled, allows the system to exist. The second subtype is an effectiveness model. It defines a pattern of interrelations among the elements of the system which would make it most effective in the service of a given goal. The survival model would not record significant changes in organizational operations; the model only asks whether the basic requirements of the organization are being met. The use of the effectiveness model evaluates changes that have occurred in the organization, and how they affect the ability of the organization to serve its goals, as compared to its earlier state or other organizations of its kind.

A third, alternative approach suggested here, which combines elements of the goal and system models, may be called a goal-effective model. Using a comparative analystical framework, it may be possible to assess the effectiveness of several organizations dedicated to the same goal. The measure of success is not the complete or even substantial attainment of the goal, but rather the relative effectiveness of each organization in its attempt to move toward its stated goal.

In the case of the open-housing movement, the recognized stated goal is equal opportunities in housing for minorities. It will be seen that each movement organization on the community level approaches this goal through different means and emphases. To the extent that each movement organization is able to effect systemic changes on the community level in reaching this goal, one can meaningfully refer to the success of that organization.

Ultimately, this study attempts to provide help in understanding the social movement as it relates to social change. Social change cannot take place without structural systemic change. Thus, this chapter is devoted to an examination of potential systemic change in four communities which contained local open-housing movement organizations: New York, Denver, Seattle, and Los Angeles.

Each of the four movement organizations was selected in terms of the factor of change from volunteer to funded (institutionalized) operation, in a further attempt to understand also the process of institutionalization as it relates to social movements. Records, reports, documents, interviews, and field visits supplied the information for this analysis of the goals, program development, and impact of these four movement organizations, examined from two time perspectives: first in 1970 and again in 1977.

In addition, brief profiles are offered of 12 current (1977) movement organizations across the country, indicating their diversity, scope, and ingenuity in confronting the open-housing issue in their own communities.

TWO THAT LIVED

As soon as it is admitted that the whites and the emancipated blacks are placed upon the same territory in the situation of two foreign communities, it will readily be understood that there are but two chances for the future: the Negroes and the whites must either wholly part or wholly mingle.[2]

Alexis de Tocqueville, 1833

The thing to do is open an office.[3]

Robinson D. Lapp
Executive Director,
Metro Denver Fair Housing
Center, Inc., 1969

New York: Open Housing Center

Time: 1970

Inception. The Open Housing Center was called Operation Open City when it began in January 1964 as a pilot volunteer project of the NCDH. Its specific purpose was to develop practical, effective methods for achieving greater dispersion of minorities throughout the five boroughs of New York City. The demonstration project of Operation Open City (OOC) tested the hypothesis that more rapid dispersion of minorities would occur if information regarding housing opportunities were made available to minorities, and if aid in securing such opportunities were provided by residents of the neighborhoods containing the available housing.

At the time OOC was launched, 15 volunteer fair-housing groups existed in New York, and 95 percent of the housing supply in New York was covered by fair-housing legislation. Rent control existed for apartments built before 1940, making these available for less than $250/ per month.

Administration of the Open City project was transferred to the Urban League of Greater New York in the fall of 1964, under a cooperation agreement with NCDH. It operated with a staff of three until February 1966, when a New York City antipoverty grant of $136,250 made possible its expansion to a staff of 22 full-time and 15 part-time workers, the opening of offices in Brooklyn and Queens, and enlargement of the Manhattan office.

The grant was renewed for the period September 1966–June 1967 in the amount of $227,660 and was then extended through the end of that year. In January 1968 the grant was increased to $381,939 for the new fiscal year, making possible the opening of a Bronx office and the increase of the total Open City staff to 33 full-time and 12 part-time workers.

In addition, $10,000 a year was received from the New York Foundation, and $30,000 a year from the Ford Foundation, through the National Urban League's Operation Equality program, to conduct two small fair-housing centers in predominantly white residential areas of Brooklyn and Queens.

The director of OOC, (Betty Hoeber) explained the link between open housing and poverty:[4]

> The freedom to move is not only a basic matter of dignity, and the right to secure better housing, but it is an important factor in breaking the poverty cycle. New York City has recognized the fact that discrimination and poverty are part of the same vicious cycle, by supporting Operation Open City for the last three years as part of its anti-poverty program. We believe this is the only city to use its anit-poverty funds in the fight against discrimination.*

Goals. Operation Open City was described by its director as

> an action program with the purpose of helping blacks and Puerto Ricans secure the same choice in housing which white New Yorkers have. It is based on the premise that equal access to housing is a fundamental right of all, and on the fact, often obscured, that desirable housing is available in neighborhoods throughout the city and the surroundings suburbs at prices residents of the ghetto can pay.[5]

The rationale for the OOC program stemmed from the social and ecological context of the New York area. New York City and New York State had open-housing laws for over ten years (see Chapter 2), but their use was been extremely limited and their enforcement very weak. Racial discrimination in housing was widespread, shutting black and Puerto Rican New Yorkers out of large residential areas in all boroughs, and out of thousands of individual buildings and blocks throughout the city. An examination of a map of racial distribution of residents in the five boroughs reveals four major ghetto areas, which are geographically quite small: Harlem, Bedford-Stuyvesant, the South Bronx, and South Jamaica in Queens. But in these areas are crowded almost two million people, while large

---

*See discussion of Akron and Los Angeles.

sections in all boroughs remain over 90 percent white. At least four-fifths of the land mass of the city is predominantly white.

Thus the stated goal of OOC was to open up these areas, in which moderate-cost, rent-controlled apartments are monopolized by whites, "where there is space, and green trees, and uncrowded schools. The families crowded in the ghettos, paying high prices to the slum lords, have the right to this housing and to any new housing that is built, and our purpose is to help them get it."[6]

Late in 1969, OOC was directed to change its goals—both stated and operative—by its funding agency, the local antipoverty organization (New York Council Against Poverty, Community Development Agency). Its proposal for 1969-70 reflected this directive by emphasizing programs of technical assistance and fund raising rather than open housing.[7]

In order to guarantee the continuation of its open-housing program, OOC prepared a separate proposal for the independent funding of an open-housing center. This proposal delinieated the problem of changed focus; calling attention to the thousands of families who would not be helped under the changed program. Those families were and are the ones who need help in combating racial discrimination in housing; who seek assistance at the rate of 800 a month. Separate funding for this project was to be sought from corporations, foundations, and government to insure the continuation of the fight for open housing in New York City.[8]

Program. The plan of action for Operation Open City is twofold. One direction is toward assisting the minority community through wide distribution of detailed and current information on units for sale or rent in predominantly white communities. In addition, information is provided on the characteristics of those communities, and on general, sound home-seeking practices. The aim is not only to draw registrants who are actively in the market for housing into the Open City office, but also to encourage blacks generally to move into the mainstream of the market by taking advantage of good housing buys in neighborhoods located outside ghetto areas and their fringes. Virtually every medium of communication is used on a continuing basis to reach nonwhite families.

The second direction of the program is toward identifying and involving residents of predominantly white neighborhoods in all sections of the city who are commited to integration. These residents form the nucleus of local fair-housing groups, which are a fundamental part of the OOC program. Sparking the formation of new local fair-housing committees and groups is an integral and continuing part of the Open City operation.

These voluntary groups perform two basic functions. First, they assemble and provide OOC with a detailed profile of their communities, giving all possible information that persons looking for a home might want to have. Open City calls these profiles "Spotlight Neighborhood #3"—or #17, and so on, and distributes them en masse.

The second role of the fair-housing group combines salesmanship with support. Personal contact is established with interested applicants, or applicants who think they might be interested; fairhousing members show the neighborhood and discuss its advantages; they may accompany the home seeker to rental and brokerage offices; where deemed advisable, they supply checkers to assure that discrimination is quickly detected and appropriate measures are taken to halt it; when needed, they supply evidence to substantiate charges of discrimination under New York's fair-housing laws. If the family moves in, the fair-housing group tries to assure that the move is made routinely and that the family's life in the new neighborhood is normal in all respects.

Since OOC is something of a mother-figure to all the other funded metropolitan fair-housing centers, the details of its specific program operation will be considered here.

Specific Procedures. OOC more closely resembles a ghetto-based organization than do most other metropolitan centers. Its main office is in the heart of Harlem, and it operates two reception centers in black ghettos in Brooklyn and Queens, and one other office in the Bronx, in addition to the two fair-housing centers in white areas of Brooklyn and Woodside. About 900 people each month find their way to these offices in search of apartments or homes. One official noted, "When they come in, we don't BS them. We tell them they may be given a tough time by landlords and real estate people. We also tell them what the law says and how they can use the law to protect themselves.[9]

Homeseekers fill out a registration form and have an interview with a housing counselor. The program is explained, the legal right to all housing is clearly spelled out, with information about how the laws work, and how OOC provides the concrete help of a white checker when discrimination is met, or suspected.

Each registrant is given a basic kit of material especially prepared by Open City—"Homeseeker's Guide," with information on how to start looking for an apartment or house, specific newspapers to look at (both well-known dailies and lesser-known neighborhood and nationality papers), "Tips on Apartment Hunting," "Your Rights Under the Law," and a number of "Neighborhood Spotlights." In addition, detailed information on some 40 neighborhoods throughout

the city is provided, as well as a list of local fair-housing committees which are ready to assist nonwhite families in securing housing
in their areas.

Additional special housing bulletins and booklets are added
according to the needs of the home seeker—for example, "Your
Housing Rights" for welfare recipients, and information on how to
apply for housing in two large rent-controlled complexes in the Bronx
(Co-op City and Parkchester, which OOC forced to open to nonwhites).

The OOC staff checks all newspapers regularly, picking out
listings which are within the price range of registrants and seem
desirable. These listings are xeroxed and given to the new registrants,
and are available at the switchboards for all registrants who phone
for them. "The purpose is to stimulate and assist families in using
these unfamiliar tools in seeking available housing."[10] All registrants are cross-indexed according to the size of apartment wanted,
the price range, and the location desired, Using this cross-index,
specific registrants are located for the listings as they occur, and
are then contacted by phone or mail so that they can apply for the
available housing.

Registrants are prepared for the types of discrimination they
may encounter. The OOC kit includes a list of ways in which landlords may discriminate: "If you are told you cannot see the apartment. . .if you are given indefinite answers about the rent. . .if
you are asked for more personal information than the checker. . . ."
Thus, if the registrant confronts an agent or landlord who says "the
apartment is already rented," or quotes a high price, or will not
take a deposit, he is prepared to immediately call OOC so that a
white checker can be sent to apply for the same apartment or house.
The checkers are carefully trained in workshops and through written
instructions prepared by OOC, in order to secure the evidence needed
for filing complaints with the Human Rights Commission or the office
of the secretary of state which issues licenses of real estate brokers.

Because the housing shortage in New York is so acute, the
checker usually puts down a deposit to hold the apartment. This is
done ostensibly until he or she can return to sign the lease, but
actually to keep the apartment from being rented while the black or
Puerto Rican applicant files a complaint of discrimination.

OOC is authorized by the New York City Commission on Human
Rights to take complaints, have them notarized, and sent with the
checker's statement to the commission for action. Their greatest
success in securing apartments has been by the technique of confrontation with the landlord or his agent.

The checker who has left the deposit makes a date to sign
a lease a few days later. On that day the checker, the

complainant and an investigator from the Commission
all arrive for the lease signing together. The landlord
is caught red-handed. In most cases he agrees to make
the apartment available to the complainant. If he refuses,
the Commission has the power to "post" the apartment,
tacking a large poster on the door stating that the unit
is under investigation of charges of discrimination, and
warning any innocent party from attempting to rent it.[11]

The legal procedures of the commission then follow, conferences
at the commission offices with the respondent, the complainant, and
a volunteer lawyer provided by OOC, and finally a commission hearing
if the case is not settled in conference. A panel of volunteer lawyers
provides legal advice and representation to the complainants at commission conferences and hearings, and works with OOC in making
use of the laws.

This case-by-case approach, requiring a panel of checkers
who are always on call, is a "clumsy and tedious way of compelling
people to obey the law. It also puts an unfair burden of time and
emotional stress upon the victims of discrimination."[12] OOC has
tried to devise more effective techniques. In 1969 it concentrated on
the Metropolitan Life Insurance Company, which owns four large
housing developments in New York. Once of them, Parkchester in
the Bronx, had a nonwhite tenancy of less than half of 1 per cent,
although OOC and other organizations have referred hundreds of
nonwhite families to it over the years. As a result of pressure from
OOC and other groups, the city Human Rights Commission has wrung
from Metropolitan Life an agreement to open its doors to nonwhite
tenants.

Similarly, OOC is currently focusing on such potentially desegregating techniques as scattered-site public housing, urban renewal,
and revision of welfare payments. OOC makes no distinctions in the
quality of service it offers, nor in the kinds of families it hopes to
attract. In New York the Welfare Department must pay the full rent
for a family on welfare, regardless of how high the rent happens to
be; this makes OOC's task somewhat easier. On the other hand,
landlords are permitted to refuse to rent to these families simply
because they are on welfare. The result is that OOC, unlike many
other groups, spends a considerable amount of time and energy
assisting families on welfare and wrangling with welfare workers,
whose putative responsibility it is to find decent housing for their
clients, but who are generally content to move them in and out of
rat-infested, segregated tenements.

Impact. The impact of any open-housing program must be viewed
against a backdrop of local constraints, two of which were cited by

OOC's director. One of the chief constraints in New York is the lack of existing housing that low-income families can afford. The other is the inadequate amount of new housing being built for low- and moderate-income families.

The Census Bureau's most recent release reports a vacancy rate in New York City's apartments of 1.23 percent. This means a very limited turnover, especially in rent-controlled apartments. Though the city is fortunate in having rent control on apartments built before 1940, there is a continuing and well-mounted attack on rent control from local landlord groups. The city administration is under heavy pressure to repeal it, and OOC is engaged in constant battle to maintain it. Rents not under control are rapidly increasing toward enormous figures.

Coupled with the low vacancy rate in existing housing, is the totally inadequate amount of new housing being built in New York to rent at moderate prices. The building of public housing is almost at a standstill, as it is in other parts of the country (Akron notwithstanding: see Chapter 4). OOC, therefore "must scramble in this tight market for available housing. Our effort to secure equal access to the housing that does exist is all the more important, while we are campaigning for building new housing."[13] Because rent controlled apartments are often not advertised, it is extremely difficult for the OOC staff to ascertain when they are available.

> Therefore, we sent 'scouts', white volunteers or paid
> part-time workers, who go to doormen, agents, supers,
> searching for available apartments. This is time-con-
> suming and tedious work, not always rewarding, but
> necessary in the situation.[14]

In the face of these constraints, the impact of the OOC program has been considerable. Since 1966, 19,420 families have applied to OOC for help, and 2,500 of them have been placed—all in predominantly white neighborhoods. In addition, according to Director Betty Hoeber, another 2,000 families have found housing as an indirect result of OOC's efforts. Since the average registrant's family has three or four members, it is estimated that approximately 15,000 people have moved through Open City to better and desegregated housing. In addition, 500 complaints of discrimination have been filed. Though no violators of municipal and state fair-housing laws in New York have as yet gone to jail, OOC has succeeded in bringing about the license suspensions of 18 real estate brokers found to be discriminating.

These totals, of course, represent only a tiny dent in New York's segregated fortress, but the dent is visible both to the guardians of the fortress, who have been compelled to pay strict attention to OOC, and to ghetto dwellers, who now know that the ramparts are assailable.

OOC's realistic stance on discriminatory practices—its insistence that in present-day society such practices are more the rule than the exception—has inspired the trust and confidence of many blacks. As one of them explained,

> Most white people just don't understand what we're facing. They keep talking about "a few bad apples in every barrel, " as if discrimination happens only once in a while. The thing about OOC is that they know most of the apples are rotten. [15]

This may be an exaggeration of OOC's sentiments, but it suggests to what an extent OOC has come to be identified with black aspirations as opposed to those of the white establishment. An OOC official was asked to explain her organization's relationship with members of "the local power structure." The reply was enlightening: "We have no relationship with them. We expect them to obey the laws like anyone else, and when they don't, we expect them to be thrown in jail. [16]

Relocation Analysis. In December 1967 a study was conducted by the Planners for Equal Opportunity on the first 600 families who had relocated through OOC's program. Entitled, "On The Move, A Survey Analysis," the study reported a number of findings based on 103 returned questionnaires. For most items of information, analysis was undertaken in reference to the degree of geographical desegregation accomplished by the move. [17] The geographical areas selected for analysis were grouped according to their proportion of nonwhite population.

The old and new addresses of respondents were plotted and connected on a map entitled "Locations of Open City Clients," which had a base showing racial distribution in school planning areas of New York City in 1964. In general the map showed a high concentration of clients located in Harlem moving to an expanded area of west, south, and central Bronx. There was a trend toward movements in Brooklyn to the south of the central ghettos. Movements in Queens were distributed widely, but tended to be made consistently toward the east. The map generally portrayed a movement from ghetto to nonghetto areas. The report[18] summarizes the data on the map. One measure of the tendency of respondents to move out of ghetto areas is that six times as many new locations as old were in white areas, and four times as many old locations as new were in ghetto areas.

Other attitude surveys in ghetto areas of New York City indicate that "the largest single problem facing Harlem residents in their own eyes is poor housing and living conditions. . . ."[19] When asked where they would like to live if they had to move, 83 percent of those questioned said outside of Harlem and none wanted their children to live in Harlem when they grew up. When respondents were asked to indicate by rank order the most important environmental features, the paramount value, to Open City's (OC) clients of better neighborhoods and buildings was emphasized.

Integration was cited by only one out of ten respondents as the most important community feature sought. Thus, although it is valued, integration is achieved more as a result of other environmental gains than as an independent ideal. The importance to OC's clients of more living space and the difficulty of obtaining it in the New York real estate market are well known to the staff of OC. In fact, more space is usually seen as accompanying the desired building and environmental features.

The survey also yielded unsolicited comments which respondents wrote on the back of the questionnaires. OOC has offered these comments ("moving statements") as a special measure of the success of its program. Though the comments are indeed a tribute to the excellence of the OOC program, a somewhat different measure of success is suggested. Specifically, the question must be raised as to what extent the Open City program has moved toward systemic change on the local level. The evidence seems to indicate that in spite of its development of a housing location service par excellence, its ability to open housing in the New York area has been limited. It is a fact that the one-to-one approach in securing housing does little to affect housing opportunities on a broad, massive scale. Yet, Open City administrators have recognized this, and have recently moved toward more comprehensive desegregating techniques. For example, an article in the New York Times indicated that a Department of Justice suit against S. J. Lefrak, one of the nation's leading builders, was based largely on investigation by Open City.

> Open City officials said yesterday that they had begun to supply the Justice Department with information on Mr. Lefrak as well as numerous other landlords, early in 1969. . . .Justice Department officials said they were concentrating on Mr. Lefrak because they believed a case against a large landlord would have more impact than charges brought against small ones. The Attorney General called it the largest housing case ever undertaken by the Federal Government. . . .Lefrak owns 21,000 apartments in Brooklyn and Queens, and was charged with discriminating against blacks.[20]

Perhaps OOC's growing concern with more sweeping desegregating techniques suggests the apparent inevitability that a listing, or housing location service with a relatively simple program will grow into a large and complex center of political action. This would seem to be called for if the group is really dedicated to the expansion of equal opportunities in housing—and Open City's entire approach suggests that it is.

Time: 1977

Late in 1970, the Open Housing Center (OHC) began as an independent agency, after it broke off amicably from OEO-funded Operation Open City.* Though still linked to the New York Urban League, (UL) its source of funding completely changed to employer contracts, which accounted by 1977 for $100,000 of its total $151,000 budget. Additional funding came from foundation and church grants. Forty major employers of New York now participate in the program, which continues to locate suitable housing for sale or rent and also combats discrimination. More than 35,000 New York employees are covered by OHC contracts with their employers. All 5,000 employees of the Federal Reserve Bank have access to the program, as do employees of companies such as the New York Stock Exchange, IBM, Exxon, General Electric, Xerox, Pfizer Inc., and Bristol-Myers. Director Betty Hoeber explains:

> Employers are beginning to realize that housing is a
> constant problem for their employees. With the lowest
> vacancy rate in the country, and the highest rents,
> employees in New York really need the expert help
> which we give.[21]

The OHC program is considered a comprehensive one by Mrs. Hoeber, whose staff now includes three full-time discrimination specialist, and two secretaries—one full-time and one part-time. An integral part of its program has been the preparation and updating of housing information in booklets and bulletins and flyers to help prospective home seekers. The titles are indicative of the focus: "Middle-Income Coops and Rentals," "Homeseeker's Guide," "Apartment

---

*OOC was appointed in 1970 as the New York City technical assistance agency for housing in 26 poverty areas. This prompted the friendly separation of the two programs, with the Open Housing Center leaving to begin its own concentrated effort to reduce housing discrimination, and to offer housing listings.

Rental Book," "Tenant Fact Book," and "Neighborhood Spotlights."
Six hundred registrants are being serviced at one time, and more
than 300 discrimination complaints a year are handled.

Audits more recently have been an important part of the OHC
program, resulting in a Department of Justice pattern-and-practice
suit against Trump Management Co. in 1973, and a consent decree
in 1975. One of the difficulties of being linked to the Urban League,
some of the staff said, was the League's reluctance to be associated
with any legal action stemming from discrimination cases. Staff
members spoke of watching five different UL directors come and go,
all of whom were uneasy about discrimination lawsuits.

This may have been one of the factors leading to the Open
Housing Center's voluntary separation from the New York Urban
League in February 1977. At that time, OHC moved back to their
earlier quarters (150 Fifth Avenue), announcing their reaffiliation
with Operation Open City, a separate antipoverty housing agency.
This affiliation is primarily one of referral and exchange, with each
program separately directed, maintained and housed.

In October 1977 the Open Housing Center submitted a proposal
to the city of New York for a grant of $150,000 under the Community
Development Block-Grant program. The proposal calls for an expanded
housing discrimination service for New York City home and apartment
seekers who are denied access to housing because of race, national
origin, religion, or sex. The proposal notes that the Open Housing
Center receives 350 discrimination complaints a year, which is the
maximum lead its small staff can handle. For this reason, the service
is not widely publicized. Despite the limited staff, both the city and
state Human Rights Commissions refer complainants to the OHC,
since they are the only organization available to help people secure
the evidence needed to file complaints with appropriate agencies or
the courts.

The need for the expansion of this service was also linked to
the evidence of housing discrimination in New York City. Cited were
the national HUD audit (June 1977), showing 90 percent racial discrimination in sales and rentals sought; and a New York Times survey
of June 28, 1976 indicating 100 building owners whose apartment were
offered in a discriminatory manner.[22]

The survival and success of the Open Housing Center is due to
steadfast, able, and dedicated leadership and direction of Betty
Hoeber. Honored for her work on open housing since 1964, she
received an award from the National Association of Housing and
Redevelopment in 1973. Commissioner Eleanor Holmes Norton,
chairperson of the city Commission on Human Rights, presented the
association's Award of Merit to Betty Hoeber with these words:

Housing is the toughest part of the civil rights struggle.
Mrs. Hoeber started as a volunteer and developed a program which has become a model in communities across
the U.S. Thousands of minority families in New York have
secured the housing of their choice only because of the
determination and persistence of Betty Hoeber and her
staff. [23]

Despite disruption and repeated change in funding sources and
amounts, affiliation, and location, all the indications are that this
determination and persistence will continue to make the Open Housing
Center effective, regardless of the external conditions affecting
funding and affiliation. Even when she almost lost all funding in
1970, Mrs. Hoeber picked up the pieces of the program, left the
antipoverty agency (Operation Open City), changed the organization's
name, moved, found new sources of support, left a second time,
moved, reaffiliated, and now is trying to enlarge the open-housing
program again. Though everything else changed, the leadership did
not. On the community level it is leadership that seems to be the
single most important factor in the success or failure of an open-
housing program.

Los Angeles: Fair Housing Congress

Time: 1970

Inception. In the fall of 1968 the Community Relations Conference of
Southern California expanded its already existing Metropolitan Fair
Housing Center into the more comprehensive Housing Opportunities
Center of Greater Los Angeles, operating on a one-year demonstration grant from OEO, with a budget of $258,300.
    The Housing Opportunities Center (HOC) has three divisions:
Metropolitan Fair Housing Division, Low Income Housing Information Division, and Low Income Housing Development Division. It is
the fair-housing division that is the most highly developed of the three,
largely because it is an extension of one of "the most effective volunteer grass roots fair housing movements in the country." [24]
    This volunteer effort began in 1960 with the formation of the
Fair Housing Council of the San Fernando Valley, a suburban area
of Los Angeles with a population of one million. In February 1967
the Community Relations Conference of Southern California expanded
the very limited area-wide fair-housing referral service it had begun
in 1965 into the Metropolitan Los Angeles Fair Housing Center. This
center was organized and operated in the beginning by volunteers

working under the overall direction of the conference's executive
director and the conference's housing committee chairman. It was
this center that was incorporated into the larger, funded Housing
Opportunities Center as one of its three divisions.

Goals. The long-term goal of the funded center is the "realization
of an adequate supply of housing available to and utilized by minority
families in all income brackets in communities throughout the Los
Angeles area."[25] The immediate goal was to begin a number of
affirmative education and action programs "designed to counteract
the major forces that have kept vast numbers of Negro and Mexican
Americans living within circumscribed areas of our city."[26] In
addition, various programs to upgrade housing opportunities within
present low-income areas of Los Angeles would be undertaken.
    The first brochure distributed by the Housing Opportunities
Center states that the HOC is "a new concept in seeking solutions
to the complex housing problems of our sprawling urban area."[27]
The three divisions were cited as comprising the Center, each devoted
to achieving different goals through a distinctive program. The Metro
(politan) Fair Housing Division was described as "a coordinator of
local fair housing and human relations groups working at the grass-
root level to promote open housing in the Los Angeles Megalopolis."[28]
It was also the contention of those operating the Center that a necessary prerequisite to achieving its long-range goal was the establishment of true freedom of choice in housing in Los Angeles—
"an absolutely open, racially unrestricted market in which housing
is affirmatively merchandised to families and persons of all racial
groups in all communities."[29]
    The predecessor of the Housing Opportunities Center, the
Metro Fair Housing Center, was sponsored by the Community Relations Conference of Southern California, as has already been noted.
This Conference was a 21-year-old association of 82 organizations
"working to promote better human relations through intergroup
cooperation." In its brochure, the earlier Metro Fair Housing Center
stated simply that it "works for free choice in housing for anyone,
anywhere." Thus, the goals of the Metro Fair Housing Division of
the funded Housing Opportunities Center were an extension and continuation of the original volunteer fair-housing movement in California.

Program. During the first nine months of operation, the Center was
contacted by 500 minority persons or families seeking housing. In
June 1967 the Center was able to employ one staff person (through
the efforts of local fair-housing councils), but "it became increasingly apparent as the months passed that the service as it was being
rendered was inadequate to meet the need."[30] Many of the programs

later carried out by the Metro Fair Housing Division of the funded HOC were conceived during the earlier phase.

The Metro Fair Housing Division currently has six staff members. Through the use of housing counselors, fair-housing field representatives, and an increasing network of grass roots fair-housing councils, this division provides an across-the-board referral service for minority families of all income levels seeking housing outside areas of racial concentration or areas in rapid racial turnover. In addition to operating this referral service, the division is engaged in an area-wide affirmative education program to promote open housing. It also is involved in action programs to deal with the problems of housing discrimination, lack of information by minority persons about housing opportunities in suburban areas, and the "widespread misconception that minority persons, especially if they are black, cannot find housing in which they will be able to live comfortably except within or on the fringes of existing ghettos.[31]

Strategy. The Metro Fair Housing Division has three departments: Housing Services, Community Organization, and Special Projects. The overall strategy of the division is to create as rapidly as possible a strong network of regional fair-housing centers to which minority home seekers can be referred. Experience gained in the San Fernando Valley volunteer effort indicated that such centers can be most effective when they maintain an office centrally located in a recognized geographic area. This facilitates extensive use of volunteers recruited from the local community to work with local groups, businesses, lending institutions, developers, local government officials, and their own neighbors, in support of a racially desegregated community. These regional offices also were viewed by division administrators as best suited for coordinating local community people to work one-to-one with individual minority home seekers referred by the Metro Center or contacting them directly.

There are no funds in the budget of the HOC for direct financial support of these regional centers or local fair-housing councils, but they are supported with program promotional materials, some equipment, central duplicating services and staff guidance. The only regional centers with offices and paid staff are in San Fernando Valley and Orange County. The Metro Fair Housing Division is working with local communities with the goal of establishing centers in ten additional Los Angeles areas.

The people in the grass roots fair housing movement of L.A. consider the Housing Opportunities Center "their" resource center. They meet with the Metro staff frequently and use it for cross fertilization of programs as

well as a focus for area-wide concerns. In addition to
helping with local problems, Center staff is working with
these community groups to catalogue profiles on housing
opportunities throughout the L.A. area. This is something heretofore unavailable in L.A. County.[32]

The Metro Fair Housing staff also provides direct assistance
to minority persons looking for housing in communities where there
are no local fair-housing groups in existence. They are developing
new direct confrontation techniques involving the home seeker, the
staff, and when possible, a community volunteer who acts as a wit-
ness in cases of suspected discrimination. The Center does not make
any special effort to maintain in its office a list of rental or sale properties. Rather, the staff and volunteers work with each individual
home seeker to explore the total housing market. With all housing
now legally open to all persons, "the assumption is that a homeseeker
should not limit his choice to a few properties that may have already
been identified as available for minorities."[33]

Discrimination complaints are handled through liaison with
cooperating attorneys and the agencies charged with enforcing the
fair-housing laws. The Center has organized an area-wide file of
lawyers who will handle housing discrimination cases in either state
or federal court. In addition, the Center has organized training sessions for these lawyers with the intent of gathering the necessary
documentation for patterns of practice suits to be filed in the courts.

Public Relations. Public relations for the Fair Housing Division have
been closely tied to a campaign in support of open housing launched
through the efforts of the Los Angeles County Commission on Human
Relations. This campaign had a commercial value estimated at
$250,000 and included radio and TV spots, newspaper ads and bill-
boards, and numerous promotional materials, all featuring the
symbol and phone number of the HOC office. During the early weeks
of the campaign, volunteers handled several hundred phone calls
requesting further information. Callers were told how they could
work for open housing in their own communities, and their names
were referred to local fair-housing councils. A number of organizations also called the Center for promotional materials.

In addition to the educational materials obtained through the
efforts of the commission, the Center produced thousands of bumper
stickers (reading, "Good Neighbors Come in All Colors"), sheets of
stamps with the HOC symbol (saying, "Support Open Housing"), HOC
lapel pins, and flyers about the Center. The original supply of promotional material purchased by HOC was offered without charge.
Subsequently, the cost of reordering was covered by donations from

those requesting the material, thus enabling the original campaign to extend beyond the limits of the HOC budget.

Various methods are used by HOC to reach the minority community with information about open housing. One considered most promising is the commitment of the Los Angeles Sentinel (largest Los Angeles black newspaper) to publish a weekly column on housing with a byline from HOC. These columns will be syndicated to other minority publications; for example, the Council for Civic Unity in San Francisco is exploring the use of the column in black publications in the Bay Area. Public-service radio spots were not found noticeably effective in attracting minority home seekers. On the other hand, classified ads placed in the Sentinel and one other weekly newspaper chain for one month produced so many home seekers that they had to be discontinued while the HOC staff caught up with the backlog. Such ads, with the message, "Fair Housing is a Fact. Find it Faster with Us, Housing Opportunities Center," will be resumed and extended to other newspapers in time. Flyers announcing service to home seekers posted on a great many government office bulletin boards locally have produced many home seekers for HOC.

In addition to the programs noted above, the Fair Housing Division initiated a monthly training session for volunteers from local fair-housing groups. Efforts have been expanded to enlist industry, large property-management firms, the California Real Estate Association, and a multitude of government and private agencies to consider open housing as a part of their responsibility. The Center has begun an investigation of possible illegal practices of rental agencies, which will culminate in a legal suit.

Impact. Viewing impact in terms of local constraints, HOC administrators listed eight which they felt hindered them in their operation.[34]

Multiplicity of government jurisdictions in the area was noted as the first constraint. The city of Los Angeles has a population of roughly four million, with an additional three million in the county. Besides the city of Los Angeles there are 77 incorporated cities within the county plus unincorporated areas. Four additional counties are serviced by the Housing Opportunities Center.

Political feuding was cited as the second constraint, referring to the long-standing feud between the mayor and some of the City Council members. Center officials felt that this situation at times blocked a more comprehensive approach to problem solving in the community.

The very size of the Los Angeles area was mentioned as the third constraint. Officials noted that suburban people never see the inner city. In addition, poor public transportation, or the complete lack of it, plus economic and racial housing segregation "keep low income persons 50 miles away from communities where there are jobs. "35

The fourth constraint cited was the lack of understanding of the intense and special housing problems of the Spanish speaking community. "Lack of understanding exists in both the Anglo and Negro community. The problem is complicated further by the Spanish-speaking community's (the largest minority group in L.A.) widespread mistrust of the outside community. "36

Multiplicity of realty boards in the area was named as the fifth constraint. As an example, the San Fernando Valley Realty Board (doing the largest volume of business west of the Mississippi) was noted as having "the most progressive attitude in the field of open housing of any Board in the California Real Estate Association. "37 Though the Valley is part of Los Angeles, it is separated physically and pyschologically from the rest of the city, according to HOC officials. There is a mountain range separating it from the city proper.

> The Valley Realty Board is not a part of the L.A. City
> Board. They have strict rules about going into each
> other's territory. Supposedly these rules have nothing
> to do with race. Since they have separate multiple listing
> services, it has the effect of keeping information about
> Valley housing out of the hands of Negro home buyers who
> by force of habit, conditioning or direction tend to deal
> with L.A. realty firms. 38

There are three major real estate boards in the city of Los Angeles, and in addition, every municipality in the area has a separate board. One local human relations council taking home-seeker referrals from HOC has to deal with six different boards in an area of 500,000 people. "Obviously this problem of too many realty boards compounds the failure of the housing industry itself to become more deeply involved in ending housing discrimination and segregation. 39

The sixth constraint was the existence of Article 34 in the Constitution of the state of California. This section, put into the constitution largely through the efforts of the California Real Estate Association, prohibits the construction of public housing units without referendum of the people in the political jurisdiction involved. The net result is that there have been no new units of public housing built in the Los Angeles area for 20 years. The Southern California Civil Liberties Union is planning a legal suit to test the constitutionality of Article 34.

The high cost of land in the Los Angeles area was named as the seventh constraint. Federal programs based upon land costs are difficult to initiate in the area for this reason.

The eighth and last constraint cited by HOC officials was "the inability to cut through the layers of public relations propaganda (including our own) to analyze what is actually happening."[40] It was stated by HOC officials that money for programs in the field of housing is so scarce that "no one wants to discuss their problems or failures or ways to correct them for fear they will not be refunded."[41] Also noted was the fact that many programs are being directed into less controversial projects with the view that it is better to solve part of the problem than nothing at all because of lack of funding. As an example, "everyone loves 202 housing for the elderly. It's so safe. Desegregated housing for poor families, especially if they are black, is another matter. Few groups are eager to handle the issues and problems involved."[42]

With some bitterness, HOC administrators commented on the situation of the local urban renewal agency:

> In applying for funds for redevelopment work, the local Community Redevelopment Agency has always been able to come up with figures to prove that there is adequate low-cost housing for all persons being displaced by the project in question. The location of this housing never seems to be as clear when the time comes for actual move-ins.[43]

In 1968, HOC had a contract with the agency to do fair-housing relocation work in an urban renewal area. Their staff members found that most people who had lived in the area had long since moved. Most of those left were so poverty stricken that "there was almost no hope of finding them housing anywhere else. . . . Most of these people sooner or later tend to disappear or be swallowed up in substandard housing in adjacent communities, thus getting the Agency off the hook."[44]

Indexes of Success. In view of these eight constraints, HOC was asked to assess the degree of success of its own program. They offered seven indexes of success, but very cautiously indicated their own lack of satisfaction with them.

> Assessing the degree of success or goal achievement in a field as subjective as the one in which HOC is working is a very subjective matter in itself. That is to say, there are all kinds of indices to use depending on how success- ful you want your program to appear. HOC has not yet found any measurements of success with which they are completely satisfied. Nevertheless, several categories

can be innumerated. Some are easy to define, others are more general in nature.[45]

The first measure of success noted by HOC was "degree of frustration in the community." It was felt by the director of Low Income Housing Information that the only honest measure of success is the degree "to which we create frustration in the community and then assist in constructively organizing it." It was explained further:

> Any program in existence today, anywhere in the country, must go faster than the articulated demand of a community that knows it has inadequate housing. Programs will be a success only if they arouse the whole community— affluent taxpayers in the suburbs, as well as residents of the inner city—to take action.[46]

The second index of success cited by HOC was the racial and ethnic head-count in the school system. Claiming that "the goal of establishing true freedom of choice in housing in L.A. can only be demonstrated when it is exercised," HOC stated that the success of this aspect of the program "must be measured in part, at least, by the degree to which minority families in significant numbers are able to and do freely move to all parts of the L.A. area."[47] HOC claimed that a yearly racial and ethnic head-count of the Los Angeles school system was the most practical and reliable measure of the degree of desegregation in the area. They noted that this had at least proved in some degree a measure of the efforts of the Fair Housing Council of the San Fernando Valley. The last head-count of schools showed over half of the 400-plus public schools there had at least some black students, and that these desegregated shcools were widely dispersed. This was seen as in marked contrast to other Los Angeles communities where there had been less fair-housing effort.

However, HOC officials admit that the yearly school count may be less than a perfect measure of the success of a fair-housing effort. For example, the Los Angeles school system has recently adopted a limited busing plan. This, along with the contention that school publications on the fringes of a ghetto do not reflect the racial composition of the surrounding community, weakens the validity of the measure.

The number of desegregated moves was cited as a third possible measure of success, but the serious limitations of this measure were openly acknowledged, with considerably detailed self-questioning:

> Even computers give out misleading information if they are programmed with conflicting data. So it is that HOC

has observed a marked inconsistency amongst fair housing
groups around the country as to what constitutes a desegregated move, an index which is so often taken as a measure of success. Is any move by a minority person (that
is, after the first one) into a community on the fringes of
an area of concentration a desegregated move? How about
the move of a Negro family into an "integrated community"?
What is an integrated community? Boundary lines on the
edge of an area of minority concentration are so fluid that
a move into a particular community yesterday may have
been a move towards successful desegregation; tomorrow
a similar move may be one that only intensifies racial
segregation. . . .

What appears to be a measure of success for one fair
housing center may be, upon closer examination, only
the result of the way they record their statistics.[48]

HOC does not record moves into already integrated neighborhoods as being desegregated, though they do assist the movement
of minorities into such areas in both their Fair Housing Division and
their Low Income Housing Information Division.

A fourth measure of success mentioned by HOC was "Degree
normal channels of acquiring housing are open." To clarify this,
HOC explained that they did not feel that the number of home seekers
being processed through the Center was a very meaningful measure
of success. In theory, quite the opposite should be true, since one
of its prime goals is to make the normal channels of acquiring housing
open to all. A better measure of success, they felt, might be the
number of real estate brokers in a given area who actually would or
do give equal service, or the number of apartments actually desegregated. As an example, they noted that the number of black home
seekers contacting the Fair Housing Council of the San Fernando
Valley has increased at a steady, slow rate since 1965. At the same
time, however, the number of apartment houses in the area known to
have been desegregated during the same period of time has jumped
from 15 in 1965 to 128 by the end of 1968. Likewise, in 1965 the
Valley Council was able to refer home seekers to only a handful of
brokers whom they knew would give equal service. By the end of
1968, over 100 real estate offices in the Valley had given a written
commitment to the council in support of equal service, The Valley
Realty Board is now a member of the Fair Housing Council, and is
joining with the council in attempting to find ways to reach the individual salesmen of its member firms, "most of whom are not as
enlightened as the Board itself."[49]

The fifth measure of success cited by HOC was "How well the law is enforced." HOC spends considerable staff time working for affirmative action with apartment house owners and managers. Although other state and federal agencies have been authorized to "engage in affirmative action," it was felt by HOC that such action was nonexistent or ineffectual. For example, the state Fair Employment Practices Commission (FEPC) was given no appropriation or staff to engage in this program, and HUD was given limited funds: "How much they can do around the country with only 2 million dollars is questionable." Therefore, HOC officials query:

> Is getting more money appropriated for HUD or FEPC so that they can be more effective a measure of success for HOC?. . .
>
> How can one measure the immediate effect of direct affirmative educational programs, other than reporting the number of people you make contact with who may or may not have been influenced by the message you convey?[50]

A sixth measure of success listed by HOC was "the number of additional housing units." They suggested that the number of additional housing units being made available to low-and moderate-income families in the Los Angeles area was so infinitesimally small that "if HOC can do anything at all to increase that number, it will be a success." But they raised further questions about this measure:

> Is success for the housing Development Division the degree to which it can find some way for the City Housing Authority to house more families under Section 23 housing? Is it helping to remove the roadblocks in the way of utilizing Section 235 and 236 of the 1968 Housing Act? Is it in being sure California legislators vote for a larger appropriation to carry out the provision of the National Housing Act?. . .Or does success lie in building 5 or 50 or 500 more units of 221-D-3 or 221-H housing in Los Angeles?[51]

Finally, their last measure of success was "increase of activity in the field." Such increases referred to general awareness of housing problems, community support for open housing, number of fair-housing groups, number of home seekers looking for housing in white areas, number of home seekers willing to seek legal recourse when faced with discrimination, number of attorneys willing to become involved in discrimination lawsuits on a contingency basis, and number of requests for speakers and fair-housing programs. In addition, they cited the increase in cooperation on the part of government agencies and community organizations as further indicators of increased activity in the field.

HOC of Los Angeles ended its discussion and consideration of success with three more questions:

> How to measure success? Compared to what? Compared
> to what would be happening if this program were not in
> existence, or what can be accomplished compared to the
> need? Obviously, these are questions that are difficult
> to resolve. [52]

Having begun as only a fair-housing center, the establishment of two field offices in the black and brown low-income ghettos of Los Angeles has forced the staff to confront appalling problems on a daily basis. The vicious cycle of poverty that leaves families with 6 to 12 children in two-bedroom apartments may seem at times to have little to do with opening up suburban housing. HOC has had to ask if they are one and the same problem, and has had to establish priorities. They admit that there is a great temptation on the part of their staff to concentrate on areas that might be easiest, or those "where we would not upset anyone who might have influence over our funding," [53] but they feel that their staff is more interested in solving the dual problem of poverty and discrimination than in job security. "We, therefore, expect to have considerable impact on the Los Angeles housing scene." [54]

End of Funding. Unfortunately, a field visit to Los Angeles in September 1969 did not warrant the same conclusion. This was not due to inadequacies in the program, but rather to the imminent loss of funding for the Fair Housing Division. A staff worker for that division (Marnesba Tackett, the Community Organization specialist) revealed [55] that HOC had been directed by OEO to emphasize the Low-Income Housing Information Division and the Housing Development Division, and to minimize or eliminate the Fair Housing Division. They had also been advised that HUD would no longer fund fair-housing programs, since it was believed that "Fair Housing is passé." Thus it was expected at the time (less than one year after funding began) that there would be no central fair-housing program or coordination, and the 60 localized, volunteer fair-housing groups would have to continue their work on their own.

Mrs. Tackett—small, energetic, middle-aged, black, and vocal—also disclosed the fact that the change to a funded operation (from a voluntary one) had, in her opinion, been traumatic for the

Los Angeles participants. She cited great tensions and frustrations during the first year. These seemed to be generated by three former volunteer leaders who hovered over the director, who had had no previous fair-housing experience. The director left after four months, by mutual agreement. Subsequently, one of the former volunteer leaders became the acting director, while a search for a permanent director continued, and held that position for five months. At the time of the field visit, the new director had just been hired.

Mrs. Tackett stressed three facets of the HOC program, all of them in the Fair Housing Division which she felt had a great impact on the area. First was the formation of the vast network of localized fair-housing volunteer groups. Sixty were in existence, of which ten had been formed during the brief funded period of the Fair Housing Division. Second was the expansion of industrial awareness of the need for open housing. With the encouragement of industrial contracts tied to the Fair Housing Division, it was felt that the base of community support was considerably enlarged. Third, the filing of 50 legal suits and 50 complaints of discrimination during the brief funded year was viewed as having great impact on the entire community. Mrs. Tackett perceived the goal of the HOC as "increasing housing opportunities for all people of all backgrounds through elimination of racial and economic barriers." She did not see how this could be achieved through the two low-income divisions alone, and planned to leave the organization if the Fair Housing Division was disbanded. She also had some harsh words for white liberals who were going along with black separatists: "It's nothing but a cop-out."

At the end of the day-long field visit, a troop of youthful fair-housers came into the office laden with bumper stickers and other promotional material. Mrs. Tackett explained with pride that this was part of the work of Community Organization, under the Fair Housing Division. The youth group had been involved in an educational campaign (under the direction of Mrs. Tackett) in their own all-white community, and had enlisted the cooperation of their city council and the Board of Education, as well as supermarket managers and parking lot attendants, to saturate the community with bumper stickers bearing the message and logo of the HOC Fair Housing Division: "Good Neighbors Come in All Colors." When they left, Mrs. Tackett wistfully murmured, "Who will see that this goes on, if we are out of the picture?"

It did appear to this observer that the only substantially effective programs of HOC were, indeed, conducted through the Fair Housing Division. Moreover, these programs seemed to be geared toward systemic change on the local level. By engaging in referrals to regional volunteer fair-housing groups, rather than conducting one-to-one placements themselves, the Fair Housing Division was

freed to devote itself to the larger task of working toward systemic
change. The sad fact that its efforts were to be aborted by the OEO
may indicate that the first task of a funded fair-housing effort is to
educate its source of funding.

Time: 1977

Marnesba Tackett described the events which led to the end of
the Fair Housing Division of the Housing Opportunity Center:

> First OEO emphasized building of homes in 1969-70, and
> named me as director of Housing Development. I tried to
> save the Fair Housing Division, and later the HOC which
> also went out of existence. Then, OEO disallowed some
> fair housing expenses, which left us with some serious
> budget balancing problems. Next, the Mexican community
> wanted its own fair housing center, and nothing pleased
> them about the way we operated. All of this was used
> against the Fair Housing Division (and the HOC) and led
> to its end. Then, Nixon's administration called for the
> Moratorium on all HUD programs—we were doomed to
> failure when funds were cut off. That's when the whole
> HOC folded.[56]

Mrs. Tackett turned her energies to several other civil rights organizations and then settled into her current position as executive director
of the Southern Christian Leadership Congress of Los Angeles.

When funds were cut off to the Fair Housing Division in 1970,
the movement did not die in Los Angeles. A new Fair Housing Congress was formed to take the place of the extinct Fair Housing Division. Under the leadership of Jim Allen, the Congress continued the
work of the fair-housing movement through ten fair-housing councils
of the metropolitan area. From 1970 to 1973, he led the program as
the first chairperson of the Congress's board of directors, functioning
with no funds.

The Congress received its first funding of $56,940 from the
city of Los Angeles in October 1974 through a HUD 701 planning grant.
The contract called for a three-part fair-housing program of public
education, complaint referral, and monitoring, to be implemented
by the central Congress office. This caused considerable distress
among the ten council groups making up the Congress. They felt
that since they were to receive some complaint referrals from the
central Congress office, they should also receive some of the grant
money. A second year of funding with the same arrangement did
nothing to relieve the hostility of some of the member groups toward
the central Congress office. This resentment spilled over to the new

Congress director, Lois Moss, who had been an active volunteer in the movement, and served without salary as director until funding was obtained.

The distress of the council groups stemmed from the nature of the funding contract: discrimination complaints were to be referred to existing government agencies, but could also be referred to member groups of the Congress. This caused resentment for two reasons: first, they felt that referrals to other agencies undercut their own services; and second, they felt that they should "get a cut of the pie."

However, a third year of funding in 1976 did include three of the member groups of the Congress in the grants. The new contract was for $178,515 and came through HCD Block Grant Funds, the current funding spark for the movement. The 1976 contract called for expansion of the program's public education segment and altered the complaint referral segment to include "the valuable investigative services provided by three of the Congress' member groups—Crenshaw Neighbors, San Fernando Valley Fair Housing Council, and Westside Fair Housing Council, all in the Los Angeles area."[57] Of the total of $178,515, $88,000 was to be divided among the three councils, and the remaining $90,000 used by the central Congress for education.

Though this reduced somewhat the resentment toward the central Congress office, it did not eliminate it. The director recognized the underlying resentment and acknowledged it in her discussion of local constraints in achieving open housing:

> I would like to see less struggle for recognition as "the one." Each group should be doing its own thing, gaining recognition as a part of a group of groups, each in its own locale. The role of the Congress is to advance issues that will help the cause for all groups. We must bring the issue of fair housing to the attention of all segments of people.[58]

Other constraints cited by the Congress director included the continued resistance of people continuing to discriminate, despite the law: occupant owners, managers, management companies, real estate companies, and lending institutions. She felt that occupant owners would be the easiest to change because of their unsophisticated methods of discrimination. Managers, too, she felt were not subtle in their methods of discrimination. Companies could change neighborhoods in a short time for profit, if they were unethical, and she felt that a significant number of companies were unethical. She also thought that the top priority of fair-housing groups should be handling complaints of discrimination in their own communities. Pending for

the next fiscal year, 1977-78, were two proposals for funding: one
to have city fair-housing councils continue service to home seeker's
discrimination complaints, and a second to have a tenant/landlord
counseling program operating out of the central Congress office.

Visits to the offices of two of the member councils of the
Congress discovered a contrast in leadership, style, program, use
of resources, and philosophy. The visits also revealed something
of a gnawing competitiveness among the councils themselves toward
each other, and continued resentment toward the central Congress
office for securing greater funding (and thus prestige) than they had.
An added factor is the difference in age between the Congress and its
member councils. The councils existed and worked in fair housing
long before the central Congress began. Yet the Congress in effect
became the parent organization when it was funded in 1974, and later
allocated part of its funding to some of the member groups. This
structure was bound to lead to conflict.

San Fernando Valley Fair Housing Council. The oldest fair-housing
group in the Los Angeles area, San Fernando's Fair Housing Council
(FHC), began in 1960 and has already been noted as the spearhead
for the entire fair-housing volunteer effort in the Los Angeles region.
Fifty-four similar groups are now organized in southern California.
FHC has grown from a simple volunteer home-finding service in a
white suburban area to a nationally known organization, recently
funded with program contracts from the government and the Ford
Foundation.

Its program has always included the traditional and necessary
discrimination complaint service, largely resolved through conciliation and legal referral. In addition, it has stressed voluntary affirmative marketing agreements, and has maintained a close working
relationship with the San Fernando Board of Realtors. FHCS's
energetic, able and long-serving director, Celia Zager, explains
the realtor relationship with a smile, "We make friends out of our
enemies."[59] A vigorous, stable board of directos raises up to
$30,000 a year. About 100 discrimination complaints a year are
handled, with only a small portion of those going to attorneys.

Perhaps the most outstanding aspect of the FHC program is
its public relations effort. The monthly newsletter is received
across the country by private and public offices; FHC has been featured in national publications such as Newsweek and the New York
Times. Numerous workshops are held for volunteers, lawyers,
realtors, and home seekers. Periodic fund-raising events are widely
publicized and attended; the active Speaker's Bureau initiates and
responds to requests from numerous civic organizations. Some
other local fair-housing leaders refer wryly to the public relations

program of FHC as "heavy, slick and much ado about nothing," implying program weaknesses and some cynicism about all the acclaim.

FHC operates a specialized fair-housing program rather than a comprehensive one. Its discrimination investigation program is based on conciliation and reaction rather than litigation and initiation. It is still a movement organization rather than just an interest group or service agency, because of its continuing focus on non-material (ideas, people's commitment) rather than material resources. However, this may change if their recent move to larger quarters, and their new budget of over $100,000 heralds a shift in values and priorities. Those who control the power and decision making will determine this.

Westside Fair Housing Council. Quite different is the Westside Fair Housing Council in the heart of Los Angeles, with Blanche Rosloff as director. This is the second oldest fair-housing group in southern California, now operating with its first major funding (through the Congress) in newly acquired office space. The directors of both organizations—San Fernando Valley Fair Housing Council, and West-Fair Housing Council—are emphatic about discrimination complaints taking top priority in their fair-housing programs. Both movement organizations specialized rather than comprehensive, both have frequent effective newsletters, both make extensive use of volunteers, and both have large involved memberships which they actively solicit. Both also are heavily involved in speaking engagements and workshops. Permeating Westside Council's program, however, is the vigorous litigative and initiative approach of its director and its board, in contrast to the conciliatory, reactive perspective of San Fernando Valley FHCS's director and board. Blanch-Rosloff had this to say, when asked to comment on the constraints interfering with the goals of open housing:

> We have to keep bucking the system (the housing industry). That system is based on discrimination and is so firmly entrenched that it will do everything possible to firmly resist efforts to make them stop discriminating. There are too many loopholes in the law. . .too many strategies that can circumvent the law. The government is not enforcing any fair housing laws. I would like to see fair housing groups enabled to use injunctions, subpoena records, and have the power of government commissions. The trouble is we have nothing in housing like employment equal opportunity monitoring. No one intends for the law to be carried out in the housing establishment. . . . I

wish we could have a massive suit against a large number
of realtors, like Bergen County's Fair Housing Council
did, I wish we could get greater monetary damages. . .[60]

The discrimination complaints coming in to Westside are
almost triple those at the San Fernando Valley Council (SFV),
amounting to about one daily and consuming most staff time. Two
housing counselors handle these discrimination complaints, an active
corps of 25 volunteer checkers, and two CETA (Comprehensive
Employment Training Act) secretaries (government-funded disadvantaged workers). Their paid membership is greater than SFV's, and
the number of lawsuits filed is more than double SFV's. Partially,
this may reflect the city location of Westside, in contrast to the
suburban one of SFV, but more likely it reflects a major difference
in philosophy. Blanche Rosloff says:

> Small realtors discriminate more than large ones. It's
> the opposite with apartments. . . .I don't mind having
> lunch with them (realtors), but I'm well aware that I'm
> having lunch with the reality of the situation, which is
> discrimination.[61]

In contrast, Celia Zager says:

> Areas that have active fair housing groups have less
> housing discrimination. It hasn't completely disappeared
> in the Valley, but our work with the realtors has cer-
> tainly cut it down tremendously.[62]

In comparing legal remedies with negotiating remedies, Blanche
Rosloff claims, "We need the clout of the first to get to the second.
First we'll sue, then we'll negotiate. I'm going to try to get voluntary
compliance, but I know I won't get it till I twist their arms." Celia
Zager would not agree that this is the best approach to achieving
what they both want so much—open housing. Zager would try every
possible means of conciliation and negotiation before recommending
legal action. Her emphasis is on "creating a favorable image of
integrated living." Again, this may be a specific response to the
situational difference of each geographical location as well as a
philosophical difference.
  Both directors agree, however, that diversity, or comprehen-
siveness of program (for example, tenant-landlord problems, low-
income housing rehabilitation and development, mortgage counseling)
dilutes the fair-housing efforts. Both, therefore, are intensively
involved in a specialized, concentrated, fair-housing program rather

than a comprehensive one. Both agree that the government itself
(HUD) makes it difficult for the movement, with no power of enforcement except through individual complaints. Both commented on their
perception of the whole movement and the role of NCDH in that movement. So also did Lois Moss, director of the Congress.

Moss felt that NCDH "could be a lot better than they are. They
don't respond unless they see it advancing their self-interest. We
asked them for help with monitoring block-grant programs, and got
no help at all. We sent them packets of stuff with copies of Community Development city proposals and plans. No response."[63] Zager
said, "I like the people at NCDH, but I wish they could do more for
fair housing groups—more field consultation." Rosloff's comment
was, "I like their literature. It motivates me. I learn from it."

Other member councils of the Southern California Fair Housing
Congress covered the spectrum of types of fair-housing organizations,
ranging from very comprehensive (Orange County includes low-
income housing development) and conciliatory-reactive to concentra-
ted-initiative-litigative. None of the groups seem to have moved out
of the movement organization classification to mere interest group
or bureaucratic agency, and all appear to be struggling valiantly to
bring open housing to southern California—in some different and some
similar ways, and with varying degrees of effectiveness and success.

TWO THAT DIED

Denver: Metro Denver Fair Housing Center (MDFHC)

Time: 1970

Inception. Metro Denver is the largest and most affluent funded
open-housing program in the nation. It grew in three years from a
small volunteer organization into one with a staff of more than 50,
a two-story office building, seven field offices, and an annual budget
of a half million dollars. Its status prompts some to make pilgri-
mages and others to make wry comments.

As with other local open-housing efforts, Denver's stemmed
from community constraints. The population of the Denver area is
1.5 million, of which 10 percent are black and 13 percent are His-
panos. Despite the passage of Colorado's first fair-housing law in
1959, residential discrimination and segregation continued to be
the prevailing pattern in the Denver metropolitan area. In 1962 a
fair-housing council was formed in response to this typical urban
situation. The council was actually preceded by a voluntary stabilization effort in one middle-class neighborhood of Denver (Park Hill),

which was gradually becoming all-black. The stabilization effort succeeded in quelling panic selling in the area, but it soon became clear that no group in one area could turn back the growth of segregation as long as the rest of Denver and its suburbs were closed to minority families. In effect, the people of Park Hill decided they could not succeed locally unless they waged a fight regionally.

Religious leaders of the city met with the mayor and subsequently formed the interfaith Council on Human Relations. The leadership of the Council and the Denver Commission on Community Relations were responsible for the eventual formation of the Metro Denver Fair Housing Center. The Center began as a private, nonprofit, totally volunteer organization in the fall of 1965, and during its formation months, received much counsel and guidance from NCDH. The Center had its first home in office space shared with the Denver Area Council of Churches in lower downtown Denver. It operated from 1965 to October 1966 with no paid staff. In October 1966 an executive secretary was hired to coordinate the work of the volunteers. Neighborhood Youth Corps trainees also became part of the staff that winter.

In late 1965, $2000 was donated by private citizens and the Religious Council on Human Relations for Metro Denver. In the summer of 1966, Governer John Love entered into a $10,000 research-grant contract with the Center. Thé purpose of the grant was to enable the Center to determine the number of minority families living in dispersed areas, as well as to make some estimate of the effect the fair-housing law was having on population patterns. Early in 1967, the mayor and the City Council of Denver collaborated to give the Center $20,000 for operations in 1967; $10,000 of this was a matching grant, designed to generate donations from the private sector of the community.

Encouraged by NCDH, the Center applied late in 1966 for an OEO grant of $172,460 for a one-year demonstration project. This was designed to launch a comprehensive attack on residential segregation, with emphasis on programs that would serve low-income families. Funding was granted by OEO, and subsequently additional funding was provided by the Ford Foundation ($300,000), by HUD, renewed by the state and city, and then enlarged by OEO (second-year grant of $259,000). In addition, special contributions from private and industrial sources amounted to $33,372. The first executive director, the Reverand Robison Lapp, was hired in April 1967 and remained in that position until 1970.

Goals. The general goals of fair housing, emphasizing the legal right to freedom of choice in housing, are delineated in one of Metro Denver's many attractive (slick) publications.[64] The specific goals of Metro Denver Fair Housing Center, Inc. are clearly stated in other publications, and reveal the belief that segregation in any form is "bad and harmful"—especially housing segregation, which perpetuates segregation in every other segment of daily life.[65]

To arrive at the goal of absolute freedom of choice in housing and the elimination of racially segregated housing patterns, the Fair Housing Center encourages all persons to make integrative moves. There are other goals: to attempt to insure that those neighborhoods that have become integrated remain integrated and do not become resegregated; to eliminate substandard housing throughout the metropolitan area; to increase home ownership among the minorities; and to increase the supply of housing for low-income families. These goals are restated in a Metro Denver publication, with somewhat different emphasis, suggesting that segregation perpetuates bigotry, prejudice, and poverty.[66]

Program. As a volunteer program, Metro Denver assisted 105 families seeking help in the finding of housing outside areas of the city considered traditional to their racial or ethnic background. Of these, 85 were satisfactorily located in new homes. Ten of these were sales, and 75 were rentals. During this same period, an estimated additional 50 families moved to nontraditional areas without help from the Center. However, Center administrators felt that the Center helped to create the climate in which such moves were both desired and possible.

The Center's volunteers also appeared before 80 groups to present fair-housing facts and possibilities in the metropolitan area. In addition, 75 news releases and 20 radio and TV appearances were made as part of the Center's motivation and education program. "Other accomplishments of volunteers in early months were those of establishing the Center as a reality and generating enough trust and faith in the Center so as to warrant grants from the State of Colorado and the City and County of Denver."[67]

As a volunteer organization, the Center thus functioned primarily as a listing service, seeking to locate desirable housing in nontraditional areas for minority families who were willing to move out. Some volunteers handled registration forms and records of available homes, while other volunteers served as housing aides or escorts. The escorts accompanied minority families on visits to homes, brokers, and mortgage institutions, "both to provide moral support and to watch for incidents of discrimination."[68] It engaged in a successful publicity program, in which minority and majority citizens were given facts on integration through public news, feature media, and the Speaker's Bureau.

As a funded operation, Metro Denver has helped 3,000 families a year find better housing. "Not all the moves are integrated, but a large majority are."[69] It has organized more than a dozen rehabilitation (221-h) projects, and completed them in record time—from three to six months. Its goals for rehabilitation is 150 houses a year. It has joined with the Catholic Archdiocese in planning a construction project covering 12 different sites, with the 300 units for low- and moderate-income families, and will offer rent supplements. It has persuaded the Model Cities planners to work for ghetto dispersion as well as for ghetto rehabilitation. It helped to organize groups in the ghetto whose purpose is to improve their housing conditions. It has filed many complaints with the Colorado Civil Rights Commission, but prefers to avoid the case-by-case approach in favor of a more sweeping attack on segregation. One observer thinks Metro Denver has already "done more to eliminate discrimination than the Civil Rights Commission could do in 100 years."[70] It has attracted 2500 rank-and-file, dues-paying members. It has bombarded the Denver public with its message—in newspapers, on television (free spots), on the bumpers of municipal buses, and even in banks.

Four Divisions. The program, strategies, and activities of the Metro Denver Center can best be described under four major headings: personal assistance efforts provided by the Community Services Division; the development of housing, carried on by the Housing Development Division; education and motivation, which is the specific responsibility of the Public Relations Department; and research and planning, which is the province of the Research Department. An examination of each of these four areas reveals the total scope of the Metro Denver Center's program.

Community Services, the largest division of the Center, helps families solve their housing problems and coordinates the work of citizens and business groups toward the goal of ending segregation in housing. Four separate departments comprise the division: Housing Services, Urban Housing Training Facility, Employer and Business Relations, and Community Coordination.

In the Housing Services Department, housing specialists, assistants, and counselors located at the main office and seven neighborhood offices in Denver, Adams, and Arapahoe Counties provide free assistance to families in search of housing appropriate to their needs. Home size, cost, schools, employment opportunities, and transportation are weighed as family and specialist evaluate available housing. The staff encourages all families to consider integrative moves. The family is aided by the specialist in making arrangements for the move. "This kind of counseling and information service provides guidelines for lower-income families who have never known any real freedom of choice in housing location."[71]

Housing counselors refer middle-income families who wish to purchase homes anywhere in the metropolitan area to representatives of the real estate industry. They maintain listings, provided by a number of Denver area realtors, of homes currently on the market. The counselors support families making integrative moves and help with any neighborhood adjustments which might be necessary.

An advocacy role is also played by Center staff in solving the housing problems of families whose needs do not involve a move from one place to another. The staff aids families in conflicts with landlords, neighbors, managers, unscrupulous lenders, and high-interest home repair agents when necessary. The Housing Services Department informs registrant families of provisions of the civil rights law and works with the Civil Rights Commission in solving injustices arising from noncompliance with the law.

The Urban Housing Training Facility is a relatively new department, established to organize moderate- and low-income families into action groups for the purpose of learning more about tenants' rights, home ownership, city service departments, home maintenance and repair, and the relationship of home location to school and employment opportunities. This department holds training sessions throughout the community in surroundings familiar to families who have the greatest need for these services.

Through the Employer and Business Relations Department, employers and businessmen of the community are given a channel through which they may express concretely their increasingly voiced desire "to do something" about the urban crisis. Employers throughout the area are approached for service contracts with the Center. Under the agreement, the Center provides housing services and assistance for all employees. Special attention is given to those interested in moving to neighborhoods closer to work in locations not traditional to their race or ethnicity. Through this department, the Center's liaison is maintained with business, area Chambers of Commerce, real estate brokers, developers and mortgage lenders. The Center generates programs and ideas on how business "may more effectively relate to ending segregation in housing."[72]

The Community Coordination Department provides creative new action programs, information, coordination, and motivation to human relations councils, action committees, civil rights groups, and private citizens. It seeks to "create a solid and unified base for social action in open housing."[73] Political action and organized citizens' lobbies are also generated through this department.

In the Housing Development Division, the guiding philosophy is that any rehabilitation or construction of homes for sale or rent to low- and moderate-income families must be done on a dispersed basis throughout the metropolitan area. The staff includes people skilled in real estate development, appraising, estimating, property acquisition, sales and loan counseling, architecture, site selection, development, and construction. The staff works with any agency, private developer, contractor, investor, or nonprofit organization to generate additional housing for low- and moderate-income families on a dispersed site basis.

This division constructs and rehabilitates housing units through the Metropolitan Housing Development Corporation, a nonprofit subsidiary of the Center. Financing for housing development is secured through various federal programs of HUD, through private and commercial investors, and through a housing development revolving fund being established by the Center.

Four basic factors affect the price a family must pay for housing each month, whether the family is renting or purchasing. They are the cost of the land upon which the dwelling is erected, the cost of materials and labor used in erecting or rehabilitating the house, the interest to be paid for mortgage money, and sales taxes on materials and property taxes on the finished product. Since the cost of interest and taxes amounts to well over half the monthly payment, the Center is concentrating on ways of reducing these two items, as well as upon ways of lowering the cost of construction. The Center subscribes to the principle that any housing constructed for low- and moderate-income families should be of good quality and standard size and should meet building codes. "Sub-code or under-sized units can become instant slums."[74]

The Public Relations Department is responsible for the creation and operation of a viable and comprehensive program for the dissemination of educational, informational, and motivational material to all publics. "Because personal attitudes based on fear, myths, and ignorance constitute the sustaining force of prejudice and discrimination, constant exposure of facts is imperative."[75]

The staff prepares and distributes news releases on Center programs and activities to the printed and electronic media and has established a strong rapport with personnel. News conferences are also arranged and coordinated for the announcement of outstanding events or achievements. The department staff creates documentary and promotional material for distribution to the public, produces audio-visual aids for use by Center staff and for special presentations, and coordinates speaking appearances for members of the staff and the speakers' bureau.

The department is responsible for planning, coordinating, and staging special events such as open houses, dedications, award dinners, banquets, and conferences. It plans publicity for and coordinates the annual membership and awareness drive. Department personnel recruit and coordinate volunteer support for the Center, both for special events and for auxiliary staff support. The department writes, edits, and produces a quarterly newsletter sent to all members, and prepares a mimeographed, monthly internal news sheet for staff, board members, area human relations councils, and related organizations.

The Center's Research Department monitors and maintains information on current housing patterns, future trends, and ethnic and racial patterns in the metropolitan Denver area, as well as other statistics related to strategy, programs, and the solution of housing problems. This department, through study of the metropolitan area, determines the location of new housing units to be built by the Center's Housing Development Division.

A chart showing program and organizational changes in 1966, 1967, and 1968 indicates the increasing scope of the Metro Denver Center program: [76]

	1966	1967	1968
Number of families served	105	711	3650
221-H Sponsors	0	0	12
221-H houses completed	0	0	31
221-D3 Units initiated	0	0	300
Staff (Paid)	1	18	45
Funding	$10,000	$202,000	$480,000
Public Appearances	224	345	1019
Integrated Moves			
Blockbusting Practices			

Impact

> These are impressive achievements. In a way, it is their very impressiveness that discourages one, because after all is said and done, the corner has not been turned, the suburbs have not been opened, and Denver is still segregating at a faster rate than Metro Denver can desegregate it. [77]

Evaluating the impact of the program and its success must be viewed in terms of the local constraints against which the Center operates. Metro Denver Center's officials noted four major areas of concern.

The first constraint mentioned was the economic factor. Many minority persons, because of job discrimination, poor education, and prejudice, do not have the economic ability to purchase a home or to rent in other then slum areas.

> We have found in many instances that a minority person
> can obtain better housing in a better neighborhood outside
> of the racial ghetto for the same amount of money. But
> the number of such units are limited and for the most part
> we are utilizing all such units now. [78]

The second constraint noted was the shortage in the housing
supply. Officials stated that while Denver is perhaps relatively
better off than other major cities in this regard, there is still a
great shortage of housing units for people of low and moderate income.
In addition, there are still on the market many substandard living
units.

The third major constraint cited was the real estate industry
itself. Though it was seen as far ahead of that in other, comparable
cities in some ways, "still, by dragging its feet, by reluctance, and
by very subtle techniques, it continues to perpetuate the patterns of
the past in discouraging integrative housing moves."[79] It was estimated by Center officials that about 10 percent of the real estate
brokers, salesmen, and managers actively supported the fair-housing
law and the efforts of the Fair Housing Center in Colorado.

> About 40% will cooperate when necessary and basically
> do obey the law or at least do not openly break the law.
> The remaining 50% range in attitude and action from one
> of subtle obstinance to open hostility. The leadership
> of the real estate industry in Colorado is slowly taking
> a more active positive role, but the results of its efforts
> have been slow and not as dramatic as hoped. [80]

The last constraint mentioned was seen by Center officials as
possibly the most serious at the time—the Denver school board and
administration. Center administrators felt that through its vacilla-
tion over the past seven years regarding the problem of segregated
education, the school board and administration had created much
hostility within the white suburban areas of Denver concerning the
efforts of integration.

> The School Board has continued to debate and flounder
> on the question of whether segregated schools should be
> eliminated and if so how. It has almost encouraged the
> formation of citizens groups in various white neighbor-
> hoods to actively fight against any attempt of Negroes to
> attend their schools. . . .

> Unless the school board assumes its position of leader-
> ship and takes those positive steps necessary to elimi-
> nate segregation within the Denver school system, the
> continued debate, the continued vacillation, the continued
> uncertainty can only lead to more and more hostility and
> open resentment among the various ethnic groups.[81]

Balanced against these constraints, some advantages were
noted by another observer. Racial lines in Denver, while visible,
were viewed as neither as hardened nor as barbed as in some older
and larger cities. Further, Denver's housing supply was seen as
relatively new—"the oldest units are only 70 years old".[82] And
although the shortage of decent housing for the poor was acknowledged,
that shortage was not considered insurmountable. A third advantage
cited for Denver was that city's civic tradition of making "The City
Beautiful" a paramount consideration. It was felt that this tradition
could not be reconciled with the maintenance of slums and ghettos.
And the fourth advantage noted was the mountains. "Any slum-dweller
will tell you it is better to live in the foothills of Denver than in the
canyons of Chicago."[83] This same observer felt that Denver had
taken the desegregation process farther than any other funded operation in the country.

However, other qualified observers have expressed varying
degrees of cautious criticism of the Denver operation. For example,
Betty Hoeber (director of New York's Operation Open City), quietly
observed that though Denver had a "most comprehensive program, it
doesn't seem to be actively fighting discrimination."[84] And Ed Rutledge (executive director, NCDH) was not veiled in his reference to
Denver as "one of the monsters we've raised".[85] He cited the Denver
program as one of the fair-housing operations that had "become part
of the establishment," and openly named the director of the program
as responsible for this. He also chided him for being "a do-gooder,"
instead of a scrapper. An examination of 11 informal guideposts for
other aspiring metros, developed by Lapp (the executive director of
the Denver Center), may be revealing in this respect. Lapp suggests:

1. Don't compete with the real estate industry. Help
    them open up a new market.

2. Don't manipulate people. White people are always
    figuring out what a Negro must do to end segrega-
    tion. The important question is, what is the white
    responsibility?

3. You can't stay volunteer very long and get anything
    done. You have to go professional fast. Get $25,000,

open an office, hire an executive and start. If you
aren't willing to pay, you're being dishonest.

4.   KISS—Keep It Simple, Stupid. The whole business
of ending segregation in housing is a simple matter.
You just have to decide that the ghettos and slums
and the separate communities and all the other related
social ills are products of racial and economic discrimination, either hidden or apparent. And you cannot accept excuses or rationalizations.

5.   Don't say your community is different because it has
no problems, or because it has problems that are too
big. That's nonsense.

6.   Ethnic background of staff is important. You should
bend over backward to seek talent from the minority
community.

7.   In hiring, look beyond the people who have been in-·
volved in your original effort. Make inroads on business, professional and university groups. Don't hire
social workers, or at least avoid the case work
approach.

8.   Make no false promises. Tell everyone how you feel.
Work hard. Very hard.

9.   Maintain genuine communications with all factions in
the community. It is no longer enough to convince
people the world is on fire. They know that. You have
to tell them how to put out the fire.

10.   Stay in touch with activist militants. It is possible to
gain at least their neutraility. Stress freedom of
choice and not forced integration.

11.   Don't respond to the out-and-out bigots. They kill
themselves with their own ludicrousness. The real
enemy is the community that doesn't give a damn but
can hurt the movement through its indifference. They
are the people who walk away with the dollars or the
votes at the crucial moment. [86]

Denver Metro has succeeded in making the community "give
a damn." Though it may have become part of the establishment in
doing so, the fact remains that the Denver Fair Housing Center has
tremendous status in the community precisely because it has broad
support from both ghetto residents and the power structure, including

city hall, major industries, and the financial community. In addition, because it is multifunded, it has a certain independence in making and executing its own policies, not being tied to any one source of funding. However, despite the good Reverend Lapp's own admonitions, the Denver Center seems to be a massive housing location agency, and offers little evidence that it has engaged in systemic desegregating techniques. Moreover, there is no evidence of its being engaged in an open fight against discrimination, and thus, it does not appear to be moving toward any real systemic change in its metropolitan area. Though its smooth public relations effort stridently claims on all its literature and buttons and window and bumper stickers that "In Denver, Fair Housing Is," it may, in fact, be concluded that in Denver, fair housing isn't—and that the city does not appear to be well on its way toward ending that situation.

Time: 1977

Robinson Lapp was dismissed as Metro Denver Center's director in 1971, and the Center closed its doors in 1973. In seven years it had completed the circle of rags to riches to rags and oblivion. What led to its death? Was it too much too soon? A combination of several related factors seemed to be responsible: internal division within staff and board (partially related to the black-power peak, nationally), inadequate administration and board leadership, goal shifts and uncertainties, and cessation of funding. Any one of these factors alone could have led to the collapse of the organization, but the combination was certain death. Each factor has been stressed to a different degree by various observers and participants and the press. Together, they tell the tale, almost like a Greek tragedy—moving swiftly and inevitably to the doomed end.

The Denver Post focused on inadequate administration in its article headlined, "Lapp, Fair Housing Chief, Dismissed," on April 23, 1971,[87] five years after the Center's inception. In those five years, Metro Denver's budget had grown from a shoestring to $500,000, and its three-member staff to 40 employees. The Post article noted the unanimous dismissal decision of 21 governing board members, and cited seven charges brought against Lapp by an investigating committee: poor management of the Center's affairs, inability to effectively develop staff potential, failure to establish a housing development fund, class discrimination, lack of support of governing board, poor administrative skills—which led to unauthorized salary increases for some employees, unreasonable workloads for some employees, unwarranted demotions and other harrassment of certain staff members—and lack of support of the Center's staff.

The article stated that 90 percent of a random sample of Center employees "agreed that the Director was a poor administrator." The

investigative committee especially noted the high rate of staff turnover, and told the governing board that "continual job changes ham-
pered the Center from accomplishing its goals." Lapp denied the
charges, according to the article, and accused the board of inadequate guidance and preoccupation with "petty issues and operation
details. . . . Seldom has the Board focused its attention on broad
and important issues of policy and on the Center's mission of
creating a truly open community."

Internal division was noted in the article's reference to the
board's action as having

> climaxed two years of strife between Lapp, staff members
> and the Board. Annual meetings the last two years have
> been disrupted by employee dissension, and monthly Board
> meetings frequently have been devoted to personnel troubles.

The impending financial collapse was mentioned at the end of the
article: "It now faces an economic crunch—because the OEO, the
Center's primary source of money, is cutting its grant from
$300,000 to $182,000 next fiscal year."

Five days earlier an article had given details of the coming
funding cuts. [88] Headlined "U.S. Funds slashed—Fair Housing
Center Cuts Seen," the article referred not only to the OEO cuts
but also to Denver's Model Cities program which had already "shut
off a flow of funds" ($60,000) to the Center. Cuts in staff and programs
were expected as a result, and Lapp stated that the reduced budget
"obviously means added headaches." One week earlier the state
legislature had moved to cut off its annual $10,000 grant to the Cen-
ter. Lapp expressed surprise at the loss of state funding, but appeared
to expect the other cuts, though he did not think the reductions would
be "so radical."

Funding loss was the primary reason given for the Center's
demise by Shed Devers, the staff member who became the Center's
acting director after Lapp left. Devers explained the funding loss
as an ironic twist to the Center's efforts to get the city involved in
housing. When the Center succeeded in motivating city officials to
begin rehabilitation and construction programs for low-income families, other departments and agencies gradually took over the tasks
of the Center, and funding was diverted into these other programs
instead of to the Center.

Devers said, however, that he "always felt it was a five-year
program, to be spun back to other agencies in the area." [89] He and
Lapp had talked about this in the beginning. Personnel problems
were acknowledged by Devers, who is black, but with sympathy for
Lapp's difficulties:

> The minority staff felt Lapp favored certain white staff.
> This was a new experience for the minority staff who
> didn't understand what it took to raise money. Lapp be-
> came a victim of circumstances.[90]

The time period was the peak of the black-power movement, it must
be recalled.

Another former staff member, the ex-business manager William
Haring, referred also to personnel problems, and put these in the context of the black-power time period: "One staff person caused a lot of
trouble, another was fired. Both were black; this led to community
clamor. Lapp was not a racist.[91] Haring, who is white, went on to
say, "But he was not a good administrator. He was a poor budget
manager. Getting money was his forte. Using it was not!" Haring
also cited the funding losses, and blamed the final closing of the
Center on the HUD moratorium in 1973. He said he had recommended
closing the Center "because there were no more programs to administer—the staff had nothing to do."

In addition to weak leadership, a shift in the goals and program
of the Center was noted by the founder and prime mover of the Center
and the fair-housing movement in Denver—Richard Young. Young
served on the board from its inception in 1966 until 1969, the first
three-year period of its fantastic growth. He stepped down from the
board presidency because he "wanted new leadership to grow. But
other individuals did not step forward to fill the breach on the Board.
No new Board leadership developed to move it ahead." Young admired
Lapp and had a good working relationship with him. But after he
(Young) left, "Lapp tried to be both leader and administrator. Fights
developed between blacks and chicanos on the board and within the
staff about everything: staff position, program priorities, etc. Lapp
was unable to handle all this."[92]

Young said that the program changed after he left. It shifted
from integration to rehabilitation—improving the quality of housing—
and construction. Zoning problems developed for the Center-sponsored
Catholic Church's nonprofit, 200-unit building project. "There was no
continuing effort to get local contributions, and finally the funding
ran out."

Changes in program were also noted by Devers, but he felt
these were justified:

> It changed from an emphasis on discrimination to basic
> rehabilitation for low-income people. As times changed,
> the direction changed. A point was reached where not
> many complaints came in. We stopped advertising that
> part of the program, and then the Civil Rights Commis-
> sion took it over.[93]

Haring further elaborated on this point: "We just had a recording device that referred discrimination complaints to the Civil Rights Commission."

The Denver story: from NCDH president Robert Carter's statement in 1968, "The Metro Denver Center has experienced the greatest success of any fair housing agency in the nation"[94]—to a recording device—and closed door in 1973.

It is suggested here that if the program had been a concentrated one, focusing on discrimination and its eradication, the Center might not have ended. Had its prime task been the one that no one else could or would do, this might have unified the staff, unified and motivated the board, and continued to appeal to the funding sources. The notion, often expressed, that infrequent discrimination complaints indicate decreasing need for such service, is incorrect. What infrequent discrimination complaints really indicate is insufficient attention to the issue. The more a fair-housing group makes this issue paramount, and concentrates on it with intensive outreach of public relations, the more the complaints will come pouring in. And the more they come in, the greater the perceived need for such service, and the greater the likelihood of eventual systemic change and success.

There is thus a snowball effect of concentration in a fair-housing program which leaks back to increased morale of staff and board, and increased potential for success. In the long run (very long—10-15 years), the complaints should decrease, but in the short run they will increase as there is greater concentration on the program aspect. This was the valuable lesson learned in the Akron summer demonstration project, and confirmed in the Long Beach, California situation.*

Seattle: Operation Equality

Time: 1970

Inception. Operation Equality is one of the eight demonstration projects sponsored by the National Urban League and financed by the Ford Foundation. Its predecessors, Harmony Homes, Inc. and the Fair Housing Listing Service, were volunteer efforts which developed in response to the segregated housing conditions in the Seattle area.

Between 1950 and 1960, the number of whites in Seattle increased 3 percent; the number of blacks increased 73 percent in Seattle as a whole and 106 percent in a 12-census-tract cental area. Almost all

---

*See Appendix D.

blacks living outside this congested central sector lived in three
public housing developments in the southern section of the city. Continued growth and concentration of blacks since 1960 has been evidenced by 12.3 percent increase in school enrollment of black students between 1962 and 1964, compared with a 6.1 percent decrease
of white pupils; and by the fact that almost all these new black pupils
were confined to the same few school zones that have traditionally
served blacks.

The rental accomodations for nonwhites in Seattle are half as
adequate as rental accomodations for white families - yet they pay
75 percent as much. Phrased another way, the typical black family
can expect to pay about 50 percent more for a rental dwelling than
a white family pays for a comparable dwelling away from the ghetto.
In effect, the typical pattern of housing exploitation exists in Seattle:
"blacks are underhoused and overcharged."[95]

In 1953 a small group of individuals attempted to secure passage of a state open-housing law, applying only to public housing,
which was declared unconstitutional by the State Supreme Court in
1954. The active thrust toward an open-housing movement began
in 1960. At that time, a member of the Greater Seattle Housing
Council recommended that an open-housing clearing house be established. In 1962 Harmony Homes, Inc. was organized "to build homes
in dozens of restricted areas, well-spaced at random,"[96] which
enabled the first black families to buy in these areas. The Fair Housing
Listing Service was the counterpart of the building group, designed
to provide information and encouragement to minorities wanting to
purchase homes outside traditional areas. Both of these organizations
were "conducted almost single-handedly by the late Sidney Gerber,
prior to his death in a tragic plane accident."[97] They were described
by Operation Equality's present director as "a remarkably successful
effort to integrate most of Seattle's major suburbs. With a really
basic, grass roots community-organized tactical organization, Gerber
helped over 200 minority families move to the white hinterlands."[98]
An average of two minority families each month purchased housing
outside the ghetto, and by 1964 the Fair Housing Listing Service
stated that it had "directly negotiated 52 sales with a dollar volume
over a million dollars."[99]

As a result of volunteer efforts, an open-housing ordinance
was adopted by the city council in 1963, but was voted down by the
people in 1964. After Gerber's death in 1965, the Urban League of
Seattle organized a rental listing service for low-income minorites,
staffed by volunteers. This organization was eventually incorporated
into Seattle's Operation Equality, after volunteers recruited from the
two earlier organizations—in conjunction with the Urban League—
were able to secure funds ($70,000) to match the first Ford Foundation

grant. This grant funded Operation Equality (OE) for three years with $138,000.

Goals. As stated in the original proposal for funding, the purpose of OE was to instigate "a three year, concerted effort to reverse the trend toward increasingly segregated housing in Seattle."[100] An evaluator of the program corroborates this: "Its intent is to desegregate the entire metropolitan area of Seattle."[101] The current director, however, states the goal as, "First, last, and always, a free and meaningful choice in housing, for everyone, everywhere. Period!"[102]

Three pieces of literature developed by OE state the goal as the erasure of discrimination in housing and the improvement of housing opportunities for minorities. The first brochure states that "OE is a new program designed to erase discrimination in housing and to improve housing opportunities for non-whites."[103] The second brochure asserts that "the Seattle Urban League's OE is a program designed to tackle discrimination and to improve housing opportunities for black people. as well as other minority group members."[104] And the third piece of educational literature is a booklet which describes the services of OE, and carries the subheading, "Equal Housing Opportunities for YOU." The lead sentences are: "Let's face it! Racial discrimination in housing, though it is against the law, still exists. And even if discrimination disappeared overnight, the economic problems facing black people, as well as other minority groups, would not be solved. The Seattle Urban League's OE was established to tackle the problem of housing with practical methods. . . ."[105]

In its own summary statement of its program, OE "was conceived as a three-year pilot program to test the thesis that professionally staffed fair housing services could have a significant impact upon breaking up segregated living patterns in the U.S."[106] Perhaps the true goal of OE is better understood in terms of the recipient of the information. It would seem that when OE is explaining its program to the general community at large, it states its goal as the desegregation of the metropolitan area. But when directing its information to the minority community, OE stresses the "freedom of choice" or "equal housing opportunities" or occasionally "tackling discrimination in housing" as its prime concern.

Program. Seattle's program has shown great flexibility and change. Changes have occurred not only from volunteer to funded program, but also within the funded program itself. They have been planned and deliberate.

The early, volunteer Fair Housing Listing Service (FHLS) was formed in a climate where there was little housing opportunity for minorities, and where there was little communication between white and black communities. All of the small, independent fair-housing committees combined under the leadership of Sidney Gerber, a past chairman of the State Board Against Discrimination and a retired businessman.

> Mr. Gerber brought about communication by bringing all of these groups together with members of the Negro community, so that fair listings didn't just accumulate in some well meaning committees' file, but an actual transaction ensued. . . .

> Members of the Service spoke to many groups about the problems minorities faced in obtaining housing. Each time several persons would reveal that their homes were for sale and they would sell regardless of race. At the same time, FHLS prepared a small brochure and delivered quantities to every church and some small businesses in the central area. The brochure simply stated that FHLS knew of homes for sale regardless of race and gave phone numbers to obtain the information. [107]

Volunteers knocked on doors of homes for sale and asked if the owner would be willing to sell regardless of race. About one out of every three was willing to do so. Some owners were found who were willing to sell, but were afraid, and asked to have appointments made after dark. Some black home seekers were afraid to use the service, for fear of another rejection:

> They were afraid of another put-down, in a life that is one continuous denial. . . .What kinds of people were these who were afraid to phone for our service? Lawyers, doctors, people who had faced the challenge and overcome the designation and fate of the majority of their background. One was a lady doctor, which itself was a challenge for a woman in this country. Yet she hesitated to call for an appointment. It might be one more false hope, one more white man who says, "I believe in your rights, my best friend is a Negro, but I won't sell you my house—I couldn't do it to my neighbors. [108]

It became apparent that the greatest void lay in new, low-cost housing which could attract minority families out of the central city,

and into new communities. Gerber then formed Harmony Homes,
Inc. as a building corporation.

> We built 25 new houses in white sub-divisions spaced
> about a mile apart, and sold them only to Negroes. This
> opened up a lot of new areas, within one year. We dis-
> continued this, as it was too much work. [109]

By 1965, the listing service was maintaining a file of 300 listings
and 30 home seekers at a time, and selling about one house a week.
The service did not accept listings close to the black district, nor
did they accept listings in the same block where blacks had recently
moved (in white areas). Over 200 black families had obtained homes
outside of the central ghetto area. "No longer are we asked to come
after dark. Often families move in and no one complains. We don't
knock on doors to get listings any more."[110] A letter from the late
Mr. Gerber, just before his death in 1965, reveals the tenacity and
determination of the man in his volunteer leadership role:

> I am enclosing our latest literature. The circular with
> the photos is used to send around the Negro district,
> churches, etc. to get Negroes to contact us. The little
> circular is used for white chuches to mail to their
> members in white districts to get owners to list with us.
>
> There are 12 Negro brokers in Seattle who are not too
> happy about our free service, although sometimes they get
> owners' names from us and make commissions. We do
> not charge anything ourselves. Our budget is about
> $300/yr, and we operate out of the basement in my
> home. . . .
>
> Most listing services fail because they don't stay in it
> long enough. It takes a year or two to get the confidence
> of Negro buyers. You have to build up a wide variety of
> listings, or else they won't buy. . . .
>
> We also provide a complete advisory service through
> volunteers: telling homeseekers how to get mortgages,
> making out earnest money offers for them, etc. It
> doesn't do any good to show a house unless you can write
> out an offer, or have a lawyer do it. The main thing is
> to get them moved there. After that they educate the
> area by themselves.
>
> This business is a practical hard matter. If you get a busi-
> nessman as a volunteer, and a lawyer, and a lot of house-
> wives to show the houses, you can become a success. . . .[111]

One of the factors of significance in securing the Ford Foundation grant was the history of the volunteer efforts, submitted by the widow of Sidney Gerber. Of the staff of six who were hired when Operation Equality first opened its doors, all had previously been involved with Seattle's volunteer efforts in fair housing. OE began with much the same program the volunteers had: securing listings, matching them with minority clients, community education.

Funded Program. The first task of OE in Seattle was to organize strong, viable, neighborhood fair-housing listing groups which could locate suitable listings, escort clients, and prepare the community to receive them, engaging in "fire-fighting efforts wherever required.[112] Sixteen such groups were organized, covering a three-county area.

A single staff member, the housing specialist, had the responsibility for organizing and staffing the 16 groups, training all of the volunteers, keeping track of the supply of housing, and "making sure that all clients were referred to suitable housing and were given every possible assistance.[113] The field representative had the responsibility of working in the ghettos, informing people of the availability of OE services, working with existing groups, organizing new ones, and generally locating and motivating clients to move from the impacted central ghettos. The housing information specialist worked with the other staff people designing promotional literature, fair-housing manuals and procedures, and maintaining the files which allowed client and seller or renter to be matched. The information specialist also initiated a public relations program with the mass media in the area, which was used by the various housing groups to educate their local communities, keeping the program and its goals in the public eye.

> In the first few months of operation, it became apparent that securing listings would be the major problem. Faced with no open housing legislation, only those who wished to participate voluntarily in an open housing program could be counted on as sources of a supply of housing. Since the pattern of support for such a program is usually middle class suburban, OE soon found itself with an adequate supply of $30,000 and $40,000 listings but very little else.[114]

After the first six months of funded operation, an evaluation was held "which clearly showed the inadequacies of the program model and the assumptions upon which it was based. The program did not lack for applicants, nor for listings. What the program did lack was a method of bridging the gap between the price of listings obtained and the limited ability to pay of the available applicants"[115] Eighty-three percent of OE's applicants required housing costing less than $120 a month, while 85 percent of their listings, both rental and sales, required monthly payments in excess of $150 a month.

> At this point, we were faced with two alternatives: either use existing staff to aggressively recruit and move middle class Negroes and minority families, thus accelerating the abandonment of the core city to the poor and powerless, or change our program strategy and direct it towards opening access to the existing supply of low and moderate priced housing, while at the same time moving to increase the inadequate supplies in this category. We had little difficulty in opting for the second alternative.[116]

This decision brought forth some opposition from the local Urban League, which resisted the change. The director of OE then went directly to the National Urban League and the Ford Foundation for approval of his changed program, which was granted despite its profound diversion from the original proposal and contract with the Ford Foundation.

Changed Program. The original proposal for funding had outlined three program areas of concern on which OE was to focus: public education and research, institutional relations, and personal housing services. Now the new program was to focus on the actual development of low- and moderate-income housing through rehabilitation or the building of new units.

The program coordinator (Director Dave Guren) accordingly called together a committee of leading law professors and practicing attorneys with the hope that existing federal and state law could be used creatively to provide access to moderate- and lower-priced accomodations. Since the time for construction of new housing was so protracted, the initial target was to open up the availability of the existing supply. The legal advisory committee designed a series of test cases which, if successful, would open major categories of housing to all purchasers or renters.

At the same time, it was determined that local fair-housing ordinances would be of value to the program, and the legal committee drafted a model ordinance which was widely circulated to the mayors, city councilmen, city attorneys, and other decision makers in the various cities, townships, and counties in the area, through the volunteer fair-housing groups. An additional parallel drive was made at the state level to encourage the state licensing commission to adopt strong, nondiscriminatory rules covering licensees. The Fourteenth Amendment and a reinterpretation of state action was used to sustain this approach.

After 39,000 signatures endorsing local open-housing ordinances were obtained by volunteer fair-housing groups, the cities of Seattle and Tacoma plus a number of other municipalities adopted open-housing ordinances. Since more than 90 percent of the geographical area of the OE program became covered by local laws, and since the state licensing board did adopt the OE request for nondiscriminatory licensing regulations, OE was able to shift its modus operandi from listing service to compliance service.

Volunteers from the fair-housing committees were retained in the role of checker as the old listing role was abandoned. Each client was escorted, and accomodations were prechecked by volunteers. All volunteers and staff received training for their new roles—training in checking techniques and the filing and filling out of formal complaints of discrimination, taking depositions, and so on, became the key functions of the volunteers.

Success in opening up to minorities access to the available supply of low- and moderate-priced housing now forced the staff to confront the depth of the housing shortage in the three-county area. "All we had been able to do was to give our clients some kind of parity in the scramble for an almost nonexistent commodity."[117] As one immediate solution, the Seattle Urban League was encouraged to become a nonprofit housing sponsor for the rehabilitation of housing units under Section 221-h of the federal housing law.

> It was our idea to demonstrate that the program could be made to function rapidly and efficiently and that good housing could be produced in 90 to 120 days. . . . Hoping to involve church groups and others in eventual sponsorship, we tried to develop a simple procedure that others could follow. . . .[118]

By enlisting the cooperation and aid of the president of the largest mortgage company in the state, a team of consulting architects and a group of attorneys, as well as the director of the local FHA, OE was able to streamline and eliminate many procedures that were only administrative guidelines. They changed the presale requirements, the eligibility requirements, the interpretation of rehabilitation, the specifications, and were thus able to obtain immediate block precommitments.

> We proceeded from the first initial closing, to the first finished house, to the first move-in, to the first blanket

mortgage closing, the the first complete spin-off of a
package. From start to finish, over 9 months were required to complete the first package of homes. Now the
time has been cut in half. We have now completely spun
off five packages totalling 30 houses, we have another
thirty in various stages of rehabilitation, and an additional
supply of packages progressing rapidly.[119]

At the same time, OE was able to locate, motivate, and assist
a number of other sponsors for the rehabilitation of housing units,
for which OE was to provide the purchasers. The rehabilitated homes
were all single-family frame residences located in nonintegrated
neighborhoods. OE was able to provide three-, four-, and five-bed-
room homes in blue-collar neighborhoods, close to jobs and good
transportation, for minority buyers at an average cost of $13,750
per house. Almost 50 percent of the houses were sold to female
heads of household, many of whom were on welfare.

Recognizing that the rehabilitation program could provide only
limited housing resources, when the need was in the thousands, OE
organized a committee of leaders in banking, construction, real
estate, government, and civil rights to deal with the overall problem
of the shortage of low-income housing in the region. This committee
contracted with Urban America for a study of low income housing
needs, and after one year of study a proposal was adopted, calling
for the creation of a private housing development corporation.

This corporation was to be capitalized at $2 million, and its
goal was to build 10,000 units of low-income housing in three counties over the next five years. Not waiting for this to occur, OE
immediately formed a coalition of churches to build new housing
units under Section 236 of the new federal housing act.

At the same time, OE prodded the Seattle Housing Authority
into a greater awareness of its responsibility. The Authority had
neither built nor acquired a single unit of family housing since 1942.
Its efforts had concentrated on the elderly. OE was able to persuade
the Authority to use some of its new 1,000 units for families.

In addition, OE played a role as advocate planner to the citizens'
housing task force of the Seattle Model Cities program. OE drafted
plans for a housing development corporation to produce and rehabilitate
5,400 units of housing during the first five years of implementation
of the plan. The proposal gave the corporation the power and the
direction to build relocation housing outside the Model Cities neighborhood, as well as within it. OE was also involved in the Seattle
antipoverty plan for a model mini-neighborhood with integrated
housing, and commercial and social activities under an OEO grant.

Most recently, OE negotiated a contract with HUD to provide counseling on credit problems for low-income families, under Section 237 of the 1968 Housing Act. They have also solicited from churches and local foundations for a secondary financing fund, to be used on a revolving basis for needy families in meeting closing costs and moving expenses.

Its latest concern has been that of restrictive zoning and land use, which effectively bar home seekers from entire neighborhoods, communities, and municipalities.

> We recognize that sophisticated concepts of land planning, urban development, taxation, land use, zoning and the like must be understood and turned to our advantage. . . . As a consequence, we are cooperating with the School of Urban Planning of the University of Washington to present a series of night classes for our volunteers. . . . [T]his will enable them to monitor local land use policy and work for change in various areas of the three counties.[120]

Impact. OE has helped over 600 families move into new or rehabilitated homes in the last three years. It serves over 1,500 families with continuing counsel on finances, home maintenance, and legal problems. In the past year, it had over 17,000 client contacts for these purposes. It processes an average of 120 to 150 new clients a month. Approximately 520 people are planning to purchase homes made available by OE, and 126 are seeking rentals. Racially, clients seeking low-income sales are 45 percent black, 50 percent white, and 5 percent "other."

OE has grown from a staff of six and a budget of $138,000 to a staff of 35 and a budget of $450,000. Its funding sources have multiplied: original Ford Foundation grant has been renewed for a second three-year period (with matching local contributions), and there have been funds from Model Cities, OEO, and an industrial contract with the Boeing company.

> Despite these accomplishments, it is our belief that the 1970 census will show that housing in this area is just as segregated as it ever was, and that at least 90% of all black families live in the overcrowded core centers of Seattle and Tacoma. . . .

> It would even be fair to say that segregation in our three county area is worse now than it was when we began. The number of families that we have moved directly and indirectly does not compare with new family formations and

in-migration to our ghetto areas in Seattle and Tacoma
in the same time period.[121]

With this sober recognition, the director of OE went on to
explain his own assessment of the program. He stated emphatically
that the staff felt that they were on the right track. The conventional
model of a fair-housing listing program was seen as inadequate to
meet the complexity of the need. "New methods and new directions
must be rapidly formulated and implemented if we are to have any
impact on the worsening problem of segregation in housing."[122]

OE has found that changing existing institutions, however, is
not enough, and insists that it is imperative to create new, innovative programs as well. For example, OE's efforts to change the real
estate industry has resulted in positive effects for many minority
families. But the concomitant creation by industry of jobs further
and further away from the inner city has resulted in very negative
effects for many other minority families. Since housing in the newer
industrial areas either is insufficient or costs more than many minorities can afford, "OE will devote a great part of its time fostering
the creation of programs to change zoning, building codes, taxation,
and other practices which prevent construction of housing for low
and moderate income families in suburban areas."[123]

From its own rehabilitated three-bedroom home that has been
turned into a warren of offices from basement to attic, Seattle's
OE has been operating an open-housing program that may be characterized as "creative flexibility in action."[124] At the open-housing
conference in Chicago in February 1969, the Seattle program was
judged to be particularly aggressive, productive, and effective in
working on the twin goals of desegregation and expanded opportunities
for low- and moderate-income minority families.

Double Strategy. OE's strategy has been twofold. Its change in focus
from a traditional fair-housing listing service to an actual construction program involved other changes in the existing institutions. To
provide the climate for its new emphasis, OE first changed the legal
framework by the enactment of a network of open-housing ordinances.
Then, in order to provide a concrete example that would induce other
potential nonprofit sponsors of building to participate in like programs,
OE completely capsized governmental regulations and procedures.

By reducing the frustrations and bureaucratic red tape that had
discouraged nonprofit sponsors up until that time, OE was able to
motivate 12 different sponsors to undertake the task of providing new
or rehabilitated housing for minorities in quantities that had not
existed before, and in nontraditional areas as well. As a by-product
of this effort in the Seattle area, HUD was so impressed with OE's

success in developing such volume with its processing changes that
it has designated pilot efforts in 15 cities to replicate the OE experience. Fifteen hundred units in multiple dwellings in the 15 cities
will be rehabilitated over for families with a rent-supplement
program.

The second strategy of OE has been equally impressive, if
not more so. In effect, this strategy has been to create new strategies by combining and permutating the OE structure with other com-
plementary agencies and programs. The OE attempt is not just to
find ways to make the present systems of housing delivery work
better, but to change them more profoundly. OE's involvement in
Model Cities, operation Breakthrough (HUD), the Housing Development Corporation, and Boeing all express this thrust. As Director
Guren notes, "If we were only a delivery program, it would be death
and disaster because the present system is so inadequate we could
not hope to meet the need." Thus, with neither the money nor the
staff to undertake all of this alone, OE is a goad to banks, industries,
and public agencies which are in positions of power. "Every man on
the staff must be a multiplier," says Guren. "Everything we do has
to have a chain reaction"[126]

In putting pressure on the power structure, Guren and the OE
staff have been compelled to pick their way through the maze of
regulations and guidelines governing the various state and federal
housing programs. Their goal has been not merely to know as much
as the officials they deal with, but to know considerably more. In
effect, they have become technical advisers to these officials, helping
to rewrite the guidelines and redraw the planning maps. As Guren
points out, if an open-housing program hopes to exercise control
over the housing supply, if it demands a say in where the houses
will be built and who will live in them, then it has no choice but to
learn "how to play the game."

> We are in housing construction development not because
> we want to build, but because we must be practitioners
> so we know the ground rules and the viewpoints of the
> participants in the process. Then when we assume an
> advocate role in behalf of change, we know what we are
> talking about. [127]

One cannot help wondering whether in learning to play the game,
OE may identify too strongly with the other players, the very people
from whom they are hoping to win concessions. But perhaps the
anodyne to creeping collusion is Guren's own professionalism.

> It sometimes gets very hard to operate and think at the
> same time. It's schizoid—half of you is the operator,

working within the system, and the other half is the
reformer, maybe even breaking down the structure
you're operating in. Yet it is the operating half that
feeds the information to be an effective reformer. A
knife-edge business, but worth it. [128]

It may be said that the professional's hallmark is an ultimate
loyalty to his creed and craft. In this case, the creed and craft add
up to equal opportunities in housing for minorities. As both a long-
range goal and an everyday process, Seattle's Operation Equality
appears to be moving toward this through a flexible, creative program geared to institutional change.

Time: 1977

In June 1970 Dave Guren was dismissed from his job as director of Operation Equality. With his dismissal, the organized fair-
housing movement in Seattle ended. Seven years later, a visit to
Seattle uncovered some facts about the demise of Operation Equality
and Guren's dismissal.

According to Dave Guren, there were two reasons for the dismissal, which seemed to be related to internal power conflicts and
external black separatism: the director of the Urban League, which
funded Operation Equality, capitulated to demands of a black contractor's group that wanted a black director for OE: and there were
conflicts over authority between Guren and the Urban League director.
Guren said: "He caved in to separatist leaders, said I'd have to go,
and gave me 24 hours to leave!"[129]

The director of the Urban League, Jerome Page, confirmed the
role of the black contractors in the dismissal:

Black contractors were very important to the Urban
League and the black community. OE was heavily involved in rehabilitation and construction. Guren wasn't
working enough with the black contractors. Being program oriented, he wanted to move quickly, and wasn't
always willing to take the time it took to deal with the
black contractors. They complained, and finally I had
to do something about it. [130]

When asked whether the black contractors' dissatisfaction was the
main reason for Guren's dismissal, the UL director quickly answered:

No, there was more to it. Dave Guren was a master
grantsman—he was super-competent. . . .OE became
too big. It got completely out of hand. Dave ran it so

completely, no one else could take it over. It was, after
all, an Urban League program—but you'd never know it.
He wouldn't listen to anybody, had to do things all his
own way. I think it wouldn't have lasted, even if he had
stayed. Anyway, we had a falling out, and he was terminated.[131]

Within one year after Guren left, Operation Equality became
the Seattle Housing Development, in a merger with Model Cities.
It was a ghetto-based program concentrating on rehabilitation and
counseling. Josephine Osby, a housing specialist who had worked
with Guren and then stayed on with Seattle Housing Development,
had some thoughts about what had happened:

After Guren left, the fair housing program floundered
and never picked up again. He knew what to do and how
to do it. Some people wanted to leave the Urban League
after he went. We've had five Directors since Guren
left—only one was any good, and he was only on loan
for one year. There are a lot of things we haven't had
since Guren left.[132]

By 1977, even the Seattle Housing Development seemed doomed.
"It's very shaky, gasping its last breath. . .there's no housing
money. . .it can't go on."[133]
    Although the organized effort for open housing died in Seattle
in 1970, in its place was left a vigorous, effective network of neighborhood councils, now united into the Central Seattle Community
Council Federation. "The big issue here is redlining. . .also zoning
and land use."[134] These issues are being confronted by the neighborhood organizations, individually and collectively, and they are, of
course, fair-housing issues, though limited.
    Neither Dave Guren nor the Urban League director, Jerome
Page, saw any critical need in 1977 for a fair-housing organization
per se. They did not perceive Seattle as having housing segregation
or much discrimination, although the director admitted: "Black im-
paction has moved south, away from the central city. There is a
large rental complex there near public housing, all of this will soon
be an instant slum."[135] He thought, however, that this was due to
poverty and choice.
    But the Urban League director of education, Tom Vassar,
lamented the housing situation in Seattle, and perceived the relationship between housing and the schools:

Housing patterns have changed in the last five years,
especially in the center and south parts of the city. The

center is still mostly black, now the south part is black
too. There's no other place to live because of discrimination. . .by real estate agents and bankers. This has
made the schools segregated. Segregated schools are
the result of segregated housing. And segregated housing
exists because of discrimination—there's no question
about it.[136]

When asked who handled discrimination complaints, UL's
Jerome Page referred to the Human Rights Department of the city,
which has its office in the UL building. This is a city-funded agency,
which also receives complaints about employment discrimination.
From what is known about other similar types of agencies, its
housing discrimination service is probably neither adequate nor
able to deal effectively with Seattle's fair-housing problems.
    Earlier, a measure for success was developed, based on the
potential for systemic change. Seattle's Operation Equality was the
most successful fair-housing organization by that measure. But it
died. Why didn't the organization continue after its leader left?
Apparently, there was no one else with the ability or will to carry
on, which suggests that the earlier analysis of success needs some
reconsideration.
    The first requirement of a successful fair-housing organization
—or any organization—is that it survive. This is a necessary, but
not sufficient, condition for success. In order to insure survival,
a leader must train others to replace him or her as needed, and must
inspire and motivate a sufficient number of others to carry on in his
absence. This necessitates task rotation and skill development, for
the temporariness of leadership in movement organizations is apparent, and must be taken into account in any planning and organization
for the future. The two dimensions of fair-housing success, then,
are survival insurance and systemic change; Seattle had it on the
second, but lost it on the first. Dave Guren was so good that no one
could replace him, and the movement folded almost immediately
after he left.
    There is no doubt that the movement is as much needed there
now as ten years ago, despite contrary perceptions of both Dave
Guren and Jerome Page. Without a vigorous watchdog on the local
level, all the varieties of discrimination tactics will not only recur,
but will thrive and expand. If the neighborhood federation does not
address this issue, the city of Seattle will continue on its way
toward massive segregation and resegregation.

ACROSS THE COUNTY—PROFILES OF
TWELVE MOVEMENT ORGANIZATIONS

Between 1970 and 1977 funded, staffed, metropolitan fair-
housing programs expanded throughout the country:

> Growth of the number of full-time, staffed housing oppor-
> tunity centers operating multi-service programs over
> large geographic areas in all regions of the nation is. . .
> one of the most encouraging civil rights developments in
> recent years. . . . There has been an expansion of acti-
> vities into new and important areas of work. . . . [137]

Brief profiles of 12 fair-housing organizations across the country
indicate their diversity, scope, and ingenuity in confronting the
issue of open housing in their own communities. Ultimately, it is
the struggle on the local level that keeps the movement alive and
justifies the existence of a national core organization.

It is probably true that community organizations could continue
indefinitely without a national organization, but unlikely that a
national organization could survive very long without the local groups.
For a vital, effective fair-housing movement, however, both are
needed. Lobbying and legislative and political activities must go on;
if there were no national organization to do this, the local groups
would soon have to create one. So their needs are mutual, and together they continue to engage in the reciprocal relationship that characterizes any movement.

It must be noted that the hundreds of fair-housing organizations omitted from the following profiles are all vital, admirable,
hard-working components of the entire fair-housing movement.
What follows here is merely a random selection of movement organizations—not in any way based on merit or size—selected as representatives of the whole body of movement organizations working for
open housing.

Chicago: Leadership Council for Metropolitan Open Communities
(LCMOC)

LCMOC, formed in 1966 as a funded organization, was an outgrowth of the Chicago Freedom Movement marches led by Martin
Luther King, Jr. When those marches were met with violence in
the Chicago area, leaders of industry, religion, labor, government,
housing, and civil rights joined together to organize the LCMOC.
Its purpose was and is to create a single, nondiscriminatory housing
market throughout the Chicago area.

Contributions from business and industry at first provided the major source of income, plus foundation grants and individual contributions. Since its inception, government contracts have significantly increased its yearly budget, which is now $600,000. Since 1977, the two major funding sources have been HUD and corporate contracts.

The program of LCMOC is extensive and has four components: legal action to enforce open-housing law, affirmative action through an affiliation of citizens' groups, brokers, and employers; a development corporation to actually build low- and moderate-income housing in the suburbs near workers' jobs; and a regional fair-share housing plan involving the regional planning commission, and mayors and citizens of surrounding suburbs.

The legal action program of LCMOC is considered one of the best in the nation, and is a model for all other fair-housing groups. The legal staff wrote the definitive "Guide to Practice Open Housing Law," which is used by fair-housing groups throughout the country. The legal action staff, headed by energetic, knowledgeable Bill Caruso, has held seminars and training sessions for attorneys and government employees in all parts of the country. They have a constant pending file of 40-60 legal cases, and average new filings of 50 cases a year, stemming from their numerous individual complaints (4-6 weekly).

In 1976 damages awarded for racial discrimination totalled $59,235 for 37 cases, an average of $1600 per case. One rental case alone resulted in settlement payments of $20,000, the highest amount awarded in a rental case anywhere. Thirty real estate licenses were suspended for racial discrimination by the state Department of Registration. Monetary damages and license suspensions are part of the council's strategy to make housing discrimination uneconomic as well as immoral and illegal.

LCMOC conducts ongoing audits which have resulted in 30 legal suits filed for racial steering in nine suburban municipalities. Through small seed-money grants, LCMOC has spurred the formation of a network of suburban fair-housing groups, which are now all funded through various foundations, churches, and businesses. Nine such groups have been formed, of which one—the Oak Park Center, begun in 1971—now received $80,000 from Community Development Block Grants to conduct its own fair-housing program in its own area.

LCMOC has promoted the extension of soft loans (about $25,000 each) to black brokers to establish real estate offices in the suburbs. These brokers cooperate with businesses, churches, and civic groups to guarantee the sale of homes in the suburbs to minority employees. More than 500 families have made open-housing moves to 80 different suburban areas, through the efforts of LCMOC. In addition, more than 600 new housing units have been built in three different areas

by Metro Housing Development Corporation, the development arm
of LCMOC, begun in 1969. These are occupied by middle-income,
moderate-income, and low-income families whose racial composition is 55 percent white, 25 percent Latino, 10 percent black, and
10 percent other minorities. Sixty-six suburban areas have begun
action to provide housing for low-income workers.

LCMOC has also sued HUD for excessive FHA and VA mortgage rates in integrated areas, which resulted in a HUD Affirmative
Action program of HUD staff counselors trained by LCMOC staff.
Kale Williams, the quiet and immensely effective executive director
of LCMOC, said, "We are beginning to see the effects of a vigorous
enforcement program."[138]

Dallas: Greater Dallas Housing Opportunity Center (GDHOC)

GDHOC began in 1968 as an outgrowth of Neighbors for Fair
Housing, a church-oriented group. Financed only by contributions,
it has remained primarily volunteer-led until the present, though it
maintains an office and a very small staff. Its budget has been about
$12,000-13,000 a year, which has allowed only part-time staffing
for most of its existence. In 1970 GDHOC first hired one paid staff
person for five hours a day, adding some clerical help in 1973. A
small HUD grant (Jaclyn) in 1975-76 provided the first outside funding
for the organization. Jane Green, past president of the board and
former office coordinator said, "We quickly saw we couldn't run only
a volunteer office. But when we got outside funding, our volunteer
support dwindled. We are now forced into thinking of other ways of
getting funding."[139]

Their thinking was productive and led to a Ford Foundation
grant in 1977-78 for $25,000, the largest funding in the history of
the organization. Their proposal to the Ford Foundation outlined an
affirmative marketing program directed to minorities living in concentrated areas. Direct mail to them, with brochures and maps of
outlying areas and vital information concerning prices, sizes, security deposits, and down payments in those areas would be beamed to
the minorities, encouraging out-movement. The program is directed
by the board, which hired a small staff to implement the plan.

A unique working relationship with the city-funded fair-housing
agency results in a highly effective fair-housing effort for the Dallas
area. HOC was instrumental in getting a local fair-housing law passed;
then they monitored it and secured greater enforcement by the city.
The newer, city fair-housing office, directed by Rick Rencher, has
five full-time workers who handle investigation of discrimination
complaints with a corps of 20-30 checkers. The suburbs are under

HOC jurisdiction, as are educational programs. There seems to be no rivalry or competitiveness between the two fair-housing groups, even though the city-funded one receives $60,000 and is relatively new. This is no doubt so because of the clear division of "turf" and program, well worked out ahead of time by the two capable and friendly leaders—HOC's Jane Green and the Dallas Fair Housing Office's Rick Rencher.

The HOC program is a traditional one of education, housing assistance for suburban areas, and monitoring and research. They receive about seven or eight discrimination complaints a month, compared to the city office's 25 a month. HOC's volunteer lawyers number ten, and the number of cases they have filed is 20, with low damages. Jane Green lamented that "Court cases in Texas have not been very successful. . .so this discourages the filing. Cases through municipal court don't turn out well."[140] She went on to discuss future program plans, indicating an emphasis on the suburbs with dispersal of low-cost housing in those areas. Educational work with the apartment house association has resulted in HOC articles in their newsletters. In addition, HOC's monitoring of housing advertising has resulted in the inclusion of minority models in picture ads.

Dallas's HOC has actively conducted audits, not for litigation, but for general systemic change. Their first audit was in 1970 and covered rentals. A second audit covered sales in 1974. After the second audit, negotiation with the real estate industry took place, resulting in a cooperation agreement with the Dallas Board of Realtors. Under this agreement, any members of the board of realtors who are guilty of discrimination and are unwilling to take positive remedial action will be dropped from board membership. HOC, with limited staff and funding, continues to be a positive force working for open housing in the Dallas metropolitan area.

Richmond, Virginia: Housing Opportunities Made Equal (HOME)

HOME is a young group that began in 1973, primarily through the efforts of James Hecht who moved to Richmond after lengthy leadership of Buffalo's 14-year-old HOME organization. Richmond's HOME began as a nonprofit, volunteer group, grew to 600 members, and is now funded by city, state and federal contracts (CDBG), foundations, corporations, and individual contributions.

Its program offers housing information and counseling (including mortgage counseling), community education, and discrimination complaint investigation and resolution. Because of the contractual provisions with its funding sources, HOME can use volunteers only for discrimination investigations. Since only about one case a week comes into the office, this does not pose any serious difficulty. HOC offers outstanding printed materials which provide housing-choice information to minority home seekers. Neighborhood profiles, for example, have been developed for areas throughout the Richmond metropolitan region. They include detailed information on price ranges and locations of homes and apartments, taxes and fees, driving times to major points, the history of the area, and names and phone numbers of HOME-member residents of the specific area who serve as volunteer guides on request.

A Guide to Real Estate Firms includes information on special services of each firm, usual sales areas, usual price ranges, and names and phone numbers of contacts for each firm. An Apartment Guide offers a comprehensive list of over 45,000 apartments in the Richmond area describing exact location, prices, and special features.

The program's excellence is largely due to the capability, knowledge, and dedication of its director, Barbara Wurtzel, who in turn claimed: "It was Jim Hecht who brought his expertise from Buffalo and offered it to Richmond. He guided us and motivated us and informed us, so that we were able to produce an effective program."[141]

Palo Alto, California: Mid-Peninsula Citizens for Fair Housing (MCFH)

MCFH was organized in 1964, after the passage of Proposition 14 "suddenly offered no protection against discrimination based on race, religion or ethnic background. Its stated goal, then and now, is to secure for all . . . equal opportunities to purchase or rent property wherever they choose."[142] In 1968 the organization began to focus on expanding the supply of housing for low- and moderate-income families. In 1970 it began its pioneering work in rental audits, which resulted in the publication of an audit handbook, widely utilized by other fair-housing groups throughout the country. Its program is a comprehensive one, involving a discrimination checking service (about 100-140 cases a year) handled by 24 cooperating attorneys, an affirmative action educational program, an employer subscription service for minority employees, and a housing rehabilitation program.

MCFH has a small budget of some $24,000, of which two-thirds comes from members and one-third from contracts with cities in 13 surrounding areas and from employer contracts. The staff consists of three full-time people and two half-time secretaries, and according to Kathy Berson, the director, "we just don't have enough staff to do all we want to do."[143] The volunteer help is very extensive, however, numbering 75 checkers alone. In 1974, because of staff limitations, the tenant-landlord counseling program was dis-

continued, and those calls were referred to other agencies. Half of
its program is low- and moderate-income housing (rehabilitation
and development promotion), half is open housing.

Despite funding and staff inadequacies, MCFH manages to
achieve a creditable legal service for discrimination cases—stronger
than in some other fair-housing groups which are much more heavily
funded and staffed. For example, in 1975 the attorney referrals
resulted in one suit filed, one won with $5,000 damages plus costs,
one suit lost, four pending, eight settlements (with from $1,000 to
$3,500) and two cases conciliated by attorneys. For a small, under-
funded organization, this is not a bad record for one year. MCFH
was rewarded in 1973 when a federal court decision, holding the
owner of 11 apartment buildings guilty of racial discrimination proved
through an audit, called the organization's testing activities: "a
reasonable means by which citizens may ascertain the compliance
status of landlords with fair housing laws, and appropriate in a proceeding of this nature."[144]

Director Berson did not seem too content with the MCFH situation. "In addition to the understaffing and underfunding", she complained wistfully, "I feel lonely—not really part of a national movement. I wish I had a chance to sit down with other fair housing groups
to talk. I wish there were more regional conferences." She wished
that NCDH would sponsor more of these, but went on to express very
positive thoughts about NCDH: "Their Newsletter and Flashes (legislative and action alerts) are fine, their monitoring of CDBG is fine,
their lawsuits are fine."[145] Since 25 percent of MCFH's discrimination cases are referred to them by Operation Sentinel (OS), also in
the San Francisco Bay area, a brief description of that fair-housing
organization logically follows.

San Francisco: Operation Sentinel (OS)

OS, which covers six counties in the Bay Area, began in May
1971 as a program to combat illegal discrimination in housing. It is
undoubtedly the most concentrated fair-housing effort in the country,
since it deals only with the one program and focuses on it completely.
OS is a program of the Stanford Mid-Peninsula Urban Coalition, which
is a private, nonprofit, action organization concerned with economic
and racial equality in Santa Clara and San Mateo Counties. The Coalition in 1971 sponsored the creation of 12 30-second films for TV
and 12 radio spots for use as public-service announcements. The goals
of the OS program are highly dependent on publicity, which also
includes billboards, bus signs, and news ads and features. The phone
number of OS is 468-7464, which spells H-O-U-S-I-N-G. The slogan,

"Discrimination in housing based on race, religion, or sex is illegal; dial H-O-U-S-I-N-G" has become a household phrase in the San Francisco Bay Area.

OS's stated goals are three: to alert the public at large and members of the housing industry in particular to the fact that discrimination in housing based on race, creed, or color is illegal and is punishable under the law; to tell the home seeker who encounters discrimination that assistance is available and is his right; and to provide that assistance by investigation of his complaint, and if necessary, to provide an attorney free of cost.[146]

Despite a modest budget for most of its existence ($20,000-25,000 per year, mostly from foundations and contributions) and a staff of only two, Operation Sentinel has investigated an average of 500 discrimination cases a year in the last five years—the most outstanding statistic in the nation for this type of activity. OS has a panel of 25 attorneys who handle cases through a revolving legal defense fund. The average cost per case is $200, paid to the attorney to cover costs when the complaint is filed. The money is set up on a revolving basis so that when the case is closed, either with a settlement or court award, $200 is refunded to the program.

"This fund has been of great assistance. It enables us to work with young attorneys who couldn't affort out-of-pocket costs, and to offer a higher caliber of service to our clients."[147] Coordinator Melinda Sacks, with the program only six months, handled the recruitment of checkers. She said that about 100 discrimination cases a year are referred to attorneys for litigation. The average out-of-court settlement has been $2,700 and the average court award $3,200. The highest court award to an OS case was $10,000, and the highest out-of-court settlement $37,000.

When asked to comment on constraints or obstacles to achieving open housing, Sacks replied:

> The problem of racial discrimination is still very much there. Fear of change is the prevailing attitude we must contend with, especially in the real estate industry. Yet, the legal cases against them (the real estate industry) are the most effective in producing the change we want to see—more compliance with the law. Long ago, the concept of "educating" landlords gave way to a more effective approach—the courts.[148]

Late in 1976, OS received an $80,000 HUD grant to conduct a massive legal enforcement program to be used as a model for the nation in enforcing fair-housing laws. Under the grant, filing and litigation costs up to $300 will be paid to attorneys for cases brought

under Title VIII of the 1968 Civil Rights Act. Attorneys will be permitted to keep 75 percent of any fees awarded by the courts, above the
costs of filing and litigation. This incentive system should work well
in ensuring the continuance of OS's vigorous program of law enforcement for open housing in the Bay Area.

Bergen County, New Jersey: Fair Housing Council (FHC)

Concerned citizens formed the FHC in 1959 in the white suburban area of Bergen County, which includes 70 municipalities and one
million people. Its annual budget then was several hundred dollars;
it is now over $150,000. Beginning as a totally volunteer organiza-
tion, it soon found that continuity was lacking and some regular
staffing was needed. Executive Director Lee Porter, after having
been with the group for fourteen years, described the early days:

> At first we met all over the county, using only volunteers.
> That was too difficult. Then we hired 1 or 2 people for 1
> or 1 1/2 days a week. But coordination was needed, and
> we had to have a Director. The first one was hired in
> 1969, but only stayed for two years, then moved away.
> I came in 1971 as Director, after having been a volunteer
> for nine years. At first I wasn't paid, so my first job
> was to raise money. [149]

FHC became a subcontractor for the Urban League, and then industries began to make contributions to the group. The FHC became part
of the United Fund, and now industries purchase service through cor-
porate memberships and affirmative action contracts for minority
employees. In addition, there has been support by foundations for
the open-housing program of FHC. In the early 1970s, their annual
budget was $20,000 a year, but only recently have they been able to
use their funding for "real fair housing," through a CDBG contract.
This "real" program supports discrimination counseling and litigation
efforts through a full-time legal staff and investigators.

Porter spoke of the current fair-housing program of FHC as
a broad one: "You can't just do a fair housing program these days.
You have to have something else added if you want funding." One
"something else" added to FHC' s program is a massive land development project covering 11 different towns. This project, developed
by Hackensack Meadowland, is being influenced by FHC pressure to
expand the supply of housing for low- and moderate-income families.

The growing emphasis on housing discrimination counseling
and litigation, however, is receiving top priority in the FHC program,

and has resulted in a multiple suit against 240 brokers of Bergen County! This unprecedented class action suit charged the brokers with racial discrimination in both sales and rentals. In a complaint filed March 8, 1976, the plaintiffs alleged that four multiple-listing services (serving 50 communities) have a policy of racial steering, use discriminatory advertising, and have discriminatory hiring practices. Porter is proud of FHC's "suit a month" (actually one every 20 days), and increasing monetary damages ($6,000 was the most recent, and the largest).

Cited as constraints by Porter were lack of money, lack of supply of housing for low- and moderate-income families, bigotry in the real estate industry, and lack of government enforcement of fair-housing laws: "If the government—HUD and the Department of Justice—would enforce their own laws, that would be a great help."

Louisville: Kentucky Commission on Human Rights

The Kentucky Commission began open-housing work in the early 1970's, when the former Housing Opportunity Center succumbed under OEO to a ghetto-based operation. Not a traditional fair-housing organization, but one which conducts a vigorous and unusual fair-housing program, the commission works under the splendid direction of Galen Martin. He has related two other critical issues to fair housing—school desegregation and subsidized housing (Section 8)—and has related them to each other as well.

When school desegregation was ordered by the courts for Louisville and its Jefferson County suburbs, the Kentucky Commission outlined a policy position for city and county governments aimed at insuring that all federally aided housing programs be used to provide desegregated housing. This would decrease rather than increase the number of children to be bused under the court-ordered school desegregation plan. The policy called on the private sector—real estate and lending institutions, business and industry—to join in an all-out effort to prevent continued use of government funds, powers, and mechanisms to increase housing segregation. "It is unfair to the people of this community to allow HUD to support different forms of housing which are segregated, while other branches of the Federal government require desegregated schools."[150] The policy was adopted by the mayor and city council of Louisville, making it the third metropolitan area in the nation to adopt similar housing desegregation plans to achieve racial balance in the schools. *

---

*The other two were Minneapolis-St. Paul and Cleveland.

The Kentucky Commission prepared and distributed widely a leaflet called "Six Ways to Avoid Busing," as part of its multipronged effort to use housing desegregation as a tool for reducing the need for busing to achieve racially balanced schools. Since the Jefferson County school desegregation plan allows children in desegregated housing areas to attend neighborhood schools, the leaflet outlines steps individual families can take to exempt their children from busing. It stresses the active role parents can take in all-white communities by welcoming new neighbors of another race, and encouraging the development of a wide range of housing in their area. Similarly, desegregated housing moves by black parents will exempt their children from busing. Martin reported that many black families were considering such moves for the first time in order to avoid having their children bused for nine or ten years.

The commission is also promoting greater use of the Section 8 subsidized housing program by both black and white low- and moderate-income families to obtain housing on a scattered-site basis throughout the county. It has initiated a counseling program to assist families in choosing locations where their children can attend neighborhood schools. "The strength of the local plan is that it enables many people to participate in desegregated housing in the area, thereby decreasing the need for student transportation."[151]

The work of the commission is critical in the Louisville area, where the tenor of local feelings is indicated in the following conversation with a taxi driver:

Driver: What building is that you're going to?

Author: Kentucky Commission on Human Rights.

Driver: Oh, them! They're responsible for all this busing we're having here. Those damn liberals —show me a liberal and I'll show you a phony. And I'll be damned if they're gonna tell me who I'm gonna sell my house to. I'll sell my house to anyone I damn please to.

Author: They're not trying to tell you who to sell to. They're just saying you have to give equal treatment—it's the law.

Driver: Well, law or not, they can't make me do it. Here we are. . . . [As I get out, he nods toward two black women crossing the street.] You think you'd like your kids to go to school with that? Imagine forcing us to do that—how would you like it?. . . .Damn phony liberals.[152]

Ohio Fair Housing Congress

A number of fair-housing groups in Ohio have joined together in a loose informal coalition, formed in 1976. This is believed to be the only current state coalition of fair-housing groups in the country. Five of the groups in the Congress are briefly profiled here, again to illustrate the "diversity in unity." Though an integral part of the Congress, Akron's FHCS is omitted here, since it has been examined intensively in Chapter 4.

Cincinnati, Ohio: Housing Opportunities Made Equal (HOME)

HOME is a 12-year-old organization which conducts a triple program of housing assistance (complaint investigation), education, and research (auditing). It has gone the usual route of voluntary to funded organization, and is currently funded through community Chest, corporation contracts, government contracts, churches, religious organizations, and individual contributions.

One unique aspect of its program is its relationship with its board of realtors. The realtors give funds to HOME to do checking and testing and conduct educational programs for real estate companies. This is a culmination of years of legal involvement with a racial steering suit brought against several large real estate companies. The monetary arrangement is part of the consent decree. Also stemming from that decree is a monitoring board set up to review and discipline agents who are found discriminatory. Finally, the consent decree led to the production by HOME of a slide show on the hazards of racial steering. This is shown to real estate companies and others as part of a community education program.

HOME received a $25,000 contract in 1977 from Hamilton County under CDBG funding, which will be used for discrimination complaint investigation in the county. The contract was given despite considerable reluctance of the county commissioners, who had balked at establishing the fair-housing program. The federal government (HUD) threatened to stop funds for all 20 community development programs in the county unless the commissioners complied. They finally did, and so enabled the county to receive $4 million in CD money.

At the same time, the Cincinnati Human Relations Commission was given $90,000 by the city for a fair-housing program, including an affirmative marketing plan and fair-housing enforcement and monitoring in the city. This dual funding in the same area of two local civic organizations may lead to conflict and tension within the movement.

There is some question as to what Community Chest funding may do to HOME's legal program. In 1974 HOME filed 16 lawsuits in federal court charging racial discrimination. In 1975 the legal program was taken over by a separate agency to which HOME can refer clients. The stability gained from the Chest affiliation may prove costly for the ultimate goal of open housing, if reduced legal action results.

Cleveland, Ohio: The Cuyahoga Plan

This fair-housing organization reversed the process of rags to riches. It began as a heavily funded organization (from two foundations of Cleveland) in 1974; in three years it was almost out of funds, looking for a new director, and in disfavor with some other fair-housing groups in the area for "not having done anything." One of its former staff members became the director of new fair-housing organization in Cleveland, Housing Advocates, Inc., and the former director of still another Cleveland organization—the Cleveland Heights Congress, a neighborhood stabilization group—left to become the new director of the Cuyahoga Plan in 1977. This musical chairs situation was accomplished while the Cleveland Urban League's fair-housing program, Operation Equality, went out of existence, and at the same time that the Cleveland Plain Dealer described the housing segregation pattern in Cleveland as worse than ever:

> The central city on Cleveland's east side grows blacker and poorer. Four integrating eastern suburbs have small percentages of black households. The remaining 48 suburbs and contiguous townships of Cuyahoga County are populated 99.8% by white households.[153]

The Cuyahoga Plan first offered a comprehensive program, with three goals: end discriminatory housing practices; desegregate neighborhoods throughout the county; and strengthen and maintain already integrated neighborhoods. This was to be accomplished through seven trustee-led task forces whose mission was to work in seven areas: business and industry, financial institutions, government affairs, community education, real estate practices, planning and evaluation, and mediation. Their early brochure stated "Yes, they're ambitious goals. Their accomplishment may take a decade—but we've begun to open the door." Apparently the door jammed somewhere, because this group has not been able to carry out an effective program to date.

Perhaps the new staff can accomplish what the former one could not. The judgment of some observers in the area seems to be that the blue-chip board of trustees does not really want systemic change and has resisted any real efforts to achieve it. The latest program change, however, should cause them no anxiety since it involves a housing information service. The Cuyahoga Plan will seek additional funding from Community Development Act (CDA) money and other sources, and may yet evolve into an effective fair-housing organization, competing with all the others in the Cleveland area for that elusive status.

Columbus, Ohio: Housing Opportunity Center (HOC)

The mammoth fair-housing organization of Ohio is Columbus's HOD, which was first funded in 1967 as a Model Cities program, and still retains much of the flavor of that venture. It is now funded heavily through CDBG money, with a budget of $270,000 for a comprehensive housing services program. The HOC program includes housing location, landlord-tenant counseling, and home ownership counseling, as well as the traditional complaint investigation and community education. The staff includes two attorneys, "who have handled 52 discrimination cases, and lost only one," as reported proudly by Director Carl White.[154] His pride in HOC's program has not been shaken by recent rumblings of discontent among his board of directors. White has been referred to by some board members as "a one-man band—not responsive to anyone else." Some of the directors are very dissatisfied with the HOC program, which does not seem to them to be doing enough to really achieve fair housing in the Columbus area. Their volunteers have dwindled, and there are indications of serious staff-board difficulties, which White has openly referred to. This will certainly need to be resolved if the organization is to conduct an effective fair-housing program.

Dayton, Ohio: Fair Housing Information Service

Newly funded under a CDBG contract, this program is operated by the Miami Valley Regional Planning Commission, nationally known for its fair-share plan. The program provides housing assistance and information and education, and is awaiting additional funding to expand its program. A proposal for $94,743 was submitted to the county, and had just been funded as of this writing. Under Dale Bertsch's expert direction, there is no doubt that a fair-housing program would be effective in the Dayton metropolitan area, as the

fair-share plan has been a model throughout the country for the
equitable distribution of low- and moderate-income housing through
voluntary agreements with area jurisdictions (see Chapter 3).

Toledo, Ohio: Fair Housing Center (FHC)

Formed as a city-funded organization with $80,000, the FHC
opened in August 1975 with a four-pronged program: public education,
assistance to victims of discrimination, assistance to the city of
Toledo, and assistance to public and private bodies on projects
affecting housing opportunities. The Center provides educational
programs on fair-housing law, how to recognize discrimination,
and the benefits of racially inclusive communities. It provides
counseling, technical assistance, and follow-up services to victims
of housing discrimination. It cooperates with area agencies in developing and monitoring programs and projects which affect housing
opportunities for low-income and minority people.
In its first year, the Center received 130 discrimination complaints, and served 450 people with housing problems. Its program
seems effective and vigorous, led by a fortunate combination of a
capable, knowledgeable board and an equally capable, knowledgeable
director. What is even more significant in its success is that the
two are close and compatible. The Toledo fair-housing leaders have
given credit to past Akron fair-housing leaders for providing a model
for them. The current Akron leaders, however, look to Columbus
for their model. But the Columbus model and the Toledo model are
very different, and these differences are often reflected in Ohio Congress disagreements over policies and procedures.
Several newly funded, fledgling fair-housing groups in Ohio,
also part of the Congress, are Canton's new Urban League fair-
housing program, Stark County's fair-housing office, and Massillon's
fair-housing program—all in the same county, all funded through
CDBG money. HUD's Equal Opportunity Division director in Columbus,
Bob Brown, has observed:

> More than $1 million dollars of CDB grants in Ohio is
> going to fair housing programs—more than any state
> in the country. Now what we need is a way of evaluating
> what they're doing. Some cities and counties are simply
> giving the money just to comply with the federal regu-
> lations of the HCDA of 1974, which call for a fair housing
> component in every program. But they don't monitor
> them once they give the money, and no one knows what
> they're really accomplishing. [155]

For that reason, on November 29, 1977 a special working conference of HUD and fair-housing groups in Ohio was held in Columbus, with Brown and Washington-HUD's Zina Greene (Equal Opportunity Division) leading the session. The purpose was to come up with guidelines for evaluating fair-housing and other programs relating to equal opportunity under CDBG programs (see Appendix D). These are badly needed to make efficient use of federal money for the fair-housing movement. In fact, without evaluation standards built into the federal regulations, the proliferation of funded fair-housing groups would be just a cruel joke.

SUMMARY

Using a goal-effective model, which combines elements of Etizioni's goal and system models, four organizations which are local manifestations of the open-housing movement in four different communities have been compared. It has been suggested that, using such a comparative analytical framework it may be possible to assess the effectiveness of different organizations dedicated to the same goal. The measure of success was not seen as the complete or even substantial attainment of the goal, but rather the relative effectiveness of each organization in its attempt to reach its stated goal.

In the case of the open-housing movement, the recognized stated goal is that of equal opportunities in housing for minorities—a goal approached by these four organizations through different means and emphases. It has been suggested that the success of each organization may be meaningfully referred to in terms of its ability to move toward systemic change in its attempt to reach this goal.

In New York, the Open Housing Center began as Operation Open City which conducted an action housing location program, funded by local antipoverty agencies. Late in 1969 it was directed to change its stated and operative goals from an open-housing focus to a technical assistance focus. In effect, this would have eliminated the entire funded open-housing program as it existed, unless other sources of funding were obtained. This program developed into a model of excellence for a one-to-one housing location service, coupled with a vigorous attack on discriminatory practices. The impact of the New York program has been considerable, in terms of the numbers of families directly or indirectly motivated to make desegregated moves. In spite of its excellence as a housing location service and discrimination fighter, the program achieved limited results in moving toward systemic change, although recent attempts toward more effective techniques of massive desegregation were noted. If the program had been terminated in 1970 through funding removal, no central coordination would exist in the vast New York area for its network of volunteer open-housing groups.

Through the determination and persistence of its founder and director, the Open Housing Center of New York has weathered loss of funding, changed affiliation and location, and repeated disruption. Survival and effectiveness of program seem to be insured with this competent leadership.

In 1970 the Los Angeles Housing Opportunities Center, funded by OEO, was comprised of three divisions, of which the Fair Housing Division was seen as having conducted the most effective programs during its brief period of funding. Though the Fair Housing Division seemed to be moving toward systemic change on the community level, this attempt was to be aborted by the imminent removal of funding. It was noted that the accomplishments of the Fair Housing Division, relative to systemic change, were made possible by the development of a huge network of localized volunteer open-housing groups. This permitted referrals from the funded central office to the local groups, freeing the staff from one-to-one service, and allowing it to work toward broad institutional change. With a loss of funding, the 60 localized volunteer groups would have had no central coordination in an area context of severe constraints.

But despite the funding loss in 1970, leadership and determination kept the movement going in the Los Angeles area until new funding was secured. A new Fair Housing Congress arose to take the place of the former program. Though the structural and funding arrangements were an initial source of conflict between the movement organizations of the Los Angeles area, the open-housing programs of the area continue to flourish and demonstrate vigor and creativity, despite different philosophical and tactical approaches.

The Denver Metro Fair Housing Center was viewed in 1970 as the largest and most affluent funded open-housing program in the nation. Conducting a huge comprehensive program, with funding from multiple sources, the program was designed to be more than a mere housing location service. Its vast public relations program stimulated greater awareness of minority housing problems in the local community. The local status of the program was high, and stemmed from a broad base of support from both ghetto residents and the power structure. However, it was concluded in 1970 that the Denver program was, in fact, a massive listing and counseling agency, which gave little evidence of moving toward systemic change relating to broad desegregation and the ending of discrimination.

Its collapse in 1971 was due to a combination of factors, mostly internal, relating to weak leadership, goal uncertainties, and cessation of funding. But as has been seen from the two cases above, cessation of funding can be overcome with strong leadership, so that factor can be eliminated as a cause of collapse. Denver's demise, then, came from weak leadership and a poor program, in the face of an external situation of black separatism.

Seattle's Operation Equality was seen in 1970 as a program of creative flexibility in action, resulting in the greatest potential systemic change of the four communities analyzed. A charismatic professional was able to educate his funding source (the Ford Foundation) to allow him and his staff to put bold innovative programs into effect. Moving almost completely away from the traditional listing service program, Seattle's OE not only provided such service, but also built and renovated the houses used for minority relocation. In order to achieve this, it first effected massive changes in the legal system and the housing industry and government systems, utilizing every available network of decision makers to accomplish this. The director of OE illustrated a broader measure of success than originally outlined here. He demonstrated that changing existing institutions was not enough, and that it was imperative to create new, innovative ones as well.

If a continuum were constructed illustrating this comparative analysis of four open-housing organizations in 1970 relative to our stated measure of success, it might appear as follows:

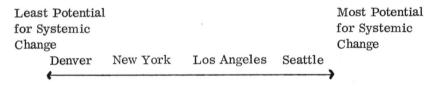

Least Potential for Systemic Change — Denver — New York — Los Angeles — Seattle — Most Potential for Systemic Change

If the case study of Akron in 1970 were added to this continuum, it would fall far to the left of the Denver point. The real tragedy of the early case study of Akron lay in the fact that its smaller geographical area could most effectively have moved toward institutional change.

It was suggested in 1970 that one of the early hypotheses had been confirmed—that institutionalization does not necessarily lead to a decline of a movement. It may, in fact, if coupled with able leadership, strengthen that movement (as in Seattle) and catapult it toward profound systemic change.

Now, seven years later, the transiency of movement organizations is even more apparent. The two that were threatened with immediate cessation of funding in 1970 managed to survive and prosper with able leadership and persistence. The other two that seemed in 1970 most entrenched and secure collapsed soon after. Analysis of the reasons for their death reveals two common factors: internal power conflicts and external black separatism in the national civil rights movement. Since the two surviving movement organizations also confronted the external black separatism factor, it must be concluded that internal power conflicts were the major cause of the demise of the open-housing movement in Denver and Seattle.

This is much too simple, however. Deeper examination of the differences in the Denver and Seattle programs and leadership indicates that Denver's administrative leadership was weak, and Seattle's was extremely strong. Denver's open-housing program was not moving toward systemic change, and Seattle's was. The reason for the internal power conflict in Seattle was precisely because of a program and leader that were too successful! However, if that leader had been able to groom others in the movement organization to take his place, the movement in Seattle might not have died.

The first requirement of a successful movement organization, it was noted, is that it must survive. A leader must train others for replacement, and must inspire and motivate others to carry on. The second requirement for success is systemic change. The tragedy here is that Seattle met the second requirement superbly, but not the first. Denver met neither condition and its loss, though regrettable is not as tragic as Seattle's.

NOTES

1. Amitai Etzioni, Modern Organizations (Englewood Cliffs, N.J.: Prentice-Hall, 1964), pp. 16-19.
2. From Alexis de Tocqueville Democracy in America (New York: Oxford University Press, 1947).
3. Confidential Report, unreleased, New York, 1969, and interview with Richard Margolis, Sept. 7, 1971, Georgetown, Conn.
4. Betty Hoeber, "Operation Open City," New York, 1969, p. 2. (Mimeographed report).
5. Ibid., p. 1.
6. Ibid., p. 2.
7. Proposal to New York Council Against Poverty, Operation Open City, New York, 1969, p. 1. Mimeographed.
8. Proposal for Open City Housing Center, New York, 1969, pp. 6-8. Mimeographed.
9. Richard Margolis, "The Metro-American Dilemma," New York, 1969, p. 13. Mimeographed NCDH report, unreleased.
10. Hoeber, op. cit., p. 4.
11. Ibid., p. 6.
12. Margolis, op. cit., p. 15.
13. Hoeber, op. cit., p. 21.
14. Ibid.

15. Margolis, op. cit., p. 14.

16. Ibid.

17. Planners for Equal Opportunity, New York Metropolitan Chapter, "On the Move: A Survey Analysis," New York, 1967, p. 2. Mimeographed.

18. Ibid., p. 6.

19. E. J. Logue, "Attitude Survey," John F. Kraft, Inc., New York, 1966, cited in Planners "Survey," op. cit., p. 2.

20. New York Times, August 7, 1970.

21. Urban League News Release, April 15, 1976.

22. Proposal to the City of New York, OHC, October 6, 1977.

23. Urban League News Release, May 7, 1973.

24. Report on the Housing Opportunities Center of Greater Los Angeles, January 10, 1969, p. 4. Mimeographed.

25. Ibid., p. 1.

26. Ibid.

27. Housing Opportunities Center, brochure.

28. Ibid.

29. Report, HOC, op. cit., p. 3.

30. Ibid., p. 4.

31. Ibid.

32. Ibid., p. 6.

33. Ibid.

34. Ibid., p. 15.

35. Ibid.

36. Ibid., p. 24.

37. Ibid., p. 25.

38. Ibid.

39. Ibid., p. 26.

40. Ibid., p. 27.

41. Ibid.

42. Ibid.

43. Ibid., p. 28.

44. Ibid.

45. Ibid., p. 16.

46. Ibid.

47. Ibid.

48. Ibid., p. 18.

49. Ibid., p. 20.

50. Ibid.

51. Ibid., p. 21.

52. Ibid., p. 22.

53. Ibid., p. 29.

54. Ibid.

55. Interview, September 5, 1969, Los Angeles.

56. Interview (telephone), July 13, 1976.
57. Fair Housing Congress News Release, August 1976.
58. Interview, Los Angeles, July 27, 1976.
59. Interview, San Fernando Valley, July 27, 1976.
60. Interview, Los Angeles, July 27, 1976.
61. Ibid.
62. Interview, San Fernando Valley, July 27, 1976.
63. Interview, Los Angeles, July 27, 1976.
64. The Comprehensive Story of Metro Denver Fair Housing Center, Inc., MDFHC, Inc., Denver, 1969, p. 7.
65. "Metro Denver Fair Housing Center, Inc.," MDFHC, Inc., Denver, 1969, p. 1. Mimeographed.
66. "What Is the Metro Denver Fair Housing Center?" MDFHC, Inc., p. 4. Lithographed.
67. "Narrative Report on Center," MDFHC, Inc., Denver, December 31, 1967, p. 4. Mimeographed.
68. Ibid., p. 2.
69. Margolis, op. cit., p. 26.
70. Ibid., p. 27.
71. MDFHC, Inc., "Narrative Report," op. cit., p. 3.
72. Ibid., p. 5.
73. Ibid.
74. Ibid., p. 7.
75. Ibid.
76. The Comprehensive Story, op. cit., p. 28.
77. Margolis, op. cit., p. 27.
78. MDFHC, Inc., "Narrative Report," op. cit., p. 12.
79. Ibid., p. 13.
80. Ibid.
81. Ibid., pp. 14-15.
82. Margolis, op. cit., p. 26.
83. Ibid.
84. Interview, New York, April 21, 1970.
85. Interview, San Francisco, August 28, 1969.
86. Margolis, op. cit., pp. 28-29.
87. Denver Post, April 23, 1971 Microfilm, Denver Public Library.
88. Denver Post April 18, 1971.
89. Interview, Denver, August 7, 1976.
90. Ibid.
91. Interview, Denver, August 7, 1976.
92. Interview, Denver, August 6, 1976.
93. Interview, Denver, August 7, 1976.
94. Denver Post, August 25, 1968, p. 4.

95. Proposal for Funding, 1966, Seattle Urban League, p. 3. Mimeographed.

96. Letter from Mrs. Frances Riley, Seattle Operation Open City, August 26, 1970.

97. Marian Pruzan, "Operation Equality, A Study of Community Organization Method," Seattle, March 9, 1970, p. 3. Mimeographed term paper.

98. Ibid.

99. Letter from Mrs. Riley, op. cit.

100. Proposal, op. cit., p. 1.

101. Margolis, op. cit., p. 16.

102. Pruzan, op. cit., p. 1.

103. Operation Equality, brochure, Seattle.

104. "The Beginning of a Better City," OE, Seattle.

105. "Let's Face It!", OE, p. 2.

106. Summary of Operation Equality Program, January 1969, p. 1. Mimeographed.

107. Hearings of Washington State Board Against Discrimination and State Real Estate Commission, October 28, 1966, p. 4. Mimeographed.

108. Ibid., pp. 4-5.

109. Letter from Sidney Gerber to author, March 26, 1965.

110. Hearings, op. cit., p. 8.

111. Letter from Sidney Gerber, op. cit.

112. Summary, op. cit., p. 3.

113. Ibid.

114. Ibid., p. 4.

115. Ibid.

116. Ibid.

117. Ibid., p. 6.

118. Ibid., p. 7.

119. Ibid., p. 8.

120. Ibid., p. 13.

121. Ibid., p. 15.

122. Ibid.

123. Newsletter, Operation Equality, Seattle, June 1969, p. 2.

124. Housing News, National Urban League, July 1970, p. 3.

125. Ibid., p. 5.

126. Margolis, op. cit., pp. 17-18.

127. Housing News, op. cit., p. 5.

128. Ibid.

129. Guren Interview, August 4, 1976.

130. Jerome Page Interview, (telephone) September 14, 1977.

131. Ibid.

132. Interview (telephone), Seattle, August 4, 1976.

133. Ibid.

134. Guren Interview, August 4, 1976.

135. Interview (telephone), September 14, 1977.

136. Vassar Interview (telephone), Seattle, August 4, 1976.

137. Trends in Housing, May-June 1974, p. 1.

138. Interview, Chicago, September 9, 1977.

140. Ibid.

141. Interview, Philadelphia, November 18, 1976.

142. Annual Report, MCFH, 1975, p. 1.

143. Interview (telephone), San Francisco, August 2, 1976.

144. U. S. vs. Youritan Construction Co., February 8, 1973.

145. Interview (telephone), August 2, 1976.

146. Flyer, OS, 1976.

147. Interview (telephone), August 2, 1976.

148. Ibid.

149. Interview (telephone), Dec. 7, 1977.

150. Trends in Housing, Winter 1975-76, p. 4.

151. Ibid., Winter 1975-76, p. 4.

152. Encounter, Louisville, June 2, 1977.

153. Cleveland Plain Dealer, May 19, 1975.

154. Interview, Columbus, March 25, 1977.

155. Interview, Ohio Fair Housing Congress, Atwood Lodge, Ohio, November 10, 1977.

6

SUMMARY AND CONCLUSIONS

OVERVIEW

A curious paradox was implied in the literature devoted to the general study of social movements. The ultimate success of a social movement was seen as symbolized by institutionalization, since unsuccessful movements usually fail before that stage is reached. However, it was repeatedly suggested that institutionalization leads to the decline and eventual failure of a movement. Thus, both unsuccessful and successful social movements must eventually fail. Institutionalization was described as the stage when a movement has achieved societal recognition, was seen as having some continuing function to perform in the larger society, and was accepted as a desirable or unavoidable adjunct to existing institutionalized arrangements.

This study has attempted the exploration of one aspect of the above paradox, namely, does institutionalization lead to the decline of a movement? From this initial query, several others emerged. How does one determine at what point a movement is institutionalized? What happens to a social movement when it becomes institutionalized? If the movement does decline after institutionalization, what factors lead to this failure? If the movement does not decline after institutionalization, what accounts for its continued growth? How can success or failure be measured?

The exploration of these varied facets of the problem has been conducted through the analysis of one specific social movement, open housing. To justify the study of open housing as a social movement, the concept of the social movement was examined. Through a synthesis of three approaches to the study of social movements—collective behaviorist, social-psychological, and sociological—an ideal-type concept of a social movement was developed. A social movement is a collectivity acting with some continuity to promote or resist change, extending beyond a local community or single event. The distinguishing features of a social movement were noted as change-oriented goals, the use of organization, durability, and geographical scope.

In view of this ideal-type concept, the study of open housing as social movement was suggested as a valid and meaningful one. However, since the study of social movements has been relatively neglected by sociologists, a systematic methodology for such study has not been developed. A few suggestions for the study of social movements have, however, been offered. Social movements are studied in terms of growth patterns or phases of development, of which institutionalization is the final phase. External influences are considered significant in the genesis and development of social movements. Internal organizational features such as leadership, membership, ideology, and strategy are of importance in considering the development of the movement and its ultimate impact, which may be viewed in terms of manifest and latent consequences. The social movement is regarded as both a product and producer of social change.

With these scant guides, and with the originally stated problem in new, this study developed the following methodology for the systematic examination of the open-housing movement. First, the movement was studied on the national level through historiography, supplemented with personal interviews with significant leaders. On this level, the movement was examined in terms of four phases of development, with the social and cultural context of each phase noted and considered. Three aspects of the movement on the national level were explored: first, the development of a national core organization, viewed in terms of goals, program, impact, and organizational changes; second, legislative development; and third, local community action development. A content analysis of 21 years of housing newspapers provided the major source for information concerning these three aspects. In addition, the national organizations's development was studied through documents and records provided by the organization.

Secondly, the movement was studied on the community level, with two approaches. One was the intensive case study of the movement as it developed over a 13-year period in one local community, examining that community's social, cultural, and ecological contexts. Involved participant observation was supplemented by historiography in the case study, which combined symbolic interaction and organizational analysis. Two early phases of development were analyzed—the voluntary and the institutionalized—each in terms of goals, program and impact, and morale. Analysis of the later development of the movement organization focused on its achievements after its return to a volunteer status, and its growth in legitimacy and prestige leading to eventual refunding.

The second approach to the community level was the comparative analysis of four movement organizations—primarily in the institutionalized phase—in four different communities. These were analyzed through historiography and supplemental field visits. Each movement organization was examined in terms of inception, goals, program and impact. Through a comparative goal-effective model, a measure of success was suggested as the relative ability of each organization to move toward systemic change in its own community. Each movement organization was reexamined seven years later, with an assessment of the factors that contributed to its success and survival or failure and demise. Brief profiles of twelve movement organizations added to this level of analysis.

The social movement was viewed throughout as a dynamic system of reciprocal influences, with each approach designed to illustrate a different aspect of this reciprocity relevant to the open-housing movement. Six emergent propositions were stated, each to be reconsidered after the presentation of findings. An attempt was to be made to develop a theory of social movements within the context of social change.

THE NATIONAL LEVEL

The significance of events in the history of a movement cannot be fully appreciated without considering the total context of those events. Thus, the social and cultural context of the general civil rights movement prior to and during the development of the open-housing movement was considered as a crucial element which constantly influenced the course of events in the movement.

In examining the open-housing movement on the national level, social and cultural context was considered in three ways. First, the general conditions leading to the development of the modern civil rights movement were briefly explored. Second, events leading to the development of the open-housing movement were noted, third, each of the three phases of development of the movement was set against a backdrop of significant events in the society at large.

Three aspects of the open-housing movement on the national level were examined: the development of a national core organization (the NCDH), legislative development, and local community action development.

Development of the National Organization: NCDH

NCDH was formed in 1950 in response to country-wide demand for a national organization to direct and coordinate the struggle for open housing. As an organization of organizations, its purpose was to establish nondiscriminatory and nonsegregated housing in the United States.

Its program during the first phase was focused primarily on federal government agency influence and field activities. Two government agencies influenced by NCDH were the Housing and Home Finance Administration and the Public Housing Authority. Of the field activities engaged in, the one involving the Levittown development had the broadest eventual impact. A national reporting service (Trends in Housing) was inaugurated toward the end of this phase, increasing NCDH impact on the local level. During this phase, NCDH changed from a volunteer group to an organization with a staff of three and a budget of $18,000, and grew from 15 to 26 member organizations.

During the second phase, three major federal housing programs were indicted by NCDH in recurrent, public, Senate testimony: Urban Renewal, FHA, and Public Housing. The growing impact of NCDH on the government and the nation was revealed by the positive action taken by federal housing agencies, by its influence on the Democratic and Republican party election platforms, and by the executive order banning discrimination in housing.

The growing impact of NCDH on the community level was indicated in the successful culmination of the Levittown case, the issuance of the Fair Housing Handbook, and the convening of three major national conferences. The third conference had an entire session devoted for the first time to grass-roots activities, indicating the extent of the growth of the movement on the community level. The NCDH grew during this phase from 26 to 37 organizational affiliates, and achieved tax exemption, which allowed it to seek foundation funding. This paved the way for the phase of institutionalization that followed.

With a greatly increased budget and staff, NCDH was able to expand its program and impact considerably during the third phase, as evidenced in the struggle against Proposition 14 in California, the Weston, Illinois atomic energy site situation, the Louisville, Kentucky Model Cities funding withholding, and the Greenburgh, New York urban renewal controversy. Of 12 national and regional conferences convened by NCDH during this phase, five were considered especially significant, in view of subsequent developments in the movement. The five were concerned with combating the growing countermovement's referendums, foundation and government financial support of community fair-housing programs, emphasis on low- and moderate-income families in open-housing efforts, the alliance with the national antipoverty agency (OEO), and the focus on metropolitan fair-housing centers.

By the end of the third phase, NCDH had grown from 37 to 51 national organizational affiliates, had moved its offices to a prestigious location, had opened two new regional offices, and had received almost one million dollars in funding from government and private sources. When fair-housing became the law of the land—largely due to NCDH pressure and influence—NCDH shifted its focus immediately to the link between jobs and housing, with land-use bias in zoning restrictions as the new target for action.

Changes in the general civil rights movement were seen as having a persistent and pervasive effect on the open-housing movement, reflected in overt and covert responses of the core organization. Yet, though it modified its public statements in response to situational demand, the NCDH clung stubbornly throughout its 20-year existence to its avowed goal of nondiscriminatory and non-segregated housing in the United States.

By its twentieth anniversary at the beginning of the fourth phase, NCDH faced financial and organizational disaster and a new national rival, National Neighbors. Administrative changes were mandated by its funding sources, and with new leadership NCDH attempted over the next five years to restore its image. During this period, marked by cautious fiscal and program management, NCDH sought to reestablish the link with local movement organizations and national government policy makers through regional conferences, legal suits, Trends, policy statements, research papers, educational programs, and consultative services. The fourth phase ended with the HUD/NCDH nationwide audit, which brought funding and a major discrimination investigation technique to 40 local movement organizations and advocates across the nation, and helped to renew the ties with the local groups.

Legislative Development

During the growth of the open-housing movement, legislative development seemed to follow a social distance scale, proceeding from public housing coverage to publicly assisted housing to private housing, with increasing resistence encountered in each step. The concomitant development of a countermovement also made the task more formidable.

At the beginning of the second phase, only three states had laws prohibiting discrimination in public housing, two had laws forbidding discrimination in public housing and urban redevelopment, and three had laws covering publicly assisted housing. Fourteen

cities had laws banning discrimination in public housing, seven
covered public housing and urban redevelopment, and only two banned
discrimination in all publicly aided housing. By the end of the second
phase, 26 government jurisdictions had adopted measures affecting
private housing, and 60 cities had laws or resolutions affecting discrimination in housing, both public and private. New York in 1957
was the first city to adopt a law banning discrimination in private
housing, with NCDH leadership spearheading the protracted struggle
that ended in the passage of the law.

The general trend of legislative development during the third
phase was the continuation of the social distance scale model indicated
earlier. The culmination of this trend was reached with the 1968
Civil Rights Act and the Supreme Court decision upholding the con-
situtionality of the 1866 Civil Rights Act. Thus it took 102 years to
merely reaffirm man's basic right to shelter. In addition, several
local and state actions barring fair-housing laws through referendum
were declared unconstitutional by state and federal supreme courts.
NCDH was active in this entire effort, submitting amicus curiae
briefs in several such cases, notably California's Proposition 14
case and the 1866 case.

Half of the 94 local laws passed since 1958 were adopted in
1967 alone. By the end of the third phase in 1970, there were 229
state and local fair-housing laws. In a period of three months after
the passage of the Fair Housing Act of 1968, the total number of local
fair-housing laws increased by 100. Though the battle for a national
open-housing law was won, the struggle for open housing as a reality
was not. NCDH shifted its legislative attack to zoning restrictions
in urban and suburban areas, and advocated replacement of the one-
by-one complaint process to the broader pattern-and-practice
approach.

The fourth phase of development was accompanied by massive
legal action brought to implement Title VIII of the 1968 Civil Rights
Act. Monetary damages were increasingly awarded in housing discrimination cases, not only to plaintiffs but also to the fair-housing
groups that supplied the data through checkers. This was a spur to
engage in more investigation and more litigation. Consent decrees
obtained through Department of Justice suits also proliferated during
this phase. A national moratorium in 1973 sharply curtailed housing
and other social and economic programs and adversely affected the
open-housing movement. Zoning decisions in legal suits vacillated
between positive and negative consequences for the movement's
goals. Fair-share plans burgeoned, but their implementation was
weakened by political and economic frustrations.

Local Community Action Development

At the beginning of the second phase, there was little evidence of local community action organizations devoted specifically to open housing, although considerable action was conducted on the local level through other civic, civil rights, and religious organizations. By the end of the second phase, more than 300 specific fair-housing committees or organizations were identified as actively working for open housing.

It was suggested that the force of national events in the civil rights field and the local constraints relative to race and housing might have spurred development on the local level even without a core organization such as NCDH. It was doubtful, however, that without it the local development would have occurred to the extent that it did. The publication of the manual and Trends in Housing were cited as propelling forces in the growth of the movement across the country.

Local community action during the third phase was marked by three trends: continuing proliferation, funding, and increased emphasis on low-income housing. Proliferation was indicated in the growth from 300 local community groups at the beginning of the phase to 2,000 at the end of the phase. Geometric progression occurred until 1966, with growth leveling off after that time. Events in the general civil rights movement leading toward separatism may have been responsible for this fact, and funding may have also been a factor, causing consolidation.

Fifteen cities across the nation were cited as having secured funding for local fair-housing organizations, formerly voluntary. Many of these indicated a new emphasis on low-income housing, either through rehabilitation efforts or the expansion of the supply of low-cost housing through the building of new units.

The three trends of proliferation, funding, and low-income focus were traced to NCDH influence. Heavy emphasis by NCDH on funding as a requisite for effective action programs on a metropolitan basis was noted throughout the third phase. The success of a few voluntary groups in securing funding also encouraged others. NCDH's growth of emphasis on low-cost housing permeated Trends and national and regional conferences, and filtered down to the local groups. Also seen as significant was the general national emphasis on the War on Poverty, which had an effect on NCDH itself as well as on the local fair-housing groups.

The fourth phase of development was marked by four aspects of local movement organization activity: an increase in auditing, an increase in legal action, an increase in citizen participation in the A-95 review process and CDBG monitoring, and an increase in funding

of metropolitan fair-housing centers under provisions of the HCD Act
of 1974. These four trends formed an additive process culminating
in the final one of funding. The reciprocal impact of the external
national situation and the NCDH on local movement organizations and
on each other was clearly evident.

THE COMMUNITY LEVEL

The Case Study

The point of view of symbolic interactionism, as advocated
by Blumer, was suggested as a necessary supplement to organizational analysis in the intensive examination of one local manifestation
of the open-housing movement. Symbolic interaction stresses the
process of interaction and interpretation among participants in organizational situations.

The similarity of certain elements of analysis in the study of
social movements and organizations was noted, for a social movement is a form of voluntary association which is, in turn, a type of
organization. The definitions of each exhibit such similarities, and
such elements of analysis as the environmental setting, goals, the
authority structure, the career, and the consideration of success
were cited as common to the study of both social movements and
organizations. The consideration of success was seen as presenting
the most difficult problem of examination and interpretation.

Although the study of social movements and the study of organizations are marked by similar elements of analysis, both seem
unable to focus on the process involved as each type responds to
changing situations. It is in this respect that the use of symbolic
interaction was thought to yield meaningful results. Thus, the fusion
of organizational analysis with symbolic interaction was seen as
possibly leading to greater understanding of the social movement as
a reflector and creator of change.

The case study, then, was an attempt to combine both modes
of analysis in an effort to understand the intricacies and complexities
of the open-housing movement as it developed in one community
over a five-year period. Using the methods of involved participant
observation and historiography, the case study illustrates the reciprocal impact of NCDII and the society at large upon the local community organization. It also illustrates the impact of the human
participants upon each other as they individually and collectively
met the situations that confronted them at the community level.

Development as a Volunteer Movement

The open-housing movement in Akron developed as a response to social, cultural, and ecological constraints which were a miniature extension and reflection of similar conditions on the national level. Such constraints represented a long history of black population growth, restricted access to housing, urban renewal leading to a shortage of housing supply, and the resultant patterns of residential segregation, compounded and reinforced and perpetruated by continuing urban redevelopment and discrimination in housing.

As a volunteer movement (the first phase of which lasted three and one-half years), the stated goals of the Fair Housing Contact Service (FHCS) were found remarkably consistent with its operative goals or program. The stated goal was equal opportunity in housing for minorities, and the program was a twofold one of education and housing assistance. The housing assistance program was a free listing service combined with a compliance service to combat discrimination in housing. The policies of the Akron organization were explicit in their directive to make housing placements in nontraditional areas only. All other requests for housing aid were to be referred to normal channels of housing service.

The education program was directed toward both the white and black communities. In the white community, the education was designed to increase awareness and understanding of the harmful effects of discrimination, and to dispel common myths and fears regarding desegregated living. In the black community, the education was primarily a publicity program, to acquaint potential black home seekers with the nature of the service, and to encourage them to make use of such a service. Education was conducted through every available medium—printed materials, newsletters, mass media, open meetings, a speaker's bureau, and special campaigns.

Three major educational campaigns had significant impact on the community; two were planned, with positive manifest consequences, and one was only partially planned, with pervading, negative, latent consequences. As a result of mass-organized FHCS pressure, stemming from its proposal for funding, the mayor was forced to develop a plan for additional low-cost housing in order to retain urban renewal funding for the city. This plan involved the local public housing agency, which was completely shaken by the publicity given to its inaction over a 20-year period. An administrative turnover resulted in a new administrator who, in response to mayoral demand, proceeded with a vigorous acquisition of funding for low-cost housing for the city. A massive building and leasing program ensued in the next three-year period, totaling $30 million of funding from HUD and resulting in 4,900 additional units of housing for low-income families.

The irony of the situation and the tragic latent consequence of this was the creation by the public housing agency, despite repeated protests, of new patterns of housing segregation, and the reinforcement and perpetuation of existent residential segregation patterns. This, of course, further compounded the difficulties of the FHCS in its attempts to desegregate the community.

Despite this, the impact of the entire first voluntary phase of the organization was positive. Two national awards and two local awards were received by the organization for outstanding volunteer service to the community. Forty different neighborhoods were opened, and 18 complaints of discrimination were filed with relevant agencies. This was achieved with no office, no staff, and a budget of some $300 a year.

The morale of the group during its voluntary phase was assessed through an examination of the quality of interaction among board of directors members, since they were the prime conducters of the organization's entire program. Using Bale's small-group analysis as a framework, the board was characterized as strong in task and and sociability factors. These were related to the instrumental-expressive and external-internal analyses of Parsons and Homans. It was suggested that the board's strength in task orientation was responsible for the high maintenance of morale. Bale's interaction categories were applied, and the group was found high in positive reactions and problem-solving attempts, and extremely low in negative reactions. Most decision making was achieved through consensus, and few formal votes were taken by the group, such formal voting as did occur eliciting unanimous response. Strong board involvement and participation characterized the entire first voluntary phase.

Toward the end of the voluntary phase, events in the national civil rights movement were seen to have an effect on some leaders of the local movement, one of whom publicly stated that blacks were no longer interested in integration. Ghetto riots occurred in Akron in August 1968, the first in the community, though among the last to occur in the nation at this time. It was at this time that the surprise announcement came that the FHCS had been granted $59,726 by OEO to administer a Fair Housing Center, to open in six weeks.

Development After First Funding (Institutionalization)

While the stated and operative goals of the organization had been completely consistent throughout the voluntary phase, this was not the case during the two-year phase of institutionalization. In the funded phase, the operative goals (program) changed almost immediately, though the original stated goals were the same. During the second year of funding, the stated goals also changed and became more consistent with the operative goals of the funded program. Throughout this period, there were differing interpretations among board and staff members of even the original stated goals, as set forth in the original proposal for funding.

The goals, both stated and operative, were clearly and specifically delineated in the original proposal for funding. The program of the new Center was intended to be an extension and expansion of the entire former volunteer program, with an added new emphasis on meeting the housing needs of the poor. Despite the clear delineation of specific detailed means of accomplishing the overall goal of equal opportunity in housing, the housing needs of the poor quickly came to be the primary focus of the entire program. All other aspects of the program were relegated to a position of minor importance.

What was not recognized by the participants for some months was that the new focus, as it came to be implemented, was in direct conflict with the original policies and goals of the organization. Even with the growing recognition of this fact, there was confusion and division among the board as to how to cope with the situation. There was, in fact, uncertainty as to whether to cope with it at all.

The negative impact of the Center on the community during its first funded year was indicated by community responses to four specific situations promulgated by the Center director and his staff, and by newspaper articles reflecting a negative image of events involving the Center. The four situations involved the organization of a real estate business, the unethical mortgage counselor engaged by the director, the rent strike, and the annual meeting report.

The annual meeting report revealed publicly the vast extent of Center placement of minority families into concentrated or already integrated areas, in direct violation of organizational policies. The placement of minority families into nontraditional areas was but a fraction of the total number of placements, and roughly equaled the number that had been placed during the last year of the voluntary phase.

The authority structure of the board, which had been viable during the voluntary phase of the organization, was found dysfunctional during the funded phase. In addition, the board found itself unable to engage in open, frank discussion at its meetings, with staff present. Two cliques eventually formed on the board: those who supported the Center program and staff, and those who did not.

Two types of individual response to organizational change were noted. Individuals loyal to the objectives of the organization will resist modification of them and may refuse to continue participating if the objectives are modified too radically. On the other hand, individuals loyal to the organization itself will support changes in the objectives if those changes are thought to promote survival and growth. It was suggested that the board members who were critical of the Center operation were more loyal to the objectives of the FHCS than those who supported the Center operation. The supporters were either more loyal to the staff, personally, or to the organization itself, and perceived the funded operation as essential to survival and growth.

Three factors were cited as significantly related to the board's inability to cope with problems stemming from the funded operation: the implicit sociability norm, role uncertainty, and goal ambiguity and eventual conflict. Inability to engage professional consultation reflected these factors, as did inability to set policies for board-staff relations. Though a questionnaire on goal consensus revealed marked perception by respondents on the disparity between goals and program, continued inability to resolve this situation further reflected the three operative factors cited.

After the budget was cut in half for the second year, and after the director had resigned from the organization, an NCDH consultant was finally engaged to study and evaluate the funded program. His strong indictment of the program prompted a reconsideration of it, resulting in a bold, innovative program recommendation by the board for the coming year. Immediately after the board reached consensus on this new program, a directive came from the local funding administrator (the antipoverty agency) that such a program could not be conducted with OEO monies. The board was unable to cope with this dilemma, and a new low in morale was reached. Indications of despair and frustration were revealed in minutes and the author's journal.

Some months after the morale-shattering event described above, the board slowly began to reactivate its volunteer efforts in a massive area-wide public relations campaign. This, coupled with progress in a nonprofit building program for low- and moderate-income families, served to increase morale. It was suggested that only when all hope was abandoned of having an effective funded operation was the board able to slowly mobilize itself toward a renewal of its volunteer efforts. Such renewed task orientation provided tension release and led gradually to increased morale, though all other basic problems remained unresolved. Toward the end of the second year of funding a new president was elected, all volunteer committees were totally reactivated, and a new plan for a program for the coming year was outlined and approved, all to be conducted by volunteers.

A final crucial item was noted. At the end of the second year of funding, despite an allocation of $34,000 from the local antipoverty agency for the continuation of the Center program, the board unanimously voted to return the funding and resume its former totally volunteer status.

It was suggested that a subtle but omnipresent contextual factor affecting the development of the organization and its participants was the change in the national civil rights movement.

The reciprocal impact of NCDH and the local organization was evident in five specific instances. In the founding of the organization, NCDH provided information and educational materials which directly aided the initial organization of the local group. In the funding of the organization, NCDH provided the initial encouragement for the FHCS to seek funding through OEO. In the development of FHCS as a legitimate and powerful pressure group, when NCDH requested local aid in securing signatures to petitions, FHCS found itself able to organize other groups in securing such support. In the expansion of the local supply of low-income housing units, when NCDH rejected the FHCS proposal because of an inadequate supply of low-income units, FHCS applied organized pressure to local decision makers, resulting in a massive expansion of public-housing units. The latent consequence was the hardening of existent patterns of residential segregation and the creation of new patterns of segregation. And in the renewed recognition and clarification of open-housing goals the NCDH consultant provided a framework in which FHCS could reexamine itself after funding had produced goal ambiguity and conflict.

Return to Volunteer Status

After its disastrous funding experience, FHCS returned to its volunteer status and its board of directors slowly took hold of the organization's program and refocused it on the original goals. A new program of auditing was begun, which became a longitudinal action-research effort with profound repercussions for other movement organizations across the country, as well as for FHCS. Three events affected the development of the organization during this period: the audits, the winning of the National Volunteer Award, and the HUD-funded summer demonstration project. Each of these contributed to the impact and success of the organization, which resulted in refunding at the end of the four-year second voluntary phase, and an important change in leadership.

Refunding. The refunded program is only briefly considered, because rapid board and staff turnover has not been conducive to program development. Some early trouble signs indicate that history may be repeating itself for Akron's FHCS. It seems likely that it will not return to a volunteer status again, because of a current leadership vacuum. It is also clear that a full-time staffed program is needed for systemic change. The new concern, then, must be how to make the funded program more effective in achieving open housing goals and objectives.

The Comparative Analysis

Using a goal-effective model, which combined elements of the goal and system models outlined by Etzioni, a comparative analysis was made of the open-housing movement in four urban communities. It was suggested that with this approach it might be possible to assess the effectiveness of several organizations dedicated to the same goal. The measure of success was viewed in terms of the relative effectiveness of each organization in its attempt to move toward its stated goal, rather than the complete or substantial attainment of the goal. It was suggested that systemic change on the community level, moving toward equal opportunities in housing, might offer a meaningful concept of success. This was justified in view of the overall focus of the study on the social movement as a reflector and creator of social change. Thus, the analysis was devoted to an examination of potential systemic change in four communities containing local manifestations of the open-housing movement.

Each of the four movement organizations was selected in terms of the factor of transition from voluntary to funded operation, since the process of institutionalization as related to social movements is also one focus of the study. The inception, goals, program, and impact of the open-housing movement in each of the four communities was examined, particularly as these related to the institutionalized phase of the movement. All four movement organizations on the community level had their genesis in a situation of social, cultural, and ecological constraints, and their organization was precipitated by a local crisis. Field visits and attendance at national conferences yielded further insight as to the singular and shared problems each organization confronted in its quest for open housing on the community level. The four movement organizations were reexamined seven years after the first analysis, through reports, news analysis, personal interviews, and on-site visits.

Two That Lived

The New York program was highly successful as the traditional mother-figure for all listing-service operations, coupled with vigorous antidiscrimination techniques. An extremely well-organized and well-implemented design for action resulted in considerable impact in the community. The numbers of relocations were impressive, and indicated a serious attempt and realization of ghetto out-movement. However, by 1970 broad systemic change had only recently been approached, and this effort, too, was threatened by removal of funding by the local source. It was doubted that the movement could sustain any meaningful impact in the community without funding for the coordination of all the scattered volunteer fair-housing groups.

Though funding for the fair-housing program was curtailed in 1970, determined efforts by the local movement leader and director resulted in new sources of funding and the continuation of an active movement organization.

The Los Angeles program also illustrated the potentiality of systemic change on the community level. Because of the development of a vast network of geographically dispersed volunteer fair-housing groups, the funded operation was able to direct referrals to such groups for housing location service. This, in effect, freed the central staff to engage in broader systemic approaches to equal opportunities in housing. Unfortunately, the attempt was an abortive one, since in 1970 the funding source was about to remove its financial support from the program. Without funding, it was doubtful that the network of volunteer groups could effectively work toward systemic change in the absence of coordination, particularly because the area constraints were seen as especially severe. Los Angeles leaders offered a number of extremely perceptive insights relative to the concept of success in open housing.

In 1970 the funding was indeed removed from the open-housing program, but the movement did not die in Los Angeles. Out of the ashes new leadership and strength emerged, and the movement kept going until new sources of funding were found. Though there are some strains in the movement organization relationships in the Los Angeles area, the open-housing program there continues to flourish. Two brief descriptions of contrasting movement organizations in the Los Angeles area illustrate "unity in diversity."

Two That Died

The Denver program, the most massively funded and staffed operation of the four, was seen in 1970 to be least effective in moving toward systemic change. Though designed to be much more than a huge listing and counseling service, it was viewed primarily as such. Its impact on the community was great, resulting from a well-oiled public relations bombardment of the public, but it did not appear to have actively engaged in combating discrimination or in changing the institutions responsible for it. Though multifunding insured its independence, and its geographical area was more circumscribed than the other communities, its leadership did not appear to be directing the operation toward systemic change.

Weak leadership and a poor program, in the face of an external black separatism, led to internal power conflicts and the removal of the administrator. The collapse of the movement organization soon after ended the fair-housing movement in Denver. Though neighborhood stabilization groups exist in the Denver area, there is no organized movement to conduct open-housing programs. As a result, much resegregation of integrated areas has occurred, and white suburban flight continues.

Of the four movement organizations studied, the open-housing program conducted in Seattle until 1970 was viewed as the most successful in moving toward systemic change on the local level. Its program was a model of creativity and flexibility, all geared toward the goal of achieving equal opportunities in housing. The professionalism and charisma of the administrator of the program were cited as significant factors leading to the success of the program. When the planned program, as set forth in the original funding proposal and contract, did not prove to be viable, the administrator was able to effectively educate the funding source to approve a bold, innovative program which diverged markedly from the traditional listing-type operation of other open-housing groups.

In order to effectuate the new program, which involved the new construction and rehabilitation of housing units on strategically scattered sites, the administrator first instituted planned systemic change. Through the utilization of every conceivable network of decision makers, he was able to achieve area-wide legal, industrial, and governmental changes, without which his program could not have been effective or even operative. The Seattle program illustrated a broader measure of success than originally defined. The program demonstrated that changing existing institutions is not enough; it is imperative to create new ones as well.

But at the peak of its success the program collapsed when the dynamic administrator was dismissed in 1970. His dismissal was the result of an internal power conflict which was caused precisely by the success of the program and leader. The first requirement of a successful movement organization, after sober reflection, must be survival. A leader must train others for replacement, and must inspire and motivate others to carry on. Only then does systemic change have lasting implications. The tragedy is that Seattle met the second requirement of systemic change superbly, but not the first. Denver met neither condition, and its loss—though regrettable—is not as tragic as Seattle's.

In Seattle, as in Denver, an active neighborhood organization network remains, but there is no sustained movement organization to tackle open-housing issues in the Seattle area. Recently, in both communities, school desegregation plans have been instituted. If administered wisely, these may do a great deal to create and maintain desegregated neighborhoods, despite the loss of the organized fair-housing effort.

National Impact on Local Level

In 1970 leaders in all four movement organizations were asked to indicate effects of the changing national civil rights movement on their program. Only New York and Seattle responded to this query, and both perceived no effects.

New York's Betty Hoeber qualified her statement somewhat:

> The move toward separation has not affected the open housing movement in N.Y.C. especially—more in talk than anything. Blacks and Puerto Ricans by the thousands are ready to move wherever the housing is, and to fight for it. What has hurt is the terrible housing shortage in this area, resulting in pressure to add to the housing supply as opposed to fighting for equal access.
>
> There is widespread frustration and despair of poor people in housing unfit to live in, with no place to move; this has caused a demand for developing and rehabilitating housing which they will control—and without the present landlords—instead, the local groups will control as non-profit sponsors.
>
> This new direction has indeed caused funding problems for open housing. Open City is being refunded by the Council Against Poverty for $392,000 October 1st, but it is all going into other groups. I am starting all over to find funds from other sources for open housing. This is the National Urban League direction, too; and most foundations at this time too. They are all wrapped up in housing development.[1]

In Los Angeles, Marnesba Tackett's interview was filled with allusions to the separatist trend, and its effect on the open-housing movement in that community. Mrs. Tackett was openly bitter about the removal of funds from open housing, and clearly attributed it to the separatist trend.

The Chicago National conference in 1971 revealed a deep concern with this issue, as indicated in the summary of the proceedings:

> One of the first and perhaps most significant of all points debated at length during the day was that of the goals of the Denver program, and, by implication, the goals of most groups represented at the conference. This debate, which was never resolved, included the following points:

1. the desirability of dispersing the ghetto as opposed to extending equal opportunity in housing.

2. whether the focus should be on improving the quality of housing everywhere rather than anything else.

3. should the goals be on strengthening and rebuilding the ghetto as opposed to open housing.

4. to what degree do the goals, however defined, extend to groups other than Negroes.

Each of these points contains at least several other topics which were also discussed at length, i.e. the ever emerging black pride and black power movement, paternalistic attitudes of whites, the definition of a ghetto and the definition of a stabilized area.[2]

Thus, on the community level, as on the national level, in 1970 and 1971 the shadowy omnipresence of separatism was a deep concern behind the on-going and persistent efforts toward open housing.

By 1977 the national civil rights movement was so fragmented that it had little or no significance for the open-housing movement, its offspring. Separatism was no longer an issue. But other external factors did affect the movement. Legislative and legal developments had profound impact on the open-housing movement, constantly reinforcing awareness of the links between general institutional racism and segregated housing, and between segregated schools and segregated housing. One piece of legislation in particular—the Housing and Community Development Act of 1974—sparked a wave of funding for local movement organizations that had grave implications for the movement. More than ever, there was a critical need for guidelines for operating effective programs, and for evaluation techniques for measuring the success of funded organizations in the open-housing movement.

Brief profiles of twelve movement organizations across the country indicate the diversity, scope, and ingenuity of the movement as it operates on the local level in response to changing national and local events.

SIX EMERGENT PROPOSITIONS RECONSIDERED

Borrowing from Beard, anyone who has studied race relations and/or social movements will hesitate to advance with firm assurance

very many conclusions.[3] This section might more wisely be entitled
"A Few General and Tentative Reflections."

Six emergent propositions, presented at the outset of this
study, are reconsidered here.

Proposition I

On both national and community levels, institutionalization of a social movement does not necessarily lead
to decline.

The evidence of the study indicates that this proposition has been
confirmed. On the national level, the increased budget, staff, legitimacy, and prestige of the NCDH only temporarily decreased the
vigor or the scope of its attack against discrimination in housing.
Such institutionalization has enabled the core organization to conduct
programs of even greater scope and impact, leading toward broad
systemic change.

On the community level, although the case study revealed a
disastrous effect of institutionalization in its first funding experience,
this was not the situation in its HUD demonstration program. It
may not even be so in the long run in its second funding experience.
In the other movement organization studied, it is certainly not the
case. Many movement organizations have been able to improve and
strengthen their programs and impact with increased funding, staff,
legitimacy, and prestige.

Proposition II

On the national level, if a movement does decline after
institutionalization, it will be due to external factors.

Two external factors are considered here in examining the validity
of this proposition. One relevant external factor might be the decrease in the number of movement organizations across the country.
It is suggested that if such numbers decline markedly, the national
core organization will be affected, and the movement may, in fact,
eventually decline. Though the core organization could still exist as
a single organized pressure group, its rationale for existence might
be weakened if it were no longer to function as an educative guide on
the local community level. Each increase in the funding of the NCDH
elicited an expanded program involving community education and
action guidelines, which must have been written into the prior funding
proposals. Thus, if the movement organizations declined on the community level, NCDH might, in fact, lose much of its funding as a
result, and the entire movement would decline.

In 1970 a second external factor of extreme relevance was the general civil rights movement, from which the open-housing movement developed. It was suggested then that if the emphasis on separatism were to increase, this would be bound to have an effect on the core organization, which could manifest itself in two ways. First, the national member organizations of the NCDH might disengage themselves from the effort toward open housing, which would, of course, weaken the support of the organization and reduce its impact. Second, if the movement organizations on the community level were to be affected by such a trend, their continued existence would be threatened, and this would also weaken the national organization and thus the entire movement. In addition, any external factors may be intertwined with a third factor, which is the possibility of actual achievement of equal opportunity in housing.

The literature has implied that a social movement may end because of success as well as failure. If its goals are realized, its raison d'etre is gone, even though other goals may be substituted. And if its goals are never achieved, it may disintegrate because of fatigue, discouragement, or internal strife. But perhaps the most interesting possibility is seen in the social movement with only partially realized goals. The activity of such a movement may become more and more organized and effective, the closer it approaches goal attainment. Then, depending on the nature of these goals, is it possible that a particular social movement may exist indefinitely?

Relating this to the open-housing movement, it would seem that in view of the current structure and functioning of this society in regard to race and housing, the actual attainment of equal opportunities in housing seems indeed remote. In spite of the fact that open housing is now the law of the land, widespread evasion of the law continues, as does outright discrimination in housing against minorities. Moreover, enforcement provisions of the laws are weak, and corroboration techniques for the verification of discrimination are complex and cumbersome. Therefore, it is suggested that the open-housing movement is one that could have a very long life span. However, the national core organization and the localized movement organizations need each other for continued existence. If the national core organization can provide sufficient guidelines for action to the local groups, the movement's existence can be extended indefinitely.

Proposition III

On the community level, if a movement organization does decline after institutionalization, it will be due to internal rather than external factors.

This proposition requires considerable rethinking, on the basis of the evidence of the case study. Generally, it would seem to be valid, yet we know that what is external may also become internal.

In 1970 the trend in the general civil rights movement toward separatism markedly affected the responses of some long-term white and black supporters of the open-housing movement on the local community level. In the case study, for example, it was observed repeatedly that one rationale for abandoning the original goal was that "black people don't want integration any more." Despite numerous national surveys indicating that a majority of black people did, in fact, prefer integrated living, the general common perception of the current situation was that they did not. And the reality, of course, lies in the perception rather than the fact. Thus the national external situation filtered down to the local internal situation, and emerged as a factor of considerable significance.

In 1970 the very question of funding, on the local community level, was relevant to this factor. In each case of threatened loss of funding, the perception of separatism as a growing preference may have been significant. In Akron, for example, it was at one point decided that the money for the Fair Housing Center would be used instead for the development of a leather-good craft employing 300 people in the heart of the ghetto. In New York and Los Angeles, the decision makers in the local funding agencies opted to divert funds from the open-housing effort to ghetto maintenance and improvement. Thus, the distinction between external and internal factors must be seen as a thin one.

This does not negate the importance of strictly internal factors in the continued growth of a movement on the local level. Such factors as morale and especially leadership are crucial, as the fourth proposition recognizes.

Proposition IV

On the community level, after institutionalization, the most important internal factor influencing a movement's success or failure is that of leadership.

The evidence of the case study and the comparative analysis seems to confirm this. It was observed throughout the case study that two types of leadership were lacking after institutionalization: administrative leadership to manage the funded operation, and board leadership to provide overall direction. Though the board leadership had been strong and effective in the voluntary phase, it was totally inadequate in the institutionalized phase. Had one or the other type of leadership been effective, the funded operation might have been successful, but without either the venture was doomed to failure. It may well be that of the two types, the more important one in the institutionalized phase is administrative leadership.

Such administrative leadership should, of course, involve managerial skills, but above all the movement organization administrator should possess skills in interpersonal relationships with board, staff, community leaders and supporters, and funding sources. This calls for healthy personalities and personally appealing people. It may be that boards of directors and other hiring groups need some specific guidelines on staff selection for open-housing programs, given the current wave of funding across the country. They may also need management consultants to guide them in successfully coping with board-staff tasks and responsibilities and divisions of labor. (See Appendix D.)

Because of what happened to two of the four movement organizations analyzed, the transiency of leadership has become painfully apparent. More than ever, the critical significance of leadership on the local level can be seen. New York and Los Angeles were threatened with loss of funding in 1970, but were able to survive and prosper with able, dedicated, stubborn leadership. Denver and Seattle seemed in 1970 most entrenched and secure—only to collapse soon after.

In both cases, internal power conflicts led to their failure, but these stemmed from different causes. In Denver the leadership and program were too weak. In Seattle the leadership and program were so strong that they became a source of tension for the local funding channel. In both cases, however, no new leadership emerged to save the movement and keep it going, when the other leaders were removed.

It is necessary to soberly reconsider the criteria of success, and it is suggested that the first requirement of a successful movement organization is survival insurance. A leader must train others for replacement, and must inspire and motivate others to carry on. The transiency of leadership necessitates task rotation and managerial skill development, and above all, knowledge and inspiration about the goals of the movement. These must all be taken into account in any planning and organization for movement survival. Systemic change is not possible if there is no movement organization to make it happen.

Proposition V

On the community level, if the leaders of a movement organization before institutionalization assume initial leadership after institutionalization, the movement will

have a greater chance of continued growth and success,
with fewer strains and tensions.

This suggests a temporal factor of significance regarding leadership.
It may be concluded, from evidence of this study and a prior study
of three other specific social movements, that leadership is of
greatest significance in the early stages of a phase, and becomes
less significant as a movement phase develops. In the voluntary
phase, the initial leadership of a movement is crucial in creating an
awareness of a situation of constraint, and in focusing on goals and
an ideology that could lead to change. Leadership in the voluntary
phase is thus needed to gain adherents. In the early stage of the
institutionalized phase, initial leadership is also a crucial factor in
developing the organizational apparatus needed to function effectively.
    In the case study, none of the initial leaders of the voluntary
phase assumed administrative leadership in the institutionalized phase.
In all of the other four communities studied, there was continuity in
administrative leadership from the voluntary to the institutionalized
phase. However, this proposition may be modified to suggest that
the leadership in the institutionalized phase does not necessarily
have to emanate from the local voluntary phase. What appears to be
important is that the administrative leadership in the institutionalized
phase should possess prior experience (either voluntary or institutionalized) in the specific type of goal-oriented organization involved.

Proposition VI

On the community level, the more structured and organized the movement organization before institutionalization,
the fewer the strains and tensions after institutionalization.

This seems to suggest that there is a developmental sequence needed
before a phase of institutionalization can be successfully managed.
The evidence of the case study and the comparative analysis seemed
at first to confirm this concept.
    In the four communities studied, each had experienced small
gradual funding prior to the phase of actual institutionalization. This
was not the situation in the case study, where the local organization
was suddenly transformed from a totally volunteer effort operating
with a budget of $300 a year to a totally staffed effort with a budget
of $59,000 a year.
    Three of the four communities studied had, prior to institutiona-
lization, developed a network of localized volunteer fair-housing
groups covering the geographical area (Denver was the exception).
In the case study, a localized network in the immediate area was not

well developed prior to institutionalization, though other cities in
the region had been aided in the formation of such voluntary groups.
This type of prior organization would seem to be essential for the
successful operation of a funded open-housing program. It is a fact
that referrals to such dispersed localized groups would relieve a
central staff from the one-to-one housing-location-type service,
and would allow it to function in terms of broader desegregation
action programs.

In addition, the evidence of the case study indicated that the
very informality and loose structure of the organization, which served
it so well during the first voluntary phase, was actually a deterrent
factor in the institutionalized phase. Had there been clearer delineations of authority and a more structured organization plan of operation
prior to funding, the first institutionalized phase might not have presented the insurmountable problems it did. Moreover, had such a
structure been incorporated into the constitution or by-laws of the
organization, some of the confusion, ambiguity, and conflict might
have been averted during the institutionalized phase. Even an initial
reexamination of such a constitution at the time of funding might have
forced the board of directors at the outset of the phase to consider
specifically the development of policies and operative goals. Instead,
the board continued with its former loose, unstructured pattern for
months after the funding began, and drifted from crisis to crisis
within the same pliable framework.

In 1970 it was acknowledged that evidence from five local movement organizations was insufficient, and it was suggested that two
additional controls were needed to strengthen the analysis. First,
studies should be conducted on those voluntary fair-housing groups
which did not become institutionalized. Second, studies should be
conducted on those institutionalized fair-housing programs which were
never voluntary. Such additional examination would yield more conclusive evidence regarding two key factors. First, more would be
known about the process of institutionalization itself; and second,
the current strength of the movement could be assessed by examining
the existing volunteer groups. Also, it might be possible to account
for other factors contributing to the growth or decline of such movement organizations on the local level.

A third control might be the examination of institutionalized
operations in terms of their funding sources. A potential factor of
relevance which appeared, was rejected, and reappeared rather persistently throughout this study was the source of funding. Is this
observer correct in thinking that OEO is the worst possible type of
funding for an open-housing program? Is HUD funding better? Is
private foundation funding even better? Would totally local funding
be best? Or worst? There is insufficient evidence on this matter.

Three of the communities studied had OEO funding, all with disastrous or abortive end results. One had multifunding, and one was funded by a private foundation. More needs to be known about this factor before the funding source can be considered significant in the success of a funded operation.

An Ironic Observation. Perhaps one thing that will insure the continuity of an effective open-housing movement is the competition for funding. If the federal regulations for funding under the HCD Act of 1974 and 1977 specify rigorous performance standards for funded fair-housing organizations, even the most inept, coopted, bureaucratic movement organizations will have to comply in order to continue to be funded. Though the staff and board may have lost sight of the goals of the movement, the regulations may force them to carry out a program that will achieve those goals.

CONCLUSIONS

Now, after seven years, a few more judgments can be made. There seem to be no more volunteer open-housing groups left to study. More and more, new open-housing groups are springing up as funded organizations. It is difficult to know where to place these in a social movement context, and it is not possible to analyze them in terms of institutionalization. This leads to the honest conclusion that today the process of institutionalization and its results may not be of great concern for the open-housing movement. What is much more critical, given the reality of funded open-housing movement organization, is how to make those movement organizations effective in achieving open-housing goals. The question now is not whether institutionalization leads to the decline of a movement, but rather how success and survival can be achieved and maintained after institutionalization.

Zald and McCarthy's views on the trends of movement professionalization and resource mobilization seem especially appropriate here. In the traditional view, social movements are dependent on participating members and supporters for their continued existence and development. Recent trends, however, indicate that member participation has been replaced by ". . .paid functionaries, by the 'bureaucratization of social discontent,' by mass promotion campaigns, by full-time employees whose professional careers are defined in terms of social movement participation. . ."[4] and by foundations and government.

In the classical model of social movements, the membership base provides money, voluntary help, and leadership. In the new model of modern social movements a membership base is dispensable, since outside financial support can provide paid staff members to perform those functions. In the new model, such support as exists is inclusive in nature rather than exclusive, meaning partial commitment and minimal requirements. Professional social movements are thus characterized by: a paid staff that devotes full time to the movement; a very small or nonexistent membership base, or a paper membership; attempts to give the image of "speaking for a potential constituency"; and attempts to influence decision makers.[5] Zald and McCarthy suggest also that the definition of "grievances" of the movement will expand to meet the funds and support the personnel available. Thus, problem definition becomes a strategy for competing for funds. Grievances of movements are created rather than mobilized in this new model of professional (paid) social movement organizations.

In addition, their funding is unstable and as personnel shift from organization to organization, a national network of potential staff develops. Recent developments indicating movement organization careers include training institutes for movement personnel, literature systematizing the knowledge required for such activity, and manuals and seminars teaching grantsmanship.

"Some movement organizations easily transform themselves into service institutions. . . .obviously, shifts in political control can lead away from movement goals."[6] Concerning survival, Zald and McCarthy suggest that the less the movement organization is tied to enduring issues, the less likely it is to survive. Since the paid movement organization is dependent on elites for funds, it is the piper that calls the tune: "Elites may have the effect of diffusing the radical possibilities of dissent."[7] They may control the direction and amount of dissent, by threatening to withold funding.

If all this is put together, one sees funding as the prevailing organizational mode, little or no member support, elite control over program, and uncertainty of funding. But Zald and McCarthy worry, as one would, about the time when funding may be cut off. What happens to a cause that has no followers? Will the paid staff assume voluntary sustained leadership in a time of crisis? This is not likely, and Zald and McCarthy advocate development of a unified membership support base for the lean times that will surely occur. They remind us again of the need for "deep interest cleavages" as enduring issues rather than multi-interest and soluble-issue movement organizations.

Relating this to the open-housing movement, five additional propositions are offered.

Proposition VII—Scope of Program

The more concentrated the open-housing program, the
more effective the movement organization will be in
achieving open-housing goals on the local level.

This also suggests that a membership base will be more readily
developed with this specialized program, and that this program will
generate exclusive membership rather than inclusive membership.

Proposition VIII—Type of Program

a.   The more the open housing program is directed
     toward the elimination of racial discrimination in
     housing, the more effective the movement organi-
     zation will be on the local level.

b.   The more the program focuses on the initiation
     of repeated, systematic data collection con-
     cerning racial discrimination in housing—that is,
     audits—the more effective the movement will be
     on the local level.

"The single most effective device for overcoming discriminatory
practices is persistent testing of the market.[8]

c.   The more the program uses feedback and follow-up
     after the audits [as described in Chapter 4], the
     more effective it will be.

d.   The more the program focuses on litigation rather
     than conciliation in individual cases of racial dis-
     crimination, the more effective the MO will be on
     the local level.

Effectiveness is defined throughout as moving toward systemic change
in the eradication of racial discrimination in housing in a metropolitan
area.

Proposition IX—Size of Community

The smaller the metropolitan area of the movement
organization's concern, the greater the potential for
achieving systemic change.

(Canton's SMSA should be easier to change than Chicago's SMSA.)
However, the existence of tighter social controls in the smaller area

and the greater difficulties of breaking through these to achieve systemic change are acknowledged. This is a paradox that calls for further study.

Proposition X—Distance from Funding Source

The further away the movement organization is from the funding source, the greater the potential for achieving open-housing goals on the local level.

This suggests that cooptation is more likely to occur if the source of funding is geographically close. Local funding may thus be more damaging to open housing goal achievement than national funding. The closer the source, the more likely the surveillance and control over the direction of the program, through threat of funding removal.

A Step Beyond. It becomes necessary to look beyond the open integrated community to the critical need for the stabilization of those already integrated neighborhoods in order to avoid resegregation. As has been noted before, these are two sides of the same coin— two movements facing many of the same obstacles and enemies. Each needs the other to succeed, and this calls for sustained cooperation of open-housing and neighborhood-stabilization groups on both national and local levels. These are two interrelated efforts that can best be handled by separate organizations on both levels, working cooperatively for maximum effectiveness. Such cooperation must be based on mutual trust and recognition, clear joint and separate goals and objectives, and avoidance of duplication of effort.

NCDH may be the only national organization able to provide training, information, and guidelines for open housing movement organizational effectiveness. In this new era of funded fair-housing groups, this is an urgent necessity. Field staff will have to be strengthened and expanded if the open-housing movement is to really amount to anything more than an elusive dream operated by paper-shuffling agencies.

National Neighbors can still function as an advisor to voluntary groups working for neighborhood stabilization, since waves of funding have not yet struck the neighborhood-stabilization movement. But NN will have to exercise care about intruding into NCDH's program and concerns. The two must work together nationally, to set a model for the groups at the local level.

In some communities there is only one organization functioning, which often plays the double role of open-housing and neighborhood-stabilization group. Consideration should be given to separating these functions for maximum effectiveness. In other communities, where both types of organizations are at work, their separate programs should be dovetailed so that each enhances the work of the other rather than intruding on it. This requires administrative skill and resourcefulness, and again calls for healthy personalities whose dedication to the larger cause overrides personal needs for power and control. It may also require professional assistance from the two national organizations.

Proposition XI—Related Programs.

The more cooperative the relations of open-housing and neighborhood-stabilization organizations on both national and local levels, the more likely it is that the goals of both will be achieved on both levels.

IMPLICATIONS FOR SOCIAL CHANGE

This study was begun with the hope that it might culminate in some development of social movement theory within the context of social change. It ends with the recognition that in the final propositions a bit of social movements theory has been applied to the specific open-housing movement and its potential for social change on both national and community levels. So the result is deductive as well as inductive. This is perhaps as it should be, in view of the major concern—systemic change to achieve equal access to housing.

The extent of residential segregation in this country has already been documented. To reinforce this:

In the urban United States, there is a very high degree of segregation of the residences of whites and Negroes. This is true for cities in all regions of the country and for all types of cities—large and small, industrial and commercial, metropolitan and suburban. It is true whether there are hundreds of thousands of Negro residents or only a few thousand. Residential segregation prevails regardless of the relative economic status of the white and Negro residents. It occurs regardless of the character of local laws and policies, and regardless of the extent of other forms of segregation.[9]

Also documented are the multiple causes of residential segregation, resulting in a massive and complex institutional network of racism in housing: government policies related to urban renewal, public housing, and suburban development; the inadequate supply of low- and moderate-income housing dispersed throughout the metropolitan area; suburban zoning regulations; and racial discrimination in the housing industry by real estate companies, lending institutions, builders, and individual owners and landlords.

Segregation in housing has had a long history, and is the result of past discriminatory practices in which all of these—the private housing industry, and federal, state, and local governments—have been active participants. These discriminatory practices have been traced from 1866 when the first open-housing law was passed, to 1968 when the constitutionality of the earlier law was reaffirmed by the Supreme Court, soon after Congress passed its first federal open-housing legislation (Title VIII).

Thus, it took 102 years to reaffirm legally the basic human right to shelter. During those 102 years, three racist textbooks for the national real estate industry were published as early as 1923 and their principles reaffirmed as late as 1950. FHA manuals from 1935 to 1940 insisted on discriminatory practices in instructions to builders of new housing developments. Federal banking agencies urged similar practices, and approved racially restrictive covenants in deeds during a 16-year period, when more than 11 million new homes were built. State courts upheld many discriminatory ordinances passed by local and state governments during these 102 years, making the legacy of discrimination complete.

It is these practices that have resulted in racial and economic separation in every metropolitan area of the country. And it is the ending of such segregation, and the beginning of real freedom of choice in housing that must be the primary goal of fair-housing movement organizations everywhere.

Years ago, Louis Wirth stated that housing is a social activity, and that it is of sociological concern as a social value—in relation to the community, and in terms of social policy:

> Everyone in our society is concerned with the realization of this value, and the quest for the achievement of this value by each affects the similar quest by all others. . . . [T]o know what is good housing involves also knowing what is a good community. . . . [10]

Extrapolating from this, it may be said that a change in the housing situation will change the community, because housing and neighborhood are among the most important symbols and rewards of status in American society, and are interrelated with all the major facets of living in that society.

> Housing is more than a physical shelter. Where a person lives bespeaks his social status, which, broadly,

324 / OPEN HOUSING

> he shares with others who occupy the same neighbor-
> hood. . . . To be a neighbor is more symbolic of equal
> status than to be a co-worker, or fellow organization
> member.[11]

It follows from this that to be denied the status of neighbor is to perpetuate a caste system. Residential segregation is a means of preventing equal-status contact. It affects not just access to housing, but also access to equal education, and access to equal economic opportunities. It creates and reinforces many other kinds of segregation. Thus, if the situation of segregated housing were changed, the major facets and patterns of living would also be changed.

Karl Taeuber notes that in recent years, despite court rulings and legislation clearly outlawing virtually all types of racial discrimination in housing, past patterns persist. Thus, "every investigation uncovers evidence that old impediments to free choice of residence by blacks continue."[12] And, more recently, a 1978 New Year's message from HEW's Secretary Califano stated: "Racism, which ravages black people from the cradle to the grave, is the nation's biggest domestic problem."[13]

Yet some still maintain that blacks do not want to live in white areas—that their concentration in ghettos is voluntary.[14] But what choice is this when movement to a nontraditional area may still be met with harassment, denial, or overt threats and actions?[15] Until racial discrimination in housing is eradicated, there can be no real freedom of choice—either to live in a black or in a white area. The task of the open-housing movement is to provide living examples of that choice throughout the metropolitan area through any program means possible: building new units, audits, litigation, fair-share plans, zoning changes, affirmative marketing; and so on. Only then can the open-housing movement's prime goal be realized—real freedom of choice in housing for minorities.

The implications of this for the open-housing movement are clear. Since it is the only organized effort to combat residential segregation in the entire society, its participants must renounce their soft shoes for real marching boots if this country is ever to begin, just begin, to heal itself.[16]

Extraordinary measures are needed to counteract the legacy of hundreds of years of racism in this country. James Farmer said recently:

> . . . an integrated society will not automatically happen.
> We've got to take deliberate counter-measures to create
> that kind of society — it won't create itself. Because of
> racism in this Nation's culture, the Nation would continue

to be segregated if left to freedom of choice alone. Many
of these counter-measures that we must take will have to
be extraordinary measures—because, in a way, we are
jumping up-stream—running against the prevailing trend
(of separation). I can't think of anything more important
than this counter-trend of working for integration.[17]

There are two biases in this entire presentation: first, that
segregation caused by discrimination is harmful to the entire society;
and second, that changes in the situation can change behavior. For
those whose concern is with attitudinal change—and the author is not
one of those—there is the comforting knowledge that attitude changes
often follow behavioral changes.

Techniques concerning reduction of discrimination are directed
toward behavior. Such techniques, when encompassed in programs of
broad institutional change, offer the only real hope of achievement
in the open-housing movement.

Just as the Black Codes, enacted after the Civil War
to restrict the free exercise of those rights, were sub-
stitutes for the slave system, so the exclusion of Negroes
from white communities became a substitute for the
Black Codes. And when racial discrimination herds men
into ghettos and makes their ability to buy property turn
on the color of their skin, then it too is a relic of
slavery. . . .

At the very least, the freedom that Congress is empowered
to secure under the Thirteenth Amendment includes the
freedom to buy whatever a white man can buy, the right
to live wherever a white man can live. If Congress cannot
say that being a free man means at least this much, then
the Thirteenth Amendment made a promise the Nation
cannot keep.[18]

NOTES

1. Letter from Betty Hoeber to Juliet Saltman, September 2,
1970.

2. Summary of the Open Housing Seminar on February 1,
1969, Leadership Council for Metropolitan Open Communities, pp.
2-3. Mimeographed.

3. Charles Beard, The Economic Basis of Politics (New York:
Vintage Books, 1957), p. 258.

4. Mayor N. Zald and John D. McCarthy, "The Trend of Social Movements in America: Professionalization and Resource Mobilization" (Morristown, N. J.: General Learning Press, 1973), p. 3.

5. Adapted from ibid., p. 20.

6. Ibid., p. 24.

7. Ibid., p. 26.

8. NCDH message to auditor trainees, HUD/NCDH Housing Market Practices Survey, 1977.

9. Karl Taeuber and Alma Taeuber, Negroes in Cities (Chicago: Aldine, 1965), p. 68.

10. Louis Wirth, "Housing As a Field of Sociological Research," American Sociological Review 12 (April 1947), pp. 137-43.

11. Commission on Race and Housing, "Where Shall We Live?" (Berkeley: University of California Press, 1958), p. 3.

12. Karl Taeuber, "Racial Segregation: The Persisting Dilemma," Annals of the American Academy of Political and Social Science 422: 87-96 (November 1975).

13. New York Times, January 1, 1977.

14. Among those emphasizing the voluntary aspects of segregation are Nathan Kantrowitz, Ethnic and Racial Segregation in the New York Metropolis (New York: Praeger, 1973); Edward Banfield, The Unheavenly City Revisited (Boston: Little, Brown, 1974); and Nathan Glazer and Daniel Moynihan, Beyond the Melting Pot (Cambridge, Mass.: M.I.T. Press, 1963). Many more scholars, however, focus on the involuntary aspects of segregation; for example, Taeuber and Taeuber, op. cit.; Raymond Franklin and Solomon Resnick, The Political Economy of Racism (New York: Holt Rinehart and Winston, 1975); Amos Hawley and Vincent Rock, eds., Segregation in Residential Areas (Washington, D.C.: National Academy of Sciences, 1973). Chester Hartman, Housing and Social Policy (Englewood Cliffs, N.J.: Prentice-Hall, 1975). Franklin and Resnik (1973), and Thomas Pettigrew Racial Discrimination in the United States (New York: Harper & Row, 1975), and Racially Separate or Together? (New York: McGraw-Hill, 1971).

15. One recent study reinforces this concept. See Reynolds Farley et al., "Chocolate City, Vanilla Suburbs." Paper presented at American Sociological Association Meetings, Chicago, August 1977.

16. The phrase has been adapted from Clarence Funnye, former NCDH consultant, in his "Critique of the Akron Area Fair Housing Center," October, 1969, p. 8. Typewritten.

17. Quoted in Juliet Saltman, ed., Integrated Neighborhoods in Action (Washington, D.C.: National Neighbors, 1978), p. 307.

18. Jones vs. Mayer, Supreme Court Decision, June 1968.

APPENDIX A:
THE NATIONAL LEVEL

APPENDIX A

THE NATIONAL LEVEL

The Changing Civil Rights Movement[a]

1966

Aside from Vietnam, the biggest single issue that divided the U.S. remained civil rights. The movement took a new turn in 1966 as civil rights organizations concentrated more and more of their fire on northern de facto segregation in housing and education. Northern cities were racked by riot after riot and were confronted with a new phrase: Black Power. Although Negro leaders were divided as to what the expression meant, the white population reacted with fear and anger. White 'liberals' withdrew their support in such droves that organizations like CORE hovered on the brink of financial ruin.

It was too early to gauge the grass-roots strength of 'black power' among the Negro masses. But there was little doubt that the slogan had exacerbated Negro-white tensions, clouded the outlook for civil rights legislation, and shattered the coalition of civil rights groups. As the year ended, the immediate outlook for race relations was undeniably bleak.

1967

It was, simply, the year that the discontent of the country's black citizens welled up and boiled over . . . All in all, the civil rights movement seemed divided and floundering. After the great success of previous years, it appeared as though the movement's future was uncertain at best.

1968

Crippled by a double assassination, Black Power widens the chasm between two separate and unequal societies . . . It was a year

---

[a]Encyclopedia News Annual (New York: Year, Inc.), Year 1967, p. 31; Ibid., Year 1968, pp. 48-49; Ibid., Year 1969, pp. 28-29.

in which the barriers of discrimination continued to break down . . .
but it became increasingly clear that black equality was inseparable
from economic equality, and with more and more funds being siphoned
off to the jungles of Vietnam, the outlook was far from hopeful.

Within the civil rights movement itself, the fate of non-violence
was in serious doubt . . . Whatever faith Afro-Americans had left
in the intrinsic worth of the American system undoubtedly received
a crushing blow in June. Two months after they lost their leader to
one assassin, they lost their candidate to another. With Robert
Kennedy's death, the chasm between the two Americas perceptibly
widened.

TABLE A.1

Average Indexes of Residential Segregation for
Regions and Census Divisions, 207 Cities, 1960[a]

Region and Division	Number of Cities	Mean Segregation Index*
Total, All Regions	207	86.2
North and West, Total	122	83.0
Northeast	39	79.2
New England	10	76.2
Middle Atlantic	29	80.2
North Central	54	87.7
East North Central	44	87.5
West North Central	10	88.4
West	29	79.3
Mountain	6	81.6
Pacific	23	78.7
South, Total	85	90.9
South Atlantic	44	91.1
East South Central	15	90.5
West South Central	26	90.8

*The index represents the percentage of nonwhites that would
have to move in order to effect unsegregated distribution, i.e., 100
represents a totally segregated area.

Source: Karl E. Taeuber and Alma Taeuber, Negroes in Cities
(Chicago: Aldine Co., 1965), p. 37.

TABLE A.2

Direction of Change in Index of Residential Segregation,
by Region, 109 Cities, 1940-50 and 1950-60

| Censal Intercensal Period | Region | Number of Cities with Change in Specified Direction | | Percentage of Cities with an Increase |
		Increase	No Change or Decrease	
1940-50	North and West	43	21	67.2
	South	40	5	88.9
1950-60	North and West	10	54	15.6
	South	35	10	77.8

Source: Taeuber and Taeuber, Negroes in Cities, p.45.

TABLE A.3

Distribution of Population Within Metropolitan
Areas by Race, 1900-1960

Year	Total	White	Negro
Percentage by Race, Inside Central Cities			
1960	100.0	82.4	16.8
1940	100.0	90.1	9.6
1920	100.0	92.9	6.9
1900	100.0	93.3	6.5
Percentage by Race, Outside Central Cities			
1960	100.0	95.0	4.6
1940	100.0	94.1	5.5
1920	100.0	93.0	6.5
1900	100.0	90.7	8.9

Source: Taeuber and Taeuber, Negroes in Cities, p.57.

TABLE A.4

Legal Coverage, June 1959[a]

State	P.H.	Publicly-Aided and/or Urb. Ren.	FHA & VA	Priv. Hous.*	Lending Inst. & R. E. Agents	Adv.
Calif.	x	x	x			
Colo.	x	x	x	x	x	x
Conn.	x	x	x	x		
Ind.	x	x				
Mass.	x	x	x	x		
Mich.	x					
Minn.	x	x		x	x	x
N. J.	x	x	x	x	x	
N. Y.	x	x	x	x	x	x
Ore.	x	x	x	x		x
Penn.	x	x	x	x	x	x
R. I.	x					
Wash.	x	x	x		x	x
Wisc.	x	x				

*Extent of private coverage: Colo.—all except owner-occupied premises; Conn.—all housing sold or leased in developments of five or more; Mass.—All apartments in multiple dwellings and houses sold in developments of 10 or more; Ore.—confined to prohibiting persons engaged in the business of selling or leasing real estate from discrimination.

Source: Trends, May-June, 1959. p. 8.

TABLE A.5

Legal Coverage, September 1961

State	P.H.	U.R.	FHA & VA	Priv. Hous.	R.E. Agents	Lend. Inst.	Adv.
Cal.	x	x	x		x		
Colo.	x	x	x	x	x	x	x
Conn.	x	x	x	x	x	x	
Ind.	x	x					
Mass.	x	x	x	x	x	x	
Mich.	x				x		
Minn.	x	x	x	x	x	x	x
Mont.		x					
N.H.	x			x			
N.J.	x	x	x	x	x	x	x
N.Y.	x	x	x	x	x	x	x
Ore.	x	x	x	x	x		x
Pa.	x	x	x	x	x	x	x
R.I.	x						
Wash.	x	x	x			x	x
Wisc.	x	x	x				

Source: Trends, July–August, 1961, p. 8.

TABLE A.6

Legal Coverage, September 1963[a]

State	P.H.	U.R.	FHA & VA	Priv. Hous.	R.E. Agents	Lend. Inst.	Adv.
Alaska	x	x	x	x	x		x
Cal.	x	x	x	x	x	x	x
Colo.	x	x	x	x	x	x	x
Conn.	x	x	x	x	x	x	
Ind.	x	x					
Mass.	x	x	x	x	x	x	x
Mich.	x	x	x	x	x	x	x
Minn.	x	x	x	x	x	x	x
Mont.		x					
N.H.	x			x	x		
N.J.	x	x	x	x	x	x	x
N.Y.	x	x	x	x	x	x	x
Ore.	x	x	x	x	x	x	x
Pa.	x	x	x	x	x	x	x
R.I.	x				x	x	x
Wash.					x	x	
Wisc.	x	x					
Virg. Is.	x	x	x	x	x		

Source: Trends, Sept.-Oct., 1963, p.7

APPENDIX B:
THE COMMUNITY LEVEL

APPENDIX B

THE COMMUNITY LEVEL: AKRON

First Announcement of GHCS, May, 1965

ANNOUNCING

A New Voluntary Non-Profit Community Organization

THE FAIR HOUSING CONTACT SERVICE

Dedicated to Providing Equal Opportunities in Housing

"We believe in encouraging freedom of residence so that all persons, regardless of race, religion, or national origin, can secure the housing they want and can afford, in the neighborhood of their choice."

Serving: The Greater Akron Area

Created By: The Citizens' Committee on Equal Opportunities in Housing, The Council on Homes

WOULD YOU LIKE TO HELP?

PLEASE CLIP AND MAIL

Date _____

Please check:

_____ I know of a house or apartment for sale or rent on an open occupancy basis.

_____ I would like to buy or rent a house or apartment on an open occupancy basis.

_____ I would like to be a volunteer worker for the Fair Housing Contact Service.

_____ I would like to become a member of the Fair Housing Contact Service.

(Form continued on next page.)

Please check one: Annual Dues

_____ Individual $ 2.00
_____ Patron $ 5.00
_____ Organization $10.00
_____ Sponsor $15.00 or more

Name_____

Address_____

Phone Number_____

Send to: Fair Housing Contact Service
         P. O. Box 8065
         Akron 20, Ohio

For further information call: 434-2524

OPEN MEMBERSHIP MEETING

Thursday—May 20—8:00 p.m.

Akron Community Service Center
250 E. Market

COME AND HEAR ABOUT OUR NEW FAIR HOUSING SERVICE

Financial Report of the Fair Housing
Contact Service, Akron

May 10, 1965 to July 15, 1966

INCOME:
Contributions and Memberships from
Individuals, Churches, and other
groups ....$1,131. $1,131.

Good Neighbor Pledge Campaign:
Individual pledge signers and
contributors...................... 1,353.

Committee on Justice and Equality
in Housing   275. $1,628

Total Income.......................$2,759. $2,759.

EXPENSES:
Operating Expenses:

Printing	$ 202.	
Postage	153.	
Telephone	92.	
Miscellaneous	20.	
	467.	$ 467.

Good Neighbor Pledge Campaign:

Printing	$1,295.	
Postage	146.	
Beacon-Journal Advertisement	746.	
	$2,187.	$2,187
Total Expenses	$2,654.	$2,654.
Bank Balance, July 15, 1966:	$ 105.	

Letter to Homeseekers, FHCS,
Akron 1965-1968

FAIR HOUSING CONTACT SERVICE
P. O. Box 8065
Akron, Ohio
Phone: 434-2524

Dear Homeseeker:

We are happy to help you in your search for a home. Now is the time to exercise your freedom to live in the neighborhood you choose, in the house you can afford.

Increasingly, your right to purchase or rent the home of your choice is being protected by state and federal laws. The state of Ohio has a new fair housing law which guarantees you equal opportunity in obtaining some of the housing which is for sale or rent. The Fair Housing Contact Service has been formed in Akron to assist you in taking full advantage of all housing available on an open basis.

Enclosed is some printed material that will be of interest to you; also enclosed is our current list of available properties. (This list is revised quite often, so check with us again soon for any new information.) Properties listed on the yellow sheets are all covered by the new law. If you should go to visit any of these, and if you should meet with discrimination, please let us know at once. The homes on the pink and blue sheets are usually owner-occupied (by friendly owners), and can only be seen by appointment. If you are interested in any of these, please let us know and we will arrange it.

If you would like one of us to go with you to see any of the above we would be happy to do so. Just call, and our telephone secretary will relay your message. Within a few days after you call one of our volunteer Escorts will contact you to arrange a day and time when you can go out together.

If there are no properties listed that are of interest, let us know if you would like one of us to accompany you to see Multiple Listings in Real Estate offices. This is a new approach we are trying.

In any case, after you have looked over the enclosed material, let us know how we can be of further assistance. Thank you for your interest and cooperation.

Sincerely,

Letter to Friendly Owners, Akron, 1965-1968

FAIR HOUSING CONTACT SERVICE
P. O. Box 8065
Akron, Ohio
Phone: 434-2524

Dear Homeowner:

Thank you for cooperating with us. We appreciate your listing and have added it to our list of available properties. This list is circulated among all of our active homeseekers. If any of these homeseekers are interested in seeing your property, we will notify you and appointments will be arranged for your mutual convenience.

If your property should be sold or rented, or conditions changed in any way, please do let us know as soon as possible.

Thank you again for your interest. We are grateful for the listing and the good will that prompted it.

Sincerely yours,

Letter to Volunteers

FAIR HOUSING CONTACT SERVICE
P. O. Box 8065
Akron, Ohio
Phone: 434-2524

Dear Volunteer:

We want you to know how much we appreciate the help you give us.
You are essential to our work, and without you it would be much more
difficult (if not impossible) to achieve our goal of equal opportunity
in housing for all.

To help us keep our records straight, will you please indicate on the
form below the type of help you are best able to give, and then return
the form to us.

Please check: Volunteer Activities:

_____   Escorting Homeseekers–Checking on
                        discrimination
_____   Phoning
_____   Checking News ads for homes
_____   Typing
_____   Addressing mail (daytime–at mailing
                        chairman's home)
_____   Assembling Newsletter (daytime–downtown)
_____   Mimeographing (daytime–downtown–we'll
                        show you how)
_____   General errands (car needed)

        NAME_____
        ADDRESS_____
        PHONE_____

Thank You so Much!

Letter to Real Estate Agents

FAIR HOUSING CONTACT SERVICE
P. O. Box 8065
Akron, Ohio
Phone: 434-2524

February 28, 1967

Dear Real Estate Agent:

Enclosed is a list of Negro homeseekers, their housing needs, and their price ranges. We are trying to expand their opportunities by contacting real estate agents in the Akron area. If you would like to cooperate with us in meeting the needs of these homeseekers, we will be glad to arrange this.

Cooperating with us means observing two of our policies. The two policies are simple:

1. These homeseekers are to be shown homes only in all-white neighborhoods. No fringe areas (we define a fringe area as within 4 blocks of an existing Negro neighborhood).
2. If there is one Negro neighbor already on a block, we do not bring another one there. We go to another all-white block.

If you have homes for this excellent market, and would like to cooperate with us, please let us know.

Yours sincerely,
John Brentall, President

Enclosures:
   Homeseeker List
   Brochure

Educational Flyer, January, 1967

Distributed as a Community Service
by the
Fair Housing Contact Service
P. O. Box 8065   Phone: 434-2524
Akron, Ohio

SELLING YOUR HOME?

There are just two sources of homes for minority buyers—properties covered by fair housing legislation, and properties offered by willing owners.

Only a small percentage of the housing for sale at any given time is covered by legislation. And ingenious methods of circumventing the laws are widely used.

Therefore, it is crucial that persons sympathetic to residential equality offer their own properties, when they sell them, on an 'open' basis.

There are property owners who say something like this: 'I would sell without discrimination, but my neighbors might object.'

This position, which sounds reasonable and humane needs careful examination. It raises the ancient question—'Who is my neighbor?' Only the man who lives geographically close to me? Or also the man of another race who may want to live in my community?

We would like to be able to say to the white homeseller:

Your neighbors weren't consulted before you were allowed to buy your home. By assuming they would object to your selling to a person of another race, you are really perpetuating prejudice. You are enabling them to continue 'typing' persons without ever having a chance to know them as individual human beings.

If you decide not to sell openly because of your 'neighbors,' this may seem to you an insignificant personal matter. But then multiply it by the thousands of Americans who reach the same decision each week, and it becomes apparent that your decision is, in effect, a part of a conspiracy which denies equality of opportunity to persons because of race.

Yes, you have an obligation to your neighbors. To those neighbors who live on your street—and to those neighbors who are trapped in ghettos by a dehumanizing system of discrimination. You discharge your obligation to both sets of neighbors by offering your home for sale without restrictions based on race.

You help your immediate neighbors to face up to their responsibilities in a multiracial world and to learn richer and deeper meanings of human living.

And you help your homeseeking minority group neighbors whose choice in homebuying is so cruelly restricted.

If you do not have a broker, list your property with the Fair Housing Contact Service. Phone 434-2524 or write P. O. Box 8065, Akron, Ohio. (NO FEES.)

If you already have a broker, insist that he show your home to all qualified home-seekers, without racial discrimination. Have an agreement such as this written into your contract: 'The Broker agrees to make every reasonable effort to procure a purchaser and further agrees that failure to show this property to any prospective purchaser because of his race or religion will render this contract null and void.'

Ask him to cooperate with any other broker who produces a qualified buyer, regardless of race, and to advertise your property in the press. Let the FHCS know your property is for sale.

When you sell property, you are in the best possible position to put your beliefs to work. Assistance is always available from the FHCS. Phone 434-2524 or write P. O. Box 8065, Akron, Ohio.

The Fair Housing Contact Service is a tax-exempt, nonprofit, educational organization of volunteers working together to provide equal opportunities.

NCDH Impact in Akron

Summit County-Greater Akron

COMMUNITY ACTION COUNCIL

William E. Fowler   72 East Market Street
Executive Director   Akron, Ohio 44308
                                                          Phone: 762-9701
Alfred T. Witcher
Deputy Executive Director

COVERING LETTER

February, 1967

Dear Friend:

We are cooperating with the Fair Housing Contact Service in seeking your support of a nationwide effort initiated by the National Committee Against Discrimination in Housing.

The National Committee Against Discrimination in Housing is composed of 39 national member organizations representing religious, civic, civil rights, and labor interests. One of these member organizations is _____C O R E_____, which is why we are appealing to you on the local level.

We need as many signatures as possible from your Board and/or membership on the enclosed letters to Federal, State and Local authorities. These letters represent a nation-wide appeal for urgent implementation of equal opportunities in housing without regard to race, religion, or nationality.

It is our hope that your local organization of _____C O R E_____
will respond warmly with this simple gesture of good faith:

SIGNATURES ! !

Please return all the enclosed material before <u>Feb. 15th</u> to the Fair
Housing Contact Service, P. O. Box 8065. The FHCS will then undertake the responsibility for mailing them to the proper authorities.

Together, we can work toward a better community and nation for all.

Sincerely yours,
Housing Specialist,
Community Action Council

AKRON, OHIO—FEBRUARY 15, 1967

We, the undersigned, support the actions of the FAIR HOUSING
CONTACT SERVICE and the NATIONAL COMMITTEE AGAINST
DISCRIMINATION IN HOUSING aimed toward attaining integration
in proper and adequate housing for all the citizens of our own community and our nation.

We, the undersigned, believe that insufficient action has been taken
in our community to provide adequate housing opportunities for all
people, regardless of race, religion, or nationality and, therefore,
urge our local administrators and state and national authorities to
intensify their concern and action to achieve an integrated community
with proper housing for all.

SIGNATURES

March 16, 1967

Mayor John Ballard
Municipal Building
Akron, Ohio

Dear Mayor Ballard:

As part of a nationwide drive sponsored by the National Committee
Against Discrimination in Housing, the Fair Housing Contact Service
and the Community Action Council respectfully request consideration
of the following petition:

We, the undersigned, submit that residential segregation by race,
color, creed and national origin is contrary to the democratic principle and is detrimental to all the groups who comprise the American
society. We further submit that it is imperative that all government

activities affecting patterns of residence be geared to preventing racial ghettos rather than to perpetuate and extend them.

It is our firm conviction that residential integration—the inclusion of both nonwhite and white families in the housing of all localities and neighborhoods of the nation—cannot and will not be achieved unless affirmative policies, regulations and practices toward this end are adopted and implemented by and through your offices.

We, the undersigned, believe that insufficient action has been taken in our community to provide adequate housing opportunities for all people, regardless of race, religion, or nationality and, therefore, urge our local administrators and state and national authorities to intensify their concern and action to achieve an integrated community with proper housing for all.

We, therefore, respectfully urge that you:

1. Publicly define the objectives of all municipal housing and planning programs and related activities, including the planning, scheduling and location of schools, in terms of positive efforts to achieve residential integration.
2. Charge directors and personnel of all municipal agencies, and their regional and local offices, to conduct their operations accordingly.
3. Employ qualified, specialized personnel with sufficient support and authority to review programs in which the municipal agencies are involved in the fields of planning, housing, and other community facilities, and to recommend revisions and modifications which will direct these programs along the lines of municipal policy and goals as reflected in the spirit of this petition.
4. Require the City Planning Commission and Metropolitan Housing Authority to plan and conduct affirmative programs to achieve residential integration and to expand the supply of low- and moderate-income housing; to use their influence to review municipal plans and programs for housing and related community programs, and to positively influence local planning, housing and other agencies to devise and conduct programs which seek affirmatively to expand the supply of low- and moderate-income housing and to achieve residential integration, and to use your authority to take action where such municipal agencies are not fulfilling this purpose.

Educational Flyer, April, 1967

Fair Housing Contact Service
P. O. Box 8065
Akron, Ohio 44320

STATEMENT ON STABILIZATION

We'd like to tell you about our new program of stabilization, which currently involves a West Hill area. What is stabilization? It is keeping a neighborhood integrated, while continuing to attract white homeseekers to the area.

We came to realize that there is no sense in integrating some all-white neighborhoods around the city, while other neighborhoods are becoming all-Negro and turning into new ghettoes at the same time. So the other side of the coin of integration is stabilization.

How does it work? Just as our integration program involves the two activities of education and housing assistance, so also does stabilization, but with a different emphasis. For example, in stabilization our work is directed toward encouraging white families to move into integrated neighborhoods, and keeping existing white families from moving out because of fears, false rumors, etc. This requires massive education directed towards white families.

Unfortunately, some real estate agents are doing the opposite job of panicking some of the white residents in West Hill. They are encouraging them to sell now and leave the area, while encouraging Negroes to move in one block at a time, thus creating new ghettoes. This keeps us very busy combating rumors, and trying to rebuild community spirit.

We work on stabilizing an area not only to keep the housing integrated, but also to keep the schools integrated. For example, you know that the Maple Valley area south of Copley Road is heavily concentrated with Negro families. (This increase took place in the last five or six years because of people relocating due to highway clearance and urban renewal projects. We must note here that if this city had provided equal access to housing in other areas, Negroes would not have felt that Maple Valley was the only section open to them, and would probably not have concentrated there in such large numbers.) The area north of Copley Road is mostly concentrated with white families. But Buchtel High School on Copley Road draws its students from both areas, and is now about 30% Negro. This is considered a desirable ratio, and we are trying to keep it that way by stabilizing the area between Copley and Delia Avenue.

So we are trying to encourage white families to stay in the Buchtel district, and trying to attract new white families to the area. At the same time, we are not encouraging Negroes to seek housing in the area between Copley and Delia Avenue, but rather doing everything possible to locate housing for them in other parts of the city, east, south, north, and west. The area we are trying to stabilize, then, is the area between Copley and Delia Avenue. The areas we are trying to integrate are all other all-white neighborhoods that are not close to concentrated Negro areas.

This takes cooperation from all sides. It will help if you spread the word about what we are trying to accomplish. Stabilization and integration are intertwined. One cannot be very successful without the other. We need your help in both.

FHCS Letter to Mayor

April 24, 1967

The Honorable Mayor John Ballard
Municipal Building
Akron, Ohio 44308

Dear Mayor Ballard:

As you probably know, these last two months we have been presenting our Proposal for a Fair Housing Center to many local organizations—civic, civil rights, religious, and service groups. Some of the housing data from our Proposal has already appeared in the Beacon Journal. A copy of this Proposal has been submitted to you.

It has come to our attention that a number of these groups, on the basis of our data, may be planning to file a complaint with Secretary Weaver, of HUD. Such a complaint would ask for a temporary cessation of Urban Renewal until more adequate plans for relocation of displaced persons are submitted.

In an effort to avert such action, we earnestly request that you, in conjunction with the Metropolitan Housing Authority and the City Planning Department, make a public commitment by May 9th to expand the supply of low-income housing in Akron.

We respectfully suggest the following commitment, based on careful research into other communities: 500 units a year, for the next five years, on scattered sites throughout the area, to be made available to low-income families, through 'Turnkey' and Leasing arrangements.

It is our sincere hope that such a public commitment will be made. Otherwise, we shall have no choice but to support the action of other local groups in lodging a formal complaint with HUD. This would be undertaken with great reluctance on our part, for it is our wish to avoid the ensuing national publicity and investigations that would result.

Our greatest concern is, as is yours, the welfare of our community. It is because of this mutual concern that we ask your most serious consideration of this urgent matter.

Sincerely yours,

John Brentall, President

Letter to HUD
(on CORE Letterhead)

June 3, 1967

The Hon. Robert C. Weaver
Secretary of Housing and Urban Development
1626 K Street, N.W.
Washington, D.C. 20410

Dear Mr. Weaver:

During the history of Urban Renewal in Akron, low cost housing for relocation has been severely limited. Racial discrimination in addition to inadequate rehousing units has resulted in the hardening of old and the establishment of new Negro ghettoes.

There have been numerous volunteer civil rights, civic, and fair housing groups which have in past years focused community and Federal attention on this problem. A few weeks ago your office acknowledged the receipt from Akron of a petition signed by hundreds of people who represented various civic and religious organizations.

This petition was a plea for your office's recognition of the fact that insufficient action has been taken in this community to provide equal opportunities in housing, plus the fact that the supply of low-income housing units in this community is shockingly low. Local urban renewal projects and highway clearance will displace thousands of families in the very near future, which indicates how crucial these facts are at this time.

Data for these statements is contained in a Proposal for a Center for Fair Housing under the Model Cities plan, recently sent to your office by the Akron City Planning Commission, and submitted to them by Akron's Fair Housing Contact Service.

Recently, the Mayor of this city was asked to formulate a plan as soon as possible for adequate low cost housing for those displaced by proposed and current urban renewal projects. Although the Mayor indicated awareness of and sensitivity to the problem, he was unable to develop such a plan.

In view of this dire local situation, we feel that the present urban renewal program perpetuates segregation, deprives Negroes of equal protection of the law, violates Title VI of the Civil Rights Act, and violates HUD's own rules.

Therefore, we of the local branch of CORE earnestly urge you to call for a temporary cessation of all Urban Renewal in Akron until the city and/or the Metropolitan Housing Authority develop a program to expand the supply of low cost housing on scattered sites in Akron.

We will appreciate the earliest possible reply.

Sincerely yours,

Educational Drive
<u>Educational Drive</u>

Fair Housing Contact Service
P. O. Box 8065
Akron, Ohio 44320
Tel. 434-2524

January, 1968

Dear Friend:

During Brotherhood Week (Feb. 12-19), we are planning to run a series of ads in the Beacon Journal. These ads will support the principle of 'Equal Opportunity in Housing,' and will repeat the Good Neighbor Pledge which was signed by thousands of people in the Greater Akron Area a year ago.

It is our hope that these ads will encourage property owners to sell and rent their properties without regard to race, religion, or nationality. It is our hope also that minority groups will be encouraged to seek more housing outside of racially concentrated areas. We are appealing to you and other community organizations for contributions to help pay for these ads.

We have just seen a summer of discontent in our nation. We hope to avoid crisis in Akron by increasing housing opportunities for minorities. Won't you join us now in this vital and unique effort in our community by contributing $50 or more toward equal opportunity in housing?

Sincerely yours,
John Brentall
President

Enclosures:
   sample ad
   brochure
   flyer

FHCS is a tax-exempt, non-profit, volunteer educational organization, Dedicated to Providing Equal Opportunities in Housing.

Letter to Homeseekers After Supreme Court Decision, June, 1968

Fair Housing Contact Service
P. O. Box 8065
Akron, Ohio
Tel. 434-2524

A Special Message for Our Homeseekers

July, 1968

Dear Homeseeker:

We're making a change! As you know, one of our services has been the printing and mailing of lists of those homes and properties covered by law. Now, the Supreme Court has declared that all housing is open and covered by law. Therefore, it would be impossible (and unnecessary) to print lists of all housing. As a special service to you, however, we will continue to print and mail lists of homes and property offered by friends of fair housing. But any and all other housing you must assume is yours for the asking!

It is more important than ever for you to get out and look at all housing and property advertised for sale or rent. Please call us any time for volunteer escort service (836-8002). It is crucial that you report to us any case of discrimination. We intend to file legal suits in cases of discrimination that you tell us about. We will also continue to file complaints of discrimination with the Ohio Civil Rights Commission and the Ohio Real Estate Commission. Together, we can put the federal laws into action, and fulfill your rights.

We will be contacting you again soon to go out with our volunteers on Open House Sundays. Now is the time to take advantage of the opportunity to look at and live in the home and neighborhood of your choice.

Yours for Open Housing,
Secretary

3 Year Cumulative Record of
Fair Housing Contact Service
Housing Aid

May, 1965—October, 1968

Total number of families assisted		300+
Buyers	96	
Renters	68	
Others	136	
Number of Successful Placements		40
Buyers	19	
Homes	14	
Lots	5	
Renters	14	
Stabilization	7	
Number of Volunteers used		65
Number of Homes Offered		117
Number of Complaints Filed (Discrimination)		18
Turnover to Center:		
Buyers	47	
Renters	20	
Homes	33	
Volunteers	65	

Three Annual Reports, FHCS

The First Year—May, 1966. The following business was conducted
by FHCS during 1965-1966:

Formation of a file of volunteers; formation of a file of information
from other volunteer fair housing groups throughout the country;
briefing of telephone secretary; briefing of groups from other communities in process of formation (Canton, Kent, Wooster, Hudson);
securing of speakers for fall open meeting and annual spring meeting;
preparation of brochures; preparation of 100 packets of material for
orientation meeting with Negro homeseekers; preparation of bimonthly
newsletters; preparation of Good Neighbor pledge envelopes and
arrangement for printing, pickup, and delivery; mailing of 750 flyers;
letters to all real estate agents not on the Board of Realtors asking
if they would like to be on our 'cooperative broker' list; letters to
50 leading citizens inviting them to be on our Advisory Council; mail-

ings of instructions for Volunteer Escorts on the contact committee; letters to 175 members and others describing plans for the Good Neighbor Pledge drive; letters and explanatory packets to Council of Churches seeking their cooperation in the Pledge drive; meeting with Mayor's Advisory Council to secure cooperation in the Pledge drive; mailings to all members concerning revisions in the Constitution, and report on progress of Good Neighbor Pledge drive; distribution of 45,000 pledge envelopes and 30,000 leaflets through churches and other organizations; thank-you notes to all involved; notification of radio stations, Beacon Journal and Plain Dealer concerning Pledge drive and meetings; mailings to 230 real estate agents listed in phone book; mailings to 280 Akron University faculty members, all FHCS members and all Advisory Council members with enclosed pledge envelopes and covering letters; letters to 137 leading citizens with leaflet and envelope enclosed; maintenance of file of all homeowners, homeseekers, volunteers, and all pertinent information for Contact work; speaking engagements on radio, TV, and for organizations on request; housing assistance for 53 families.

This was a lot of work. Three things made it bearable. First, the knowledge that we were doing something greatly needed in the community. Second, the wonderful people we had contact with all the time—the Board, the volunteers, the homeseekers, and the homeowners. Third, knowing that the first year is always the hardest, and that some day the second year would begin!

The Second Year—May, 1967. During 1966-1967, FHCS did the following:

Finished sticking pins in a huge wall map showing the location of pledge signers; continued cooperating with Negro real estate agents, CAC and UR relocation workers; tried to secure cooperation with Akron Bd. of Realtors (haven't gotten it yet; sent letters to 75 leading real estate brokers suggesting a plan for cooperation (response from 5); received tax-exemption from Internal Revenue as a non-profit educational organization; also granted non-profit bulk mailing permit for special postage rates (after long hard battle); sent samples of our materials to various groups in Ohio and 6 other states; sent out over 100 packets and brochures to homeseekers and homesellers on request; gave TV talks, had panel discussions for churches and other organizations; gave assistance to other volunteer fair housing groups just organizing in Canton, Alliance, Wooster, and Wadsworth; distributed 3000 educational flyers and brochures, printed 10,000 new educational flyers; distributed 7500 Newsletters; circulated 15 petitions to Federal, state, and local authorities, pleading for increased action towards equal opportunities in housing, signed by over 300 people;

wrote Proposal for Fair Housing Center, presented to various local groups for endorsement, included also in Model Cities planning and CAC budget; began exploring the possibility of building low-income units as non-profit sponsor; filed two complaints with Ohio Civil Rights Commission on cases of discrimination, which were conciliated without public hearings; increased our activity in housing assistance with aid to 150 families, with 13 minority families moving to 13 different all-white neighborhoods, and 4 white families moving to integrated areas for stabilization; received the local Urban League annual award for our efforts toward open housing.

Does this sound like a lot of activity? It is, but it's not enough. We've figured it out with pencil and paper, and at this rate it will take us 799 years to desegregate the city of Akron!

Let us repeat what we said two years ago when we began. When we see that local real estate brokers and agents are playing fair and truly providing equal opportunities in housing for Negroes all over the area, we'll be glad to fold up our housing operations. Until that time, we continue, with your help and support, to try to make this an open city.

The Third Year—May, 1968. Three years ago we were an embryo. We are now out of the infancy stage and into the toddler stage. A rather healthy sturdy toddler. But even an embryo depends on its environment for growth. Whatever progress we have made has been due to external factors as well as strengths from within. Ten years ago, we probably could not even have been conceived, let alone born. So the times have been good for us. But the external factors that have helped us grow are not all positive by any means. We have found ourselves gaining strength from unfavorable conditions as well as favorable ones. For example, inaction on the part of the city and wrong action on the part of certain groups has spurred us on to greater action. Here are the highlights of what we have done this past year;

We wrote a proposal for a Fair Housing Center. It took us about 7 months to do the research and preparation for this proposal. We submitted it to OEO, Model Cities, and the Ford Foundation for funding. We were turned down finally by all three, with words of encouragement to try again and keep working. This is perhaps less significant than the fact that as a result of our proposal, certain facts about housing in this city were publicized. As a result, CORE sent a complaint to HUD asking that Urban Renewal be halted until plans were developed for the expansion of the supply of low-income housing in the area. After this, we mobilized the support of thirteen leading organizations in this city for this goal. As a result, public housing officials (MHA) announced plans for 500 units for low-income families.

Other actions taken this year: We helped launch West Side Neighbors, as an outgrowth of our stabilization program. We are on the Mayor's Minority Group Housing Committee. We prepared one minute public service radio announcements. We had an open fall meeting on "Moving Out of the Ghetto". We were part of a 2 day Human Relations Institute in Columbus.

With increased demands for our service, we found a volunteer to handle all rentals. We put out a new manual for escorts and volunteers. We filed 6 complaints with the Board of Realtors Ethics Committee, concerning unscrupulous agents and companies. We filed 15 complaints with the Ohio Civil Rights Commission.

Our series of ads ran in the Beacon Journal during February (Brotherhood Week). The response was tremendous. All bills were paid, and we have more in the bank than ever before.

We had a mass meeting with residents of Opportunity Park, with the cooperation of Urban Renewal Relocation authorities. We showed the film strip 'It's Your Move,' with our own revised script (courtesy of American Friends Service Committee). It was well received by our audience of some hundred people.

As a result of a news feature about us in the Toledo Blade, we were called by Toledo people who want to form their own fair housing group. We have also been asked to come to Battle Creek, Michigan to help them start a fair housing group.

We were included in the citizen groups who helped the city with its Model Cities application. Our position is that any planning for improvement of one section of the city must take into account the desegregation of the total metropolitan area.

We submitted a statement with the Blueprint for Schools to the Akron Superintendent of Schools. Since housing and schooling are so intertwined, we felt a responsibility here. We called for quality integrated education for the entire city, and warned about sins of omission being just as serious as sins of commission regarding racial imbalance in schools.

We ran ads in the real estate section calling for homes in all-white areas. We had a few responses, but not $30 worth.

We are seeking seed money from local sources to go ahead with our sponsorship of building low-income units on scattered sites.

We are seeking a meeting with the Board of Realtors to see how they plan to implement the new federal law.

We are represented on a new County Coalition for human rights action, with people from outlying areas and Akron banding together.

We have distributed and mailed 10,000 Newsletters, 300 Homeseekers Kits, and have met with groups from Canton, Wooster, Alliance, Hiram College, Wadsworth, as well as many local churches, youth groups, and other organizations. We have also distributed hundreds of our brochures and flyers.

We have helped Youth for Fair Housing get started. Young people who wanted to 'do something' after the death of Martin Luther King have been going door-to-door in all-white areas getting pledge signatures.

We have been nominated for a national Lane Bryant Volunteer Service of $5000. We received a citation from the local chapter of NAACP for outstanding volunteer service in Akron.

None of this could have been accomplished without our Volunteers, including the Urban League staff, our telephone secretary, volunteer typists, mailers, phoners, escorts, and all of you who come to our meetings and give us your support and encouragement—and even sometimes money.

So much for our accomplishments. What about our failures? This list is shorter, but it's just as important. We are troubled about our inability to help low-income families. It pains us when our home-seekers end up moving to concentrated areas, because we didn't respond fast enough or with not enough selections to meet their needs. We have not done enough to encourage large numbers of homeseekers to get out and look. We need to get to more black organizations and groups. We don't answer our mail fast enough. We don't have enough homes offered by friendly owners. We have not been able to effect any real changes in real estate actions. We never have enough volunteers when we need them. We have not recruited actively for membership. It takes too long to effect a move-in. And we wish we could have a crash program of moving 200 families at once, because we are not moving enough people fast enough.

But we do think we have needled many of the decision-makers in Akron into improving their goals concerning housing. We think we have helped to create an awareness of the needs of this community concerning equal opportunities in housing. And we still think the best education about integration is to live it. The movement of 33 families into 33 different all-white neighborhoods has a far greater impact than we can recognize. Every time a move-in occurs and neighbors see that the world doesn't fall apart, and then settle in for co-existence, this is progress.

Someone once said, 'There is nothing more powerful than an idea whose time has come.' We think our time has come.

Akron FHCS—Questions About
Akro-Met (Proposed Real
Estate & Loan Co.)

1. Why is it needed at this time?

   a. For rehabilitation and loans, we have: Model Cities
   b. For building new units, and loans, and purchases: Housing Foundation (Inpost)
   c. For bringing owners and homeseekers together: Fair Housing Center
   d. All the above are newly funded.

2. Is it in the best interest of the Fair Housing Center to have its staff involved in the formation of Akro-Met?

   a. A separate real estate co. may not make the best use of federal laws, since it would not need to make existing real estate & loan firms confront the law. One real function of the Center is to force existing agencies to face the law, and break their patterns of discrimination.
   b. The goal of the Center is to expand equal opportunity in housing and provide freedom of choice. In order to do this, the patterns of discrimination must be broken. And in order to break these, large numbers of minority families must be encouraged to get out and look at available housing. Only then is discrimination uncovered, and only then can you fight it.
   c. Therefore, why isn't the Center actively engaging now in bringing Negro homeseekers out in droves to look at existing homes, & visiting existing real estate & loan firms, in order to implement the federal laws?

3. If the Center is unable to do this adequately, why isn't money being raised to strengthen and support and expand it, instead of spending the time and effort and money to form a separate new real estate co?

   a. If we are ever to make our Fair Housing Center a permanent community supported agency, why don't we all pull together for it? There are only so many $100 shares of sympathetic people to be had; why divert this from the Center? Why not make all this one joint effort for the Fair Housing Center— so it could do the job it's supposed to?

December, 1968

Memorandum to Staff,
March 4, 1969

TO: Fair Housing Center Director and Staff
FROM: J. B., President, Board of Directors
RE: Development of Board policies relating to the Center

Our Board has begun to develop some policies relating to the Center. We would like to keep you posted on decisions as soon as they are reached.

On Sunday, March 2, the Board voted to include the following in our policies:

1. Channels of Communication

   It is recognized that Board-Center communication between Board meetings is necessary. Therefore, it is suggested that when Board approval is needed by the Center, the Director will contact the President, who will then poll the Executive Committee, and notify the Director.

   Communication from the Board to the Center will go through the President to the Director.

2. Public Relations

   Wherever possible, any public relations material or activity by the Center (public appearances, news ads, articles, printed matter, etc.) should include reference to the Fair Housing Con-tact Service as the Sponsor of the Fair Housing Center.

   As a result of your request for a policy statement from the Board, we are also studying program priorities, which we will develop with your cooperation.

   In addition to the above, the Board voted to set up a committee to re-examine and standardize the Center monthly reports. S.P. and J.S. were appointed to meet with the Center Director and/or Assistant Director to carry out this task.

   Board members present were: _____ (Fifteen Board members attended, including three open and constant admirers of the Center staff and its operation.)

Letter Accompanying Questionnaire

844 Frederick Blvd.
Akron, Ohio 44320
April 1, 1969

Dear

I need your help in completing a study for a course (Organization Analysis) I'm taking at Case Western Reserve University.

Would you be good enough to answer the enclosed questionnaire as well as you can, and return it to me (in the stamped addressed envelope) before April 15?

This will be treated as anonymous data, and you need not sign your name.

I'm grateful for your help. Thanks so much.

Yours,
Julie Saltman (Mrs. William)

Akron FHCS—Organization Questionnaire,
April, 1969

1. How long have you been a Board member? (Please check)

___4 yrs, ___3 yrs, ___2 yrs, ___1 yr, ___less than 1 yr.

2. What do you think the goal of the Fair Housing Center should be? Below are listed some goals. Please number these in order of importance: 1=most important, 2=next, etc.

___a. Helping the poor with day-to-day housing problems (evictions, tenant-landlord complaints, repairs, etc.)
___b. Increasing the supply of housing units for the poor.
___c. Educating the community about open housing.
___d. Influencing local decision-making to further our goal.
___e. Fighting discrimination.
___f. Ending segregation by making housing available on a dispersed basis.
___g. Other (please specify)

3. Which goals do you think the Fair Housing Center is now emphasizing? Please number these in order of present emphasis: 1=most emphasis, 2=next, etc.

___a. Helping the poor with day-to-day problems (evictions, tenant-landlord complaints, repairs, etc.)
___b. Increasing the supply of housing units for the poor.

   __c. Educating the community about open housing.
   __d. Influencing local decision-making to further our goal.
   __e. Fighting discrimination.
   __f. Ending segregation by making housing available on a dispersed basis.
   __g. Other (please specify)

4. Do you think there are any problems that exist in the present Center-FHCS situation? __No, __Uncertain, __Yes. (Please check)

If you checked YES, please describe briefly any problems as you see them, and indicate (if possible) any suggestions you have for reducing these. (Use the back of this sheet if necessary.)

Thank you very much.

Break 'Amicable'

FAIR HOUSING UNIT
SPLITS WITH CAC

Refuses to Give Reasons

By Dianne Coughlin

The Fair Housing Contact Service Board has decided to end its affiliation with the Summit County Community Action Council (CAC) and refuse the $34,000 that CAC had budgeted for it during 1971.

The Fair Housing Contact Service has been a delegate agency of the CAC since October 1968. Previously it operated largely as a volunteer agency with little paid staff. It is expected to revert to that status.

CAC is expected in turn to set up some kind of housing service for the poor to replace Fair Housing, possibly absorbing some of the service's present five-member paid staff. The CAC money earmarked for Fair Housing would go to this new service.

The split between the two organizations was described as an "amicable one" by a Fair Housing board member.

Although Fair Housing board members refused to release reasons for the split until a joint meeting today with CAC Director Don Ellis, it is known that the two organizations have long had a difference in philosophy about housing services.

Fair Housing has had integration as one of its major goals, placing blacks in formerly all-white neighborhoods. But the CAC board has put top priority on finding homes for poor people, no matter in what neighborhood.

In past years some CAC board members have called on their board to entirely cut off Fair Housing funds because of this difference.

Ellis and Sidney Reaven, a CAC and Fair Housing Board member, were expected to release a joint statement this afternoon on reasons for the split.

Source: Akron Beacon Journal, September 10, 1970.

Voice Of The People

END DISCRIMINATION,
OPEN HOMES TO ALL,
GOALS OF FAIR HOUSING

To The Editor:

At a special Board of Directors meeting (September 8) we unanimously passed the following resolution (with one abstention):

"After Oct. 1, the control and operation of the Center Housing Program will be given directly to the Community Action Council with the name and symbols of Fair Housing being returned to the Fair Housing Contact Service, thereby relinquishing our role as a delegate agency of the Community Action Council."

It is important that the community understand our reasons for doing this, which were not reported in your article of Sept. 10.

This action reflects a belief in the self-determination of people: self-determination for the Community Action Council, and self-determination for the Fair Housing Contact Service. It is hoped that this action will be mutually beneficial to both of these organizations, and to the entire community.

We strongly urge the continuation of a housing service program by the Community Action Council, in the interest of meeting day-to-day housing needs of the hard-core poor. The FHCS will continue to work cooperatively with such a program, and will engage in mutual referrals.

This action will free the Fair Housing Contact Service to devote itself to working with those moderate-income and working class families whose needs cannot be met under present anti-poverty regulations.

Our goal is, as it has been in the past, the expansion of equal opportunities in housing so as to provide maximum freedom of choice

in housing for minorities of all income-levels. We will pursue this
goal by fighting discrimination whenever and whereever it occurs.
Since fair housing is now the law of the country, the state, and this
city, we will seek total compliance with the law from the entire housing industry as well as from individuals.

The FHCS will continue to seek funding from other sources,
and will operate as a volunteer program until such funding is secured.

We regard this as an expansion of housing service to the community, and hope to gain the vigorous cooperation of all those concerned with equal opportunities in housing. The real fight for open
housing in this community is far from won, and the task is a difficult
one.

Housing is still the only commodity not freely offered on the
open market, without regard to race, religion, or nationality. Our
work will continue until this basic commodity is made available to
all, without the widespread evasion of the law and out-right discrimination that continue to plague this community.

BOARD OF DIRECTORS
Fair Housing Contact Service

SIDNEY REAVEN
President

Source: Akron Beacon Journal, September 19, 1970.

FAIR HOUSING IS TOP ORGANIZATION

New York subway riders often see a public service advertisement which announced: "Unfair housing isn't just unfair. It's illegal."

The sign reminds them of something residents of Akron, Ohio
already know. And they know it thanks to the work of the Fair Housing Contact Service, a non-profit, tax-exempt organization dedicated
to providing equal opportunities in housing for minority groups.

In 1965, the Fair Housing Contact Service was formed by
citizen volunteers as a response to segregation and discrimination
in housing in the Akron area. It conducts a triple program of education, research and housing assistance.

The organization is bi-racial and interfaith, and receives no
outside funding. It is financed solely by the dues and donations of
its 1,800 supporters.

Some of the residents of Akron once questioned the need for
such an organization, but Fair Housing responded with a brochure
that put an end to the question.

OPEN HOUSING IS THE LAW

USE IT!   *SUPPORT IT!*

For information or assistance...call

434-2524

FAIR HOUSING CONTACT SERVICE

WORKING FOR EQUAL OPPORTUNITIES IN HOUSING

Volunteer operated   **Non-profit**

The brochure stated that:

Residential segregation creates a divided society;
children must not grow up in a city where prejudice
and discrimination are a way of life; Black homeseekers in Akron are denied freedom of choice.

Source: Voluntary Action Center News, Washington, D.C.,
February 1973, p. 7.

TABLE B.1

Black Population in the Akron Metropolitan Area, 1960 and 1970

Akron Metropolitan Area[a]	1960		1970	
	Number	Percent	Number	Percent
City of Akron				
Total population	290,351	100.0	275,425	100.0
Negro population	37,636	13.0	48,205	17.5
Suburban areas[b]				
Total population	223,218	100.0	277,946	100.0
Negro population	3,620	1.6	3,417	1.2
Total metropolitan area				
Total population	513,569	100.0	553,371	100.0
Negro population	41,256	8.0	51,622	9.3

[a] Akron metropolitan area defined as all of Summit County.

[b] Suburban areas defined as all of Summit County excluding the City of Akron.

Source: Population characteristics for 1960 from 1960 Census of Population. Population characteristics for 1970 from 1970 Census of Population.

APPENDIX C: AUDITS

AUDIT I

Summary of Audit Reports

Company #1

Three counts of discrimination were indicated in this real
estate company: in access to listings (reported by both black and
white volunteers), and in courtesy (reported by the black volunteer).
Concerning access to listings, the black volunteer never saw
the multiple listing file, though she requested this repeatedly. The
white volunteer did have access to the listings, but only when the
agent was with her.
Concerning courtesy, the black volunteer had to make five
times as many phone calls to this company as the white volunteer,
in order to receive assistance with housing. The black volunteer
repeatedly left messages for the agent, who seldom returned her
calls. She made 13 phone calls and two personal visits to the company. The white volunteer made two phone calls and one visit in
order to receive comparable service.

Company #2

Two counts of discrimination were indicated: in locations
offered (black) and in racial remarks (white). Concerning locations
offered, the black volunteer was consistently offered housing in an
already integrated area, and had to insist on other locations—which
she selected herself from the multiple listing file (with no cooperation
from the agent). The black volunteer had to make 11 phone calls and
four personal visits, while the white volunteer made only two phone
calls and two visits to receive comparable assistance.
Concerning racial remarks, the white volunteer was told by
the agent of some integrated housing on two streets in a predominantly
white area, and the remark was made by the agent that "she didn't
want a bomb thrown at her house" (presumably for becoming involved
with such housing).

Company #3

Two counts of discrimination were indicated: in locations
offered (black) and in courtesy (black). Concerning locations offered,
the black volunteer was repeatedly offered housing in black or already
integrated areas. When he insisted on two other specific white areas,
he was given several addresses and told to drive by to see if he liked
these. When one of these was selected by the volunteer for viewing,

an appointment was arranged by the agent. But when the volunteer met the agent at the given address, he was told the owners were not at home. He was then offered housing in an integrated area.

Concerning courtesy, at no time did the agent offer to accompany the volunteer in his search for housing. The white volunteer was immediately offered housing in all-white areas. The black volunteer made five phone calls and two personal visits; the white volunteer made four phone calls and one visit.

Company #4

Four counts of discrimination were indicated: in locations offered (black), in courtesy (black), in price differentials (black) and in racial remarks (white). For locations offered, the black volunteer was offered a house in an all-black area, when he had specifically requested a particular all-white area. The prices of other housing offered were consistently below his range ($25,000). He was given little or no encouragement or assistance. The white volunteer was asked in the initial phone contact whether she was "interested in an all-white area." Though she replied that this was not her concern, she was immediately offered housing in three all-white areas.

Company #5

Six counts of discrimination were indicated: in locations offered (both black and white volunteers), in access to listings (black and white), in price differentials (black), and in courtesy (black).

For locations offered, the black volunteer (who sought a two-bedroom apartment, up to $250/month) was first offered a low-rent apartment in a black area. When he specifically asked for a suburban area (near his work, which was professional), the agent reluctantly offered to meet him there the following week. When the volunteer called the following week, the agent told him all their apartments in that area were already rented. No other units were offered; in fact, the agent said no others were available.

The white volunteer was offered five immediate apartment listings in all-white areas. Concerning access to listings, neither volunteer was given access to multiple listing files. Concerning price differentials, the black volunteer was offered a unit at a price much lower than what he said he could afford to pay. Concerning courtesy, the black volunteer was never asked his name nor asked to be seated during his personal visit.

Company #6

Three counts of discrimination were indicated: in locations offered (black and white), in forms required (black), and in courtesy (black). Concerning locations offered, the black volunteer was offered no housing on the phone, but was asked to come in to the office. The white volunteer was offered five locations (all-white areas) on the phone, and was told there were no units available in the integrated area she asked for.

Concerning forms required, the black volunteer was told he could file an application for housing only by qualifying for a Master Charge credit card through the Akron National Bank. The white volunteer was offered housing which was immediately available to her, with no application required.

In addition, courtesy was not shown to the black volunteer, who was given little assistance or encouragement in seeking housing aid.

Company #7

Four counts of discrimination were indicated: in locations offered (black), in access to units (black), in forms required (black), and in courtesy (black).

The black volunteer was told that no agents were available on Saturdays or evenings, which was the only time the volunteer was able to see housing outside of working hours. No other information was given on the phone. The white volunteer was offered four locations on the phone (all-white areas), and was told no apartments were available in integrated areas or close to downtown. She was told, "There is nothing desirable, nothing you would like there." When the white volunteer said she wanted to decide for herself, and would not mind an older building, she was told "we don't have anything" in such an area.

A second black volunteer was offered housing in an older integrated area near downtown. A second white volunteer was offered several locations on the phone (all-white areas). In addition, when she said she was available only evenings and Saturdays (as the first black volunteer), she was told the names and phone numbers of various building superintendents would be furnished to her on request, and she could make any arrangements to see these evenings or weekends.

Concerning forms required, the second black volunteer was told in a personal visit that she would have to fill out an application, which would be kept on file. The white volunteers were not required to do this.

Company #8

The report for the black volunteer was never turned in. The white volunteer's report gave no evidence of possible discrimination. There was, however, no basis for comparison.

Company #9

One possible indicator of discrimination was reported by the white volunteer. She reported a remark by the agent which indicated the schools in two areas were good, and that these were all-white. The black volunteer's report (same as above) was not turned in for this company, so there was no basis for comparison.

Company #10

One indicator of discrimination was reported by the black volunteer, who was consistently offered housing in the $40,000 to $50,000 price range when he had asked for housing at $20,000-30,000. This was noted as a price differential.

Company #11

One possible indicator of discrimination—again in price differentials—was reported by the black volunteer. He was shown two homes, one for $44,500 and another for $55,900, when his stipulated range was $20,000-30,000. The white volunteer reported that she was asked her preference regarding integrated areas. When she replied she had no restrictions, she was shown three homes in one such area. However, she was then immediately offered six homes in all-white areas. All the homes she was shown were in her stipulated price range of $20,000-30,000.

Company #12

One possible indicator of discrimination was found concerning locations offered. The white volunteer reported that the agent asked how she felt about living in an integrated area. When the volunteer responded that this was not a concern of hers, the agent then made an appointment for the next day to show her homes. She was taken to two homes in all-white suburban areas. The black volunteer was shown two homes in an integrated area, and two in an all-white area close by.

TABLE C.1

Discrimination Types, Audit I, Akron, Ohio

Company	Locations Offered B	Locations Offered W	Forms Required B	Forms Required W	Price Differential B	Price Differential W	Access to Units B	Access to Units W	Access to Listings B	Access to Listings W	Courtesy B	Courtesy W	Racial Remarks B	Racial Remarks W	Total by Type
1									x	x	x				3
2	x													x	2
3	x										x				2
4	x				x						x			x	4
5	x	x			x				x	x	x				6
6		x	x								x				3
7	x		x				x				x				4
8															0
9														x	1
10					x										1
11														x	1
12														x	1
13														x	1
Total by Race	5	2	2	0	3	0	1	0	2	2	6	0	0	6	29

Source: Compiled by the author.

Company #13

A racial remark was made by the agent to the white volunteer.
The agent referred to an integrated area as "becoming a mixed area—
and the houses have already suffered somewhat as a result of it."
She also said, "I'm not prejudiced—I just wouldn't want to put you
where you would be uncomfortable." She also referred to the "colored"
problem several times. All this was counted as one indicator of discrimination. The black volunteer did not make a personal visit to
this company, so there is no valid basis of comparison on other factors.

AUDIT II: APARTMENT DISCRIMINATION IN AKRON, OHIO

Summary

The audit period covered the three months from November 1971
through January 1972. Five teams of auditors visited 37 assigned
apartment complexes, covering a total of 3,719 units. The apartment
complexes were selected on the basis of size (over 20 units), known
vacancies (as advertised in the Beacon Journal), listing in the classified section of the telephone directory, and geographical scope.
Each audit team consisted of one black person and one white
person, with matching family compositions and qualifications. Each
auditor visited independently the assigned complexes, after telephone
contact had been made to ascertain 1- or 2-bedroom vacancies and
arrange appointments. Both auditors visited a given complex within
a few hours of each other, the black auditor usually preceding the
white auditor. Each auditor filled out a standard form to record his
experience at each complex. These written reports provided the data
for this summary report. (Note: auditors were instructed to proceed
up to the point of deposit.)
Of the 3,719 units audited, 1,849 indicated discrimination, or
49 percent of the total number of units. Of the 37 complexes audited,
17 indicated discrimination, or 46 percent of the total number of
complexes. An apartment complex was considered as indicating
discrimination only if evidence obtained appeared to be conclusive.
Discrimination was defined as any difference in treatment on the basis
of race.*

---

*Seven types of discrimination were indicated in the case
descriptions. These concerned differentials in access to units,

Descriptions of Specific Cases of
Discrimination Reported by Audit Teams

Team 1

Team 1 audited eight complexes covering 944 units. Of these,
four complexes (50 percent), or 420 units (44.4 percent), indicated
discrimination.

In the first complex (complex designated 1b, 214 units; see
Table C.2), the black auditor was told there were no 2-bedroom units
available, while the white auditor was told these were available. The
white auditor was told by the manager that no blacks were in the complex, and that they were "screened." The manager also referred
negatively to the prior visit of the black auditor. The black auditor
was shown a 3-bedroom unit for $370/month. The white auditor was
shown a 2-bedroom unit for $250.

In the second complex indicating discrimination (1c, 96 units),
the black auditor was shown a 2-bedroom unit in a different building
from the one shown to the white auditor. The white auditor was told
by the manager that some buildings in the complex were reserved
for whites, others were "mixed." The manager stated that "that is
the way the company wants it." The "whiteness" of the complex
shown to the white auditor was pointed out by the manager three times.

In the third complex (1a, 24 units), the black auditor was told
no unit was available; the white auditor was told the unit was available.

In the fourth complex (1e, 86 units), the black auditor was told
there was no vacancy, despite being told on the phone that three or
four vacancies existed. The white auditor was shown two units, which
were immediately available. The manager stated to the white auditor
that if apartments were scarce, she would tell any blacks that none
were available.

Team 2

Team 2 audited eight complexes, covering 919 units. Of these,
660 units (72 percent), or 4 complexes (50 percent), indicated discrimination.

In the first complex indicating discrimination (2b, 120 units),
the black auditor was told no units were available, and was not shown

---

locations offered, quality of units, prices, information requested,
and courtesy. A seventh category concerned racial remarks, made
to white auditors about blacks.

any. An application was taken. The white auditor was shown an apartment and was told it was available immediately.

In the second complex (2a, 500 units), the black auditor was told there were no units available, and was shown none, despite being told on the phone that several vacancies existed. The white auditor was offered two units. A $25/month reduction in rent was offered to the white auditor if she would take a unit instead of the black, who was still there at the time. The white auditor was urged to take a unit and not to indicate to the black that any units were available. The reduction in rent was offered "for being a good sport." The manager stated that "they'll probably report me. I don't care. I've been reported before. I have a friend that's been reported 3 times and been to court once." The two vacant units were shown to the white auditor after the black auditor left.

In the third complex (2d, 20 units), the black auditor reported that a credit check was required. The white auditor reported that it was not required. The same apartment was shown to both auditors.

In the fourth complex (2c, 20 units), the black auditor visited and saw the vacant unit one day. When he called the owner back the next day to say he wanted the apartment, he was told it was no longer available. The white auditor phoned one-half hour later and was told the apartment was available.

Team 3

Team 3 audited eight complexes, covering 731 units. Of these, one complex (12 percent) or 60 units (8 percent) indicated discrimination.

In the one complex indicating discrimination (3h, 60 units), the black auditor was asked information concerning the name of her employer and the name of her husband's employer. The white auditor was not asked these questions. The white auditor was told by the manager that a "colored had been to see the apartment today, but I don't know whether they will rent to her." She indicated the decision was made in Cleveland, and the application would be sent there. She also stated that if the "colored" returned and wanted the apartment, she would call the white auditor to see if she wanted it first.

Team 4

Team 4 audited seven complexes, covering 510 units, of which three complexes (33 percent) or 189 units (37 percent) indicated discrimination.

In the first complex (4d, 18 units), the black auditor was told no vacancy was available at the location specified. The white auditor was shown a unit at the specified address and was offered the unit.

TABLE C.2

Discrimination Types, Audit II, Akron, Ohio

No. of Units	Complex No.	Type of Discrimination[a]							Total Acts of Discrimination
		1	2	3	4	5	6	7	
214	1b	*			*			*	3
96	1c		*					*	2
24	1a	*							1
86	1e	*						*	2
120	2b	*				*			2
500	2a	*			*				2
20	2d					*			1
20	2c	*							1
123	3f	*				*			2
60	3h					*		*	2
18	4d	*							1
130	4c					*			1
41	4a	*							1
90	5a	*	*	*	*		*		5
68	5b					*			1
190	5c					*			1
20	5d					*			1
103	5e					*			1
144	5f				*				1
Total 2,075[b]	19[b]	10	2	1	4	9	1	4	31

[a]Types of discrimination: 1—Access to units, 2—Locations offered, 3—Quality of units, 4—Prices, 5—Information requested, 6—Courtesy, 7—Racial remarks.

[b]There were 3,110 units in 30 complexes audited.

Source: Compiled by the author.

In the second complex (4c, 130 units), the black auditor was told a credit check was needed. The white auditor was told none was required.

In the third complex (4a, 41 units), the black auditor was told no apartments were available. The white auditor was told three vacancies were available, and saw two units.

Team 5

Team 5 audited six complexes, covering 615 units, of which five complexes (83 percent), or 512 units (84 percent), indicated discrimination.

In the first complex (5a, 90 units), the black auditor saw a vacancy at a different address from the one shown to the white auditor. The black auditor was not shown the unit, but had to view it with no assistance from the manager who would not show her around. The black auditor was told there were no other vacancies, but the white auditor was offered four additional vacancies. The apartment seen by the black auditor was in poor condition, requiring paint and repairs. The white auditor was given different terms for paying the security deposit from those given the black auditor. The black auditor was told she would have to pay the complete month's rent in advance. The white auditor was told her deposit could be divided over a period of months.

In the second complex (5b, 68 units), the black auditor was asked to give personal information concerning number of children, occupation of self, and occupation of spouse. The white auditor was not asked for any such information.

In the third complex (5c, 190 units), the black auditor was also asked to furnish information concerning the name of her employer and the name of her husband's employer. The white auditor was not asked for this information.

In the fourth complex (5d, 20 units), the black auditor had to fill out an application blank. The white auditor was not required to do this.

In the fifth complex (5f, 144 units), the black auditor was told one month's rent was required for a security deposit ($230). The white auditor was told that the security deposit was $100.

AUDIT III: SURVEY OF MINORITY HOUSING OPPORTUNITIES IN THE AKRON METROPOLITAN AREA

Introduction

There are two major reasons that blacks and the poor are concentrated in central cities: racial discrimination, and inadequate supply of low- and moderate-income housing throughout the metro-politan area. This audit documents and analyzes the first factor, and acknowledges the importance of the second factor in its recom-mendations.

Two previous audits have been conducted by the Fair Housing Contact Service: Audit I surveyed minority housing opportunities in real estate companies (February–June 1971); Audit II surveyed minor-ity housing opportunities in apartment complexes (November–January 1972). In this audit report, for the first time the previous results can be compared with those of Audit III, which surveyed both real estate companies and apartment complexes. These comparisons are revealed in the figures and tables at the end of the report.

The recommendations reflect an acute recognition of the forces which have created and perpetuated racial discrimination in housing: past federal government policies, urban renewal practices, public housing practices, real estate industry practices, and lending industry practices. But another force which has perpetuated racial discrimi-nation in housing has been the inaction of relevant decision makers on the local and metropolitan level. Perhaps some inaction was caused by lack of awareness. It is in the hope of increasing the level of awareness so as to bring about constructive social change that this audit report is offered.

Summary

General Description

The audit period covered the four months from July 1973 through October 1973. Five auditors visited 43 assigned apartment complexes, with a total of 2,343 units. In addition, they visited seven real estate companies,* in an effort to purchase homes in the $25,000–35,000 price range. The two principal auditors were actually in the market for housing at the time of the audit.

All apartment complexes had known vacancies, ascertained from newspaper advertisements and phone calls. Auditors sought 1- or 2-bedroom units, up to $280/month. Auditors were instructed to proceed up to the point of deposit.

---

*These figures represent only those contacts that provided usable data. Several additional companies and complexes were con-tacted, which did not yield data adequate for this analysis.

Method

Apartment complexes and real estate companies were visited
by one white auditor and one black auditor, with matching family
compositions and income qualifications. Each auditor visited independently the assigned complex or company, after telephone contact
had been made to ascertain vacancies and appropriate visiting times.
Apartment complexes were visited within the same hour by both
auditors. Some complexes and companies were visited by additional
auditors to confirm information gathered by previous auditors. Each
auditor wrote a summary of each contact. The written summaries
provided the basis for this final report and analysis. All auditors
participated in an initial training session, in which both verbal and
written instructions were provided.

Results (See Table C.2, and Figures C.1 and C.2)

Of the 43 apartment complexes audited, 29 (67 percent) indicated
discrimination on the basis of race. Of these, 6 were owned or managed by real estate companies, one by an investment company, and
the others by individual businessmen and builders. A total of 53 acts
of racial discrimination were encountered in the 29 apartment complexes. Eighteen complexes audited were in suburban locations, of
which 15 (83 percent) indicated racial discrimination. Twenty-five
complexes were in Akron, of which 14 (59 percent) indicated racial
discrimination.

Of the seven real estate companies audited, six (85 percent)
indicated racial discrimination. A total of 13 different acts of racial
discrimination were encountered in the six real estate companies.
Two of these companies also indicated racial discrimination in an
earlier survey (Audit I, conducted from February to June 1971).

Types of Discrimination (See Figure C.1)

Discrimination was defined as any difference in treatment on
the basis of race. Six different types of discrimination were indicated
in Audit III:

Unequal Treatment Regarding Availability of Units. Blacks were
told nothing was available, either at present or in the near future,
whereas whites were told one or more units were available at present
or in the immediate future. In real estate companies, blacks were
not given access to listings, and whites were given such access. Of
the 29 apartment complexes where discrimination was found, 20 (62
percent) indicated racial discrimination regarding availability of units.

Of the six real estate companies where discrimination was found, one
(16 percent) indicated racial discrimination regarding availability of
housing.

Unequal Treatment Regarding Prices. Prices or deposit costs quoted
were different for blacks and for whites. Of the 29 complexes where
discrimination was found, 11 (37 percent) indicated racial discrimination regarding prices. Of the six real estate companies where discrimination was found, two (33 percent) indicated racial discrimination
regarding prices.

Unequal Treatment Regarding Requirements. Blacks were told credit
checks and/or applications were required, or a second interview;
whites were not given such requirements. In addition, blacks were
asked for personal information not asked of whites. Of the 29 complexes where discrimination was found, 11 (37 percent) indicated
racial discrimination regarding requirements.

Discrimination in Racial Remarks. Negative and disparaging remarks
about blacks were made to white auditors, or remarks were made
concerning the racial composition of the neighborhood or complex.
Of the 29 complexes where discrimination was found, six (20 percent)
made discriminatory racial remarks. Of the six real estate companies where discrimination was found, 4 (66 percent) made discriminatory racial remarks.

Unequal Treatment Regarding Locations. Locations of available units
differed for blacks and whites, either within the same complex, or
in separate geographical areas. Of the 29 complexes where discrimination was found, three (10 percent) offered different locations to
blacks and whites. Of the six real estate companies where discrimination was found, three (50 percent) offered different locations to
blacks and whites. (This is "steering," and is in violation of the
federal fair-housing law.)

Unequal Treatment Regarding Courtesy. Blacks were told to drive
themselves out to see various suggested properties, or were not
escorted to rental units, or were not asked to be seated during office
visits, or received poor or no response to their phone messages.
Of the 29 complexes where discrimination was found, one (3 percent)
indicated discourtesy in one or more of these respects. Of the six
companies where discrimination was found, three (50 percent) indicated such discourtesy.

Case Descriptions of Housing Discrimination:
Real Estate Companies

Company #4. Black auditor was never shown listings, despite repeated requests for them. Agent used "personal listings," also not made available to auditor. Black auditor was quoted higher price for suburban home than white auditor. (Discrimination: availability, prices.)

Company #5. Black auditor steered to West Side for $13,000 home, despite asking for $25,000-35,000 home in suburbs. Agent told black auditor that homes listed with other companies could not be shown by this company. The white auditor was told that the company did not deal with West Akron properties. Agent said property values were down in West Akron, and the situation was unsettled. Agent said, "not allowed to refer to racial make-up of neighborhoods—it's against the law." (Discrimination: locations, remarks, prices.)

Company #6. Black auditor was offered home in West Akron, despite asking for suburban location. Agent asked auditor to drive out to see the outsides of three homes selected from listings, then to call for appointment to see insides of homes. Agent questioned black auditor as to advisability of daughter changing schools from inner city to suburbs. White auditor was accompanied by agent to all properties, located in suburbs. Agent said West Akron in "too much of a state of change to be a sound investment." (Discrimination: locations, remarks, discourtesy.)

Company #7. Black auditor not asked to be seated, despite fact that husband was on crutches. Referred to home in West Akron, despite asking for Fairlawn. Was discouraged from seeing homes in Cuyahoga Falls, told schools were terrible there. Discouraged from seeing homes in Portage Lakes area, where agent lived. Was told of prejudice in area. Agent also mentioned being shot at by residents of Copley area for showing homes to blacks. Agent unable to locate address of listing in Tallmadge area. White auditor shown homes in various suburban locations. Was told West Akron not advisable for a sound investment. (Discrimination: locations, remarks, discourtesy.)

Company #8. White auditor was told properties in West Akron had gone down in value, were not kept up, and that the schools were not good. (Discrimination: remarks.)

Company #9. Black auditor given no appointments to see homes, despite repeated requests. Told to drive out alone to see exterior of properties and to call back for appointments. White auditor given listings in her home, and escorted by agent to all properties selected. (Discrimination: discourtesy.)

Case Descriptions: Apartment Complexes

Case #2 (in Akron all-white area). Black auditor was told there would be no vacancies for four months, and was told a $100 security deposit was required. White auditor was told an apartment was available immediately and no deposit was required. (Discrimination: availability, prices.)

Case #3 (Suburban). The black auditor was told an apartment was not available till the following month. The owner refused to accept a security deposit from this auditor, saying that a second interview would be necessary, with both the owner and his wife present. The white auditor was told an apartment was available immediately. The owner said that another person had just been there, and "we don't want her" and "would use whatever means required to avoid renting to this person." (Discrimination: availability, requirements, remarks.)

Case #9 (Suburban). The black auditor was told only basement apartments were available. Was not taken to see model apartment, but had to find this herself. Was told application must be reviewed by out-of-town owner, to check place of employment to determine whether applicant could afford to pay rent. White auditor was told of other apartments available on second floor. Was not told of application review. (Discrimination: availability, discourtesy.)

Case #8 (Suburban). The black auditor was told no apartment was available until the following month, and that a credit check and application were required. When an application was requested by black auditor, owner said they were "all out of them." The white auditor was told an apartment was available immediately, and that no credit check or application were needed. (Discrimination: availability, requirements.)

Case #10 (Akron, all-white area). The black auditor was told that a security deposit was $265, and that no other apartments would be available for 30 days. The white auditor was told the security deposit was $100, and other units were available immediately. (Discrimination: availability, prices.)

Case #11 (Akron, all-white area). Black auditor was told the rental price was $250/month plus a $50 deposit, plus $255 security deposit, and a $200 pet deposit. Black auditor was told the credit check was run by Master-Charge and OKd by them. The white auditor was told the rental price was $225, plus a $235 security deposit. (Discrimination: prices, requirements.)

Case #12 (Suburban). The black auditor was told an apartment was not available until after two weeks. Was told no other units were available in that building, but some would be available in West Akron. The white auditor was told an apartment would be available in one week, and was told other units would be available in same complex in a few weeks. (Discrimination: availability, locations.)

Case #13 (Akron). The black auditor was given a higher price of $274/month rental, plus a $50 deposit and a security deposit. Was shown a higher priced unit. The white auditor was shown a lower priced unit at $260/month with no other deposit required besides a security deposit. (Discrimination: prices, locations.)

Case #15 (Suburban). Black auditor was told apartment had already been rented, and that a credit check was required, and the security deposit was $200. The white auditor was told by owner (after black auditor arrived) that owner had not known "they were colored when they called, and she had told them the place was just rented." Also, no credit check was required of the white auditor, and the security deposit was $185. (Discrimination: availability, prices, requirements, remarks.)

Case #17 (Suburban). The black auditor was told an apartment was not available for two weeks. Was given a price of $235/month. The white auditor was told an apartment was available immediately. Was given a price of $215/month. (Discrimination: availability, prices.)

Case #67 (Suburban). The black auditor was told a $50 "cleaning deposit" was required. The white auditor was not given such a cost. (Discrimination: prices.)

Case #18 (Akron). The black auditor was told no units were available. The white auditor was told an apartment was available immediately. (Discrimination: availability.)

Case #20 (Akron). The black auditor was asked for information concerning the length of the employment of spouse, current address, sale of current home, and so on. The white auditor was not asked for this information. (Discrimination: requirements.)

Case #21 (Suburban). The black auditor was told no apartments would be available for another month. Was told the security deposit was $330, and a credit check took several days to complete. The white auditor was told an apartment was available immediately, the security deposit was $245, and a credit check would be completed in one day. (Discrimination: availability, prices, requirements.)

Case #23 (Akron, Ellet). The black auditor was told by the manager on the phone that "this is an all-white neighborhood" and "there are some pets in the apartments but we want no coloreds there." (Discrimination: remarks.)

Case #24 (Suburban). Black auditor did not see vacant unit. White auditor did. (Discrimination: availability.)

Case #26 (Akron, Ellet). Black auditor was told a credit check was required, and no other units were expected to be available. The white auditor was told no credit check was required, and two other units would be available very soon. Manager told white auditor that "we don't have any colored here." (Discrimination: availability, requirements, remarks.)

Case #31 (Suburban). The black auditor was told no units were available. The white auditor was told by the manager that she had been instructed by the owner "to do everything possible to discourage any black from renting—quote higher prices, anything. . . . " Owner stated he had already been sued for discrimination in other buildings he owns. (Discrimination: availability, remarks.)

Case #35 (Suburban). The black auditor was told the unit was just rented. A tenant misrepresented himself as the owner. The white auditor confirmed true owner's appearance, who was seen running from the premises when the black auditor arrived. (Discrimination: availability.)

Case #36 (Suburban). The black auditor was told no units were available for one month. Auditor's deposit offer was refused. Auditor was told by owner that both husband and wife must come in together to file an application, and make a deposit. Black auditor was also asked place of husband's employment and length of employment. White auditor was told apartment was available immediately, and was also told of other available vacant units. White auditor was not asked for any other information. (Discrimination: availability, requirements.)

Case #37 (Suburban). Black auditor was told an apartment was not available for two weeks. Was told $100 deposit was required plus one month's security deposit. Was told a credit check took two weeks to complete. White auditor was told an apartment was available immediately, no deposit was required, and a credit check took only one day. (Discrimination: availability, prices, requirements.)

Case #38 (Suburban). The black auditor was told the security deposit was $350. The white auditor was told the security deposit was $300. (Discrimination: prices.)

Case #47 (Akron, integrated area). Black auditor was told an apartment would be available in three days. Was told no others were available. White auditor was told an apartment was available immediately, and other units were also available immediately. (Discrimination: availability.)

Case #49 (Akron, integrated area). Black auditor was told a credit check was required, and would take two weeks to complete. White auditor was told no credit check was required, and was shown a vacancy at a different location from the one shown the black auditor. (Discrimination: requirements, locations.)

Case #52 (Akron, integrated area). The black auditor was told a $25 or $50 deposit was required. The white auditor was not given such a requirement. (Discrimination: prices.)

Case #53 (Akron). The black auditor was told a credit check was required, and was asked for place and length of residence. White auditor was told no credit check was required, and was not asked for any additional information. (Discrimination: requirements.)

Case #54 (Suburban). The black auditor was told no other units were available. The white auditor was told other vacancies were available immediately. (Discrimination: availability.)

Case #56 (Suburban). The black auditor was told no other units were available, and a credit check took five days. The white auditor was told another unit was available immediately, and a credit check took one day. White auditor was told by the manager that "when colored come" she "has nothing to show them." (Discrimination: availability, requirements, remarks.)

Case #64 (Akron). The black auditor was told no apartments were available. The white auditor was told several apartments were available. (Discrimination: availability.)

Conclusions and Recommendations

Despite the passage of federal, state and local open
housing laws, it is apparent from the results of Audit
III that racial discrimination in housing is a pervasive
and crucial problem in the Akron metropolitan area.
Moreover, a comparison of the results of two previous
Audits (Figures C.2 and C.3) indicates that the practice
of racial discrimination in housing shows little substantial change in either real estate companies or apartment
buildings over the past three years. It is particularly
significant that the amount of racial discrimination in
suburban areas is substantially higher than within the
city (Tables C.1 and C.2). The implications of this
for future metropolitan growth and development are
extremely serious, and gravely reminiscent of the
Kerner Commission's Report that we are "a divided
society—separate and unequal."

There are only three basic human commodities: food,
clothing, and shelter (housing). Most people would
think it incredible to find food and clothing offered
selectively on the basis of race, with dual markets,
prices, qualities, and locations for each—according to
race. Yet we seem to calmly accept the fact that housing continues to be the only basic human commodity not
offered on the open market, without regard to race.

The findings of our studies do not and can not reveal
the actual extent of personal humiliation, disrespect
for law, and human injustice which are implicit in these
results. Our findings cry out for action by area-wide
public bodies and citizen groups. We call on all concerned officials, organizations, and citizens to respond
with prompt affirmative action to correct these inequities.
Specifically, we recommend the following:

1. To the Akron Area Real Estate Board: Although you
have worked with us [the FHCS] cooperatively for some
months, and although you have a 2 year old Human Relations Committee with some 33 members (which now
includes one of our FHCS board members), you have not
really begun to eradicate racial discrimination within
your own industry. Since you control access to most
of the housing in the area, we think you are one key to
solving this problem. We therefore urge you to:

(a) Design and implement as soon as possible an affirmative marketing plan for your industry. We offer our
resources, research materials and manpower to
assist you in every possible way to bring this into
action.

(b) Encourage the real estate companies which have been
audited and found discriminating to respond affirmatively to our certified letter inviting them to meet
with us privately and individually to learn what we
found in their companies. (When we made this same
offer after Audit I, only one company out of twelve
met with us.)

(c) Notify us in writing of the action you have taken after
we turn over to you the complete list of discriminating
companies and our findings in this Audit.

(d) In future handling of discrimination complaints, continue to follow the procedures outlined in the Court's
Order in the 1968 Mercer Bratcher case. (We note
that these procedures were followed for the first time
in the recent West Side solicitation case involving
Ranell-Self Realty Co.)

(e) Immediately instruct all agents that "steering" and
"racial statements and remarks" are in violation of
the federal Fair Housing Law, as interpreted by the
courts and the Department of Justice.

2. <u>To the Goals for Greater Akron Committee</u>: We
urge you to incorporate into its recommendations to the
relevant agencies and officials of the area the crucial
goal of Equal Opportunities in Housing for the entire
metropolitan area. Without this, we cannot achieve a
healthy, viable metropolitan community for all our
citizens.

3. <u>To the City of Akron and County Commissioners</u>:
It is essential that you cooperate in an effort to fund
an on-going open-housing program in the metropolitan
area. In our work as volunteers over the past $8\frac{1}{2}$ years,
we have found that most discrimination occurs and continues to occur because owners, agents, and managers
believe that: (a) Blacks don't know when they are being
discriminated against, (b) They will not complain if
they do realize they are being discriminated against,
and (c) The apartment or house will be gone before
action will be initiated. It is crucial, therefore, that
potential minority renters and buyers know their hous-

ing rights, know where they can go for assistance, and seek and receive such assistance as soon as the act of discrimination occurs. To achieve this level of awareness, an educational outreach effort must be constantly maintained throughout the metropolitan area.

An adequate open-housing program should also include area-wide education on open-housing laws in the majority community as well as in the minority community, systematic continuous research Audits on the actual availability of housing for minorities throughout the metropolitan area, and the on-going investigation and referral of individual complaints of racial discrimination in housing.*

In addition, an open-housing program should promote the formation of Affirmative Action voluntary citizen groups in all the suburbs of the Akron metropolitan area. This is especially vital to the success and implementation of the recently approved COG Housing Development plan, which calls for the dispersal of low and moderate income housing throughout the metropolitan area.

Both the city and the county should take immediate steps to see that such a program is funded well enough to move this area forward in the direction of real freedom of choice in housing for all minorities, and true equality of opportunity in that basic human commodity of housing. The time has come for community leaders to respond to this Audit report—not with the old inertia, apathy, and neglect—but rather with a new sense of responsibility and urgency, calling for prompt meaningful affirmative action.

---

*Note: The only existing funded agency able to investigate complaints of housing discrimination on an area-wide basis is the Ohio Civil Rights Commission. However, since they investigate so many other types of complaints unrelated to housing, they are seriously understaffed for housing investigations. In fact, they sometimes turn to FHCS to provide volunteer checkers for them. Also, they are not structured to conduct community education or on-going research on housing availability.

FIGURE C.1

Discrimination Types, Audit III, Akron, Ohio

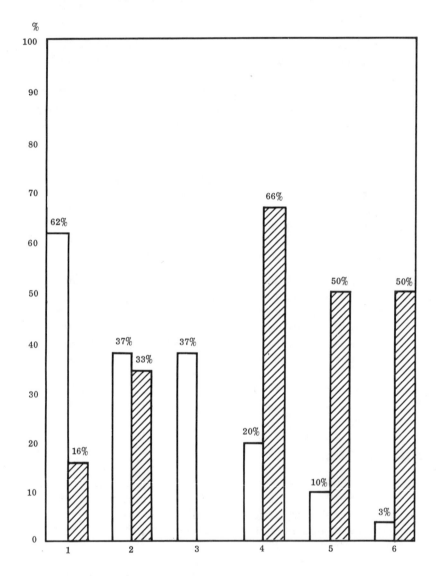

Note: The numbers 1-6 indicate type of discrimination: 1-availability, 2-prices, 3-requirements, 4-remarks, 5-locations, and 6-discourtesy. Open areas indicate apartments, shaded areas indicate companies.

Source: Compiled by the author.

FIGURE C.2

Discrimination Types, Audit I and Audit III,
Akron, Ohio (Sales)

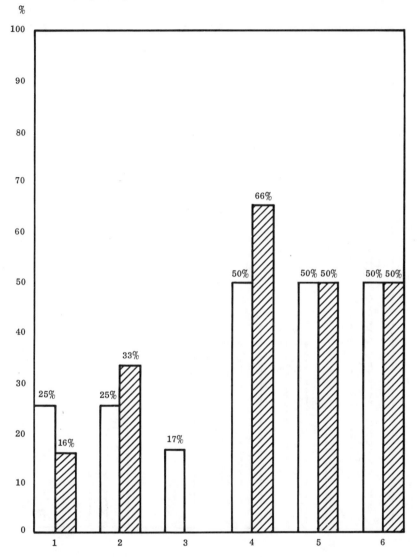

Note: The numbers 1-6 indicate type of discrimination:
1—availability, 2—prices, 3—requirements, 4—remarks, 5—locations,
6—discourtesy. Open areas are from Audit I (February-June, 1971),
shaded areas are from Audit III (July-October, 1973).
    Source: Compiled by the author.

FIGURE C.3

Discrimination Types, Audit II and Audit III,
Akron, Ohio (Rentals)

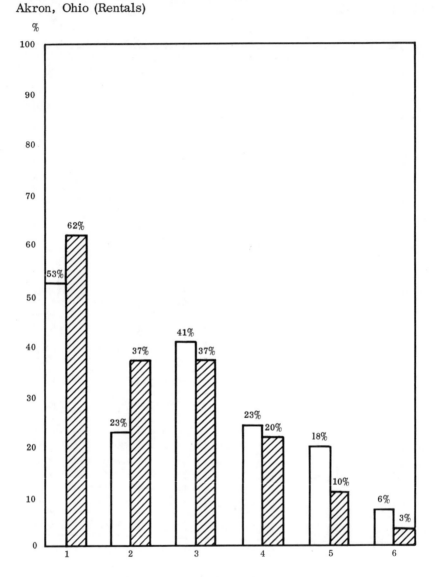

Note: The numbers 1-6 indicate types of discrimination:
1–availability, 2–prices, 3–requirements, 4–remarks, 5–locations,
6–discourtesy.   Open areas are from Audit II (November 1971–
January 1972), shaded areas are from Audit III (July–October 1973).
    Source: Compiled by the author.

TABLE C.3

Apartment Discrimination by Location:
Audit II, November 1971–January 1972,
Akron, Ohio

	Discriminating	Nondiscriminating	Total Complexes
Akron	56 percent (10)	44 percent (8)	100 percent (18)
Suburban	75 percent (9)	25 percent (3)	100 percent (12)
Total	63 percent (19)	37 percent (11)	100 percent (30)
	2075 units	1035 units	3110 units

Source: Compiled by the author.

TABLE C.4

Apartment Discrimination by Location:
Audit III, July–October 1973,
Akron, Ohio

	Discriminating	Nondiscriminating	Total Complexes
Akron	59 percent (14)	41 percent (11)	100 percent (25)
Suburban	83 percent (15)	17 percent (3)	100 percent (18)
Total	67 percent (29)	33 percent (14)	100 percent (43)
	1550 units	793 units	2343 units

Source: Compiled by the author.

AUDIT RENTAL FORM

Fair Housing Contact Service, Akron, Ohio

PLEASE ANSWER FULLY

Building Name_____ Address_____

Units _____ Name of Auditor_____ Dress_____

Date & Time of Phone Contact_____ _____
Date & Time of Personal Contact_____ _____

Apartment Available?____When?_____ # BR_____ Price_____

    Gas & Elec. Included?___ Furnished?___ Length of Lease_____
    How much deposit required?___ Am't of Security deposit?_____
    Any refund of deposit?_____ Application required?_____
    Credit check required?_____ How long does it take?_____
    Can you move in before credit check?_____ Ap't #_____

Was any apartment seen?_____ If not, why not?_____
When could you see it?_____

Any other ap'ts available or expected to be vacant?____ When?_____
    Price?_____ Type? (#BR, Furn., etc.)_____
    Waiting list required?_____ Were you put on waiting list?_____

Name of Person you saw_____ Position_____

    Address_____ Sex_____ Age_____ Race_____

Personal Information Given (If any):

    Marital Status_____
    No. Children_____
    Occupation of self_____
    Occupation of spouse_____
    Employer of self_____
    Employer of spouse_____
    How long employed_____
    Salary_____
    Address_____ Name_____ Phone_____

Additional Comments: (USE BACK OF SHEET IF NECESSARY)

AUDIT FOLLOW-UP: AFFIRMATIVE ACTION

Letter to Discriminators*

March 14, 1974

Dear _____

Our recent Housing Audit III indicates that racial discrimination was encountered in one or more of your apartment houses. We are informing you of this fact because you, as owner, are legally responsible for the real estate actions of those in your employ, and you may not be aware of their actions in this regard.

As you probably know, discrimination because of race, religion, or nationality is illegal under local, state and federal laws. Individuals, both black and white, who are deprived of their right to live where they choose can file complaints with HUD or the courts under Titles VIII and IX of the 1968 Civil Rights Act, or civil suits under the Civil Rights Act of 1866 as interpreted by the Supreme Court in the Jones vs. Mayer decision of 1968.

FHCS has long dedicated itself to providing equal opportunities in housing by eliminating discrimination in housing rentals and sales in this area. We are a group of over 2000 concerned citizens with the full support of many churches and area-wide organizations. We have had extensive experience in monitoring housing discrimination, working closely with volunteer lawyers and state and federal agencies.

We would be happy to meet with you to discuss our findings in Audit III, as they pertain to your apartments. If you would be interested in such a meeting, please call me after 3 p.m. to arrange a time that is mutually convenient. We hope that we can enlist your cooperation in assuring fair housing practices in the entire metropolitan area.

Sincerely yours,

Dr. Juliet Saltman,
President
(864-2227)

_____

*The letter to the real estate companies was identical to this one, except that the word "offices" was substituted for "apartments" in the last paragraph.

Letter to Non-Discriminators

March 14, 1974

Dear _____

We are pleased to inform you that our recent Housing Audit III of minority housing opportunities in area apartment buildings indicated that your apartment manager was not engaged in racial discrimination at the time of the audit.

As you probably know, discrimination because of race, religion, or nationality is illegal under federal and state fair housing laws. Unfortunately, our information indicates that this type of discrimination still occurs in the Akron metropolitan area.

FHCS has dedicated itself to eliminating discrimination in housing rentals and sales in this area, and we are pleased to find you offering equal housing opportunities to all home seekers.

We hope our on-going Audits will continue to show minorities receiving fair and equal treatment in renting your apartments.

Sincerely yours,

Dr. Juliet Saltman,
President

SAMPLE AFFIRMATIVE ACTION COMMITMENT

Glendon Realty Company

MEMO

To: George Evans, Vice President
From: Robert Glendon, President
Subject: Fair Housing

I have recently studied the Fair Housing Law and other federal civil rights laws and executive orders relating to fair housing. It occurs to me that we have not sufficiently stressed the importance of each of our people following this law in both letter and spirit.

Please be sure to discuss with each of our associates the necessity of so doing and that we will not begin to tolerate any exceptions. This is a very serious matter and we cannot allow any deviations based on any individual's personal feelings or interpretations.

Please follow thru and furnish me with a copy of this memo signed and dated by each of our associates regardless of their position or duties.

APPENDIX D:
PROGRAM EVALUATING

Some Fair-Housing Groups Receiving Community Development Funds

Group[a]	Source of Funds	Activities	Amount of Funding
Housing Assistance Center of Niagara Frontier (Buffalo, N.Y.)	City of Buffalo	Housing counseling	$ 80,000 and
	Erie County		$ 19,505
Housing Council of Monroe County, (Rochester, New York)	City of Rochester	Monitoring, testing, tenant/ landlord counseling	$ 12,000
New York City Commission on Human Rights (N.Y.)	New York City	Antisolicitation Fair-housing law enforcement	$ 82,000
Housing Opportunities Made Equal, Housing Counseling & Informa- tion Center (Richmond, VA)	City of Richmond	Housing information service	$ 46,000
Urban League of Pittsburgh (Pittsburgh, PA)	City of Pittsburgh	Comprehensive counseling	$134,584
Fair Housing Contact Service (Akron, OH)	Summit County	Women's outreach program	$ 14,500 and
	City of Akron	Affirmative marketing, metro- politan outreach program	$ 55,000

(continued)

TABLE D.1 (continued)

Group[a]	Source of Funds	Activities	Amount of Funding
Housing Opportunities Center (Columbus, OH)	City of Columbus Franklin County	Comprehensive housing services: discrimination complaints, legal assistance, testing, educational service to municipal agencies	$136,000 and $ 24,000
Housing Opportunities Made Equal (Cincinnati, OH)	City of Cincinnati Human Relations Commission	Testing, educational service to real estate brokers on fair-housing laws	$ 45,000
Miami Valley Regional Planning Commission (Dayton, OH)	Montgomery County	Information service only	$ 29,590
Toledo Community Housing Residence Board Fair Housing Center (Toledo, OH)	City of Toledo	Educational campaign, investigation and litigation of discrimination complaints	$100,000
ECHO (Eden Council for Hope and Opportunity) (Hayward, CA)	City of Hayward	Home seekers' service for minorities, investigation of discrimination complaints	$ 44,000
The Southern California Housing Congress (Los Angeles, CA)	City of Los Angeles	Tenant/landlord information service, information, investigation and processing of complaints	$281,515

CDA–Funded Fair Housing Groups, 1978[b]

Lynn, (Mass.) Community Development Agency	$ 85,000
Connecticut Housing Investment Fund (Hartford)	$ 18,700
Housing Assistance Center of Niagra Frontier (Buffalo, N.Y.)	$ 50,000
Housing Council of Monroe County (Rochester, N.Y.)	$139,000
Fair Housing Council of Bergen County (Hackensack, N.J.)	$ 11,000
Morris County Fair Housing Council (N.J.)	$ 22,288
Baltimore Neighborhoods, Inc.	$ 10,000
Housing Opportunities Made Equal (Richmond, VA)	$ 46,000
Urban League of Pittsburgh	$290,000
City Housing Agency (Paducah, Kentucky)	$ 9,000
Memphis Urban League	$ 50,000
City Housing Agency (Kingsport, TN)	$ 4,000
Fair Housing Contact Service (Akron, OH)	$128,000
City Department of Community Development (Alliance, OH)	$ 14,750
City Department of Community Development (Berea, OH)	$ 15,000
Canton Urban League (OH)	$ 10,000
Cincinnati Human Relations Commission	$ 43,595
Housing Opportunities Made Equal (Cincinnati)	$ 79,335
Cincinnati NAACP	$ 12,279
Joseph E. Batle & Associates (Cleveland)	$105,000
Housing Opportunity Center of Columbus (OH)	$165,000
Human Relations Department (Hamilton Co., OH)	$ 1,970
Toledo Fair Housing Center	$100,000
City of Toledo Community Development Department	$ 32,000

(continued)

TABLE D.1 (continued)

Group	Amount of Funding
Wayne County Community Action (OH)	$ 2,600
Department of Human Resources (Middletown, OH)	$ 19,700
Hamilton County CD Department (OH)	$ 3,000
Miami Valley Regional Planning Commission	$102,743
Massilon Urban League (OH)	$ 17,500
Painesville Fair Housing Board (OH)	$ 5,000
Stark County Fair Housing Department (OH)	$ 50,000
Oak Park Housing Center (ILL)	$ 20,000
Greater Housing Information Center, Inc. (Kansas City, MO)	$ 45,500
Normandy Residential Service (St. Louis, MO)	$ 8,760
Southern California Housing Congress (Los Angeles)	$212,610
Eden Council for Hope & Opportunity (Hayward, CA)	$ 92,000
Mid–Peninsula Citizens for Fair Housing (Palo Alto, CA)	$ 5,500
Total:	$2,026,831

[a]Source: Fair Housing Center, Detroit, Michigan.
[b]Source: Trends in Housing, May, 1978.

400

FIGURE D.1

FHF-Assisted Move-ins, 1965-72

Number of Move-ins

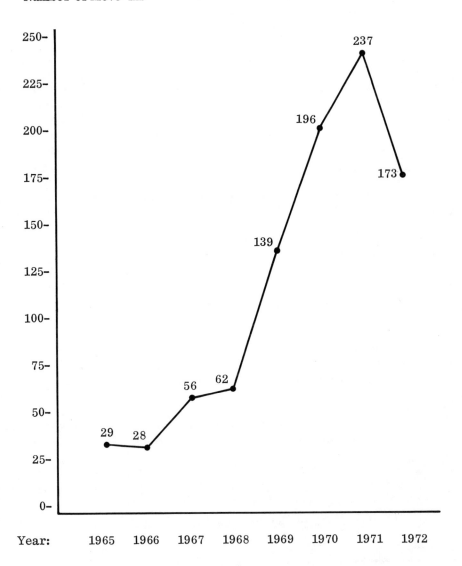

TABLE D.2

Effectiveness as a Function of Paid Staff,
Selected Los Angeles Area Fair-Housing
Councils, 1971

Community	Inquiries Received	Move-ins	Paid Staff
Long Beach	780	237	3 full-time
Westside	200	85	1 part-time
San Fernando	108	42	3 part-time
Orange County	201	51	1 full-time
			1 part-time

Source: Fair Housing Congress of Southern California.

EVALUATING FAIR HOUSING PROGRAMS
(ANNUALLY)*

1. Who will evaluate?
2. Who will analyze results?
3. Who will use results for decision making?

I. Objectives

   A. Major Goal: To reduce and eliminate discrimination (as
       covered by law) in the sale and rental of housing (primarily
       racial).

       1. Action: Directed primarily toward behavior and institu-
           tional change, rather than toward attitudes and individual
           change.

II. Measurement (In order of priority)

       1. Program 1. Research and Monitoring

           a. Longitudinal ongoing audits, maxi and mini.

---

*Author's draft, submitted to HUD EO Division Working Con-
ference, Columbus, Ohio, November 29, 1977.

(1) For each audit: when were audits initiated and conducted by the organization?
(2) What was the sample used? How selected?
(3) How many pairs of auditors were used? Ages? Sexes? Races? Characteristics assigned?
(4) Type and length of training? Paid or volunteer? Amount paid?
(5) Controls used? (Daily call-backs, report reviews?)
(6) Forms used? (Attach) Control charts?
(7) Data findings?
(8) Data analysis conducted by whom? Qualifications?
(9) Extent of discrimination indicated? In sales? In rentals? In city? In suburbs? By income levels? By auditor pairs? By firm or company?
(10) Number of staff or volunteers assigned to this program:
    (a) qualifications
    (b) titles and names
    (c) description of duties
    (d) time and budget allocation

b. Audit Follow-up: Program 1A: Affirmative Action

(1) How many general open meetings held to publicize audit findings? When and where? Attendees? How notified? (Copies of notices.)
(2) How many letters were sent to nondiscriminators? Names, addresses. (copy)
(3) How many letters were sent to discriminators? Names, addresses. (copy)
(4) How many meetings were held privately with discriminators? Dates, names, titles, attendees.
(5) How many fair-housing memos and agreements were obtained? (copies)
(6) How many EO (equal opportunity) words or logos in ads were agreed to? (copies)
(7) How many ads actually appeared with EO words or logos as per agreement? (copies)
(8) How many public agencies received final audit reports? Names, dates, cover letter copies.
(9) Number of staff or volunteers assigned to this program
    (a) qualifications
    (b) titles, names

(c) duties

(d) time and budget allocation

2. Program 2. Complaint Investigation of Discrimination

   a. Outreach to community: minority (racial primarily)

     (1) Number of ads, dates, sources (copies)

     (2) Literature distribution: when, where, what, how many? (copies)

     (3) Talks given: when, where, what, notices. (copies)

     (4) Media announcements, programs, etc. (copies)

     (5) Billboards: when, where, what, how many? (copies)

     (6) Number of staff and volunteers assigned to this program

       (a) qualifications

       (b) titles and names

       (c) duties

       (d) time and budget allocation

     (7) No. lawyers affiliated

       (a) volunteer or staff

       (b) names

       (c) meetings: no., dates, subjects, attendees

   b. Response from minority community

     (1) Number of phone calls re discrimination per week?

     (2) Number of investigations of complaints per week?

     (3) Disposition of cases?

       (a) number of court cases: filing dates, decision dates, and content

       (b) referrals to state commissions

       (c) referrals to lawyers; follow up: dates, results

       (d) no evidence

       (e) client would not pursue

       (f) conciliation

       (g) injunctions: number, dates, results

3. Program 3. General Public Education

   a. Media presentations: number, dates, subjects, station

   b. News articles about organization: dates (copies)

   c. Public meetings: number, dates, subject (copies of programs or announcements)

   d. Meetings with relevant organizations: number, names of organizations, dates, (copies of agendas)

e. Number of ads: dates, sources (copies)

4. Program 4. General Institutional Monitoring

   a. EO logos in re companies, banks, apartment complexes: number, dates, participants, results, follow-up letters, and meetings
   b. Affirmative marketing: number of showings and moves of pro-integration type (that is, whites to integrated areas, blacks to white areas), by tract number, company, agent, and date, sales or rentals.

      (1) Explain method of obtaining data and personnel used and dates obtained
      (2) Number of staff and volunteers assigned to this program
         (a) names, titles, duties
         (b) qualifications
         (c) time and budget allocation

5. Other Programs (specify)

   a. Title and description
   b. Number of staff and volunteers assigned
      (1) names, titles, qualifications
      (2) time and budget allocation
   c. State explicitly how each program is directly related to major goal

TEN CHARACTERISTICS OF HEALTHY ORGANIZATIONS*

1. All individuals and groups manage work against goals and plans for goal achievement.
2. Form follows function (the task determines the organization).
3. Decisions made by and near sources of information (regardless of table of organization).
4. Rewards for short-term production or performance, growth and development of subordinates, creation of effective working groups.
5. Communication undistorted and open.
6. Minimum of win-lose activities between individuals and groups.

---

*Adapted from R. Beckhard, Organization Development Strategies and Models (Reading, Mass.: Addison Wesley, 1969).

7. High conflict about tasks and projects and little energy spent in interpersonal difficulties.
8. Organization and its parts see themselves as interacting with each other and with a larger environment. The organization is an "open system."
9. Shared value of helping each person in organization maintain integrity and uniqueness in interdependent environment (management-supported).
10. Organization and its members operate in "action-research" way. Constant feedback so that individuals and groups can learn from own experience.

SYNTHESIZED LIST OF POSSIBLE INDICATORS OF ORGANIZATION EFFECTIVENESS (30)*

1. Overall effectiveness (based on (1) archival performance records, (2) judgments of persons who know about organization).
2. Productivity (quantity or volume of major service, at three levels: individual; group; total organization measured by records, ratings, and individual observation).
3. Efficiency (performance/costs).
4. Profit (percent return on investment).
5. Quality.
6. Accidents (minimal).
7. Growth.
8. Absenteeism.
9. Turnover.
10. Satisfaction (summed across people) re job outcomes.
11. Motivation (individual sums).
12. Morale (group commitment, effort, involvement, goal consensus).
13. Control (degree and distribution of organization for influencing and directing behavior of organization members).
14. Conflict/cohesion (verbal clashes, poor coordination, ineffective communication versus liking one another, working well together, communicating openly, coordinated work efforts).
15. Flexibility/adaptation (change of procedures in response to environmental changes).

---

*Adapted from John P. Campbell, "Contributions Research Can Make In Understanding Organization Effectiveness," in <u>Organization Effectiveness</u>, ed. S. Lee Spray (Kent, Ohio: Kent State University Press, 1976).

16. Planning and goal setting.
17. Goal consensus (perception by all individuals of same goals for organization).
18. Role and norm congruence—agreement re which supervisory attitudes best, performance expectations, morale, role requirements, and so on.
19. Managerial interpersonal skills—level of skill and efficiency in dealing with subordinates, superiors, peers, and so on. Support for goals and performance achievement.
20. Managerial task skills—overall levels of leaders for performing tasks to be done.
21. Information management and communication—collection, analysis, and distribution of critical and relevant organization information.
22. Readiness (to perform some specified task, if asked).
23. Utilization of environment—successful interaction with environment—acquisition of steady supply of people power and financial resources.
24. External evaluations (loyalty, confidence, support by general public).
25. Stability (maintenance of structure, function, and resources through time—even in stress).
26. Internalization of organization goals (acceptance, not understanding).
27. Value of human resources (worth of individual members of the organization).
28. Participation and shared influence (individual participation in decision making).
29. Training and development emphasis (amount of effort for development of human resources).
30. Achievement emphasis—organization value on achieving major new goals.

PROGRAM EVALUATION*

1. Criteria of performance
   a. For what decision?
      (1) To decide whether some aspect of a program is desirable or undesirable.

---

*Adapted from John Campbell, op. cit., and Thomas K. Glennan, "Evaluating Federal Manpower Programs," in Evaluating Social Programs, ed. Peter Rossi (New York: Seminar Press, Harcourt, Brace, Jovanovich Subsidiary, 1972)

       (2) To diagnose why the program is in the state it is in.

       (3) To plan on actions to be taken to change the state of the program.

  b. Who will use the data to make the decisions?

  c. Under what conditions will the decisions be made?

2. Two models of organizational effectiveness
    a. Goal-centered model
       (1) Develop criteria measures to assess extent and quality of goal achievement.
       (2) Dependent on: clearly stated goals, few enough in number to be manageable, and well defined.
    b. Natural systems model
       (1) Develop criteria measures to assess best use of resources to maintain existence of program and organization.
       (2) Focus on: internal consistency, nature of communication, level of tension, level of satisfaction; that is, overall viability and strength of organization.

Both need to know which tasks are the important ones to evaluate.

3. Alternative views of organization effectiveness (5)
    a. Cost/benefit analysis (relative effectiveness of different strategies or programs).
    b. Management by objectives (aggregation of specific quantifiable achievements per time period).
    c. Organizational development model (Ten Characteristics of Healthy or Effective Organization).
    d. The Likert ISR [Institute for Social Research, University of Michigan] model (similar to organization development above, but more concerned with links between variables and criteria; that is, profitability and turnover; more research-oriented).
    e. Industrial-organizational psychology criterion model (individual contributions toward goals of organization—many criteria based on task descriptions and evaluated by qualified experts).

What Kind of Evaluation?

    1. Impact-only evaluation best in later development of program.

    2. Impact-plus evaluation best in early years of program, when adaptation is taking place. (What is working for whom?) (Less effective in producing change, more open to differing interpretation.) Takes more time to set up.

Purpose of Evaluation?

    1. To guide resource allocation.

    2. Improve program; for example, redefine objectives, change target population, modify services or aspects of program, change personnel.

Conducting an Evaluation

1. First, do a contingency analysis (pose questions about decisions to be made if one or another result is obtained).
2. Propose set of hypotheses that have implications for program planning. This provides guidance to planner, and indicates how program's impact can be improved.
3. Alternative approach: identify "exemplary projects"; these can indicate directions for less effective projects.
4. Specify objectives (seldom explicit) and criteria for measuring degree of achievement of objectives. (complex)
5. Consider marginal versus average effects. (generally impossible)
6. Develop set of conventions for specific program evaluation. (FH)
7. Improve data systems. (regional computer centers?)
8. Longitudinal studies preferred, but costly and time consuming.
9. Systematic experimentation with various program designs desirable. (demonstration programs)

Conclusions

1. Most programs and agencies are reluctant to be evaluated.
2. If they must be evaluated, they will try to find evaluation designs that have the greatest probability of supporting the status quo.
3. Evaluations should be related to planning all along.

BIBLIOGRAPHY

BOOKS

Abrams, Charles. The City is The Frontier. New York: Harper &
Row, 1965.

Ash, Roberta. Social Movements in America. Chicago: Markham,
1972.

Babcook, Richard F. The Zoning Game. Madison, Wisc.: University of Wisconsin Press, 1970.

Barzun, Jacques, and Graff, Henry. The Modern Researcher.
New York: Harcourt Brace, 1957.

Banfield, Edward. The Unheavenly City Revisited. Boston: Little,
Brown, 1974.

Beard, Charles. The Economic Basis of Politics. New York:
Vintage Books, 1957.

Bennet, Lerone, Jr. Before the Mayflower. Baltimore: Penguin
Books, 1966.

Bennis, Warren G. Changing Organizations. New York: McGraw-
Hill, 1966.

Blalock, Herbert. Toward a Theory of Minority Group Relations.
New York: Wiley, 1967.

Blau, Peter, and W. Richard Scott. Formal Organizations. San
Francisco: Chandler, 1962.

Blumer, Herbert. Symbolic Interactionism. Englewood Cliffs, N.J.:
Prentice-Hall, 1969.

_____. Review of Sociology. New York: Wiley & Sons, 1957.

Cameron, William. Modern Social Movements. New York: Random
House, 1966.

Cantril, Hadley. The Psychology of Social Movements. New York:
Wiley, 1941.

Clark, Kenneth. Dark Ghetto. New York: Harper & Row, 1965.

Etzioni, Amitai. Modern Organizations. Englewood Cliffs, N.J.:
Prentice-Hall, 1964.

411

____. The Active Society. New York: The Free Press, 1968.

Gerth, Hans, and Saul Landau. Readings in Sociology. New York: Crowell, 1967.

Glazer, Nathan, and Daniel Moynihan. Beyond the Melting Pot. Cambridge, Mass.: M.I.T. Press, 1963.

Gordon, Milton. Assimilation in American Life. New York: Oxford University Press, 1964.

Gusfield, Joseph. "The Study of Social Movements," in International Encyclopedia of the Social Sciences, edited by David L. Sills. New York: Crowell Collier and Macmillan, 1968.

Hartman, Chester W. Housing and Social Policy. Englewood Cliffs, N.J.: Prentice-Hall, 1975.

Hawley, Amos, and Vincent Rock, eds. Segregation in Residential Areas. Washington, D.C.: National Academy of Sciences, 1973.

Heberle, Rudolf. Social Movements. New York: Appleton-Century, 1951.

Helper, Rose. Racial Policies and Practices of Real Estate Brokers. Minneapolis: University of Minnesota Press, 1969.

Hobsbawm, Eric J. Primitive Rebels. New York: Free Press, 1963 ed.

Hoffer, Eric. The True Believer. New York: Harper Bros., 1951.

Homans, George. Social Behavior. New York: Harcourt, Brace and World, 1961.

____. The Human Group. New York: Harcourt, Brace and World, 1950.

Housing Opportunities Council of Metropolitan Washington. Housing and Justice. Washington, D.C., 1974.

Kantrowitz, Nathan. Ethnic and Racial Segregation in the New York Metropolis. New York: Praeger, 1973.

Killian, Lewis. Handbook of Modern Sociology. Chicago: Rand McNally, 1964.

King, C. Wendell. Social Movements in the U.S. New York: Random House, 1956.

Lang, Kurt, and Gladys Lang. Collective Dynamics. New York: Crowell, 1961.

Lauer, Robert. Social Movements and Social Change. Carbondale, Ill.: Southern Illinois University Press, 1976.

Massotti, Louis, and Jeffrey Hadden. The Urbanization of the Suburbs. Beverly Hills, Calif.: Sage, 1973.

Merton, Robert. Social Theory and Social Structure. Glencoe, Ill.: Free Press, 1957.

Milgram, Morris. Good Neighborhood. New York: Norton, 1977.

Myrdal, Gunnar. An American Dilemma. New York: Harper Bros., 1944.

Oberschall, Anthony. Social Conflict and Social Movements. Englewood Cliffs, N.J.: Prentice-Hall, 1973.

Palen, John. The Urban World. New York: McGraw-Hill, 1975.

Parsons, Talcott. Structure and Process in Modern Societies. Glencoe, Ill.: The Free Press, 1957.

____. Toward a General Theory of Action. Cambridge, Mass.: Harvard University Press, 1951.

Pettigrew, Thomas. Racial Discrimination in the United States. New York: Harper & Row, 1975.

____. Racially Separate or Together? New York: McGraw-Hill, 1971.

Roberts, Ron, and Robert Kloss. Social Movements. St. Louis: Mosby, 1974.

Rush, Gary, and R. Serge Denisoff. Social and Political Movements. New York: Appleton-Century-Crofts, 1971.

Saltman, Juliet. Open Housing As A Social Movement: Challenge, Conflict and Change. Lexington, Mass.: Heath, 1971.

____, ed. Integrated Neighborhoods in Action. Washington, D.C.: National Neighbors, 1978.

Sjoberg, Gideon, and Roger Nett. A Methodology for Social Research. New York: Harper & Row, 1968.

Smelser, Neil. Theory of Collective Behavior. New York: Free Press, 1963.

Taeuber, Karl, and Alma Taeuber. Negroes in Cities. Chicago: Aldine, 1965.

Toch, Hans. The Social Psychology of Social Movements. New York: Bobbs-Merrill, 1965.

Turner, Ralph, and Lewis Killian. Collective Behavior. Englewood Cliffs, N.J.: Prentice-Hall, 1957.

Weber, Max. <u>Theory of Social and Economic Organization</u>, edited by Talcott Parsons. Glencoe, Ill.: Free Press, 1964.

ARTICLES AND PERIODICALS

Akron <u>Beacon Journal</u>. 1965-1970.

Associated Press. <u>The World in 1965</u>. New York, 1966.

Bales, Robert F. "Task Roles and Social Roles in Problem-Solving Groups." <u>Readings in Social Psychology</u>, edited by Eleanor F. Macoby, Theodore M. Newcomb, and Eugene Hartley. New York: Holt, Rinehart and Winston, 1958.

Barnard, Chester B. "A Definition of Authority." In <u>Reader in Bureaucracy</u>, edited by Robert Merton et al. New York: Free Press, 1952.

Becker, Howard. "Inference and Proof in Participant Observation." <u>American Sociological Review</u> 23 (December 1958): 652-67.

Blumer, Herbert. "Collective Behavior." In <u>New Outline of the Principles of Sociology</u>, edited by Alfred Lee. New York: Barnes Noble, 1951.

____. "Collective Behavior." In <u>Review of Sociology</u>, edited by B. Gittler. New York: Wiley, 1957.

Carter, L. F. "Recording and Evaluating the Performance of Individuals as Members of Small Groups." <u>Personnel Psychology</u> 7 (1954): 477-84.

Coleman, James. "The Methods of Sociology." In <u>A Design for Sociology: Scope, Objectives, and Methods. Annals of the American Academy of Political and Social Science</u>. Monograph 9, April 1969.

<u>Encyclopedia Britannica Book of the Year, 1971-1977</u>. Chicago: Encyclopedia Brittanica, Inc.

<u>Encyclopedia News Annual</u>. <u>Year 1967</u>. New York: Year, Inc.

____. <u>Year 1968</u>. New York: Year, Inc.

____. <u>Year 1969</u>. New York: Year, Inc.

Erber, Ernest. "Housing Allocation Plans: A National Overview." Washington, D.C.: NCDH, 1974.

Fair Housing Congress News Release. August 1976.

Farley, Reynolds, et al. "Chocolate City, Vanilla Suburbs." Paper presented at American Sociological Association Meetings, Chicago. August 1977.

Freeman, Jo. "Resource Mobilization and Strategy—A Model for Analyzing Social Movement Organizations." Paper presented at Social Movements Symposium, Vanderbilt University, Nashville, Tenn., March 17, 1977.

Gerth, Hans, and Saul Landau. "The Relevance of History to the Sociological Ethos." In Readings in Sociology, edited by E. Schuler, T. Holt et al. New York: Crowell, 1967.

Gouldner, Alvin. "Organizational Analysis." In Sociology Today, edited by Robert Merton, Robert Broom, and F. Cottrell. New York: Basic Books, 1959.

Gusfield, Joseph. "The Study of Social Movements." In International Encyclopedia of the Social Sciences, edited by Joseph Gusfield. New York: Crowell Collier and Macmillan, Inc., 1968.

____. "Functional Areas of Leadership in Social Movements." Sociological Quarterly Vol. 7 (Spring 1966): 141.

Killian, Lewis. "Social Movements." In Handbook of Modern Sociology, edited by Robert E. Faris. Chicago: Rand McNally, 1964.

Leadership Council for Metropolitan Open Communities. Guide to Practice Open Housing Law. Chicago, 1974.

Miller, Loren. "The Protest Against Housing Segregation." The Annals 357 (January 1965).

National Urban League. Housing News, July 1970.

National Committee Against Discrimination in Housing, "Toward Democracy in Housing," Trends in Housing, July–August, 1960.

Nelson, Harold. "Intrusive Movement Organizations: A Preliminary Inquiry." Paper presented at American Sociological Association Meetings, Montreal, Canada, August 1974.

Perrow, Charles. "The Analysis of Goals in Complex Organizations." American Sociological Review 26 (December 1961): 854–66.

Saltman, Juliet. "Three Strategies for Reducing Involuntary Segregation." Journal of Sociology and Social Welfare 4, No. 5 (May 1977): 806–21.

____. "Implementing Open Housing Laws Through Social Action." Journal of Applied Behavioral Science 11, No. 1 (January–March 1975): 39–61.

____. "Funding, Conflict and Change in an Open Housing Group."
Journal of Voluntary Action Research, Vol 2, No. 4 (October
1973): 216-23.

____. "Integration Attitude Differentials and the Social Situation."
Phylon Vol. 32 (Fall 1971): 312-25.

____. "Organizational Analysis and the Study of Social Movements."
Paper presented at the Ohio Valley Sociological Society Meetings,
Akron, Ohio, May 1, 1970.

Scott, W. Richard. "Theory of Organizations." In Handbook of
Modern Sociology, edited by Robert E. Faris. Chicago: Rand
McNally, 1964.

Simon, Herbert. "Inducements and Incentives in Bureaucracy."
In Reader in Bureaucracy, edited by Robert Merton et al. New
York: Free Press, 1952.

Taeuber, Karl E. "Residential Segregation." Scientific American
Vol. 213 (August 1965).

____. "Racial Segregation: The Persisting Dilemma." Annals of
the American Academy of Political and Social Science 422: 87-96,
November 1975.

Thompson, Daniel C. "The Rise of the Negro Protest." The Annals
Vol. 357 (January 1965).

Trends in Housing. National Committee Against Discrimination in
Housing, 1956-78.

Urban League News Release. May 1973.

VanderZanden, James. "Resistance and Social Movements." Social
Forces 37 (May 1959): 312-15.

Whyte, William F. "Corner Boys: A Study of Clique Behavior."
American Journal of Sociology 46 (March 1941): 647-64.

Wirth, Louis. "Housing As a Field of Sociological Research."
American Sociological Review 2 (April 1947), 137-43.

Zald, Mayer, and Roberta Ash. "Social Movement Organizations:
Growth, Decay and Change." Social Forces 44 (March 1966): 329.

____. "Tactical Considerations in Social Movement Organizations."
Paper presented at Annual Meeting of American Sociological Association, Montreal, Canada, August 1974.

Zald, Mayer, and John McCarthy. "Resource Mobilization and Social Movements: A Partial Theory." American Journal of Sociology Vol. 82 (May 1977): 1212-41.

____. "The Trend of Social Movements in America: Professionaliza-tion and Resource Mobilization." Morristown, N.J.: General Learning Press, 1973.

DOCUMENTS

Akron Area Housing Market, Federal Housing Administration, April 1965.

Akron Community Service Center and Urban League. Brief on Urban Renewal, March 1961.

Community Action Council. Letter from Jordan Miller. October 27, 1969.

Denver Public Library. Microfilm, Denver Post, 1970-71.

Department of Planning and Urban Renewal, Akron, Ohio. Com-munity Improvement Program, 1964.

Fair Housing Contact Service. Proposal for a Fair Housing Center, 1967.

____. Proposal for a Fair Housing Center, 1969.

____. Proposal for a Fair Housing Center, 1970.

____. Proposal for Funding, 1974, 1975, 1976.

Fair Housing and Funding. Washington, D.C.: HUD, 1976.

FHCS. Brochure, December 1965.

Fuller, Blanford. Letter to Board of Directors, Fair Housing Contact Service, Akron, October 27, 1969.

Gerber, Sidney. Letter to Juliet Saltman, March 26, 1965.

Hearings of Washington State Board Against Discrimination and State Real Estate Commission, October 28, 1966.

Hoeber, Betty. Letter to Juliet Saltman, September 2, 1970.

Housing Opportunities Center of Greater Los Angeles. Report, January 10, 1969. (Mimeographed).

Jones vs. Mayer, Supreme Court Decision, June, 1968.

Leadership Council for Metropolitan Open Communities. Summary of the Open Housing Seminar on February 1, 1969. Mimeographed.

Metro Denver Fair Housing Center. The Comprehensive Story, 1969.

_____. Narrative Report on Center, December 31, 1967.

Minutes of Meetings of the Board of Directors. Fair Housing Contact Service, 1965-70. Mimeographed.

National Committee Against Discrimination in Housing. "A Descriptive Overview of Its Organization and Activities." 1969. Mimeographed.

_____. Director's Action Report, 1952.

_____. Executive Director's Report, May, 1956.

_____. Funnye, Clarence. "A Directional Critique of the Akron Fair Housing Center." Mimeographed.

_____. "Ghettos—The Last Barrier," estimated 1955.

_____. Margolis, Richard. "The Metro-American Dilemma," 1969. Mimeographed, unreleased.

_____. "Opening a New Frontier," estimated 1954.

_____. "Statement of Principles," estimated 1950.

_____. "Thirty Thousand Americans Need Your Help," 1952.

_____. Weaver, George. Letter to The Links, June 14, 1955.

National Association for the Advancement of Colored People (Akron Branch). "The Status of Civil Rights in Akron." 1961.

Open Housing Center, Proposal to the City of New York, October 6, 1977.

Operation Equality, Seattle. Newsletter, June 1969.

_____. Summary of Program, January 1969. Mimeographed.

Operation Open City, New York. Report on Program, 1969.

_____. Proposal to New York Council Against Poverty, 1969.

_____. Proposal for Open City Housing Center, 1969.

Planners for Equal Opportunity, New York Metropolitan Chapter. "On the Move: A Survey Analysis." 1967.

Pruzan, Marian. "Operation Equality, A Study of Community Organization Method." Seattle, March 9, 1970. Mimeographed Term Paper.

Riley, Frances. Letter to Juliet Saltman, August 26, 1970.

Seattle Urban League. Proposal for Funding, 1966.

Task Force (of mayor) on Human Relations. Report, Akron, September 1, 1962.

U.S. Department of Commerce. U.S. Censuses of Population and Housing: 1960. Final Report PHC(1)-2, Census Tracts, Akron, Ohio.

INDEX

Akron, Ohio, 116-213; audits in, 181-95; [summary of, 194-95]; back to total volunteers, 201; change and transition of, 202-03; community level action of, 339-96; complaints filed in, 128-30; cultural context of, 119-24; education program in, 131; Fair Housing Contact Service, 124-213; Fair Housing Ordinance (1064), 123; funding in, 132, 142-46; HOMES council in, 123; housing assistance program in, 126; HUD Demonstration Project, 198-201; [conclusions, 201]; National Volunteer Award, 196-98; NCDH, 124; organizational policy, FHCS in, 164; public housing, history of in, 134-35; refunding of, 1975, 205-07; return to volunteer status of, 180; stabilization statement of, 347-48; urban renewal funds of, 132-33

antipoverty program, 65
antisegregation campaign, 51
armed forces: segregation banned in, 43
Atlanta, Georgia: racial unrest in, 49
audit: nationwise, 103-07
auditing and legal action, 91-96; in Baltimore, 94; in Chicago, 95; in Cleveland Heights, 95; in Palo Alto, 93; in St. Louis, 93

authority structure: definition of, 118

Baton Rouge, Louisiana: racial tension in, 49
Bedford-Stuyvesant: race riot in, 50
Bergen County: Fair Housing Council, 279-80
Birmingham, Alabama: racial tension in, 44, 50
Black Panthers: harassment of, 61
black population: mobility of, 40-41
Black Power, 60
Bogalusa, Louisiana, 59
Boston, Massachusetts: racial unrest in, 50, 59
Brown, H. Rap, 60
building trades unions: discrimination in, 50
buses: segregation banned on, 43

Cairo, Illinois: racial unrest in, 49
Capahosic Conference, 64
Carmichael, Stokeley, 60
caste system: perpetuation of, 324
Chattanooga, Tennessee: racial tension in, 48
Chicago, Illinois: racial unrest in, 43, 60
Chicago: Leadership Council, 272-74
Cicero, Illinois: racial unrest in, 42
Cincinnati: HOME, 282-83

421

HUD Manual, 99-102; comprehensive agencies in, 100; funding possibilities of, 100; inconsistency of, 102

impact: of programs, 33
inner-city blight, 41
instant funding: in Akron, 142-46
integration, 43, 44
internal morale, 33
institutionalization, 1-3, 24-25; in Akron, development after, 146-210; decline and, 311-17; of social movement, 294; strains and tensions, 316

Johnson, President Lyndon B., 50

Kennedy, President John F., 49
Kennedy, Attorney-General Robert, 49
Kentucky Commission on Human Rights, 280-81
King, Rev. Martin Luther, 43, 47, 50, 61
KKK violence, 59

law: inadequacies in, 127
leadership, 9-12; importance of, 314-15
legislative development: 1956-1964, 54-56; 1964-1970, 69-70
Levittown development: in Pennsylvania, 46
Local Community Action Development: in Akron, 339-65; 1956-1964, 56-59; 1964-1970, 72-74
Los Angeles, California: open housing in, 227-44
Louisville, Kentucky: funding withheld from, 63

Malcolm X, 59
mass movements, 10-11
McKissick, Floyd, 60
McLaurin case, 42
Meredith, James, 49
Metro Denver Fair Housing Center, 244-57
migration: of black population, 40-41
minorities: exclusion of, 41; equal opportunity housing for, 215
Mississippi: civil rights workers murdered in, 50
Montgomery, Alabama: racial unrest in, 43
morale: internal, 33
Muhammed, Elijah, 48

Nashville, Tennessee: racial unrest in, 48
National Association for the Advancement of Colored People: attack on segregation of, 42
National Association of Real Estate Boards, 70
National Committee against Discrimination in Housing, 29; in Akron, 124; impact of in civil rights movement, 67-69; development of: [legislative and legal action in, 85-90; (consent decrees, 86, damages, 85, moratorium, 88-89, Trafficante Case, 89, Upper Arlinton Case, 89, zoning challenges, 86); 1956-1964, 53-55; 1964-1970, 70; 1970-1977, 74-111]; fund appeals of, 337-38; organization of, 44-47; program enlarged, 47
National Neighbors, 79; and Intrusive Movement Organization, 79-80

New York City: Fair Housing Practice Law in, 48; housing struggle in, 43; open housing in, 216-27; racial discrimination prohibited in, 42; racial quotas in, 49; racial tension in, 50

Nixon, Richard, 61

Office of Economic Opportunity: antipoverty program of, 65

Ohio Civil Rights Commission: complaints filed with, 128

Ohio Fair Housing Congress, 282-86

Oklahoma City, Oklahoma: racial tension in, 48

Operation Equality in Seattle, 257-71

Operation Open City in New York, 216-25

Open Housing: in Akron, 116-213; on community level, 214-71; cultural context of, 39-42; in Denver, 244-57; development in: [first phase, 42-47; second phase, 47-59; third phase, 60-74]; in Los Angeles, 227-44; in New York, 216-27; in Seattle, 257-71; social context of, 40-42

Open Housing Center: in New York, 225-27

open housing movement: community development of, 301-11; national development of, 296-301

organizational careers: definition of, 118

Palo Alto: MCFH in, 276-77

participant observation, 34-35

Poor People's March, 61

population: Akron's nonwhite, 120

Prince Edward County: integration in, 48

private housing: discrimination banned in, 298

process: in social movement, 16-25

Proposition 14: in California, 61-63

public housing: in Akron, 134

Public Housing Administration, 45

Public Housing Authority: NCDH influence on, 299

race riots: nationwide, 60

Richmond: HOME in, 275-76

Rochester, New York: racial tension in, 50

San Fernando: Fair Housing Council in, 241-42

San Francisco: Operation Sentinel in, 277-79

school and housing desegregation, 84

Seattle, Washington: open housing in, 257-71

segregation, 42; extent of residential, 322

Selma, Alabama, 59

sit-in movement: size of, 48

social change: implications of, 322-25

social context: in Akron, 119-24

social movement, 1-26; concept of, 3-25; decline in, 1-2, 311; definition of, 5-8; emergent propositions of, 30; five new propositions of, 319-21; historiography in, 35-37; institutionalization of, 294; models of emergence of, 22-24; participant observation in, 34-35; research design in, 31-37; six propositions reconsidered, 311-17; types of, 15-16

424

ABOUT THE AUTHOR

DR. JULIET SALTMAN is a Professor of Sociology at Kent State University, where she was a Finalist for the Distinguished Teaching Award in 1974 and 1975. She is the author of <u>Open Housing as a Social Movement</u> (Heath, 1971) and editor of <u>Integrated Neighborhoods in Action</u> (National Neighbors, 1978), a monograph, and many articles and studies which have been published in professional and lay journals. She has been a university teacher since 1957.

She has been active in community and national affairs concerning urban problems, race relations, and peace. Dr. Saltman was a founder in 1965 of the Akron area Fair Housing Contact Service, winner of the National Volunteer Award in 1973, a $5000 prize presented in Washington, D.C. by the National Center for Voluntary Action. The Fair Housing Contact Service (FHCS) is now funded by the city and county, and provides equal housing opportunities for minorities. Dr. Saltman was also a founder of West Side Neighbors, organized in 1967 to promote stabilization and to provide a demonstration model of effective integrated living.

Dr. Saltman received her Ph.D. in Sociology from Case Western Reserve University, an M.A. in Sociology from the University of Chicago, and a B.A. from Rutgers University. She is married to Dr. William Saltman, a manager in the Research Division of Goodyear Tire & Rubber Co. They have three children, now grown.

In 1974, Dr. Saltman was nominated by the editors of the <u>Ladies' Home Journal</u> for one of their Woman of the Year Awards, for her community service. In February 1975, she won the 1975 Brotherhood Award for the greater Akron area. In March 1975 she won the Citizen of the Year Award from the National Association of Social Workers, North Central Ohio Chapter. In June 1975 she was named one of four "Outstanding Ohio Women in Housing" by the HUD Federal Women's Unit of Columbus. In April 1976 she received the Douglass Society Distinguished Alumna Award from Douglass College of Rutgers University for career and community achievements.

Dr. Saltman has served as a consultant to numerous government agencies and community organizations. Most recently, she was a consultant and regional coordinator for the HUD/NCDH nation-wide audit in 1976-77. Her biography is listed in <u>American Men & Women of Science</u>, <u>Who's Who in the Midwest</u>, and <u>Who's Who of American Women</u>.

RELATED TITLES

HOMESTEADING IN URBAN U.S.A.
                              Ann Clark
                              Zelma Rivin

HOUSING COSTS AND HOUSING NEEDS
                              edited by
                              Alexander Greendale
                              Stanley F. Knock, Jr.

NEIGHBORHOOD CHANGE: Lessons in the
Dynamics of Urban Decay
                              Charles L. Leven
                              James T. Little
                              Hugh O. Nourse
                              and R. B. Read

THE RIGHT TO HOUSING: Constitutional
Issues and Remedies in Exclusionary Zoning
                              Mary Sullivan Mann

THE POLITICS OF HOUSING IN OLDER
URBAN AREAS
                              edited by
                              Robert E. Mendelson
                              Michael A. Quinn